ENDURANCE PERFORMANCE IN SPORT

D1610861

Athletes participating at all levels of endurance performance can relate to the impact of psychological factors. Whether it is motivation, self-belief, feeling nervous before a race, exercise-induced pain, sticking to a pacing strategy, or thoughts around what to focus on, there are a vast number of psychological factors which can affect endurance performance.

Bringing together experts in the field from around the world, this is the first text to provide a detailed overview of the psychology of endurance performance where there is a research and an applied focus looking at both main theoretical models as well as how interventions can support an athlete's efficacy and well-being. The authors look at regulatory processes around pain, decision-making, self-belief, emotions, and meta-cognition, before examining a range of cognitive strategies, including the use of imagery, goals, self-talk, and mindfulness techniques. With a final section of the book outlining issues related to mental health that are relevant to endurance performance, the book shows that the future of research and application of psychological theory in endurance performance in sport is bright and thriving.

Aimed at researchers, students, coaches, and athletes themselves, this is essential reading for anyone wishing to better understand how our minds experience endurance in performance arenas, and what psychological techniques can be used to make us more efficient.

Carla Meijen is a chartered sport and exercise psychologist and a senior lecturer in applied sport psychology at St Mary's University, UK. She has a keen interest in endurance performance inspired by her work providing brief mental support at running events. She researches and teaches in sport psychology, and also works as a sport psychology practitioner.

ENDURANCE PERFORMANCE IN SPORT

Psychological Theory and Interventions

Edited by Carla Meijen

Routledge
Taylor & Francis Group

LONDON AND NEW YORK

First edition published 2019
by Routledge
2 Park Square, Milton Park, Abingdon, Oxon, OX14 4RN

and by Routledge
52 Vanderbilt Avenue, New York, NY 10017

Routledge is an imprint of the Taylor & Francis Group, an informa business

British Library Cataloguing-in-Publication Data
A catalogue record for this book is available from the British Library

Library of Congress Cataloging-in-Publication Data
Names: Meijen, Carla, 1982- editor.
Title: Endurance performance in sport : psychological theory and
    interventions / edited by Carla Meijen.
Description: Abingdon, Oxon ; New York, NY : Routledge, 2019. |
    Includes bibliographical references and index.
Identifiers: LCCN 2018061156 (print) | LCCN 2019009878 (ebook) |
    ISBN 9781315167312 (ebook) | ISBN 9781138053199 (hardback) |
    ISBN 9781138053212 (pbk.) | ISBN 9781315167312 (ebk)
Subjects: LCSH: Endurance sports–Psychological aspects. | Physical
    education and training–Psychological aspects. | Athletes–Psychology.
Classification: LCC GV749.5 (ebook) | LCC GV749.5 .E65 2019 (print) |
    DDC 613.7/1–dc23
LC record available at https://lccn.loc.gov/2018061156

ISBN: 978-1-138-05319-9 (hbk)
ISBN: 978-1-138-05321-2 (pbk)
ISBN: 978-1-315-16731-2 (ebk)

Typeset in Bembo
by Swales & Willis Ltd, Exeter, Devon, UK
Printed by CPI Group (UK) Ltd, Croydon CR0 4YY

CONTENTS

List of illustrations   *viii*
List of contributors   *x*

1 An introduction to *Endurance Performance in Sport:*
   Psychological Theory and Interventions   1
   Carla Meijen and Samuele Marcora

PART I
Determinants of endurance performance   **13**

2 Psychobiology of fatigue during endurance exercise   15
   Samuele Marcora

3 Exercise-induced pain: a psychophysiological perspective   35
   Alexis R. Mauger

4 Decision-making, pacing, and performance in
   endurance sport   47
   Dominic Micklewright

5 Regulating emotions to go faster!   70
   Andrew M. Lane, Daniel T. Robinson, and Ross Cloak

6 Metacognitive processes in the self-regulation of
endurance performance   81
Noel Brick, Mark Campbell, and Christian Swann

7 Self-efficacy and endurance performance   96
Paul Anstiss

PART II
Psychological interventions in endurance
performance   **107**

Prelude: interventions for endurance performance   109
Carla Meijen

8 Attentional focus and cognitive strategies during
endurance activity   113
Noel Brick, Tadhg MacIntyre, and Linda Schücker

9 Goal striving and endurance performance   125
Wanja Wolff, Maik Bieleke, and Julia Schüler

10 The theoretical and applied implications of using
imagery to improve the performance and well-being
of endurance performers   138
Sheree McCormick, Francesco di Gruttola, and
Maurizio Bertollo

11 Self-talk and endurance performance   153
Alister McCormick and Antonis Hatzigeorgiadis

12 Mindfulness in endurance performance   168
Emilie Thienot and Danielle Adams

Appendix 12.1   183

Appendix 12.2   185

PART III
Future directions for research and practice   **187**

13 Clinical issues in endurance performance   189
Jennifer E. Carter and James Houle

14 Application to recreational settings: working with the
    public, psyching team activities, and suggestions   201
    Chelsi Day

15 Pursuing the next challenges: directions for research on
    the psychology of endurance performance   212
    Carla Meijen and Alister McCormick

Index   *225*

ILLUSTRATIONS

Figures

2.1 Graphical representation of how perception of effort and potential motivation interact to determine time to exhaustion during endurance exercise 19

2.2 Graphical representation of the corollary discharge model of perception of effort 24

2.3 Grand averages of the motor-related cortical potential (MCRP) at electrode Cz (vertex) for a) muscle fatigue and b) weight during submaximal voluntary contractions of the elbow flexors (N = 16), and for c) caffeine and d) time-on-task during submaximal voluntary contractions of the knee extensor muscles (N = 16) manipulations. Time 0 s is electromyogram onset and contractions lasted approximately 2 s. ★ Significant simple main effect of condition based on Holm-Bonferroni corrected α-levels. 26

4.1 Example pacing pattern of a 10-mile (16.1 km) cycling time trial with 4 km segment averaging and continuous data with simple exponential smoothing (b) 60

6.1 Illustration of the hierarchical organisation of the meta-level and the object-level 83

6.2 A metacognitive framework of attentional focus and cognitive control in endurance activity 86

6.3 Integrated model of flow and clutch states in sport 90

9.1 The steps involved in forming an implementation intention 131

10.1 The Motor Imagery Integrative Model 143

10.2 Tailored imagery programme to meet the needs, abilities and preferences of the athlete 147

12.1   Practice of self-observation   176
12.2   Practice of acceptance   178

Tables

4.1   Variations in expected utility associated with different
        permutations of acts and states   49
4.2   The interaction between uncertainty and complexity in
        endurance sport   55
11.1 A framework for recording self-talk that you notice you
        are using   161
11.2 The IMPACT approach to self-talk   161
11.3 Example instructional and motivational self-talk statements   162
11.4 An exercise for practising choosing self-talk statements   162
11.5 An example self-talk plan for a half-marathon   165

CONTRIBUTORS

Danielle Adams is an Applied Practitioner lending Sport Psychology support to the British Canoe Slalom programme. She received her MSc in Performance Psychology from the University of Edinburgh, and her PhD from Brunel University with a research focus on attentional processes governing optimal skill execution.

Paul Anstiss received his PhD in Sport and Exercise Psychology from the University of Kent. His research primarily focuses on investigating how self-efficacy beliefs are formed and altered, and how we can develop more effective interventions to change self-efficacy.

Maurizio Bertollo received his PhD from Universidade de Tras-os-Montes Alto Douro and he is currently Associate Professor in Motor Behaviour and Sport Psychology at the University G. d'Annunzio of Chieti-Pescara. He is part of the FEPSAC MC and a Chartered Psychologist and Psychotherapist in Italy. His research activity focuses on the processes and mechanisms underlying the development, maintenance, and improvement of human motor behaviour and performance.

Maik Bieleke is a Postdoctoral Researcher at the University of Konstanz and affiliated with the Department of Psychology and the Department of Empirical and Educational Research. His research focuses on the self-regulation of human performance and decision making, with a particular emphasis on how motivation and emotions influence performance. Most recently, he has started to investigate the psychological and neurophysiological underpinnings of self-regulatory strategies in endurance contexts.

Noel E. Brick is a Lecturer in Sport and Exercise Psychology at Ulster University, Northern Ireland. He received his PhD from the University of Limerick, Ireland.

His research primarily addresses the effects of attentional focus, cognitive strategy use, and metacognitive processes on endurance performance and endurance exercise adherence. Noel's research also focuses on endurance activity and cognitive functioning in adults.

Mark Campbell is a Senior Lecturer and Course Director for the MSc Sport, Exercise and Performance Psychology in the Department of Physical Education and Sport Sciences at the University of Limerick, Ireland. Mark is a Science Foundation Ireland Funded Investigator (SFI-FI) and his primary research interests focus on exploring the neurocognitive characteristics of expertise in skilled performers.

Jennifer E. Carter received her PhD from the University of Notre Dame and is currently the Lead Sport Psychologist and Associate Professor, clinical, at Ohio State University Wexner Medical Center. As a former university swimmer and volleyball player, Jen is a board-certified counselling psychologist with specialities in sport psychology and eating disorders.

Ross Cloak is a Senior Lecturer in Sport and Exercise Science at the University of Wolverhampton, UK, where he also received his PhD. His research interests are primarily around injury prevention and performance enhancement in elite sport and he is also involved in a number of interdisciplinary projects around health promotion and physical activity.

Chelsi Day is a Clinical and Sport Psychologist. She currently serves as the Director of Counselling and Sport Psychology for sports medicine in the athletic department at Indiana University. In this role she provides mental health services and performance services to student-athletes on all 24 teams. She obtained her PsyD in Clinical Psychology at Antioch University, New England and her Masters in Sport Psychology from the Chicago School of Professional Psychology. She is the founder of the Psyching Team for the Nationwide Children's Hospital Columbus Marathon in Columbus, Ohio, USA.

Francesco di Gruttola received his PhD from the University of Pisa and is currently a Senior Research Collaborator in Neuroscience at IMT School for Advanced Studies, Lucca. His research focuses on the development of innovative psychophysiological techniques to improve sports and work performance. Specific topics include motor imagery assessment, life skills training, biofeedback and neurofeedback interventions.

Antonis Hatzigeorgiadis is a Professor at the Department of Physical Education and Sport Science at the University of Thessaly, Greece, and the Course Director for the department's MSc in Psychology of Sport and Physical Education. He received his PhD from Loughborough University, UK. His research primarily focuses on athletes' cognitive activation and in particular self-talk. Other interests include socio-moral aspects of sport and motivation. He is currently Associate Editor for the journal *Sport, Exercise and Performance Psychology* (APA), and serves on the Managing Council of the European Federation of Sport Psychology.

James Houle received his PhD from the Auburn University and is currently a Sport Psychologist and Assistant Professor, clinical, at Ohio State University Wexner Medical Center. As a former university gymnast, Jamey is a board-certified coun-selling psychologist with specialities in sport psychology and eating disorders.

Andrew M. Lane is a Professor of Sport Psychology at the University of Wolverhampton. He is a fellow of the British Association of Sport and Exercise Sciences (BASES), and Chartered Sport and Exercise Scientist. He is Health Professional Council registered and a British Psychological Society Chartered Psychologist. He has authored more than 200 peer refereed journal articles and edited five books, the most recent of which is on sport psychology and nutrition in running. Andy has also provided self-help material for runners at the London Marathon on how to use psychological strategies such as if-then planning.

Tadhg MacIntyre is a Lecturer in Sport, Exercise and Performance Psychology in the Department of Physical Education and Sport Sciences at the University of Limerick, Ireland. He is a British Psychological Society Chartered Psychologist and a Health Care Professionals Council accredited Practitioner Psychologist. Tadhg's primary research interest applies the strength-based approach to investigating key questions in cognitive psychology and performance psychology. These include the role of motor imagery in expert performance and the interplay between physical activity and positive emotions.

Samuele Marcora is a Professor of Sports Science at the University of Kent (UK) and the University of Bologna (Italy). He holds a PhD in Clinical Exercise Physiology, an MSc in Human Performance, and a Bachelor's degree in Physical Education. His field of research integrates exercise physiology, motivation psy-chology, and cognitive neuroscience in order to better understand endurance performance, physical activity behaviour, and the interplay between physical and mental fatigue.

Alexis R. Mauger received his PhD from Exeter University and is currently a Senior Lecturer and the Director of Innovation at the School of Sport and Exercise Sciences in the University of Kent. His research looks at the psychophysiologi-cal factors affecting exercise performance, with a specific focus on how exercise-induced pain impacts on fatigue and task cessation.

Alister McCormick is a Lecturer and Sport and Exercise Psychologist at Plymouth Marjon University, UK. He completed his PhD at the University of Kent, focusing on how psychology can be used to improve the performances of people completing endurance events and competing in endurance sports. His research focuses on how psychology can be used to benefit people involved in endurance sports, such as through improving performance or encouraging sustained involvement. He is passionate about making psychology research findings practical and useful for the public.

Sheree McCormick received her PhD from Manchester Metropolitan University and is currently a Postdoctoral Researcher in Neuroscience and Experimental Psychology at the University of Manchester. As a Chartered Cognitive Psychologist, her research centres on the development of passive and adjunctive therapies to improve health and well-being, and the cognitive processes underlying human behaviour.

Carla Meijen is a Senior Lecturer in Applied Sport Psychology at St Mary's University, UK. She is a Health and Care Professions Council registered Sport and Exercise Psychologist and a British Psychological Society Chartered Psychologist. She received her PhD from Staffordshire University where she focused on challenge and threat states in athletes. She has a keen interest in endurance performance inspired by her work providing brief mental support at running events. Her research focuses on self-regulatory factors of endurance performance and implementing psychological strategies in endurance settings.

Dominic Micklewright is a Professor of Sport Psychology at the University of Essex, UK. His research focuses on perceptual and decision-making processes associated with fatigue and performance among endurance athletes. He is a Chartered Psychologist of the British Psychological Society and a Fellow of the American College of Sports Medicine and the British Association of Sports and Exercise Sciences.

Daniel T. Robinson is a Doctoral Student at the University of Wolverhampton. His research is focused on developing psychology-based interventions to allow endurance athletes to cope with in-event fatigue. He coaches a number of elite athletes, particularly in the marathon. He is also supporting England Athletics' endurance programme in both physiology and psychology.

Christian Swann received his PhD from the School of Sport and Exercise Science, University of Lincoln and is currently a Senior Lecturer in Psychology at Southern Cross University in Australia. He is accredited with both the British Association of Sport and Exercise Sciences, and Exercise and Sports Science Australia. Christian's research focuses on the psychology of exceptional performance, goal-setting, and enjoyment of sport, exercise, and physical activity.

Linda Schücker is a Postdoctoral Researcher in Sport Psychology at the University of Münster, Germany, where she also received her PhD. Her research interests include attentional focus effects in endurance performance, effects of cognitive fatigue on physical tasks and colour effects in sports.

Julia Schüler received her PhD from the University of Wuppertal, Germany and is currently Professor in the Department of Sport Science (Sport Psychology) at the University of Konstanz, Germany. Her current research addresses motivational and volitional aspects of sport and exercise with a special focus on individual differences (e.g., implicit motives, trait self-control).

Emilie Thienot received her MSc in Psychology from the Paris School of Psychology and her PhD in Sport Psychology from the University of Western Australia. Her research area focuses on attention and mindfulness in elite sport performances. She is currently in charge of the coordination and delivery of sport psychology services for French Swimming and French Rowing. She is also a research partner of the Laboratory of Vulnerabilities and Innovation in Sport, Claude Bernard University Lyon 1 and a board member of the French Society of Sport Psychology.

Wanja Wolff received his PhD in Psychology from the University of Potsdam, Germany, and is now a post-doctoral researcher at the University of Konstanz, Germany and the University of Bern, Switzerland. His research interests focus on psychological, neuronal, and physiological aspects of self-regulated performance.

1

AN INTRODUCTION TO *ENDURANCE PERFORMANCE IN SPORT: PSYCHOLOGICAL THEORY AND INTERVENTIONS*

Carla Meijen and Samuele Marcora

What is endurance performance?

The focus of this book will be on endurance performance defined as "performance during whole-body, dynamic exercise that involves continuous effort and lasts for 75 seconds or longer" (McCormick, Meijen, & Marcora, 2015, p. 998). This kind of endurance performance, often referred to as cardiorespiratory or aerobic endurance, includes the most popular endurance sports such as road cycling, middle-distance running, marathons and ultra-marathons, many swimming events, triathlons, rowing, and cross-country skiing. Performance during tasks involving sustained or repeated submaximal contractions of a single muscle or muscle group (e.g., sit-ups, weight holding, hand-grip tasks, and leg-raise tasks) is referred to as muscular endurance (Kenney, Wilmore, & Costill, 2015). Although we may draw on some research related to muscular endurance, the focus of this book is on whole-body endurance performance and the application of knowledge to endurance performance at all levels, including competitive, elite, and recreational athletes, as well as those participating in mass-participation endurance events.

Like any other kind of physical performance, endurance performance can be investigated from different disciplinary perspectives, the main ones being physiological, biomechanical, and psychological. Because most books on the science of endurance performance have focused primarily on physiology, biomechanics, sports medicine, physical training, and nutrition (Shephard & Astrand, 2000) we felt it was timely to compile a book focusing on psychological aspects of endurance performance. Nevertheless, we believe that a multidisciplinary and interdisciplinary approach should be adopted by researchers and practitioners involved in endurance sports. As a result, the book will also provide several examples of the complex interactions between psychology and the biomechanical/technical, tactical, physiological, and coaching/training methodology aspects of endurance performance.

We will first provide a brief introduction to some more physiology-based models to help explain how the research in the area has developed historically.

Models of how the brain can limit endurance performance

The traditional physiological model of endurance performance proposes that endurance performance is determined primarily by three physiological constructs: maximal oxygen consumption (VO_{2max}), the 'lactate threshold' (the $\%VO_{2max}$ at which lactate starts to accumulate in the blood) and gross mechanical efficiency (the oxygen cost to generate a given velocity or power) (Joyner & Coyle, 2008). Although the role of the brain in physical fatigue has been recognised for more than a century (Giulio, Daniele, & Tipton, 2006), constructs related to brain function or psychology are not included in this traditional physiological model. Over the past 20 years, however, exercise physiologists have paid more attention to the brain/mind and included related constructs in their endurance performance models. These models can be classified as 1) the central fatigue model, 2) the central governor model, and 3) the psychobiological model.

The central fatigue model is based on the observation that the muscle fatigue that progressively develops during endurance exercise (Marcora & Staiano, 2010) is not solely caused by metabolic factors or muscular damage if eccentric contractions are involved (peripheral fatigue). The progressive reduction in maximal voluntary force or power induced by endurance exercise is, in part, due to a reduction in the capacity of the central nervous system (CNS) to recruit the locomotor muscles (central fatigue) (Millet & Lepers, 2004). The specific mechanisms of central fatigue depend on the task. For example, during high-intensity endurance exercise in normoxia (i.e., at sea level) or mild hypoxia, it has been proposed that the main cause of central fatigue is feedback from Group III–IV afferents that sense fatigue-related metabolites in the locomotor muscles (Amann & Calbet, 2008). These afferents are thinly myelinated (Group III) and unmyelinated (Group IV) nerve fibres located within the muscle and receive sensory information. This afferent feedback inhibits the descending drive to the locomotor muscles at spinal and/or supraspinal (above the spine) level, and it is believed to limit endurance performance when peripheral locomotor muscle fatigue reaches a critical threshold (Amann, 2012). On the contrary, during high-intensity exercise in severe hypoxia (high altitude), the main mechanism of central fatigue seems to be the direct effect of limited convective oxygen delivery to the brain (Amann & Calbet, 2008). During endurance exercise in the heat, it has been proposed that central fatigue is caused by changes in the activity of the dopaminergic system and inhibitory signals from the hypothalamus, a region in the brain, when brain temperature increases (Nybo, 2008). Although there are different task specific-mechanisms (such as the altitude one may be exercising at), the assumption of this model is that central fatigue, together with peripheral fatigue, directly limits the capacity of the athlete to sustain endurance exercise (Nybo, 2008). Although the motor function of the brain is included in this central fatigue model, there are no specific psychological constructs. Therefore, it is difficult for the central fatigue model to explain the effects of psychological variables on endurance performance. Furthermore, a model based on simple inhibitory reflexes cannot explain the complex decision-making processes that determine the self-regulation of velocity and power (pacing) during endurance events (Amann & Secher, 2010).

The central governor model is a very influential model originally popularised by Noakes (1997) and further developed by Noakes and colleagues (Noakes, 2012; Noakes, St Clair Gibson, & Lambert, 2005). The core idea is that a subconscious intelligent system in the brain, the central governor, senses the physiological conditions of the body (e.g., myocardial oxygenation) and regulates endurance performance by continuously modifying the number of motor units that are recruited in the exercising limbs. The purpose of this teleoanticipatory control system is to ensure that humans terminate endurance exercise before there is a catastrophic failure of bodily homeostasis (e.g., myocardial ischemia) (Noakes, 1997, 2012; Noakes et al., 2005). In its original formulation, the positive influence of psychological variables like the placebo effect on endurance performance was considered to be in conflict with the core idea that endurance performance is regulated at a subconscious level to prevent conscious override that may damage the human (Noakes, 2000). Over the years, however, psychological constructs like perception of effort (Noakes et al., 2005) and self-belief (Noakes, 2012) have been added to the model. Although an interdisciplinary approach is to be applauded, it has been argued that these post-hoc modifications of the model can make the central governor appear like an all-knowing homunculus and unfalsifiable in principle, which reduces the validity of this model as a scientific explanation of fatigue during physical and mental tasks (Inzlicht & Marcora, 2016).

The psychobiological model is a model of endurance performance based on psychological theory, specifically the motivational intensity theory proposed by Brehm and Self (1989). In this model, the athlete, rather than a subconscious central governor, is the agent that self-regulates the velocity/power during endurance exercise (Marcora, 2007, 2008) and the capacity to sustain endurance exercise is not directly limited by locomotor muscle fatigue (Marcora, Bosio, & de Morree, 2008; Marcora & Staiano, 2010). What limits endurance performance is a decision-making process based on perception of effort and potential motivation. Potential motivation is the maximum effort an individual is willing to exert in order to succeed in the task. Specifically, the model postulates that an athlete decides to terminate endurance exercise (or slow down, i.e., disengage from the task) when sustaining the required or desired velocity/power is perceived as impossible or excessively difficult in relation to what they are willing to offer to achieve the particular outcome. More details about this model will be provided in Chapter 2.

The role of psychology in endurance performance

Before we further introduce the role of psychology in endurance performance, let us first take a step back and define (sport) psychology. Sport psychology is about understanding the performance, mental processes, and well-being of people in sporting settings, taking into account psychological theory and methods (Moran & Toner, 2017). Within this we need to consider the thoughts, feelings, and behaviours of individuals. The reason we go back to this definition is to initiate an awareness that although the role of the brain is integral to the regulation of endurance performance as outlined by the central fatigue model, the central governor model, and the psychobiological model, we do need to focus on a much wider range of psychological variables if we want to understand and improve endurance performance from a psychological perspective. The constructs and processes explored in sport psychology are 'emergent' properties of the brain. Endurance activities share psychological demands that makes it such as fascinating field to study. For example, consider the motivation that is needed to go out for long and physically demanding training sessions on a dark and windy winter morning. To be able to perform well in endurance events, practice is an important predictor of performance (for example see Baker, Deakin, & Côté, 2005). There are no shortcuts in terms of the time commitment required to perform optimally in endurance activities, and training sessions can be lonely and repetitive. Also inherent to endurance activities are the pain and discomfort experienced by endurance athletes when exerting themselves and pushing their exercise tolerance to the limit, and this can also influence an athlete's affective state. Endurance activities also require complex decision-making to optimise pacing during endurance events. In addition to these variables, dealing with environmental factors, such as varying weather conditions, or mechanical failures, as well as other competitors can play a role in endurance performance (McCormick, Meijen, & Marcora, 2018a).

Endurance athletes and coaches are aware of the interdisciplinary nature of endurance performance, yet it is striking how much physiology has dominated research in the field of endurance performance. On the one hand, this is odd considering that physiological aspects are not able to fully predict endurance performance (e.g., see O'Connor (1992)), but on the other hand it can be explained by the line of thinking that optimal performance in endurance activities is primarily determined by physiological capacity and muscle fatigue, in which, typically, psychological factors were referred to fleetingly (Joyner & Coyle, 2008). Many endurance athletes at all levels of performance, from recreational to Olympic level, have, however, emphasised the important role of psychological variables (for example see Fitzgerald (2015)). Perhaps, we should also be surprised that within the field of sport psychology endurance activities are under-researched compared to sports such as golf, football, and tennis, especially considering that the paper that is often referred to as one of the first sport psychology studies (Triplett, 1898) discusses an endurance activity. Most of the research outputs examining endurance performance rely on the application of sport psychology concepts to endurance activities (Simons, 2012).

The focus of research in endurance performance is, however, shifting and more of a movement towards the inclusion of a variety of psychological variables in endurance performance research is emerging. Initially, the majority of studies on psychological variables focused on attentional strategies. In their seminal paper, Morgan and Pollock (1977) explored the attentional strategies of elite and non-elite marathon runners. They suggested that elite marathon runners used more associate strategies, such as focusing on how their body feels, to help dictate their pacing, whereas non-elite marathon runners tended to adopt more dissociative strategies (i.e., focusing on aspects away from bodily sensations, such as counting the number of dogs on a training run). There was, however, no empirical evidence to assess whether these associative and dissociative attentional strategies have distinct, differential, effects on performance. The area of attentional strategies has received much attention from researchers, but those researchers who have attempted to better understand the distinct effects of attentional strategies on performance failed to arrive at a consistent conclusion (for a review see Masters & Ogles 1998; Salmon, Hanneman, & Harwood 2010). The distinction between associative and dissociative strategies is, indeed, overly simplistic. Athletes may rely on both strategies at different parts of an endurance activity; for example, when the task intensity is high endurance athletes rely more on associative strategies (Hutchinson & Tenenbaum 2007; Salmon et al., 2010). More recently, a new model has been introduced where Brick, MacIntyre, and Campbell (2014) have endeavoured to categorise these cognitive processes more specifically. During endurance activities there is a lot of time to think, and it is no surprise that research has continued to focus on the role of thoughts (Baker, Côté, & Deakin, 2005; Stevinson & Biddle, 1998). Meta-cognitive processes ('thinking about thinking') and cognitive processes will be covered in Chapters 6 and 8 of this book.

The perception of psychological demands is evident in a range of endurance activities. When we interviewed competitive recreational athletes from a range of endurance sports about the types of things that can make their sport challenging, we found that endurance athletes were worried about whether they had done enough preparation. Moreover, they experienced pre-event stressors such as practical worries about how to get to the course. Feeling guilty about the time investment and lifestyle sacrifices, as well as the commitment to training that is required were also considered to be demands as part of endurance training. During the event athletes experienced demands such as worries about optimising pacing and remaining focused despite adversity (McCormick, Meijen, & Marcora, 2018a). When working with runners before long distance running events (Meijen, Day, & Hays, 2017) we also find that athletes are anxious and worried about the upcoming event, some have concerns about optimising their pacing and sticking to their race plan, and runners often mention that they feel tense as a result of their nerves. The impact of an endurance athlete's thoughts on their emotional responses and behaviours have been reported by others (Hammermeister & Burton, 1995; Philippe, Rochat, Vauthier, & Hauw, 2016). It is evident that emotions can play a role in performance (for example see Baron, Moullan, Deruelle, & Noakes, 2011; Lane et al., 2016). The role of emotions and emotion regulation will be discussed in Chapter 5.

The increasing interest in the role of psychological variables in the field of endurance performance is exciting. During our journey in the field of endurance performance we did, however, feel that some of the research on the psychological determinants of endurance performance was fragmented. Therefore, we wanted to better understand what the effects of psychological skills interventions were on performance, and to identify which additional psychological factors influenced performance. In our systematic review (McCormick et al., 2015), we identified studies that used practical psychological interventions that aimed to improve endurance performance using an experimental design. Psychological interventions that were accessible to use, such as imagery, attentional strategies, goal-setting, and self-talk, improved performance in endurance activities including running, rowing, gymnasium triathlon, swimming, and cycling. There was, however, no evidence to suggest that one psychological intervention was more effective compared to others. In addition to these psychological interventions, self-efficacy and motivational factors including extrinsic rewards, head-to-head competition, and verbal encouragement benefitted performance; mental fatigue, on the other hand, undermined performance.

With this increased focus on psychological variables in endurance performance we feel that it is timely to share psychological theories and interventions for endurance performance and feed the increasing interest in this research topic. Although it is important to look at the function of the brain, and to consider the physiology of endurance performance, we also need to consider psychological factors such as self-efficacy, motivation, and affective responses as these impact endurance performance. Moreover, we endeavour to acknowledge the interdisciplinary nature of endurance performance, and where applicable we refer to this.

Quality of the studies conducted in the area of endurance psychology

The psychology of endurance performance is an upcoming field, and we are only just starting to embrace the inclusion of psychological variables. Many of the novel research findings are published in physiology journals; this may escape the attention of those who are not based in sport science departments and these studies are not necessarily reviewed by those with a background or expertise in psychology. To give the reader an example as to why this could be problematic, we return to the systematic review on the psychological determinants of endurance performance (McCormick et al., 2015). A modified version of the Effective Public Health Practice Project (EPHPP) Quality Assessment Tool for Quantitative Studies (Thomas, Ciliska, & Dobbins, 2004) was used to assess the quality of the studies. Of the 46 reviewed studies only two were classified as strong in quality. In addition, only three studies were informed by a theoretical framework *and* measured whether the intervention also had an impact on this psychological variable. Let us illustrate this with an example as to why this affects the quality of a study. Imagine a study that aims to examine a goal-setting intervention with the aim of increasing an athlete's confidence to stick to a race plan. It is helpful to actually measure changes in confidence as well as measuring performance. Similarly, if a researcher is using an incentive to increase motivation, you want to measure if this in fact changes the motivation of the participants if you are to draw the conclusion that *because* of a change in motivation the performance increased. We hope that with this book we can encourage our readers to inform their practice by theory, and a wider range of underpinning theoretical frameworks will be covered in this book.

The systematic review provided us with a comprehensive overview of the psychological determinants of endurance performance, but it also highlighted the need to consider the moderators and mediators of endurance performance. We felt that it is important to outline what these are and how these can influence endurance performance, so that the reader can refer back to this throughout the book. Moderators are variables that can influence the strength or direction of a relationship (Baron & Kenny, 1986). For example, when assessing the relationship between the use of imagery and performance, a factor that can influence this is the type of endurance activity. Although the review was not able to evaluate the influence of moderators such as the gender of the participants, or their athletic ability/skill level, observational research from other sports suggests that the skill level of an athlete can play a role in the use of a psychological skills intervention in relation to performance (for an overview see Krane & Williams, 2010).

Mediators are variables that can help explain the relationship between two other variables, that is, the how or why of an effect (Baron & Kenny, 1986). Going back to the previous example of measuring the relationship between the use of imagery and performance, a mediating variable could be an athlete's level of self-efficacy. That is, when we consider mediators we are focusing on the psychological mechanisms that underpin improvements in performance. Increasing motivation, strengthening efficacy, or decreasing perception of effort are examples of psychological mechanisms that can be the focus of practical psychological interventions (McCormick et al., 2015). This can help practitioners, athletes, coaches, and researchers to understand why an intervention does, or does not, work.

There are also challenges that come with the use of performance measures in endurance performance research. Although endurance sport is unique in that performance can typically be measured in a fairly objective manner, we need to be critical in when and how performance is assessed and how we define performance. Some researchers have measured performance using a 'subjective' measure of performance where participants were asked to rate their satisfaction with their performance or where the sport psychology consultant reviewed the day's performance as part of their sessions (Bull, 1989), whereas others have used physical measures of performance such as maximal oxygen intake or a time-based (such as time taken to complete a 5 km run) or distance based (such as a time-trial where one is asked to cycle for 20 minutes) measure of performance. Although it is beyond the scope of this chapter to critically discuss the different ways and intricacies of measuring endurance performance, we felt it appropriate to at least raise this as it can influence how one may interpret the findings of research that is covered in the various chapters. For example, one can consider how much the task meant to the participant, when the performance measure was taken in the training cycle of an athlete, and how well findings from a lab experience translate to less controlled settings (for a critical review see McCormick, Meijen, Anstiss, & Jones, 2018). In fact, very little 'real-life' field research has been conducted where performance measures from outside of a controlled lab setting have been used when considering psychological factors in endurance performance. This is not surprising considering the challenges of doing field research. For example, in our study examining the effects of a motivational self-talk intervention in an ultramarathon (McCormick, Meijen, & Marcora, 2018b), there were various confounding variables such as people getting lost during the event (considering it was a self-supported race), injuries, and running together with others (thus not focusing on performing optimally in terms of time, and instead more focusing on running and supporting a friend). An additional consideration of this study was how to ensure that the control group, who received an alternative control intervention, kept engaged with the study, and to match the two groups in terms of 'expectancy effects' to help avoid that the control group would actively seek out what intervention the other (self-talk) group had received. On a more general note, focusing too much on performance as an outcome measure will also do injustice to research that uses qualitative designs and mixed-methods designs, for example to better understand emotion regulation, the reasons for participating in endurance events, and goal-pursuit processes, to name just a few topics of interest that will be covered in this book.

The book in a nutshell

This book is divided in three parts. The first part will focus on key determinants of endurance performance, with a particular focus on self-regulatory processes. Self-regulatory processes are goal-driven processes, where an individual can be moving towards or away from goal representations by changing their responses or inner states (Carver & Scheier, 2009). For example, athletes may decide to slow down during a training run to avoid injury, or use metacognitive processes to evaluate how their body feels and speed up accordingly. When considering these self-regulatory processes it is important to identify what the psychological determinants of endurance activities are that can influence this feedback loop process. We believe that this is not only a cognitive process, but that it is also influenced by psychophysiological and motivational processes. Therefore, in this part of the book there will be a focus on perception of effort and potential motivation, exercise induced pain, decision-making processes and pacing, emotions and emotion regulation, meta-cognitive processes, and self-efficacy.

The second part of the book provides an overview of psychological interventions aimed to improve endurance performance. In the prelude to this part, a basic introduction to what interventions are will be provided. The interventions that will be covered in this part are cognitive strategies to help with altering pace control, goal-setting and goal-striving, the use of imagery to improve the performance and well-being of endurance performers, self-talk, and mindfulness in endurance performance.

The third part of this book focuses on future directions for research and applied practice. Clinical issues such as injury, burnout, and eating and substance use disorders are prevalent in endurance performance. What do we know about this, and how can this inform our research and practice? As the interest in and uptake of endurance activities is on the rise, we also need to focus on the application of psychological support when working with the public, and this will be discussed through the evaluation of mental support provision at mass participation events. Finally, we will provide suggestions on directions of research in this field.

References

Amann, M. (2012). Significance of Group III and IV muscle afferents for the endurance exercising human. *Clinical and Experimental Pharmacology and Physiology, 39*(9), 831–835.

Amann, M., & Calbet, J. A. (2008). Convective oxygen transport and fatigue. *Journal of Applied Physiology, 104*(3), 861–870.

Amann, M., & Secher, N. H. (2010). Point: Afferent feedback from fatigued locomotor muscles is an important determinant of endurance exercise performance. *Journal of Applied Physiology, 108*(2), 452–454.

Baker, J., Côté, J., & Deakin, J. (2005). Cognitive characteristics of expert, middle of the pack, and back of the pack ultra-endurance triathletes. *Psychology of Sport and Exercise, 6*(5), 551–558.

Baker, J., Deakin, J., & Côté, J. (2005). On the utility of deliberate practice: Predicting performance in ultra-endurance triathletes from training indices. *International Journal of Sport Psychology, 36*(3), 225–240.

Baron, B., Moullan, F., Deruelle, F., & Noakes, T. D. (2011). The role of emotions on pacing strategies and performance in middle and long duration sport events. *British Journal of Sports Medicine, 45*(6), 511–517.

Baron, R. M., & Kenny, D. A. (1986). The moderator–mediator variable distinction in social psychological research: Conceptual, strategic, and statistical considerations. *Journal of Personality and Social Psychology, 51*(6), 1173–1182.

Brehm, J. W., & Self, E. A. (1989). The intensity of motivation. *Annual Review of Psychology, 40*, 109–131.

Brick, N., MacIntyre, T., & Campbell, M. (2014). Attentional focus in endurance activity: New paradigms and future directions. *International Review of Sport and Exercise Psychology, 7*, 106–134.

Bull, S. J. (1989). The role of the sport psychology consultant: A case study of ultra-distance running. *The Sport Psychologist, 3*(3), 254–264.

Carver, C. S., & Scheier, M. F. (2009). Action, affect, multitasking, and layers of control. In J. P. Forgas, R. F. Baumeister, & D. M. Tice (Eds.), *Psychology of self-regulation: Cognitive, affective, and motivational processes* (pp. 109–126). New York: Psychology Press.

Fitzgerald, M. (2015). *How bad do you want it?: Mastering the psychology of mind over muscle.* Boulder, CO: VeloPress.

Giulio, C. D., Daniele, F., & Tipton, C. M. (2006). Angelo Mosso and muscular fatigue: 116 years after the first congress of physiologists: IUPS commemoration. *AJP: Advances in Physiology Education, 30*(2), 51–57.

Hammermeister, J., & Burton, D. (1995). Anxiety and the ironman: Investigating the antecedents and consequences of endurance athletes' state anxiety. *The Sport Psychologist, 9*, 29–40.

Hutchinson, J. C., & Tenenbaum, G. (2007). Attention focus during physical effort: The mediating role of task intensity. *Psychology of Sport and Exercise, 8*(2), 233–245.

Inzlicht, M., & Marcora, S. M. (2016). The central governor model of exercise regulation teaches us precious little about the nature of mental fatigue and self-control failure. *Frontiers in Psychology, 7*, 656.

Joyner, M. J., & Coyle, E. F. (2008). Endurance exercise performance: The physiology of champions. *The Journal of Physiology, 586*(1), 35–44.

Kenney, W. L., Wilmore, J., & Costill, D. (2015). *Physiology of sport and exercise*. Champaign, IL: Human Kinetics.

Krane, V., & Williams, J. M. (2010). Psychological characteristics of peak performance. In J. M. Williams (Ed.), *Applied sport psychology: Personal growth to peak performance* (pp. 169–188). New York, NY: McGraw-Hill.

Lane, A. M., Devonport, T. J., Friesen, A. P., Beedie, C. J., Fullerton, C. L., & Stanley, D. M. (2016). How should I regulate my emotions if I want to run faster? *European Journal of Sport Science, 16*, 465–472.

Marcora, S. M. (2007). Entia non sunt multiplicanda praeter necessitatem. *The Journal of Physiology, 578*(Pt 1), 371.

Marcora, S. M. (2008). Do we really need a central governor to explain brain regulation of exercise performance? *European Journal of Applied Physiology, 104*(5), 929–931.

Marcora, S. M., Bosio, A., & de Morree, H. M. (2008). Locomotor muscle fatigue increases cardiorespiratory responses and reduces performance during intense cycling exercise independently from metabolic stress. *American Journal of Physiology – Regulatory, Integrative and Comparative Physiology, 294*, R874–R883.

Marcora, S. M., & Staiano, W. (2010). The limit to exercise tolerance in humans: Mind over muscle? *European Journal of Applied Physiology, 109*(4), 763–770.

Masters, K. S., & Ogles, B. M. (1998). Associative and dissociative cognitive strategies in exercise and running: 20 years later, what do we know? *The Sport Psychologist, 12*(3), 253–270.

McCormick, A., Meijen, C., Anstiss, P. A., & Jones, H. S. (2018). Self-regulation in endurance sports: Theory, research, and practice. *International Review of Sport and Exercise Psychology*. DOI: 10.1080/1750984X.2018.1469161.

McCormick, A., Meijen, C., & Marcora, S. (2015). Psychological determinants of whole-body endurance performance. *Sports Medicine, 45*(7), 997–1015.

McCormick, A., Meijen, C., & Marcora, S. (2018a). Psychological demands experienced by recreational endurance athletes. *International Journal of Sport and Exercise Psychology, 16*(4), 415–430.

McCormick, A., Meijen, C., & Marcora, S. (2018b). Effects of a motivational self-talk intervention for endurance athletes completing an ultramarathon. *The Sport Psychologist, 32*(1), 42–50.

Meijen, C., Day, C., & Hays, K. F. (2017). Running a psyching team: Providing mental support at long-distance running events. *Journal of Sport Psychology in Action, 8*(1), 12–22.

Millet, G. Y., & Lepers, R. (2004). Alterations of neuromuscular function after prolonged running, cycling and skiing exercises. *Sports Medicine, 34*(2), 105–116.

Moran, A. P., & Toner, J. (2017). *A critical introduction to sport psychology*. London: Routledge.

Morgan, W. P., & Pollock, M. L. (1977). Psychologic characterization of the elite distance runner. *Annals of the New York Academy of Sciences, 301*(1), 382–403.

Noakes, T. D. (1997). 1996 J.B. Wolffe Memorial Lecture. Challenging beliefs: ex Africa semper aliquid novi. *Medicine and Science in Sports and Exercise, 29*(5), 571–590.

Noakes, T. D. (2000). Physiological models to understand exercise fatigue and the adaptations that predict or enhance athletic performance. *Scandinavian Journal of Medicine & Science in Sports, 10*(3), 123–145.

Noakes, T. D. (2012). Fatigue is a brain-derived emotion that regulates the exercise behavior to ensure the protection of whole body homeostasis. *Frontiers in Physiology*, *3*, 82.

Noakes, T. D., St Clair Gibson, A., & Lambert, E. V. (2005). From catastrophe to complexity: A novel model of integrative central neural regulation of effort and fatigue during exercise in humans: summary and conclusions. *British Journal of Sports Medicine*, *39*(2), 120–124.

Nybo, L. (2008). Hyperthermia and fatigue. *Journal of Applied Physiology*, *104*(3), 871–878.

O'Connor, P. J. (1992). Psychological aspects of endurance performance. In R. J. Shepard & P. O. Astrand (Eds.), *Endurance in sport* (pp. 139–145). Oxford, England: Blackwell Publishing.

Philippe, R. A., Rochat, N., Vauthier, M., & Hauw, D. (2016). The story of withdrawals during an ultra-trail running race: A qualitative investigation of runners' courses of experience. *The Sport Psychologist*, *30*(4), 361–375.

Salmon, P., Hanneman, S., & Harwood, B. (2010). Associative/dissociative cognitive strategies in sustained physical activity: Literature review and proposal for a mindfulness-based conceptual model. *The Sport Psychologist*, *24*(2), 127–156.

Shephard, R. J., & Astrand, P.-O. (Eds.). (2000). *Endurance in sport*. Oxford: Blackwell Science Ltd.

Simons, J. (2012). Endurance psychology. In I. Mujika (Ed.), *Endurance training: Science and practice* (pp. 201–210). Vitoria-Gasteiz: Iñigo Mujika SLU.

Stevinson, C. D., & Biddle, S. J. (1998). Cognitive orientations in marathon running and 'hitting the wall'. *British Journal of Sports Medicine*, *32*(3), 229–234.

Thomas, B., Ciliska, D., & Dobbins, M. (2004). A process for systematically reviewing the literature: Providing the research evidence for public health nursing interventions. *Worldviews on Evidence-Based Nursing*, *1*(3), 176–184.

Triplett, N. (1898). The dynamogenic factors in pacemaking and competition. *The American Journal of Psychology*, *9*(4), 507.

PART I

Determinants of endurance performance

2

PSYCHOBIOLOGY OF FATIGUE DURING ENDURANCE EXERCISE

Samuele Marcora

Introduction

The aim of this chapter is to describe the psychobiology of fatigue during endurance exercise. Endurance exercise can be defined as whole-body, dynamic exercise that involves continuous effort and lasts for 75 s or longer (McCormick, Meijen, & Marcora, 2015). This operational definition includes the most popular endurance sports such as road cycling, middle-distance running, marathons and ultra-marathons, most swimming events, triathlons, rowing, and cross-country skiing.

The definition of fatigue is more challenging because this term is used when referring to many different phenomena ranging from feeling tired after a prolonged and vigorous bout of exercise (Loy, O'Connor, & Dishman, 2013) to the reduction in maximal force of an isolated muscle fibre induced by continuous electrical stimulation (Allen, Lamb, & Westerblad, 2008). For the purpose of this chapter, I adopt the definition of fatigue as an acute impairment in performance that includes both an increase in the perceived effort necessary to exert a desired force or power and an eventual inability to produce this force or power (Enoka & Stuart, 1992). This definition of fatigue includes three different phenomena that can be observed during endurance exercise (Marcora & Staiano, 2010). The first one is muscle fatigue defined as the exercise-induced impairment in muscle performance measured as the force or power produced during a brief maximal voluntary contraction (MVC). The second phenomenon is the progressive increase in perception of effort experienced during endurance exercise. The third phenomenon is the eventual inability to produce the required velocity/power that occurs at the point commonly called exhaustion or task failure.

Since the time of A. V. Hill (1926), the mainstream assumption among exercise physiologists has been that highly-motivated people terminate endurance exercise when their fatigued neuromuscular system is no longer able to produce the velocity/power required by the endurance task despite a maximal voluntary effort (Allen et al., 2008; Burnley & Jones, 2018; Hepple, 2002). Because of this assumption, most research has been on the cardiorespiratory, central (within the brain and spinal cord), and peripheral (within the muscles) mechanisms of locomotor muscle fatigue (Allen et al., 2008; Amann & Calbet, 2008; Burnley & Jones, 2018; Hepple, 2002; Taylor & Gandevia, 2008) with relatively little attention to perception of effort (Barry & Enoka, 2007). However, in recent years, several studies have shown that, immediately after exhaustive endurance exercise, the maximal voluntary power of the locomotor muscles is significantly higher than the power required by the endurance task (Cannon et al., 2016; Ferguson, Wylde, Benson, Cannon, & Rossiter, 2015; Marcora & Staiano, 2010; Morales-Alamo et al., 2015; Morales-Alamo, Martin-Rincon, Perez-Valera, Marcora, & Calbet, 2016; Staiano, Bosio, de Morree, Rampinini, & Marcora, 2018). These findings challenge the assumption that locomotor muscle fatigue directly causes exhaustion during endurance exercise. Furthermore, models that include only physiological constructs like oxygen transport, central fatigue, and peripheral fatigue fail to explain why psychological manipulations can affect endurance performance (McCormick et al., 2015). The ergogenic effects of psychological manipulations like placebo (Ross, Gray, & Gill, 2015) and motivational self-talk (Blanchfield, Hardy, De Morree, Staiano, & Marcora, 2014) also argue against the central governor model which postulates that locomotor muscle recruitment and endurance performance are regulated at a subconscious level to prevent conscious override that might damage the human (Noakes, 2000; St Clair Gibson & Noakes, 2004). Therefore, a different theoretical framework is required (Inzlicht & Marcora, 2016; Marcora, 2007, 2008).

In this chapter I describe a psychobiological model (PBM) to explain why perception of effort increases over time and how this fatigue interacts with motivational factors to determine for how long an individual can sustain endurance exercise at a given velocity/power. This basic endurance is measured in the laboratory using time-to-exhaustion tests (Amann, Hopkins, & Marcora, 2008) and it is associated with performance level in professional endurance athletes (Sassi, Marcora, Rampinini, Mognoni, & Impellizzeri, 2006). This association is not surprising because time to exhaustion at a given velocity/power is the main factor determining whether an athlete can sustain (or not) the pace required to win a mass-start endurance competition (de Koning et al., 2011) or to set a new personal, national, or world record (Padilla, Mujika, Angulo, & Goiriena, 2000).

Basic principles of the psychobiological model

The first basic principle of the PBM is to consider endurance performance as a goal-directed behaviour rather than just the output of a biological engine that transforms chemical energy into mechanical energy. The theoretical consequence of this approach is that endurance performance should be explainable by psychology, the scientific study of the human mind and behaviour. Indeed, at the first level of explanation, the PBM includes only psychological constructs (perception of effort and potential motivation) to explain for how long an individual can sustain endurance exercise at a given velocity/power. This is the psychological level of explanation.

The second basic principle of the PBM is that the mind emerges from lower-level neurobiological processes in the brain (Searle, 1998). Therefore, the PBM includes the neurophysiological/neuroanatomical correlates and other biological aspects (e.g., neurochemistry and genetics) of the psychological constructs that determine endurance performance at the psychological level of explanation. This is the biological level of explanation.

Psychological level of explanation

Psychological constructs and theory

At the psychological level of explanation, the PBM postulates that time to exhaustion during endurance exercise is determined primarily by two psychological constructs: perception of effort and potential motivation (Figure 2.1). Perception of effort, also known as perceived exertion or sense of effort, is the conscious sensation of the effort exerted to perform a physical task (Marcora, 2009, 2010), and its intensity is commonly measured using the scales developed by Borg (1998). As an example, the 15-point rating of perceived exertion (RPE) scale ranges from 6 ('no exertion at all') to 20 ('maximal exertion') with additional verbal anchors for some of the intermediate ratings; for example, 7 on this scale corresponds to 'hard (heavy)'. During endurance exercise, overall perception of effort has two main components that can be measured separately (de Morree & Marcora, 2015): the conscious sensation of how hard one is driving the locomotor muscles (e.g., leg effort) and the conscious sensation of how heavily one is breathing, a type of dyspnea called respiratory effort or exertional dyspnea (Gigliotti, 2010). Perception of effort should not be confused with discomfort or other conscious sensations experienced during endurance exercise, such as muscle pain and thermal sensation (Marcora, 2009). Indeed, discomfort refers to the affective dimension of any conscious sensation (Cabanac, 1979) whilst exercise-induced muscle pain is both phenomenologically and neurophysiologically different from perception of effort (Hamilton, Killian, Summers, & Jones, 1996; O'Connor & Cook, 1999).

Notwithstanding momentary fluctuations (Balagué et al., 2015), RPE at a given velocity/power progressively increases over time (Garcin & Billat, 2001; Kearon, Summers, Jones, Campbell, & Killian, 1991; Nakamura et al., 2009) and it can predict time to exhaustion during endurance exercise at different intensities and in various physiological and environmental conditions (Crewe, Tucker, & Noakes, 2008; Horstman, Morgan, Cymerman, & Stokes, 1979; Noakes, 2004). These findings are consistent with our proposal that perception of effort is one of the two main determinants of time to exhaustion during endurance exercise. However, to generate experimentally testable hypotheses, a theoretical framework is needed to explain how the progressive increase in perception of effort experienced during endurance exercise can eventually cause exhaustion.

Previous attempts at providing such explanation have been limited to brief references about people stopping when perception of effort and/or other sensations experienced during endurance exercise become "more intense than is tolerable", "maximally tolerable", or "sufficiently unattractive", the so-called 'sensory tolerance limit' (Amann et al., 2006; Gandevia, 2001; Kayser, 2003; Tucker, 2009). The PBM is based on a more sophisticated psychological theory developed by Brehm to explain mobilisation of effort during any goal-directed behaviour: motivational intensity theory (Wright, 2008).

With regard to endurance performance, the PBM adopts two components of motivational intensity theory. The first one is the psychological construct of potential motivation defined as the maximum effort an individual is willing to exert in order to succeed in the task. Potential motivation is determined by motivational variables like the incentive value of the anticipated outcome(s), the need for the anticipated outcome(s), and the instrumentality of the task with respect to achieving these outcome(s). In other words, the more rewarding or instrumental success on a task is, the more effort is justified to succeed in that task. Unlike other motivation theories, motivational intensity theory is not about the quality of motivation, such as the differences between intrinsic and extrinsic motivation (Deci & Ryan, 2011). Any motivational variable that makes success more or less important has basically the same effect on potential motivation which is more about the quantity of motivation (Gendolla & Richter, 2010).

The second component of motivational intensity theory adopted by the PBM is its prediction that when success in the task is perceived as impossible or excessively difficult, people disengage from the task. When applied to time-to-exhaustion tests, motivational intensity theory postulates that people decide to stop endurance exercise (i.e., disengage from the task) when sustaining the required velocity/power is perceived as impossible or excessively difficult. Perception of effort plays a major role in this decision-making process because one of its functions is to provide information about task difficulty (Preston & Wegner, 2009). In other words, in conditions of relatively low potential motivation, people decide to stop endurance exercise when perception of effort exceeds the maximum effort they are willing to exert in order to succeed in the task (Figure 2.1a). In conditions of high potential motivation, people decide to stop endurance exercise when effort is perceived as maximal and sustaining the required velocity/power seems impossible (Figure 2.1b).

At the psychological level of explanation, the PBM of endurance performance makes the following experimentally testable predictions. With regard to perception of effort, it postulates that (assuming the same potential motivation) any physiological or psychological manipulation that reduces perception of effort during endurance exercise would increase time to exhaustion (Y vs X in both Figure 2.1a and Figure 2.1b). Conversely, any physiological or psychological manipulation that increases perception of effort during endurance exercise would reduce time to

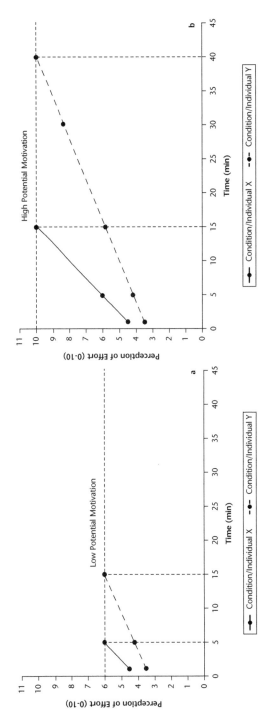

FIGURE 2.1 Graphical representation of how perception of effort and potential motivation interact to determine time to exhaustion during endurance exercise

exhaustion (X vs Y in both Figure 2.1a and Figure 2.1b). Changes in perception of effort refer to both its initial intensity and/or how quickly perception of effort increases over time during endurance exercise.

With regard to potential motivation, the prediction of the PBM is that any experimental manipulation that increases potential motivation would increase time to exhaustion assuming the same perception of effort during endurance exercise (Figure 2.1b vs Figure 2.1a for both X and Y). When potential motivation is high enough to justify a maximal effort, motivational intensity theory predicts that a further increase in the incentive value of the anticipated outcomes (or other motivational factors that increase potential motivation) will not result in further improvements in time to exhaustion. The following three sections provide some examples of experiments testing these hypotheses using both physiological and psychological manipulations.

Physiological manipulations of perceived effort

At the psychological level of explanation, the PBM includes only psychological constructs (Figure 2.1). However, this theoretical approach does not mean that physiological manipulations cannot affect endurance performance; it simply means that their negative or positive effects on time to exhaustion are mediated by changes in perception of effort (a psychological construct) rather than being direct.

A striking example is locomotor muscle fatigue. As I have argued in the introduction to this chapter, locomotor muscle fatigue does not directly cause exhaustion during endurance exercise. Nevertheless, we demonstrated experimentally that locomotor muscle fatigue reduces endurance performance (Marcora, Bosio, & de Morree, 2008). In this study, we induced significant locomotor muscle fatigue in ten participants using an eccentric exercise protocol before a high-intensity time-to-exhaustion test performed on a cycle ergometer. Compared to the control condition (resting before the time-to-exhaustion test), locomotor muscle fatigue significantly reduced time to exhaustion by 15 per cent (locomotor muscle fatigue 636 s vs. control 750 s). In both conditions, our participants stopped cycling despite their maximal voluntary locomotor muscle force being well above the force required by high-intensity cycling exercise (Löllgen, Graham, & Sjogaard, 1980). So why did they stop cycling earlier in the locomotor muscle fatigue condition compared to the control condition? Our explanation was that, because because perception of effort was higher when cycling with pre-fatigued locomotor muscles, our participants reached the point at which they perceived the task to be impossible or excessively difficult earlier than in the control condition. Whilst supporting the predictions of the PBM, this study also demonstrates that, albeit indirectly, locomotor muscle fatigue remains an important determinant of endurance performance in humans. The PBM can also explain why respiratory muscle fatigue reduces time to exhaustion during high-intensity cycling exercise: breathing with fatigued expiratory/inspiratory muscles significantly increases exertional dyspnea, an important component of overall perception of effort (Romer & Polkey, 2008). Via complex pathways, respiratory muscle fatigue can also exacerbate locomotor muscle fatigue and, thus, further increase overall perception of effort (Romer & Polkey, 2008).

With regard to physiological manipulations that reduce perception of effort and improve endurance performance, the most effective by far is physical training. Traditionally, the positive effect of physical training on endurance performance has been explained physiologically: physical training induces cardiovascular and muscular adaptations leading to an increase in maximal oxygen consumption, improved exercise economy, and a reduction in blood lactate accumulation at a given velocity/power (Joyner & Coyle, 2008). However, it is also possible to provide a psychological explanation: physical training reduces perception of effort during endurance exercise. For example, Ekblom and Goldbarg (1971) tested eight participants on a cycle ergometer before and after eight weeks of physical training consisting mostly of outdoor cross country running. Compared to the pre-training values, RPE at each corresponding stage of the incremental exercise test was significantly lower after physical training, and participants stopped later. Similarly, a reduction in exertional dyspnea may mediate the positive effect of respiratory muscle training on endurance performance (Romer & Polkey, 2008).

The effects of nutritional and environmental manipulations on endurance performance can also be explained psychologically. For example, it is now widely accepted that the improvement in time to exhaustion observed after caffeine ingestion is mediated by perception of effort (Doherty & Smith, 2005) rather than higher fat oxidation and glycogen sparing originally postulated (Graham, 2001). The negative effects of hypoxia (Romer et al., 2007) and heat (Crewe et al., 2008) on time to exhaustion can also be explained by the higher effort perceived when exercising in these environmental conditions.

Psychological manipulations of perceived effort

Importantly, the PBM can also explain the effects of psychological manipulations that do not affect the physiological systems (e.g., cardiorespiratory and neuromuscular) traditionally associated with endurance performance (Amann & Calbet, 2008; Joyner & Coyle, 2008). One example of such manipulations is mental fatigue defined as the psychobiological state of fatigue induced by prolonged mental effort (Van Cutsem et al., 2017). In a seminal study, we induced mental fatigue experimentally by asking 18 participants to perform a cognitively demanding computerized task for 90 min before a high-intensity time-to-exhaustion test performed on a cycle ergometer (Marcora, Staiano, & Manning, 2009). Compared to the control condition (watching documentaries for 90 min before the time-to-exhaustion test), mental fatigue significantly reduced time to exhaustion by 15 per cent (mental fatigue 640 s vs. control 754 s). However, mental fatigue did not affect the cardiovascular, respiratory, and metabolic responses to high-intensity cycling exercise. In a subsequent study, we demonstrated that mental fatigue does not affect the development of central and peripheral fatigue induced by high-intensity cycling exercise either (Pageaux, Marcora, Rozand, & Lepers, 2015). The only effect of mental fatigue that could explain its negative effect on endurance performance was the higher perception of effort. As a result, when mentally fatigued, our participants reached the point at which they perceived the task to be impossible or excessively difficult earlier than in the control condition.

Psychological manipulations can also reduce perception of effort and, thus, delay exhaustion during endurance exercise. For example, we conducted a ran-domised controlled trial of motivational self-talk in 24 participants. In the group of participants who were taught and practised the use this psychological skill, time to exhaustion increased significantly from pre-test to post-test (637 to 750 s) whilst no significant change was observed in the control group (486 to 474 s). This positive effect of motivational self-talk on endurance performance was associated with a significant reduction in perception of effort as postulated by the PBM. Interestingly, perception of effort and endurance performance can also be changed using psychological manipulations of which the person being tested is not con-sciously aware (Blanchfield, Hardy, & Marcora, 2014).

Manipulations of potential motivation

Like perception of effort, potential motivation can be manipulated both physi-ologically and psychologically. For example, starvation (and related hunger) would increase potential motivation if endurance exercise was the task instrumental to obtaining food. This was most likely the case when persistence hunting (i.e., chas-ing an animal until it is run to heat exhaustion) was one of the most efficient forms of hunting (Liebenberg, 2006). Nowadays, the factors that determine potential motivation for endurance exercise are primarily psychological, such as competition and monetary reward in endurance athletes.

Although it is widely accepted that motivation is important for endurance per-formance, very little experimental research has been published on its effects on time to exhaustion. With regard to the effect of competition, Wilmore (1968) demon-strated that time to exhaustion during high-intensity cycling exercise is significantly longer when competing against an opponent than when cycling solo. With regard to the effect of monetary reward, I am not aware of any experimental study using time-to-exhaustion tests whilst running or cycling. However, over five different testing sessions, Cabanac (1986) gave ten male participants 0.20, 0.50, 1.25, 3.125, 7.8125 French francs for every 20 s they lasted during an isometric leg endurance exercise (wall squat test). As predicted by motivational intensity theory, the amount of contingent monetary reward was correlated with time to exhaustion, and the effect tended to plateau at higher amounts of contingent monetary reward.

Biological level of explanation

The central governor model (Noakes (2012) and another almost identical theoreti-cal model (Tucker, 2009)) postulate that, at the beginning of endurance exercise, a subconscious central governor/controller in the brain receives afferent feedback about the physiological conditions of the body and skin temperature, and uses it to calculate for how long the individual can sustain a given velocity/power without catastrophic failures of bodily homeostasis. The linear increase in perception of effort over time is then set as a consequence of this subconscious teleoanticipatory calculation of the safe duration of endurance exercise, with some ongoing adjustments based on continuous afferent feedback. In short, time to exhaustion and perception of effort are both based on a subconscious decision taken at the beginning of endurance exercise.

As described in detail at the psychological level of explanation, the PBM postulates the exact contrary: time to exhaustion is limited by a conscious decision taken at the end of endurance exercise on the basis of perception of effort. Furthermore, at the biological level of explanation of the PBM, there is no central governor/controller (Marcora, 2007, 2008); like any other conscious sensation, perception of effort is generated at any given moment by brain processing of the relevant neural signals. Therefore, rather than reflecting a subconscious teleoanticipatory calculation of time to exhaustion, the progressive increase in perception of effort experienced during endurance exercise reflects a progressive increase in the magnitude of the neural signals processed by the brain to generate perception of effort, and/or changes in the way the brain processes these neural signals (Marcora, 2008).

Progressive increase in the magnitude of the neural signals processed by the brain to generate perception of effort

The first step to understand the neurophysiology of perception of effort is to identify the neural signals processed by the brain to generate it. Some authors have proposed that perception of effort is generated by brain processing of afferent neural signals providing information about heart rate, oxygen uptake, ventilation and respiratory rate, lactic acid production, muscle glycogen content, mechanical strain, skin temperature and core temperature (Hampson, St Clair Gibson, Lambert, & Noakes, 2001; Noakes, 2012; Noakes, St Clair Gibson, & Lambert, 2005; Tucker, 2009). According to this afferent feedback model, blockade of afferent neural signals from the skeletal muscles, heart, and lungs along their pathways to the brain using surgical or pharmacological procedures should significantly reduce RPE during exercise. However, this is not the case (Barbosa et al., 2016; Marcora, 2009; Smirmaul, 2012). Furthermore, the intramuscular injection of hypertonic saline (Khan, McNeil, Gandevia, & Taylor, 2011) or of various mixtures of protons, lactate, and ATP to stimulate group III–IV afferents elicits pain and other conscious muscle sensations, but not perception of effort (Khan et al., 2011; Pollak et al., 2014). Overall, it seems clear that afferent neural signals from the body are processed by the brain to generate exercise-induced muscle pain (O'Connor & Cook, 1999), thermal discomfort (Filingeri, 2016) and other conscious sensations experienced during endurance exercise, but not perception of effort.

Current evidence supports the proposal that perception of effort is generated by brain processing of neural signals (called corollary discharges) originating from a) the premotor/motor areas of the cortex that directly or indirectly drive the motoneurons innervating the locomotor muscles (and during heavy breathing, the respiratory muscles), and b) from the medullary centres that drive the motoneurons innervating the respiratory muscles (Figure 2.2) (de Morree & Marcora, 2015; Gigliotti, 2010; Marcora, 2009). In other words, at any given moment,

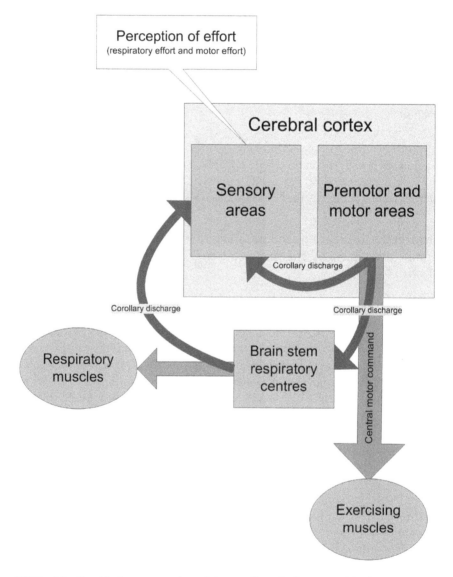

FIGURE 2.2 Graphical representation of the corollary discharge model of perception of effort (Reprinted with permission from de Morree & Marcora, 2015)

the magnitude of the cortical and medullary drives to the locomotor and respiratory muscles determines the magnitude of the corollary discharges and, through brain processing, the intensity of perception of effort during endurance exercise. Although there is anatomical and neurophysiological evidence that corollary discharges from premotor/motor to sensory areas of the cortex do exist (Christensen et al., 2007; Poulet & Hedwig, 2006), it is also possible that the anterior cingulate cortex (ACC) and other premotor/motor areas of the cortex can directly generate subjective feelings of effort (Shenhav et al., 2017), or that corollary discharges traverse efferent and then afferent pathways via the muscle spindles (reafferent corollary discharges) (Luu, Day, Cole, & Fitzpatrick, 2011). Regardless of the specific mechanism, an increase in the activity of premotor/motor areas during voluntary muscle contractions (the so called 'central motor command') should be perceived as an increase in effort.

According to this corollary discharge model (Figure 2.2), the most obvious reason for the progressive increase in perception of effort experienced during endurance exercise is the progressive increase in central motor command necessary to compensate for the progressive development of locomotor muscle fatigue (Enoka & Stuart, 1992; Marcora & Staiano, 2010). Indeed, the reduced responsiveness of the spinal motoneurons innervating the locomotor muscles (central fatigue) and of the locomotor muscles themselves (peripheral fatigue) should force people to increase central motor command (and thus perceived effort) in order to sustain a given velocity/power (Marcora, 2008). However, as lamented by Enoka and Stuart (1992), there is little research on the relationship between the amplitude of the motor-related cortical potential (MRCP, an electrophysiological measure of central motor command) and perception of effort in the context of muscle fatigue. We addressed this gap by measuring MRCP amplitude and RPE during repeated submaximal voluntary contractions of the elbow flexor muscles (de Morree, Klein, & Marcora, 2012). Before these repeated submaximal voluntary contractions (weight lifting), the elbow flexor muscles of one of the two arms were fatigued using an eccentric exercise protocol similar to that used in our cycling study (Marcora et al., 2008). As expected, lifting the same weight with the fatigued arm required a higher central motor command as shown by higher MRCP amplitude during movement execution compared to the non-fatigued arm (Figure 2.3a). The amplitude of this MRCP correlated significantly with RPE across the four experimental conditions which also included two different amounts of weight lifted (Figure 2.3b). These findings support the hypothesis that the increase in perception of effort caused by increasing power/speed (Kearon et al., 1991) and inducing locomotor muscle fatigue (Marcora et al., 2008) during endurance exercise is due to an increase in central motor command.

Although the progressive increase in central motor command necessary to compensate for the progressive development of locomotor muscle fatigue is certainly a very important mechanism, the progressive increase in perception of effort experienced during endurance exercise should not be considered simply as an epiphenomenon of locomotor muscle fatigue. For example, Taylor and Gandevia (2008)

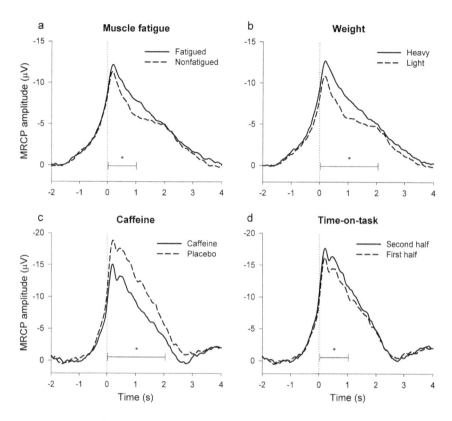

FIGURE 2.3 Grand averages of the motor-related cortical potential (MCRP) at electrode Cz (vertex) for a) muscle fatigue and b) weight during submaximal voluntary contractions of the elbow flexors (N = 16), and for c) caffeine and d) time-on-task during submaximal voluntary contractions of the knee extensor muscles (N = 16) manipulations. Time 0 s is electromyogram onset and contractions lasted approximately 2 s. ★ Significant simple main effect of condition based on Holm-Bonferroni corrected α-levels (Reprinted with permission from de Morree & Marcora, 2015)

observed that RPE during repeated submaximal voluntary contractions of the elbow flexor muscles increases disproportionately more than the increase in effort necessary to compensate for the exercise-induced reduction in MVC force. In a second electroencephalography (EEG) study, we found that MRCP amplitude during movement execution (Figure 2.3d) and RPE increased significantly over time during repeated submaximal voluntary contractions of the knee extensor muscles despite no significant muscle fatigue (de Morree, Klein, & Marcora, 2014).[1] But why should the central motor command/perceived effort necessary to exert the desired force or power increase over time if there is no muscle fatigue to compensate for? To answer this question, it is important to note that perception of effort seems to reflect the activity of premotor and motor areas upstream of the primary motor cortex (M1) rather than of M1 itself (Proske & Gandevia, 2012). Two important components of this 'perceived effort network' are the supplementary motor area (SMA) (Zénon, Sidibé, & Olivier, 2015) and the anterior cingulate cortex (ACC) (Williamson, 2015). Both the SMA and the ACC contribute significantly to the direct cortical control of skeletal muscle output (Dum & Strick, 2002; Nielsen, 2016). However, they also have important cognitive and motivational functions, for example the ability to inhibit prepotent responses and urges in order to pursue a goal (inhibitory control) (Bonnelle, Manohar, Behrens, & Husain, 2015; Botvinick & Braver, 2015). My suggestion is that the increase in central motor command/ perception of effort that occurs over time in excess of muscle fatigue (de Morree et al., 2014; Taylor & Gandevia, 2008) reflects the inhibitory control required to resist the 'urge to quit' when sustaining a given velocity/power becomes unpleasant due to fatigue, pain, thermal discomfort, or boredom (Baumeister, Vohs, & Tice, 2007; Brick, MacIntyre, & Campbell, 2016; Shenhav et al., 2017; van der Linden, 2011). This proposal is corroborated by an EEG study showing that the largest change in cortical activity accompanying fatigue during high-intensity cycling exercise to exhaustion is seen the frontal areas associated with inhibitory control and other effortful cognitive processes (Enders et al., 2016). Over time, the mental effort required by endurance exercise may also lead to mental fatigue which, as discussed earlier, significantly increases perception of effort (Marcora et al., 2009; Pageaux, Lepers, Dietz, & Marcora, 2014).

Finally, the respiratory component of overall perception of effort (as measured indirectly by breathing frequency) should not be ignored as it is highly correlated with RPE during endurance exercise (Nicolò, Marcora, & Sacchetti, 2016). Therefore, the various factors that stimulate the medullary centres and higher cortical areas to increase their drive (and related corollary discharges) to the respiratory muscles can indirectly increase the perception of effort. These factors include some that can increase over time during endurance exercise, for example afferent feedback from metaboreceptors in the locomotor muscles and core body temperature (Wasserman, Whipp, & Casaburi, 1986). The progressive increase in central motor command that occurs during endurance exercise because of locomotor muscle fatigue can also indirectly increase the respiratory component of overall perception of effort (Marcora et al., 2008). Indeed, corollary discharges from premotor/motor areas of the cortex to the medullary centres (Figure 2.3) are considered an important stimulus for hyperpnea during exercise (Wasserman et al., 1986). Furthermore, the respiratory muscle fatigue that can develop during endurance exercise can also increase exertional dyspnea (Romer & Polkey, 2008).

Changes in brain processing during endurance exercise

Perception of effort, like any other conscious sensation, is not simply a reflection of the magnitude of the neural signals processed by the brain to generate it; the neurocognitive processing of these neural signals can also profoundly affect perception (Goldstein, 2009). Therefore, the progressive increase in perception of effort experienced during endurance exercise may also be caused by changes in the way the brain processes the corollary discharges from premotor/motor and respiratory areas of the brain. Unfortunately, there is little research on how the brain processes these corollary discharges to generate perception of effort. Therefore, I can only speculate about the potential changes occurring during endurance exercise.

As for pain, the gain in perception of effort may be due to activation-dependent plasticity (Woolf & Salter, 2000) or other neurobiological changes including those induced by mental fatigue (van der Linden, 2011). Furthermore, brain processing of corollary discharges includes cognitive processes (e.g., attention and the way people interpret and rate their perceived exertion) that can also change over time. For example, over time, attention during endurance exercise shifts internally and becomes narrow and associative (Balagué, Hristovski, Aragonés, & Tenenbaum, 2012). This change in attentional focus can increase perception of effort if an individual focuses excessively on locomotor effort and respiratory effort (Brick et al., 2016). Many other psychological factors can affect how the conscious sensation of effort is processed, interpreted, and reported (Morgan, 1994).

Conclusions

> Granted that psychology is a special phase of brain physiology, it is nevertheless useful to speak of physiologic and psychologic factors. Physiologic factors set the relatively fixed and outermost limits, psychologic factors, the more proximate ones. In this sense it is appropriate to speak of a physiologic and a psychologic limit. Capacity is the always undetermined measure of the former. Performance is always limited by the latter.
>
> *(Ikai & Steinhaus, 1961, p. 157)*

This quote from Ikai and Steinhaus perfectly summarises the basic principles of the PBM of endurance performance described here. The practical implication of this theoretical approach is that interventions that reduce perception of effort should improve the performance of highly motivated endurance athletes over and above what can be accomplished by solely improving their maximal oxygen consumption, lactate threshold, and exercise economy (Joyner & Coyle, 2008). Examples of such psychobiological interventions include the systematic use of various psychological strategies (McCormick et al., 2015), minimisation of mental fatigue before and during endurance competitions (McCormick et al., 2015), nutritional interventions that influence the adenosine-dopamine system (Salamone, Yohn, López-Cruz, San Miguel, & Correa, 2016), brain stimulation (Angius et al., 2017; Zénon et al., 2015), and a new training method that combines physical and cognitive workload during endurance exercise (Marcora, Staiano, & Merlini, 2015). Future improvements in endurance performance will be achieved by better understanding the psychological and neurobiological mechanisms underlying perception of effort during endurance exercise and the high potential motivation required to be an endurance athlete (Henning, Khamoui, & Brown, 2011).

Acknowledgements

I would like to thank Dr Andrea Nicolò and Dr Israel Halperin for their useful comments on earlier versions of this manuscript.

Note

1 In this study, we also observed a significant reduction in MRCP amplitude during move-ment execution (Figure 2.3c) and RPE after caffeine ingestion. This finding provides further evidence that the positive effect of this adenosine antagonist on perception of effort is because of its effects on the central nervous system.

References

Allen, D. G., Lamb, G. D., & Westerblad, H. (2008). Skeletal muscle fatigue: Cellular mechanisms. *Physiological Reviews*, *88*(1), 287–332.

Amann, M., & Calbet, J. A. L. (2008). Convective oxygen transport and fatigue. *Journal of Applied Physiology*, *104*(3), 861–870.

Amann, M., Eldridge, M. W., Lovering, A. T., Stickland, M. K., Pegelow, D. F., & Dempsey, J. A. (2006). Arterial oxygenation influences central motor output and exer-cise performance via effects on peripheral locomotor muscle fatigue in humans. *The Journal of Physiology*, *575*(3), 937–952.

Amann, M., Hopkins, W. G., & Marcora, S. M. (2008). Similar sensitivity of time to exhaustion and time-trial time to changes in endurance. *Medicine and Science in Sports and Exercise*, *40*(3), 574–578.

Angius, L., Mauger, A. R., Hopker, J., Pascual-Leone, A., Santarnecchi, E., & Marcora, S. M. (2017). Bilateral extracephalic transcranial direct current stimulation improves endurance performance in healthy individuals. *Brain Stimulation*, *11*(1), 108–117.

Balagué, N., Hristovski, R., Aragonés, D., & Tenenbaum, G. (2012). Nonlinear model of attention focus during accumulated effort. *Psychology of Sport and Exercise*, *13*(5), 591–597.

Balagué, N., Hristovski, R., García, S., Aguirre, C., Vázquez, P., Razon, S., & Tenenbaum, G. (2015). Dynamics of perceived exertion in constant-power cycling: Time- and work-load-dependent thresholds. *Research Quarterly for Exercise and Sport*, *86*(4), 371–378.

Barbosa, T. C., Vianna, L. C., Fernandes, I. A., Prodel, E., Rocha, H. N. M., Garcia, V. P., . . . Nobrega, A. C. L. (2016). Intrathecal fentanyl abolishes the exaggerated blood pres-sure response to cycling in hypertensive men. *The Journal of Physiology*, *594*(3), 715–725.

Barry, B. K., & Enoka, R. M. (2007). The neurobiology of muscle fatigue: 15 years later. *Integrative and Comparative Biology*, *47*(4), 465–473.

Baumeister, R. F., Vohs, K. D., & Tice, D. M. (2007). The strength model of self-control. *Current Directions in Psychological Science*, *16*(6), 351–355.

Blanchfield, A. W., Hardy, J., De Morree, H. M., Staiano, W., & Marcora, S. M. (2014). Talking yourself out of exhaustion: The effects of self-talk on endurance performance. *Medicine and Science in Sports and Exercise*, *46*(5), 998–1007.

Blanchfield, A. W., Hardy, J., & Marcora, S. M. (2014). Non-conscious visual cues related to affect and action alter perception of effort and endurance performance. *Frontiers in Human Neuroscience*, *8*, 967.

Bonnelle, V., Manohar, S., Behrens, T., & Husain, M. (2015). Individual differences in premotor brain systems underlie behavioral apathy. *Cerebral Cortex*, *26*(2), 807–819.

Borg, G. (1998). *Borg's perceived exertion and pain scales*. Urbana-Champaign, IL: Human Kinetics.

Botvinick, M., & Braver, T. (2015). Motivation and cognitive control: From behavior to neural mechanism. *Annual Review of Psychology, 66*, 83–113.

Brick, N. E., MacIntyre, T. E., & Campbell, M. J. (2016). Thinking and action: A cognitive perspective on self-regulation during endurance performance. *Frontiers in Physiology, 7*, 159.

Burnley, M., & Jones, A. M. (2018). Power-duration relationship: Physiology, fatigue, and the limits of human performance. *European Journal of Sport Science, 18*(1), 1–12.

Cabanac, M. (1979). Sensory pleasure. *The Quarterly Review of Biology, 54*(1), 1–29.

Cabanac, M. (1986). Money versus pain: Experimental study of a conflict in humans. *Journal of the Experimental Analysis of Behavior, 46*(1), 37–44.

Cannon, D. T., Coelho, A. C., Cao, R., Cheng, A., Porszasz, J., Casaburi, R., & Rossiter, H. B. (2016). Skeletal muscle power and fatigue at the tolerable limit of ramp-incremental exercise in COPD. *Journal of Applied Physiology, 121*(6), 1365–1373.

Christensen, M. S., Lundbye-Jensen, J., Geertsen, S. S., Petersen, T. H., Paulson, O. B., & Nielsen, J. B. (2007). Premotor cortex modulates somatosensory cortex during voluntary movements without proprioceptive feedback. *Nature Neuroscience, 10*(4), 417–419.

Crewe, H., Tucker, R., & Noakes, T. D. (2008). The rate of increase in rating of perceived exertion predicts the duration of exercise to fatigue at a fixed power output in different environmental conditions. *European Journal of Applied Physiology, 103*(5), 569–577.

Deci, E. L., & Ryan, R. M. (2011). Self-determination theory. In P. A. M. Van Lange, A. W. Kruglanski, & E. T. Higgins (Eds.), *Handbook of theories of social psychology* (Vol. 1, pp. 416–433). London: SAGE.

de Koning, J. J., Foster, C., Bakkum, A., Kloppenburg, S., Thiel, C., Joseph, T., . . . Porcari, J. P. (2011). Regulation of pacing strategy during athletic competition. *PloS One, 6*(1), e15863.

de Morree, H. M., Klein, C., & Marcora, S. M. (2012). Perception of effort reflects central motor command during movement execution. *Psychophysiology, 49*(9), 1242–1253.

de Morree, H. M., Klein, C., & Marcora, S. M. (2014). Cortical substrates of the effects of caffeine and time-on-task on perception of effort. *Journal of Applied Physiology, 117*(12), 1514–1523.

de Morree, H. M., & Marcora, S. M. (2015). Psychobiology of perceived effort during physical tasks. In G. H. E. Gendolla, M. Tops, & S. L. Koole (Eds.) *Handbook of biobehavioral approaches to self-regulation* (pp. 255–270). New York: Springer.

Doherty, M., & Smith, P. M. (2005). Effects of caffeine ingestion on rating of perceived exertion during and after exercise: A meta-analysis. *Scandinavian Journal of Medicine & Science in Sports, 15*(2), 69–78.

Dum, R. P., & Strick, P. L. (2002). Motor areas in the frontal lobe of the primate. *Physiology & Behavior, 77*(4–5), 677–682.

Ekblom, B., & Goldbarg, A. N. (1971). The influence of physical training and other factors on the subjective rating of perceived exertion. *Acta Physiologica Scandinavica, 83*(3), 399–406.

Enders, H., Cortese, F., Maurer, C., Baltich, J., Protzner, A. B., & Nigg, B. M. (2016). Changes in cortical activity measured with EEG during a high-intensity cycling exercise. *Journal of Neurophysiology, 115*(1), 379–388.

Enoka, R. M., & Stuart, D. G. (1992). Neurobiology of muscle fatigue. *Journal of Applied Physiology, 72*(5), 1631–1648.

Ferguson, C., Wylde, L. A., Benson, A. P., Cannon, D. T., & Rossiter, H. B. (2015). No reserve in isokinetic cycling power at intolerance during ramp incremental exercise in endurance-trained men. *Journal of Applied Physiology, 120*(1), 70–77.

Filingeri, D. (2016). Neurophysiology of skin thermal sensations. *Comprehensive Physiology*, *6*(3), 1429.

Gandevia, S. C. (2001). Spinal and supraspinal factors in human muscle fatigue. *Physiological Reviews*, *81*(4), 1725–1789.

Garcin, M., & Billat, V. (2001). Perceived exertion scales attest to both intensity and exercise duration. *Perceptual and Motor Skills*, *93*(3), 661–671.

Gendolla, G., & Richter, M. (2010). Effort mobilization when the self is involved: Some lessons from the cardiovascular system. *Review of General Psychology: Journal of Division 1, of the American Psychological Association*. Retrieved from http://psycnet.apa.org/record/2010-17363-003.

Gigliotti, F. (2010). Mechanisms of dyspnea in healthy subjects. *Multidisciplinary Respiratory Medicine*, *5*(3), 195–201.

Goldstein, E. B. (2009). *Sensation and perception*. Belmont, CA: Cengage Learning.

Graham, T. E. (2001). Caffeine and exercise. *Sports Medicine*, *31*(11), 785–807.

Hamilton, A. L., Killian, K. J., Summers, E., & Jones, N. L. (1996). Quantification of intensity of sensations during muscular work by normal subjects. *Journal of Applied Physiology*, *81*(3), 1156–1161.

Hampson, D. B., St Clair Gibson, A., Lambert, M. I., & Noakes, T. D. (2001). The influence of sensory cues on the perception of exertion during exercise and central regulation of exercise performance. *Sports Medicine*, *31*(13), 935–952.

Henning, P. C., Khamoui, A. V., & Brown, L. E. (2011). Preparatory strength and endurance training for U.S. army basic combat training. *Strength & Conditioning Journal*, *33*(5), 48.

Hepple, R. T. (2002). The role of O_2 supply in muscle fatigue. *Canadian Journal of Applied Physiology = Revue Canadienne de Physiologie Appliquee*, *27*(1), 56–69.

Hill, A. V. (1926). *Muscular activity*. Baltimore, MD: Williams & Wilkins Company.

Horstman, D. H., Morgan, W. P., Cymerman, A., & Stokes, J. (1979). Perception of effort during constant work to self-imposed exhaustion. *Perceptual and Motor Skills*, *48*(3 Pt 2), 1111–1126.

Ikai, M., & Steinhaus, A. H. (1961). Some factors modifying the expression of human strength. *Journal of Applied Physiology*, *16*, 157–163.

Inzlicht, M., & Marcora, S. M. (2016). The central governor model of exercise regulation teaches us precious little about the nature of mental fatigue and self-control failure. *Frontiers in Psychology*, 7, 656.

Joyner, M. J., & Coyle, E. F. (2008). Endurance exercise performance: The physiology of champions. *The Journal of Physiology*, *586*(1), 35–44.

Kayser, B. (2003). Exercise starts and ends in the brain. *European Journal of Applied Physiology*, *90*(3–4), 411–419.

Kearon, M. C., Summers, E., Jones, N. L., Campbell, E. J., & Killian, K. J. (1991). Effort and dyspnoea during work of varying intensity and duration. *The European Respiratory Journal*, *4*(8), 917–925.

Khan, S. I., McNeil, C. J., Gandevia, S. C., & Taylor, J. L. (2011). Effect of experimental muscle pain on maximal voluntary activation of human biceps brachii muscle. *Journal of Applied Physiology*, *111*(3), 743–750.

Liebenberg, L. (2006). Persistence hunting by modern hunter-gatherers. *Current Anthropology*, *47*(6), 1017–1026.

Löllgen, H., Graham, T., & Sjogaard, G. (1980). Muscle metabolites, force, and perceived exertion bicycling at varying pedal rates. *Medicine and Science in Sports and Exercise*, *12*(5), 345–351.

Loy, B. D., O'Connor, P. J., & Dishman, R. K. (2013). The effect of a single bout of exercise on energy and fatigue states: A systematic review and meta-analysis. *Fatigue: Biomedicine, Health & Behavior*, *1*(4), 223–242.

Luu, B. L., Day, B. L., Cole, J. D., & Fitzpatrick, R. C. (2011). The fusimotor and reafferent origin of the sense of force and weight. *The Journal of Physiology, 589*(Pt 13), 3135–3147.

Marcora, S. M. (2007). Entia non sunt multiplicanda praeter necessitatem. *The Journal of Physiology, 578*(1), 371.

Marcora, S. M. (2008). Do we really need a central governor to explain brain regulation of exercise performance? *European Journal of Applied Physiology, 104*(5), 929–931.

Marcora, S. M. (2009). Perception of effort during exercise is independent of afferent feedback from skeletal muscles, heart, and lungs. *Journal of Applied Physiology, 106*(6), 2060–2062.

Marcora, S. M. (2010). Effort: perception of. In E. B. Goldstein (Ed.), *Encyclopedia of perception* (Vol. 1, pp. 380–383). Los Angeles, CA: SAGE.

Marcora, S. M., Bosio, A., & de Morree, H. M. (2008). Locomotor muscle fatigue increases cardiorespiratory responses and reduces performance during intense cycling exercise independently from metabolic stress. *American Journal of Physiology. Regulatory, Integrative and Comparative Physiology, 294*(3), R874–R883.

Marcora, S. M., & Staiano, W. (2010). The limit to exercise tolerance in humans: Mind over muscle? *European Journal of Applied Physiology, 109*(4), 763–770.

Marcora, S. M., Staiano, W., & Manning, V. (2009). Mental fatigue impairs physical performance in humans. *Journal of Applied Physiology, 106*(3), 857–864.

Marcora, S. M., Staiano, W., & Merlini, M. (2015). A randomized controlled trial of brain endurance training (BET) to reduce fatigue during endurance exercise. *Medicine & Science in Sports & Exercise, 47*(5S), 198.

McCormick, A., Meijen, C., & Marcora, S. M. (2015). Psychological determinants of whole-body endurance performance. *Sports Medicine , 45*(7), 997–1015.

Morales-Alamo, D., Losa-Reyna, J., Torres-Peralta, R., Martin-Rincon, M., Perez-Valera, M., Curtelin, D., . . . Calbet, J. A. L. (2015). What limits performance during whole-body incremental exercise to exhaustion in humans? *The Journal of Physiology, 593*(20), 4631–4648.

Morales-Alamo, D., Martin-Rincon, M., Perez-Valera, M., Marcora, S. M., & Calbet, J. A. L. (2016). No functional reserve at exhaustion in endurance-trained men? *Journal of Applied Physiology, 120*(4), 476–476.

Morgan, W. P. (1994). Psychological components of effort sense. *Medicine and Science in Sports and Exercise, 26*(9), 1071–1077.

Nakamura, F. Y., Okuno, N. M., Perandini, L. A. B., de Oliveira, F. R., Buchheit, M., & Simões, H. G. (2009). Perceived exertion threshold: Comparison with ventilatory thresholds and critical power. *Science & Sports, 24*(3–4), 196–201.

Nicolò, A., Marcora, S. M., & Sacchetti, M. (2016). Respiratory frequency is strongly associated with perceived exertion during time trials of different duration. *Journal of Sports Sciences, 34*(13), 1199–1206.

Nielsen, J. B. (2016). Human spinal motor control. *Annual Review of Neuroscience, 39*, 81–101.

Noakes, T. D. (2000). Physiological models to understand exercise fatigue and the adaptations that predict or enhance athletic performance. *Scandinavian Journal of Medicine & Science in Sports, 10*(3), 123–145.

Noakes, T. D. (2004). Linear relationship between the perception of effort and the duration of constant load exercise that remains. *Journal of Applied Physiology, 96*(4), 1571–1572; author reply 1572–1573.

Noakes, T. D. (2012). Fatigue is a brain-derived emotion that regulates the exercise behavior to ensure the protection of whole body homeostasis. *Frontiers in Physiology, 3*, 82.

Noakes, T. D., St Clair Gibson, A., & Lambert, E. V. (2005). From catastrophe to complexity: A novel model of integrative central neural regulation of effort and fatigue during exercise in humans: summary and conclusions. *British Journal of Sports Medicine, 39*(2), 120–124.

O'Connor, P. J., & Cook, D. B. (1999). Exercise and pain: The neurobiology, measurement, and laboratory study of pain in relation to exercise in humans. *Exercise and Sport Sciences Reviews, 27*(1), 119–166.

Padilla, S., Mujika, I., Angulo, F., & Goiriena, J. J. (2000). Scientific approach to the 1-h cycling world record: A case study. *Journal of Applied Physiology, 89*(4), 1522–1527.

Pageaux, B., Lepers, R., Dietz, K. C., & Marcora, S. M. (2014). Response inhibition impairs subsequent self-paced endurance performance. *European Journal of Applied Physiology, 114*(5), 1095–1105.

Pageaux, B., Marcora, S. M., Rozand, V., & Lepers, R. (2015). Mental fatigue induced by prolonged self-regulation does not exacerbate central fatigue during subsequent whole-body endurance exercise. *Frontiers in Human Neuroscience, 9*, 67.

Pollak, K. A., Swenson, J. D., Vanhaitsma, T. A., Hughen, R. W., Jo, D., White, A. T., . . . Light, A. R. (2014). Exogenously applied muscle metabolites synergistically evoke sensations of muscle fatigue and pain in human subjects. *Experimental Physiology, 99*(2), 368–380.

Poulet, J. F. A., & Hedwig, B. (2006). The cellular basis of a corollary discharge. *Science, 311*(5760), 518–522.

Preston, J., & Wegner, D. M. (2009). Elbow grease: When action feels like work. *Oxford Handbook of Human Action*, 569–586.

Proske, U., & Gandevia, S. C. (2012). The proprioceptive senses: Their roles in signaling body shape, body position and movement, and muscle force. *Physiological Reviews, 92*(4), 1651–1697.

Romer, L. M., Haverkamp, H. C., Amann, M., Lovering, A. T., Pegelow, D. F., & Dempsey, J. A. (2007). Effect of acute severe hypoxia on peripheral fatigue and endurance capacity in healthy humans. *American Journal of Physiology. Regulatory, Integrative and Comparative Physiology, 292*(1), R598–R606.

Romer, L. M., & Polkey, M. I. (2008). Exercise-induced respiratory muscle fatigue: Implications for performance. *Journal of Applied Physiology, 104*(3), 879–888.

Ross, R., Gray, C. M., & Gill, J. M. R. (2015). The effects of an injected placebo on endurance running performance. *Medicine and Science in Sports and Exercise, 47*(8), 1672–1681.

Salamone, J. D., Yohn, S. E., López-Cruz, L., San Miguel, N., & Correa, M. (2016). Activational and effort-related aspects of motivation: Neural mechanisms and implications for psychopathology. *Brain: A Journal of Neurology, 139*(Pt 5), 1325–1347.

Sassi, A., Marcora, S. M., Rampinini, E., Mognoni, P., & Impellizzeri, F. M. (2006). Prediction of time to exhaustion from blood lactate response during submaximal exercise in competitive cyclists. *European Journal of Applied Physiology, 97*(2), 174–180.

Searle, J. R. (1998). How to study consciousness scientifically. *Philosophical Transactions of the Royal Society of London. Series B, Biological Sciences, 353*(1377), 1935–1942.

Shenhav, A., Musslick, S., Lieder, F., Kool, W., Griffiths, T. L., Cohen, J. D., & Botvinick, M. M. (2017). Toward a rational and mechanistic account of mental effort. *Annual Review of Neuroscience, 40*(1), 99–124.

Smirmaul, B. P. C. (2012). Sense of effort and other unpleasant sensations during exercise: Clarifying concepts and mechanisms. *British Journal of Sports Medicine, 46*(5), 308–311.

Staiano, W., Bosio, A., de Morree, H. M., Rampinini, E., & Marcora, S. (2018). The cardinal exercise stopper: Muscle fatigue, muscle pain or perception of effort? *Progress in Brain Research, 240*, 175–200.

St Clair Gibson, A., & Noakes, T. D. (2004). Evidence for complex system integration and dynamic neural regulation of skeletal muscle recruitment during exercise in humans. *British Journal of Sports Medicine, 38*(6), 797–806.

Taylor, J. L., & Gandevia, S. C. (2008). A comparison of central aspects of fatigue in submaximal and maximal voluntary contractions. *Journal of Applied Physiology, 104*(2), 542–550.

Tucker, R. (2009). The anticipatory regulation of performance: the physiological basis for pacing strategies and the development of a perception-based model for exercise performance. *British Journal of Sports Medicine, 43*(6), 392–400.

Van Cutsem, J., Marcora, S., De Pauw, K., Bailey, S., Meeusen, R., & Roelands, B. (2017). The effects of mental fatigue on physical performance: A systematic review. *Sports Medicine, 47*(8), 1569–1588.

Van der Linden, D. (2011). The urge to stop: The cognitive and biological nature of acute mental fatigue. In P. L. Ackerman (Ed.), *Cognitive fatigue: Multidisciplinary perspectives on current research and future applications* (pp. 149–164). American Psychological Association.

Wasserman, K. W. B. J., Whipp, B. J., & Casaburi, R. (1986). Respiratory control during exercise. *Handbook of Physiology. The Respiratory System. Control of Breathing, 2*(pt 2), 595–620.

Williamson, J. W. (2015). Autonomic responses to exercise: Where is central command? *Autonomic Neuroscience: Basic & Clinical, 188*, 3–4.

Wilmore, J. H. (1968). Influence of motivation on physical work capacity and performance. *Journal of Applied Physiology, 24*(4), 459–463.

Woolf, C. J., & Salter, M. W. (2000). Neuronal plasticity: Increasing the gain in pain. *Science, 288*(5472), 1765–1769.

Wright, R. A. (2008). Refining the prediction of effort: Brehm's distinction between potential motivation and motivation intensity. *Social and Personality Psychology Compass, 2*(2), 682–701.

Zénon, A., Sidibé, M., & Olivier, E. (2015). Disrupting the supplementary motor area makes physical effort appear less effortful. *The Journal of Neuroscience, 35*(23), 8737–8744.

3

EXERCISE-INDUCED PAIN

A psychophysiological perspective

Alexis R. Mauger

Introduction

> Obviously, there is a big difference between the exertion pain and any other physical kind of pain. The exertion pain I would term as a kind of fire . . . a burn pain. I have never had a severe burn from a fire but if it were to be like that, it would be throughout your whole body. Every square inch of it. If you are really exerted and you are going flat out, I can't think of much worse. It's like a burn or an electric shock type thing. It's there and it really hurts. Your lungs are gasping for air while your legs are on fire . . . or worse.
>
> *(Quote from athlete Ivan; Kress & Statler, 2007, p. 438)*

For anyone who has trained for, or competed in, an endurance sport like running, swimming, or cycling, this description of how it feels to be working maximally will probably resonate. Pain is something the majority of us will try to avoid throughout our lives, yet it will inevitably find us at some point, regardless of age, sex, ethnicity, or any other stratification we can think of. It is curious then, that so many of us are willing to engage in the level of suffering that intense and prolonged exercise exposes us to. Perhaps this is human nature and part of sport – we are willing to make great sacrifices to reap the multitude of other physical and psychological rewards that sport and exercise provide. Indeed, listen to coverage of any endurance-based event and it is likely that you will hear some reference to the competitor's battle with pain and how overcoming this pain will dictate their performance – we think we know about this relationship because of moments like these and the adages that follow; '*No pain, no gain*', '*Pain is weakness leaving the body*'. But pain is a complex phenomenon, and the determinants of endurance performance are likely multiple and will certainly be argued over for decades to come. So, the answer to 'does pain limit endurance performance' is not a simple

one and this is compounded by a relatively small, and often flawed, scientific literature base pertaining this specific area. Therefore, the aim of this chapter is to
approach this question from a performance perspective, by considering the current
understanding and evidence underpinning how the pain associated with exercise
affects both the approach we take in competition and, ultimately how we perform.
For this chapter a wide and rich base of literature on pain will be drawn from, and
this will be discussed in the context of the recent literature on exercise-induced
pain. Factors that cause pain during exercise will be reviewed, and I will discuss
how these may contribute to exercise-induced fatigue (defined here as any exercise-
induced reduction in the ability to exert muscle force or power, regardless of
whether or not the task can be sustained (Bigland-Ritchie & Woods, 1984)) and
inform decisions to alter work rate, and evaluate whether this relationship may be
different between athletes and non-athletes.

Pain and exercise-induced pain

Pain is defined by the International Association for the Study of Pain (IASP) as
an unpleasant sensory and emotional experience that is associated with actual
or potential tissue damage or described in such terms (Merskey & Spear, 1967).
This definition implies that pain is subjective, that it elicits an emotional reaction
because it is unpleasant (Hadjistavropoulos & Craig, 2002) and that there is not
always a proportional relationship between severity of physical injury and pain
experienced. At this point, it is important to reiterate that the type of pain that will
be discussed in this chapter is exercise-induced pain (EIP), which is very different
from the pain one may experience from an acute injury (e.g., a pulled muscle),
or from the micro-trauma and inflammation arising from delayed onset muscle
soreness. The distinction is a significant one, because EIP occurs naturally without
causing lasting damage and will usually diminish or completely disappear shortly
after exercise is ceased or intensity is reduced. In addition, this type of pain will
also occur in the presence of a variety of other emotions associated with exercise,
which may be both positive and negative (Bąbel, 2016) and have the potential to
affect the degree of pain experienced. Therefore, this complex psychophysiological environment caused by exercise likely exacerbates the already highly individual
and subjective experience of pain, and thus makes examining its impact on performance all the more challenging. However, a first step to understanding why pain
may affect performance is to identify what causes the pain receptors (nociceptors)
to fire during exercise.

Causes of exercise-induced pain

The experience of EIP is often associated with a 'burning' sensation in the muscles
or a dull ache, soreness, or heaviness which can be akin to muscle cramp (Cook,
O'Connor, Eubanks, Smith, & Lee, 1997; Miles & Clarkson, 1994). The intensity
of this pain has been shown to increase alongside increases in exercise intensity,

and it can be distinguished from other sensations induced by exercise such as the sense of effort (Cook et al., 1997). The observation that EIP can be produced by an exercise intensity of as little as 50 per cent VO_{2max} suggests that high-force muscle contractions or muscle damage are not necessary to elicit muscular pain (Cook et al., 1997). Whereas the exact mechanisms of muscle pain resulting from endurance type exercise are still not yet agreed, it is suggested that it likely arises from one, or a combination, of an accumulation of noxious biochemicals, increased intramuscular pressure, or deformation of tissue due to muscular contractions (Dannecker & Koltyn, 2014).

Exercise, especially at an intensity above the gas exchange threshold, leads to a build-up of metabolic by-products which stimulate and/or sensitise group III (myelinated) and IV (unmyelinated) afferent nociceptive fibres (Mense, 2009; O'Connor & Cook, 1999). It is likely that the most prominent of these is a fall in pH, caused by proton accumulation when oxygen supply is not sufficient to meet demand at the muscle (Mense, 2009). Although this will inevitably occur more readily at exercise intensities above the gas exchange threshold, at a local level muscle ischaemia from blood vessel occlusion (leading to a shortfall in oxygen), caused by low-force, repetitive, tonic muscular contractions, can lead to an increased concentration of protons (Mense, 2009). This can partly explain why EIP is still observed in sports and exercise modalities where sub-threshold exercise intensities are maintained over a long period of time (McCormick, Meijen, & Marcora, 2018), or where a low intensity, repetitive muscle action is performed using a smaller muscle mass (Angius, Pageaux, Hopker, Marcora, & Mauger, 2016). In addition to protons, an inflammatory 'soup', caused by intense exercise and likely consisting of a combination of biochemicals including histamine, potassium, prostaglandin E_2, bradykinin, and substance P are likely responsible for the aetiology of EIP, as these substances either sensitise or stimulate the nociceptors (O'Connor & Cook, 1999; Rotto, Hill, Schultz, & Kaufman, 1990). Indeed, Pollak et al. (2014) showed that a similar metabolic 'soup', injected into a muscle in concentrations equivalent to those found in resting muscle and in muscle during low intensity contractions did not cause any pain. But, when concentrations were increased to be equivalent to moderate intensity exercise and above, participants started to report sensations of pain similar to that of EIP ('ache', 'hot'), and reported some descriptors that are consistent with the sensations of fatigue ('tired', 'shaking').

So far, we have established that endurance exercise can result in naturally occurring EIP, and that this is largely caused by an accumulation of deleterious metabolites. The magnitude of this sensation is increased by higher levels of exercise intensity, and relieved by a reduction in work-rate or cessation of exercise. Furthermore, a link between EIP and verbal descriptors akin to the sensation of fatigue have also been presented. However, just because EIP is often present alongside fatigue during exercise, and that the perception that one can feel like the other, does not necessitate a causal relationship. Indeed, there are plenty of examples where exercise-induced fatigue is present without the perception of pain (Amann, Proctor, Sebranek, Pegelow, & Dempsey, 2009) and where changes in pain perception elicit no change in the occurrence of fatigue during exercise (Flood, Waddington, Keegan, Thompson, & Cathcart, 2017). However, there are several mechanisms that could provide a plausible explanation for why EIP is a factor limiting some types of endurance performance; these are explored in the following section.

Mechanisms explaining the negative impact of EIP on endurance performance

Differences between pain perception and nociception

To understand the role EIP may play in exercise-induced fatigue, it is first important to highlight a key difference between pain perception (i.e., the unpleasant sensation we feel and recognise as pain) and nociception (the unconscious detection, encoding, and transmission of the potentially tissue threatening nociceptive stimulus) – nociception is a physiological process and as such may occur in the absence of consciousness, whereas pain perception is the product of the conscious brain; a sensory and emotional experience which is usually (but not always) the consequence of nociception (Turk & Melzack, 2011). A nociceptive stimulus can evoke a protective (nocifensive) response that does not have to be intentional or volitional; a behaviour that is popularly exemplified by the immediate removal of the hand from a hot stove. Whether there is an additional but more subtle protective physiological response arising from nociception during exercise is a notion discussed later in this chapter. Because the nociceptive signal is largely transmitted alongside other forms of afferent feedback via the Group III and IV fibres, it is hard to separate a fatiguing effect of nociception specifically from the multiple other sources of afferent feedback experienced during exercise. For example, there are multiple classes of nociceptor that respond to thermal, chemical, and mechanical stimuli, but only when these stimuli reach a noxious intensity or duration. The same type of stimuli at a lower intensity would activate other classes of A and C fibre (still resulting in afferent feedback), but not evoke a nociceptive response (Dubin & Patapoutian, 2010). Therefore, identifying the type/cause of the nociceptive stimulus is extremely important, particularly when trying to exacerbate or alleviate EIP in experimental studies.

Psychologically, the conscious experience of exercise-induced pain can be influenced by a variety of top-down and affective aspects, all of which have the potential to drive a change in behaviour that is usually the result of considered judgement. Furthermore, because there is not a one-to-one relationship between the nociceptive signal and the pain experienced, a person could receive a large nociceptive signal but experience little/no pain, or process a small nociceptive signal but feel a significant level of pain. Therefore, considering psychological factors in exercise/pain experiments is important. Evidently, pain as a complete construct (i.e., nociception and pain perception) is complex because it has both physiological and psychological elements (Hadjistavropoulos & Craig, 2004; Price, 2000) and this makes its potential effects during exercise a challenge to investigate. In spite of this, I believe there is a theoretical basis to suggest that both the nociceptive signal and the conscious experience of pain *may* contribute to fatigue during exercise, and so fatigue arising from EIP may have both physiological and/or psychological origins – the basic premise underpinning these two notions are discussed here.

Afferent feedback

As alluded to in the previous paragraph, muscle nociceptors are connected to the central nervous system via group III and IV afferent fibres. Group III fibres are responsible for conducting pain signals that are rapid, sharp and localised in nature, whereas group IV fibres conduct a pain signal that is felt as slow, dull and aching. Importantly, about 40 per cent of group IV fibres transmit non-nociceptive information (Hoheisel, Unger, & Mense, 2005) which is used to help mediate pressure sensations (Graven-Nielsen, Mense, & Arendt-Nielsen, 2004; Light & Perl, 2003) and make adjustments in the cardiovascular response to exercise (McCloskey & Mitchell, 1972). It is suggested that increased afferent feedback via group III and IV fibres constrains voluntary neural drive to working locomotor muscle (Blain et al., 2016) and promotes the development of central fatigue (Gandevia, 2001; Goodall, Charlton, Howatson, & Thomas, 2015). However, whether this effect is one driven by all types of afferent feedback, or more specifically feedback which is noxious (i.e., nociception) is hard to deduce. Experiments that moderate all afferent feedback in order to explore its effects on exercise performance are often compounded by an inhibited cardiovascular control (arising from blocking afferent feedback), do not report perceptual data relating to pain experience (Amann et al., 2009; Sidhu et al., 2017), and so provide limited insight. Therefore, a more focussed experimental approach, where pain is specifically manipulated in the experimental design, can provide better insight into whether EIP (rather than afferent feedback more broadly) affects fatigue and performance.

Sensory-discriminative and affective-motivational components

Pain is a multidimensional construct and can be described in both sensory-discriminative and affective-motivational components (Treede, Kenshalo, Gracely, & Jones, 1999). The sensory-discriminative component (i.e., sensory pain) informs the individual about the location, modality, and intensity of stimuli, whereas the affective-motivational component (i.e., pain unpleasantness or emotional pain) refers to the emotional response to a painful stimulus, or accompanying feelings of fear, exhaustion, anxiety, and an avoidance drive (Auvray, Myin, & Spence, 2010). These latter sensations motivate the individual to escape or reduce the source of pain, and thus provide an important protective and survival function. The distinction of these components is important, because they have implications for how methods of inducing experimental pain (e.g., contact heat, pressure) are compared and applied to EIP. It is also likely that the sensory and affective elements of EIP provide very different information and motivations for behaviour drive during exercise, so study design should try to account for and measure these components separately.

It has been shown that the unpleasantness of the pain associated with ischaemic exercise (i.e., exercise with restricted blood flow) is considerably greater than that of contact heat or electric shocks, despite a given perceived intensity of the stimuli (Rainville, Feine, Bushnell, & Duncan, 1992). This is an important point, because in studies investigating the factors affecting exercise performance, even when pain perception is reported (which is infrequently), attempts are not usually made to separate the intensity and unpleasantness of the pain. Consequently, evidence of the specific impact of the affective-motivational component of pain during exercise is limited, and this is significant given that it is this aspect which correlates with the personal significance of pain to the individual, and thus causes a motivational demand that drives a thought or behaviour to escape the pain (Fields, 1999). In an exercise context, escaping the pain is most easily achieved by the individual reducing their work-rate or stopping the exercise, because as already discussed, EIP is proportional to exercise intensity. Therefore, during exercise in the presence of EIP, there is a powerful psychological drive to decrease exercise intensity, because doing so means a reduction in the pain and the unpleasantness associated with it. However, the affective-motivational component of pain is a 'higher-order' function, produced by the processing of 'lower-order' sensory-discriminative information, and as such requires additional information to contextualise it (Lee, Watson, & Frey Law, 2010). The context matters, and can affect the degree of unpleasantness experienced by a given stimulus (Moseley & Arntz, 2007). For example, the unpleasantness of the pain of child birth is significantly less than that of cancer pain or lower back pain, despite the intensity of the pain being far greater (Price, Harkins, & Baker, 1987). Furthermore, Bąbel (2016) found that marathon runners who recalled exercise-induced pain underestimated pain intensity three and six months after the event. So, for those individuals training for, or competing in sporting events, there are a plethora of different contexts, motivations, and memories that could moderate the higher-order processing of the unpleasantness of EIP in either direction. As such, undertaking experimental studies that investigate the psychological (and performance) effect of EIP is important because the impact could vary between individuals and environments, and have potential to respond to a range of ergogenic and psychological interventions.

The impact of EIP on pacing and performance

So far I have presented a case to suggest that there is a theoretical basis that EIP impacts on exercise performance through both unconscious physiological and conscious psychological mechanisms. This section will explore the empirical evidence that substantiates this notion. However, as alluded to earlier in the chapter, there are likely a host of individual differences (e.g., competitive level) and study design decisions (e.g., time to exhaustion or self-paced tests) which may moderate the relationship between EIP and exercise performance, all of which are further compounded by the varying inhibitory/facilitatory effects of afferent feedback. Consequently, application of the findings of the following studies, to athletes and exercise types which are significantly different to those detailed in the study methods, should be treated with caution.

There has long been recognition that athletes are able to withstand pain better than non-athletes, and some have partly attributed this to sporting success. Although not always the case (Tesarz, Schuster, Hartmann, Gerhardt, & Eich, 2012), the weight of most cross-sectional studies supports this notion, with good examples from both competitive rowers (Ord & Gijsbers, 2003) and swimmers (Scott & Gijsbers, 1981). However, in these studies differences between trained and untrained groups were only apparent for measures of pain tolerance, not pain threshold. This appears to be a common finding (Tesarz et al., 2012), and may suggest that it is a better tolerance (i.e., maximum intensity or duration of pain a person is able to tolerate) of a given pain, rather than a higher pain threshold (i.e., smallest stimulus eliciting pain) that is important for the sportsperson. Some studies go further, and demonstrate that prolonged (>6 weeks) aerobic (Anshel & Russell, 1994; Jones, Booth, Taylor, & Barry, 2014) but not strength training (Anshel & Russell, 1994) actually increases pain tolerance, which indicates that pain tolerance can be trained. The authors of these studies suggest that the observed improvements in pain tolerance are due to an improved psychological status that is developed through a higher self-efficacy and improved coping strategies resulting from prolonged exposure to painful stimuli during intense aerobic training, this is a conclusion which is also drawn from cross-sectional studies (Ord & Gijsbers, 2003). This interpretation was arrived at largely because no changes in pain threshold were observed and because the pain tolerance tests were performed on a non-exercising limb. Consequently little to no physiological adaptation at the site of nociception would be expected, and the observed no change in pain thresholds suggest that pain signalling was unaffected by the training. Although one of the training studies accounted for changes in mood (Anshel & Russell, 1994), neither recorded changes to psychological measures such as self-efficacy or pain coping, which future studies should seek to do because it is known that these factors have a significant influence on pain perception (Hadjistavropoulos & Craig, 2004). Furthermore, the possibility that changes to pain signalling could occur following aerobic training should not be dismissed, as the rationale that these adaptations are purely specific to the site of the exercising muscle is questionable as the relationship with pain threshold and nociception is more complex (Flood, Waddington, Thompson, & Cathcart, 2017).

Although these studies provide strong evidence to demonstrate that pain tolerance is improved by endurance training, they do not tell us whether pain tolerance is actually an important determinant for athletic success. Astokorki and Mauger (2016) addressed this question by using a novel test to assess tolerance of EIP, and compared this to the predictive value of traditional physiological markers of endurance performance (VO_{2max}, gas exchange threshold, peak power output) in time trial cycling. In the group of 32 recreationally active males and females, only peak power output and EIP tolerance were significant predictors of endurance performance, with peak power output accounting for 75 per cent variance and EIP accounting for 7.5 per cent. From these results, it is clear that EIP tolerance is of lesser importance, although it is still meaningful. Indeed, in the study cohort, a person whose time trial time was in the third quartile could progress into the upper second quartile, purely on the basis of performance variation explained by EIP tolerance. However, on the basis of the differences in pain tolerance between individuals of different training status observed in previous studies (Anshel & Russell, 1994; Jones et al., 2014; Ord & Gijsbers, 2003; Scott & Gijsbers, 1981), and the fairly homogenous group of participants in Astokorki & Mauger's study, it is likely that the relative predictive capacity of EIP tolerance is variable. Furthermore, the measure of EIP tolerance used in this study relied on assessing pain response to exercise at a fixed perception of effort, and so a possible co-correlation effect with perception of effort should be considered. More recently, O'Leary, Collett, Howells, and Morris (2017) examined changes in pain tolerance response and its impact on endurance performance following aerobic continuous and interval cycling training in 20 untrained but healthy males and females. The results of this study demonstrated that whereas 6 weeks of total work matched continuous and interval training both improved markers of aerobic fitness by similar amounts, only the interval training group improved their pain tolerance of ischaemic muscle pain. Interestingly, the interval group showed a superior improvement in the performance of a time to exhaustion test (148 per cent vs. 38 per cent improvement) and the changes in pain tolerance showed a positive relationship with changes in time to exhaustion ($r = 0.44$). These findings support the conclusions of those studies discussed previously, and provides further evidence that not only does endurance training improve pain tolerance, but that the increase in pain tolerance is also important for driving better endurance performance independent of physiological markers of aerobic fitness.

If improvements in pain tolerance result in a superior endurance performance, we should be able to test this relationship by experimentally increasing or decreasing pain perception across an exercise task. Several studies have attempted to do this, with mixed results, but the same warnings about generalising conclusions apply, with the added issue that pain response is difficult to experimentally moderate independently of other physiological and psychological parameters that may affect exercise (e.g., cardiovascular control, placebo effect, perception of effort). Mauger, Jones, and Williams (2010) used acetaminophen (paracetamol) to induce analgesia in a group of well-trained cyclists (13.4 ± 3 h/wk cycling training) prior to the performance of a 10-mile cycling time trial in a placebo controlled, cross-over study. Following the ingestion of paracetamol, the cyclists performed the time trial significantly faster (mean 2 per cent improvement), owed to a higher power output that was maintained in the middle section of the race. Foster, Taylor, Chrismas, Watkins, and Mauger (2014) observed a similar effect in recreationally active males performing a repeated sprint cycling task following the ingestion of the same quantity of paracetamol (1.5 g). Notably, the participants in these studies reported the same intensity of pain between experimental and placebo conditions, despite maintaining a higher power output under greater physiological strain (higher heart rate and blood lactate concentration) in the paracetamol condition. The authors attributed this to the participants being more willing to produce a higher work-rate when this resulted in relatively less EIP (in conditions of analgesia), and therefore an assumption that the participants had a pacing strategy that partly relied on basing work-rate on perceptions of EIP. Although the analgesic effect of paracetamol is well-reported (Yuan et al., 1998), the authors of these studies did not directly test that the paracetamol dose induced analgesia. Furthermore, there are other side-effects (e.g., hypothermic action) from paracetamol that could have influenced the changes in performance (Foster, Mauger, Chrismas, Thomasson, & Taylor, 2015; Mauger & Hopker, 2013). To address this, Astokorki and Mauger (2017) used transcutaneous electrical nerve stimulation (TENS) to induce analgesia in recreationally active (n= 18) and trained (n = 22) males and females prior to both a single arm contraction time to exhaustion, and in a 10-mile time trial cycling task. In this study, EIP was significantly reduced (as measured in the isometric task), and this led to an improved performance in both the single arm task and the self-paced cycling time trial. It is likely that both paracetamol and TENS act by blocking the nociceptive signal at a spinal level (Anderson, 2008; Sluka & Walsh, 2003), and so it is not clear from these studies if the performance enhancing effect can be attributed to a reduction in the negative impact on central drive from the activation of group III and IV afferents (Kennedy, Fitzpatrick, Gandevia, & Taylor, 2015) or a reduction in the unpleasantness of the exercise due to a reduced nociceptive signal reaching the brain (Rainville et al., 1992). The recent application of novel neurophysiological techniques such as transcranial direct current stimulation (tDCS) may help us to deduce this (Mauger, 2013), but as we are already finding out, this can bring about more questions than answers (Angius, Hopker, Marcora, & Mauger, 2015). Indeed, the current evidence suggests that tDCS of the motor cortex (M1) can reduce pain perception during a cold-pressor test but not cycling exercise, and that the ergogenic effect of tDCS of the motor cortex in time to exhaustion cycling is likely related to changes in perception of effort and not pain perception (Angius et al., 2018).

Conclusions

In conclusion, the psychophysiology of pain is complex, and it seems there are no easy ways of examining whether the putative impact of EIP on endurance performance is physiological or psychological in origin. There is likely a role for both, but that the relative contribution of these is dependent on the individual, the task performed and the context of the exercise. What is clear, is that it is difficult, if not impossible, to fully understand the mechanisms and implications solely from a physiological or psychological perspective, and so interdisciplinary collaboration in this area is essential. Whereas there have been a variety of studies that attempt to moderate physiological aspects of pain during exercise, little work has been done to explore the potential to use psychological manipulations to moderate the affective and behavioural aspects of exercise-induced pain. This avenue presents some exciting and potentially fruitful opportunities that can only expand our understanding and appreciation of this complex area.

References

Amann, M., Proctor, L. T., Sebranek, J. J., Pegelow, D. F., & Dempsey, J. A. (2009). Opioid-mediated muscle afferents inhibit central motor drive and limit peripheral muscle fatigue development in humans. *The Journal of Physiology*, *587*(1), 271–283.

Anderson, B. J. (2008). Paracetamol (acetaminophen): mechanisms of action. *Paediatric Anaesthesia*, *18*, 915–921.

Angius, L., Hopker, J. G., Marcora, S. M., & Mauger, A. R. (2015). The effect of transcranial direct current stimulation of the motor cortex on exercise-induced pain. *European Journal of Applied Physiology*, *115*(11), 2311–2319.

Angius, L., Pageaux, B., Hopker, J., Marcora, S. M., & Mauger, A. R. (2016). Transcranial direct current stimulation improves isometric time to exhaustion of the knee extensors. *Neuroscience*, *17*(339), 363–375.

Angius, L., Mauger, A. R., Hopker, J., Pascual-Leone, A., Santarnecchi, E., & Marcora, S. M. (2018). Bilateral extracephalic transcranial direct current stimulation improves endurance performance in healthy individuals. *Brain Stimulation*, *11*(1), 108–117.

Anshel, M. H., & Russell, K. G. (1994). Effect of aerobic and strength training on pain tolerance, pain appraisal and mood of unfit males as a function of pain location. *Journal of Sports Sciences*, *12*(6), 535–547.

Astokorki, A. H., & Mauger, A. R. (2017). Tolerance of exercise-induced pain at a fixed rating of perceived exertion predicts time trial cycling performance. *Scandinavian Journal of Medicine and Science in Sports*, *27*(3), 309–317.

Auvray, M., Myin, E., & Spence, C. (2010). The sensory-discriminative and affective-motivational aspects of pain. *Neuroscience & Biobehavioral Reviews*, *34*(2), 214–223.

Babel, P. (2016). Memory of pain induced by physical exercise. *Memory*, *24*(4), 548–559.

Bigland-Ritchie, B., & Woods, J. J. (1984). Changes in muscle contractile properties and neural control during human muscular fatigue. *Muscle Nerve*, 7(9), 691–699.

Blain, G. M., Mangum, T. S., Sidhu, S. K., Weavil, J. C., Hureau, T. J., Jessop, J. E., . . . Amann, M. (2016). Group III/IV muscle afferents limit the intramuscular metabolic perturbation during whole body exercise in humans. *The Journal of Physiology*, *594*(18), 5303–5315.

Cook, D. B., O'Connor, P. J., Eubanks, S. A., Smith, J. C., & Lee, M. (1997). Naturally occurring muscle pain during exercise: assessment and experimental evidence. *Medicine and Science in Sports & Exercise*, *29*(8), 999–1012.

Dannecker, E. A., & Koltyn, K. F. (2014). Pain during and within hours after exercise in healthy adults. *Sports Medicine*, *44*(7), 921–942.

Dubin, A. E., & Patapoutian, A. (2010). Nociceptors: the sensors of the pain pathway. *The Journal of Clinical Investigation*, *120*(11), 3760–3772.

Fields, H. L. (1999). Pain: An unpleasant topic. *Pain*, *6*, S61–69.

Flood, A., Waddington, G., Keegan, R. J., Thompson, K. G., & Cathcart, S. (2017). The effects of elevated pain inhibition on endurance exercise performance. *PeerJ*, *5*, e3028.

Flood, A., Waddington, G., Thompson, K., & Cathcart, S. (2017). Increased conditioned pain modulation in athletes. *Journal of Sports Sciences*, *35*(11), 1066–1072.

Foster, J., Mauger, A. R., Chrismas, B. C., Thomasson, K., & Taylor, L. (2015). Is prosta-glandin E2 (PGE2) involved in the thermogenic response to environmental cooling in healthy humans? *Medical Hypotheses, 85*(5), 607–611.

Foster, J., Taylor, L., Chrismas, B. C., Watkins, S. L., & Mauger, A. R. (2014). The influence of acetaminophen on repeated sprint cycling performance. *European Journal of Applied Physiology, 114*(1), 41–48.

Gandevia, S. C. (2001). Spinal and supraspinal factors in human muscle fatigue. *Physiological Reviews, 81*(4), 1725–1789.

Graven-Nielsen, T., Mense, S., & Arendt-Nielsen, L. (2004). Painful and non-painful pressure sensations from human skeletal muscle. *Experimental Brain Research, 159*(3), 273–283.

Goodall, S., Charlton, K., Howatson, G., & Thomas, K. (2015). Neuromuscular fatigability during repeated-sprint exercise in male athletes. *Medicine and Science in Sports and Exercise, 47*(3), 528–536.

Hadjistavropoulos, T., & Craig, K. D. (2002). A theoretical framework for understand-ing self-report and observational measures of pain: A communications model. *Behaviour Research and Therapy, 40*(5), 551–570.

Hadjistavropoulos, T., & Craig, K. D. (2004). *Pain: Psychological perspectives*. NJ, USA: Lawrence Erlbaum Associates.

Hoheisel, U., Unger, T., & Mense, S. (2005). Excitatory and modulatory effects of inflam-matory cytokines and neurotrophins on mechanosensitive group IV muscle afferents in the rat. *Pain, 114*(1–2), 168–176.

Jones, M. D., Booth, J., Taylor, J. L., & Barry, B. K. (2014). Aerobic training increases pain tolerance in healthy individuals. *Medicine & Science Sports & Exercise, 46*(8), 1640–1647.

Kennedy, D. S., Fitzpatrick, S. C., Gandevia, S. C., & Taylor, J. L. (2015). Fatigue-related firing of muscle nociceptors reduces voluntary activation of ipsilateral but not contralat-eral lower limb muscles. *Journal of Applied Physiology, 118*(4), 408–418.

Kress, J. L., & Statler, T. (2007). A naturalistic investigation of former Olympic cyclists' cognitive strategies for coping with exertion pain during performance. *Journal of Sport Behavior, 30*(4), 428–452.

Lee, J. E., Watson, D., & Frey Law, A. (2010). Lower-order pain-related constructs are more predictive of cold pressor pain ratings than higher-order personality traits. *The Journal of Pain, 11*(7), 681–691.

Light, A. R., & Perl, E. R. (2003). Unmyelinated afferent fibers are not only for pain any-more. *Journal of Comparative Neurology, 461*(2), 137–139.

Mauger, A. R. (2013). Fatigue is a pain-the use of novel neurophysiological techniques to understand the fatigue-pain relationship. *Frontiers in Physiology, 4*, 104.

Mauger, A. R., & Hopker, J. G. (2013). The effect of acetaminophen ingestion on cortico-spinal excitability. *Canadian Journal of Physiology and Pharmacology, 91*(2), 187–189.

Mauger, A. R, Jones, A. M., & Williams, C. A. (2010). Influence of acetaminophen on performance during time trial cycling. *Journal of Applied Physiology, 108*(1), 98–104.

McCloskey, D., & Mitchell, J. H. (1972). Reflex cardiovascular and respiratory responses originating in exercising muscle. *The Journal of Physiology, 224*(1), 173–186.

McCormick, A., Meijen, C., & Marcora, S. M. (2018). Effects of a motivational self-talk intervention for endurance athletes completing an ultramarathon. *The Sport Psychologist, 32*, 42–50.

Mense, S. (2009). Algesic agents exciting muscle nociceptors. *Experimental Brain Research, 196*(1), 89–100.

Merskey, H., & Spear, F. G. (1967). The concept of pain. *Journal of Psychosomatic Research, 11*(1), 59–67.

Miles, M. P., & Clarkson, P. M. (1994). Exercise-induced muscle pain, soreness, and cramps. *The Journal of Sports Medicine and Physical Fitness*, *34*(3), 203–216.

Moseley, G. L., & Arntz, A. (2007). The context of a noxious stimulus affects the pain it evokes. *Pain*, *133*(1), 64–71.

O'Connor, P. J., & Cook, D. B. (1999). Exercise and pain: The neurobiology, measurement, and laboratory study of pain in relation to exercise in humans. *Exercise and Sport Sciences Reviews*, *27*(1), 119–166.

O'Leary, T. J., Collett, J., Howells, K., & Morris, M. G. (2017). High but not moderate-intensity endurance training increases pain tolerance: A randomised trial. *European Journal of Applied Physiology*, DOI 10.1007/s00421-017-3708-8.

Ord, P., & Gijsbers, K. (2003). Pain thresholds and tolerances of competitive rowers and their use of spontaneous self-generated pain-coping strategies. *Perceptual and Motor Skills*, *97*(3 Pt 2), 1219–1222.

Pollak, K. A., Swenson, J. D., Vanhaitsma, T. A., Hughen, R. W., Jo, D., Light, K. C., . . . & Light, A. R. (2014). Exogenously applied muscle metabolites synergistically evoke sensations of muscle fatigue and pain in human subjects. *Experimental Physiology*, *99*(2), 368–380.

Price, D. D. (2000). Psychological and neural mechanisms of the affective dimension of pain. *Science*, *288*(5472), 1769–1772.

Price, D. D., Harkins, S. W., & Baker, C. (1987). Sensory-affective relationships among different types of clinical and experimental pain. *Pain*, *28*(3), 297–307.

Rainville, P., Feine, J. S., Bushnell, M. C., & Duncan, G. H. (1992). A psychophysical comparison of sensory and affective responses to four modalities of experimental pain. *Somatosensory & Motor Research*, *9*(4), 265–277.

Rotto, D. M., Hill, J. M., Schultz, H. D., & Kaufman, M. P. (1990). Cyclooxygenase blockade attenuates responses of group IV muscle afferents to static contraction. *American Journal of Physiology-Heart and Circulatory Physiology*, *259*(3), H745–H750.

Scott, V., & Gijsbers, K. (1981). Pain perception in competitive swimmers. *British Medical Journal (Clin Res Ed)*, *11*;*283*(6284), 91–93.

Sidhu, S. K., Weavil, J. C., Mangum, T. S., Jessop, J. E., Richardson, R. S., Morgan, D. E., & Amann, M. (2017). Group III/IV locomotor muscle afferents alter motor cortical and corticospinal excitability and promote central fatigue during cycling exercise. *Clinical Neurophysiology*, *128*(1), 44–55.

Sluka, K. A., & Walsh, D. (2003). Transcutaneous electrical nerve stimulation: basic science mechanisms and clinical effectiveness. *The Journal of Pain*, *4*(3), 109–121.

Tesarz, J., Schuster, A. K., Hartmann, M., Gerhardt, A., & Eich, W. (2012). Pain perception in athletes compared to normally active controls: a systematic review with meta-analysis. *Pain*, *153*(6), 1253–1262.

Treede, R. D., Kenshalo, D. R., Gracely, R. H., & Jones, A. K. (1999). The cortical representation of pain. *Pain*, *79*(2), 105–111.

Turk, D. C., & Melzack, R. (2011). *Handbook of pain assessment*. NY, USA: Guilford Press.

Yuan, C. S., Karrison, T., Wu, J. A., Lowell, T. K., Lynch, J. P., & Foss, J. F. (1998). Dose-related effects of oral acetaminophen on cold-induced pain: a double-blind, randomized, placebo-controlled trial. *Clinical Pharmacology & Therapeutics*, *63*(3), 379–383.

4

DECISION-MAKING, PACING, AND PERFORMANCE IN ENDURANCE SPORT

Dominic Micklewright

Introduction

Pacing is a generic term used to describe changes in speed during an athletic task. It has been argued that pacing is a behavioural strategy that athletes adopt in an attempt to produce their best possible overall performance (de Koning, Bobbert, & Foster, 1999; Foster et al., 2003). Whereas pacing measurements, presented as either continuous or segment-averaged speed data, reveal something about the outcomes of pacing decisions they have limited utility in the investigation of pre-decisional or contemporaneous cognitive processes. In this chapter, an overview of judgement and decision-making theory will be given in the context of the pacing and performance of endurance tasks with some attention on research methods and measurement issues. The aim of the chapter is to consider how endurance athletes make decisions about their pace as a strategy for performing at their best, as well as how advanced process-tracing methods might be used to further our understanding of the underlying cognitive processes. The chapter is intended to provide a rudimentary introduction to judgement and decision-making in endurance sport, and has been written with scholars, students, and coaches in mind who may be new to this area of study. It is hoped that the later part of the chapter on measurement issues and methods will be of interest to established scholars in the field as a primer to embarking upon sophisticated new avenues of research that will advance our understanding of athletic judgement and decision-making processes.

There is something captivating and intriguing about endurance athletes and the sports they participate in such as cycling, marathon running, triathlon, and other long-distance physical tasks. Perhaps it is the abiding physical discomfort to which these athletes subject themselves that is cause for admiration. Benignly masochistic but nonetheless rewarding and self-actualising. If not admiration, then perhaps bemusement. Why would any rational individual voluntarily subject themselves to the discomfort and pain associated with enduring physical activity? Maybe such athletes are motivated by the desire to stand out, after all, endurance sport provides the perfect opportunity for those individuals, fearful of being labelled average or normal, to project themselves as extraordinary? In recent years the popularity of endurance sport has swollen with, for example, marathon finishers in the United States increasing from 25,000 in 1976 to just over half a million in 2016 (RunningUSA, 2016). With this growth of 'standard' endurance formats, those wishing to stand out as exceptional need to push the boundaries even further which perhaps explains the increasing prevalence of ultra-distance events or those involving extreme environments. Where will it stop? Perhaps it is the arresting reminder of our evolutionary past that draws interest in endurance sport; energetically adaptive bipedal australopithecines who, unlike many other animals, mastered persistence hunting as a means of survival (Carrier et al., 1984; Liebenberg, 2006; Lieberman, Bramble, Raichlen, & Shea, 2007). Although these and many other reasons might explain the growing appeal of endurance sport, I believe it is the higher degree of outcome uncertainty associated with long-duration athletic events that ultimately distinguishes them from short-duration tasks or those that depend on high levels of skilled motor performance. The long distances and protracted time periods over which such events occur constitutes conditions of uncertainty that no spectator or pundit can easily predict, and which require participating athletes to make decisions that have many associated risks. To be successful, athletes not only have to think in the moment, they need to anticipate the future and be ready to defer to a contingency plan should the future not unfold according to their expectations. The important point is that the interaction between highly-trained individuals and the uncertain conditions associated with most endurance situations, catalyses an engaging, interesting, and unpredictable athletic spectacle. As such, to be a successful endurance athlete, it is insufficient to be in peak physical condition, what is also needed is good judgement and decision-making (JDM) with the adaptive characteristics needed to respond effectively to uncertain and changing conditions. In recent years there has been growing interest in JDM research in the context of endurance sport (Micklewright, Kegerreis, Raglin, & Hettinga, 2017a; Renfree, Martin, Micklewright, & St Clair Gibson, 2014; Smits, Pepping, & Hettinga 2014) and it is this relatively new and exciting topic that I will focus on in this chapter.

Judgement and decision-making

For well over half a century JDM has been a distinct and recognised scholarly field spanning many academic disciplines including psychology, economics, philosophy, law, and medicine to name a few. Investigating how decisions are made not only has the potential to make significant theoretical contributions towards human cognition, but also has a practical importance that can improve society and enrich the lives of those exposed to it, from better flight safety to less volatile financial markets, from safer medical practices to better designed cars. In one way or another, virtually all aspects of our lived societal experience is influenced by human JDM. Endurance athletes make decisions too, for instance whether to speed up or slow down, where to position themselves, how often to take on fuel, whether to respond to an attacking competitor or show restraint, and other decisions that can have a profound effect on their performance. An important question is whether endurance performance can be improved through an enhanced understanding of athletic decision-making? First it is important to appreciate how decision-making theory has evolved.

Theoretical developments in decision-making

Rational decision-making theory

Decision-making theory has, in a relatively short period of time, undergone considerable transformation that has challenged traditional computational models of human cognition. Rational Decision-Making Theory (RDM) (Simon, 1957) is one of the earliest propositions about the underlying cognitive processes that enable humans to make decisions. According to RDM, individuals calculate the likelihood of all possible outcomes, evaluate the utility (or advantage) of each outcome, and choose the option which delivers the most beneficial combination of likelihood and utility, sometimes referred to as expected utility (Bernoulli, 2011). For example, at the beginning of a race a marathon runner could decide to run at a slow, moderate, or fast pace. These potential behaviours I shall refer to as *acts*. Now suppose that during the race either a strong head wind could develop or there will be no wind. These potential conditions I shall refer to as *states*. Each combination of act and state leads to a unique outcome (expected utility) as illustrated in Table 4.1.

In deciding how to act, an athlete must balance the likelihood of a head wind against the expected utility of each act. Adopting a slow pace results in underperformance but guarantees completion no matter what wind conditions arise. A medium pace threatens completion if a head wind develops but guarantees completion with average performance if there is no wind. Providing there is no head wind, selecting a fast pace will lead to a personal best – however, if a head wind does develop, this will result in not finishing. So, the decision depends on the

TABLE 4.1 Variations in expected utility associated with different permutations of acts and states

		STATE	
		No Wind	*Head Wind*
ACT	**Slow Pace**	Will finish but underperforms	Will finish but badly underperforms
	Medium Pace	Will finish but no personal best	May finish but no personal best
	Fast Pace	May finish & achieve personal best	Will not finish

relative value the runner places on completion compared to achieving a personal best, and their appraisal of how likely it is a head wind will occur. Thus, an athlete who values completion above all else should select a slow pace. An athlete who values personal best should only select a fast pace if they asses the likelihood of a head wind to be low, otherwise they should accept that a personal best will not be possible and settle for a medium pace to guarantee completion which offers better expected utility than not finishing. By assigning values (utility) to each outcome and a probability of each outcome associated with each act it is mathematically possible to calculate the best expected utility and the theoretically superior decision. Readers interested in the complexities of modelling expected utility are referred to Hey and Orme (1994).

The number of ways an athlete could act, and the number of states associated with endurance sports are much more numerous and complex than those given in Table 4.1. For instance, temperature, terrain, competitor behaviour, feelings, injury, and other states might need to be considered by an athlete in deciding how to act. The complexity associated with many situations requiring a decision created a real problem for RDM because the number of potential acts and states generates so many outcome permutations that it would very easily exceed human computational processing capacity. Even if such extensive and methodical processing were possible, it would consume so much cognitive effort and take so much time that making decisions in an efficient and pragmatic way in changing situations would be impractical. The theory also assumes that all individuals, including athletes, are rational actors who will act according to the rules of probability. If that were true, sport would be predictable, uninteresting to watch and bookmakers probably would not exist. Finally, RDM is limited because it assumes actors are always fully aware of, and have accurate information about, every state that could influence action outcomes, something most unlikely given the complexity of their environment and the constraints associated with human perception. What was needed then, was a theoretical perspective that could equally account for decision-making in simple as well as complex, confusing or unknown circumstances, and one that could explain good as well as poor decisions. The issue of complexity and uncertainty is considered further later in this chapter.

Bounded rationality

In recognising some of the limitations of RDM, most notably the pragmatic implausibility of full rationality, the concept of bounded rationality was introduced (Simon, 1957). According to bounded rationality, actors make decisions based on partial or imperfect information which lead to satisfactory but not necessarily optimal decisions. Partial or imperfect information is, in fact, an inevitable consequence of situational uncertainty, mentioned earlier as a differentiating feature of endurance sport. Suppose our example runner adopted a fast pace at the start of the marathon based on a favourable weather forecast but then could not finish because, contrary to the forecast, a strong headwind developed. Although disappointing for the runner, the decision to set off with a fast pace was probably optimal given the information they had access to at the time which subsequently turned out to be imperfect. In other words, decisions are bounded by the constraints associated with situation complexity, human awareness, and cognitive processing.

Prospect theory

An alternative theory, and a turning point in decision-making research, occurred when it was recognised that, contrary to previous beliefs, individuals are not always fully rational when making decisions but are instead influenced by emotion, experience, perception, and social context. A novel concept of prospect theory was dual-processes or the distinction between fast/intuitive thinking and slow/ deliberative thinking, influenced by economic decision theory (Kahneman & Tversky, 1973, 1979; Tversky & Kahneman, 1973, 1974, 1986, 1991, 1992), social judgment theory (Nisbett & Wilson, 1977; Petty & Cacioppo, 1984) and cognitive psychology (Evans & Over, 1996, 2003; Klaczynski, 2000; Osman, 2004; Shiffrin & Schneider, 1977; Sloman, 1996; Stanovich, 1999). The introduction of dual pro- cesses allowed a new way of conceptualising how decisions are made, namely that individuals are not always fully rational but instead used cognitive shortcuts under- pinned by emotion, previous experience, perception, and social context. In the context of endurance performance, prospect theory has intuitive appeal because, as highlighted previously (Micklewright et al., 2017a), the necessity to integrate a wide array of situational cues and sensory-perceptual information places signifi- cant cognitive demand on athletic decision-making processes. Thus, rather than attempting to calculate the expected utility of numerous possible ways of acting in even more numerous potential situations, consistent with dual process theory, endurance athletes are able instead to make quick decisions or approximations based upon experience, instinct, and intuition. Whereas in most endurance situations an athlete has time to make decisions, there are instances where the ability to make quick, intuitive pacing decisions is advantageous – for instance, how to respond to or counterattack a break-away attempt by a competitor. Most likely, endurance athletes use both intuitive and deliberative decision-making processes in an adaptive way according to the complexity of available cues or the time available to decide.

Intuitive decision-making is automatic and quick because it relies very little on working memory resources (Shiffrin & Schneider, 1977), facilitates parallel functions (Holyoak & Simon, 1999; Simon, Krawczyk, & Holyoak, 2004), and is associative such that complex tasks, problems and uncertain situations can be responded to by drawing on previous experience and beliefs (Bowers, Regehr, Balthazard, & Parker, 1990; Stanovich, 1999). Deliberative decision-making is slower, sequential, requires greater cognitive effort (Haidt, 2001; Mynatt, Doherty, & Dragan, 1993; Wang, 2006), utilises working memory (Gilinsky & Judd, 1994; Bröder, 2003) and relates to general intelligence (Evans, 2010; Colom, Rebollo, Palacios, Juan-Espinosa, & Kyllonen, 2004). The distinction between intuitive and deliberative decision- making can be interpreted in the context of previous endurance pacing research.

For example, studies that have linked experience (Mauger, Jones, & Williams, 2010; Micklewright, Papadopoulou, Swart, & Noakes, 2010) to pace suggest factors other than present cues can influence decisions perhaps indicating similar efficiencies proposed with intuitive decision-making. A tendency to selectively attend to a few cues during an endurance task (Boya et al., 2017) suggests pacing decisions are sometimes made by reducing complex environments into simpler propositions, also characteristic of intuitive decision-making. In contrast, deliberative thinking does facilitate the kind of abstract and hypothetical thinking needed to anticipate and mentally model different scenarios that might transpire during the course of an endurance task. The two central concepts underpin prospect theory that make intuitive decisions possible are heuristics and biases.

A heuristic is best thought of as mental shortcut that allows individuals to approximate a decision in circumstances where there is complex, confusing, contradictory, missing, or partial information. The significance of heuristics is that they vitiate the need to notice and process all information sources thus reducing complex scenarios into simpler decision-making propositions: a pragmatic trade-off between cognitive effort and accuracy. Two of the classic heuristics introduced by Kahneman and Tversky were availability and representativeness (Tversky & Kahneman, 1974). For example, an endurance athlete's decision about how much and how often to drink during a race is most likely to be influenced by memorable negative images or footage of dehydrated athletes who collapse that are more *available* to remember than images of athletes where dehydration has had no discernible effect on them. Hydration decisions might also be influenced by how *representative* an athlete's perceived current situation is compared to previous races where collapse from dehydration occurred. As evident in both examples, the availability and representativeness heuristics depend on memory, something which might partly explain the known effects of experience on pacing (Micklewright et al., 2010; Mauger et al., 2010). The systematic influence of a heuristic on decision-making is referred to as a bias. In many effort regulation theories (Coquart et al., 2012; de Koning et al., 2011; Faulkner, Parfitt, & Eston, 2008; Marcora, 2010; Noakes, St Clair Gibson, & Lambert, 2004; St Clair Gibson, Swart, & Tucker, 2018; Tucker, 2009; Venhorst, Micklewright, & Noakes, 2018a), it is predicted that perceived exertion influences athletic pace in a systematic way such that unsustainable rises in rate of perceived exertion (RPE) cause athletes to slow down. In this regard, perceived exertion might be conceived of as a bias, it allegedly having a systematic influence on pacing decisions. Perceived exertion, although not classically defined as an emotion, is nevertheless a feeling state and therefore its influence on pacing decisions will be considered in the next subsection.

Perceived exertion and decision-making during endurance activity

Until a few decades ago, relatively few researchers had investigated how athletes pace themselves (Morgan & Pollock 1977; Siegel & Johnson 1992) but there has since been interest in identifying optimal patterns of energy expenditure for performance (Abbiss & Laursen, 2008; Foster et al., 2003), using pacing measurements to investigate theories of homeostatic exercise regulation (Noakes et al., 2005; St Clair Gibson et al., 2018; Ulmer 1996), and the extent to which pacing behaviour is decided upon through conscious or subconscious processes (Marcora, 2010; Micklewright et al., 2017a; St Clair Gibson et al., 2006). Perceived exertion has emerged as having an influential role that is common to most models of exercise regulation.

In central governor theory (Noakes et al., 2005), perceived exertion constitutes part of a homeostatic feedback loop that represents global integration of afferent feedback from the active muscles and organs during exercise, which then influences efferent control of further muscle activation. In central governor theory, perceptual experience impedes access to theoretical motor reserves, thus giving the brain a protective function in effort regulation. This idea can be compared to the way a rev-limiter protects the engine of a motorcar. Various mechanisms of how perceived exertion influence pacing behaviour have since been proposed. For instance, Tucker (2009) proposed a template-matching model where pace is modified according to how well experienced and anticipated RPE compare, considering distance remaining to the end of the task. Faulkner et al. (2008) proposed that athletes modify their pace to maintain a scalar linear increase in RPE whereby peak RPE coincides with the endpoint. By multiplying RPE by percentage of distance remaining, De Koning et al. (2011) created a single metric they called hazard score, apparently representing the likelihood of a pacing modification. Garcin, Coquart, Salleron, Voy, and Matran (2012) put forward an estimated time-limit model whereby a pace is set according to whether it, and the corresponding perceived exertion, can be maintained for the estimated time required to reach the endpoint. All these accounts of how pace is determined and modified throughout an endurance task are not dissimilar from the decision-making systems previously discussed. For instance, they all describe information processes that always occur prior to selecting a behavioural action, in this case pace, in conditions where there is a choice. The extent to which perceived exertion has heuristic properties in facilitating pacing decisions among endurance athletes will be returned to later. First, I will discuss how the complexity of an endurance task and uncertainty influence anticipatory pacing decisions.

The effects of uncertainty and complexity on anticipatory pacing decisions

The concept of teleoanticipation was first coined by Ulmer (1996) who recognised the need to regulate energy expenditure in anticipation of being able to cope with future demands of an exercise task. As discussed, many of the exercise regulation models have since explained anticipatory pacing in terms of the combined influence of perceived exertion and athlete awareness of distance remaining. Whereas our mental representation of the past is a memory and our mental representation of the present is a perception, our ability to pre-experience or mentally simulate the future is referred to as prospection (Gilbert & Wilson, 2007). Prospective thought is an important concept in anticipatory pacing, for without this ability, athletes would not be able to either approximate future demands of an endurance task or, in adjusting to the anticipated demand, be able to adopt an appropriate pattern of energy expenditure. This requires the ability to think in abstract terms, without which, it has been shown, young children adopt a very fast starting pace apparently without regard for the duration of a task (Micklewright et al., 2012). Even older teenagers, with a developing ability for abstract thought, experience difficulties in anticipating the demands of, and pacing themselves to, a time-based running task compared to a more visibly tangible distance-based run. Furthermore, athletes do not only have to predict the circumstance of a task but also how their perceptions of effort will respond to the pacing strategy they choose to adopt. When faced with a pacing decision then, mental simulation provides a way of previewing and pre-feeling its consequences. The degree of difficulty an athlete experiences in making such anticipatory pacing decisions may depend on the level of uncertainty and complexity of the situation.

Forecasting and scenario planning are influenced by the uncertainty and complexity of a situation (Schoemaker, 2008). Complexity refers to the number of factors present and the extent to which they interact. Uncertainty relates to the availability of information and the degree of confidence felt about predicting events. A matrix is provided in Table 4.2 illustrating circumstances of an endurance task typically associated with each permutation of complexity and uncertainty. According to Schoemaker (2008), approaches to forecasting and decision-making differ according to how complex and uncertain a situation is. Using this framework, the most straightforward scenario is where the complexity and uncertainty associated with an endurance task are both low; an experienced, well-informed athlete completing a simple course under stable environmental conditions with little competitor interference. In such circumstances, a pre-planned point-estimate approach to pacing strategy will probably work best since forecasting is simple, the conditions stable, and the likelihood of having to make impromptu decisions is low. Where complexity is low but uncertainty is high, a ballpark range approach to forecasting and decision-making would be appropriate i.e., it is still relatively easy to make predictions about an uncomplicated endurance task but, given the high uncertainty, bounded between best- and worst-case scenarios. With low uncertainty and high complexity, deterministic modelling would be better whereby a variety of outcomes to decisions are conceived of depending on how particular variables have a combined influence. In contrast, an endurance task with high complexity and uncertainty will require a different decision-making approach because deterministic models that require low uncertainty, ballparks which need low complexity, and pre-planned strategies which rely on both low complexity and uncertainty are unlikely to work well in such unpredictable conditions. A stochastic approach to making decisions would be better, continuously weighing up several possible pacing strategies and, as they progress, being willing and able to switch in an adaptive way according to any emerging situation.

TABLE 4.2 The interaction between uncertainty and complexity in endurance sport

	UNCERTAINTY	
COMPLEXITY	**LOW**	**HIGH**
HIGH	Complicated course with difficult navigation and many waypoints. Changeable weather, variable terrain and other unpredictable conditions. Position or outcome goal referenced against other competitors. High competitor crowding with other course obstacles. Self-aware experienced athlete with solid knowledge of the course and navigation. Access to reliable and accurate information about weather and environmental conditions. Access to relibale real-time feedback about their own progress and performance. Good intelligence about competitors and experienced at reading their tactics.	Complicated course with difficult navigation and many waypoints. Changeable weather, variable terrain and other unpredictable conditions. Position or outcome goal referenced against other competitors. High competitor crowding with other course obstacles. Inexperienced athlete. Knowledge of the course and navigation lacking. Limited or no information about weather and environmental conditions. Little or no real-time feedback about their own progress and performance. Little or no intelligence about competitors and inexperienced at reading their tactics.
LOW	Uncomplicated course with easy navigation. Very stable weather, terrain and other conditions. Simple goal(completion or self-referenced time). Minimal competitor crowding or course obstacles. Self-aware experienced athlete with solid knowledge of the course and navigation. Access to reliable and accurate information about weather and environmental conditions. Access to relibale real-time feedback about their own progress and performance. Good intelligence about competitors and experienced at reading their tactics.	Uncomplicated course with easy navigation. Very stable weather, terrain and other conditions. Simple goal (completion or self-referenced time). Minimal competitor crowding or course obstacles. Inexperienced athlete. Knowledge of the course and navigation lacking. Limited or no information about weather and environmental conditions. Little or no real-time feedback about their own progress and performance. Little or no intelligence about competitors and inexperienced at reading their tactics.

Any endurance sport situation might be defined by one of the four extremes provided in Table 4.2 or somewhere in between. In using this framework, it is possible to understand how particular endurance situations demand different approaches to making pacing decisions. For example, one might imagine that tasks characterised by high complexity and high uncertainty would require lots of deliberation involving high levels of cognitive effort and the use of working memory to simulate, hold, and compare different pacing scenarios. In complete contrast, it is easy to see how the intuitive execution of very well practised and tested pacing strategies would be fine for an uncomplicated endurance task with high levels of certainty. It is also possible to see how poor pacing decisions might be made, for instance if an athlete attempted to use a pre-planned pacing strategy in a highly complex and highly uncertain situation or attempted to use deterministic mental models in situations of high uncertainty. The ability to make good pacing decisions is also influenced by a variety of intrinsic factors such as perceptual fidelity, risk-taking traits, and affect.

Intrinsic factors influencing pacing decisions

Most decisions involve risk. When an endurance athlete decides upon a pace, there are two apparent risks. The first is that they do not complete the task because of exhaustion. The second is that they complete the task with a slower time or lower position than intended. Choosing an appropriate pacing strategy is about balancing these opposing risks which is difficult because a fine line exists between putting in the best possible performance and failing to finish. A variety of individual factors influence decision-making under risk.

Early decision-making theory, including prospect theory, largely ignored the influence of emotions on decisions. However, it has since been shown that emotions unrelated to the task can impact decisions (Lerner & Keltner, 2000) and negative emotions can degrade the quality of decisions (Wilson et al., 1993). There are two ways in which emotions can affect decision-making. The concept of expected emotions assumes that individuals try to forecast how they will respond emotionally to each choice available to them and then select a decision that produces the most favourable outcome (Loewenstein & Lerner, 2003). This bears some resemblance to RPE template models (de Koning et al., 2011; Faulkner et al., 2008; Tucker, 2009), which predicts athletes will make pacing decisions to produce the most favourable RPE trajectory. What this also highlights is the intertemporal dimension to pacing decision-making in that the benefits of any decision are delayed rather than immediate.

Emotions can also have an indirect immediate effect on decision-making (Loewenstein & Lerner, 2003). Lerner and Keltner (2000) found further effects of emotions on risk perception and attribution. For example, it was found that individuals experiencing anger had a low perception of risk, felt future events were predictable and felt strongly in control of outcomes. Individuals experiencing anxiety or fear had a high perception of risk, felt future events were not predictable, and that they were not in control of outcomes. Thus, endurance athletes that experience anger may be more willing to decide upon a risky, aggressive pacing strategy, whereas those experiencing anxiety might decide to act more conservatively. In two separate experiments involving novice time-trial cyclists and experienced endurance runners, a much faster more aggressive starting pace was found among those with low risk perceptions compared to those with high risk perceptions (Micklewright et al., 2015).

Decisions involving risk are not just based upon a rational objective analysis of the circumstances, referred to as risk-as-analysis, but are also influenced by emotions associated with experience, referred to as risk-as-feelings (Slovic, Finucane, Peters, & MacGregor, 2004). A further interesting development was the introduction of an affect heuristic (Slovic, Finucane, Peters, & MacGregor, 2007) which, it has been proposed, influences decision-making. The idea is that the mental representations that people access while imagining future scenarios all have affective tags, either positive or negative, pleasant or unpleasant, which serve as decision-making cues or cognitive shortcuts as previously described. Perhaps most compelling is that in deciding whether to adopt a potentially hazardous behaviour, emotions were associated with the inverse relationship found between deliberations of perceived risk and perceived benefit (Alhakami & Slovic, 1994), an effect found to be strong even under time-pressure (Finucane, Alhakami, Slovic, & Johnson, 2000). It was also found that changing information about risks and benefits could influence people's emotions towards a behaviour and their subsequent preference for it (Finucane et al., 2000). In deciding whether to increase pace, it may come down to whether the negative emotions associated with failure and collapse (emotion-influenced perceived risk) are more dominant within an endurance athlete than the positive emotions associated with winning or success (emotion-influenced perceived benefit). Furthermore, it may be that when under sudden pressure to respond to a competitor it is the emotional tagging of imagined behavioural consequences (affect heuristic), that enables athletes to act intuitively rather than having to rely on slower deliberation about the pros and cons of various actions.

Perceived exertion and heuristic based decision-making

The application of decision-making theory to athletic pacing is relative recent (Micklewright et al., 2017a; Renfree et al., 2014; Smits et al., 2014) which has provided a different but complementary perspective on effort regulation during endurance activity which, hitherto, has gravitated around perceived exertion-endpoint interactions. A question of interest is where perceived exertion-endpoint interactions sit within a decision-making perspective of pacing and performance of endurance tasks? At face value, the similarities with decision-making theory are that it comprises both an affective component, since perceived exertion is a feeling state, and a cognitive component in the form of anticipation and the processing of endpoint information. Yet, as many deception studies have shown (Jones et al., 2013), RPE templates are most effective in those conditions where both complexity and uncertainty are relatively low. For instance, in a complex multi-discipline event like an ironman triathlon, RPE trajectory is no longer linear but instead follows a more oscillatory pattern (Parry, Chinnasamy, Papadopoulou, Noakes, & Micklewright, 2011). When uncertainty is increased by asking participants to exercise without stating an endpoint (Micklewright et al., 2010; Swart et al., 2009), athletes understandably adopt a very conservative pace to maintain a much shallower RPE trajectory. The role that RPE plays in endurance situations of varying complexity and uncertainty, might be usefully reframed in terms of its heuristic function or association with heuristic principles.

The extent to which perceived exertion might be considered an affective state is interesting, not least because, unlike classic emotions such as fear, joy, and anger, it emerges from intrinsic physiological origins. Nevertheless, perceived exertion shares many of the characteristics used to define emotion. For instance, it meets the definition put forward by Watson (2000), of being a distinct, integrated psychophysiological response system. Perceived exertion also satisfies Watson's four criteria in that it is a distinctive feeling state that provokes adaptive behaviour and has associated autonomic responses and facial expressions (see fascinating perceived exertion and facial electromyogram work (de Morree & Marcora, 2010)). In this sense, models such as CGM (Noakes et al., 2005), RPE template (Tucker, 2009), hazard score (De Koning et al., 2011) and RPE trajectory all essentially describe how changing patterns of perceived exertion provoke an adaptive pacing response, comparable in nature to the way decisions of many other kinds are influenced by the affect heuristic. However, although it is a feeling state, perceived exertion cannot be considered an emotion in the classical sense because of one fundamental difference. This is because, whereas affective experience endures once the cause that stimulated it has been removed, this is not true of perceived exertion which immediately ceases once exercise is stopped. Interestingly, perceived fatigue does endure (Micklewright, St Clair Gibson, Gladwell, & Al Salman, 2017b) and may be a more useful construct in terms of its affect heuristic properties.

While there is no doubt from the evidence (Jones et al., 2013; Williams et al., 2014) that perceptions of exertion and knowledge of the endpoint are important, some evidence is beginning to suggest that this may not be exclusively or universally the case. In a recent study using eye-tracking technology, researchers found differences of information uptake between experienced cyclists, who preferred feedback about speed, and novice cyclists, who preferred feedback about distance (Boya et al., 2017). The experienced cyclists in this study were also found to be much more selective in their information-seeking behaviour, looking at fewer sources of information, doing so less frequently than novices but for longer. The effects of experience on the pacing and performance of an endurance task have been well reported (Mauger et al., 2010; Micklewright et al., 2010) although little is known about the causes. In an earlier study, we also showed that experienced endurance athletes were more likely to adopt a relatively faster starting pace than novice athletes, indicating a different, more confident approach to risk and uncertainty (Micklewright et al., 2015). Recent work has also shown that competitor behaviour can strongly influence pacing, which is a long overdue development in pacing research so that theory is no longer exclusively based on data gathered in the alone condition (Noorbergen, Konings, Micklewright, Elferink-Gemser, & Hettinga, 2016; Venhorst, Micklewright, & Noakes, 2018b). The notion that a range of information cues, wider than endpoint-RPE interactions, might inform pacing decision is also theoretically consistent with adaptive decision-making strategies put forward in dual processes theory (Gigerenzer, Todd, & ABC Research Group, 1999).

How do endurance athletes select from several available heuristics in any given situation to make the best pacing decision? Ecological rationality as an overarching principle of heuristic selection was put forward (Gigerenzer et al. 1999, p. 13). which predicts that a heuristic is adapted to the structure of the environment. Thus, in endurance sport, this would enable athletes to use one type of heuristic to determine pace at the beginning of a task when completion risks and uncertainty are at their greatest, yet a different heuristic in the latter half of a task as such risks and uncertainties begin to diminish. It would also accommodate the idea that, contrary to logic, athletes might temporarily abandon a sustainable endpoint-targeted RPE trajectory in certain circumstances such as, i) the beginning of a race when sustainable pace is sometimes sacrificed in favour of establishing position, ii) when reacting to a competitor or attacking competitors, for instance peloton breakaways in cycling, iii) negotiating challenging environments or terrains such as headwinds or hills. Thus, consistent with the idea of an adaptive heuristic toolbox underpinned by ecological rationality (Gigerenzer & Gaissmaier, 2011), of great interest are the dynamic processes of selecting, changing, and using heuristics in ways that produce optimal pacing and performance.

Methodological considerations for decision-making research in endurance sport

So far, this chapter has attempted to explore how effort is regulated during endurance tasks through the lens of decision-making theory. This perspective of endurance performance, although relatively new in comparison with other domains, has heuristic potential but requires additional measurement and methodological techniques to those already commonly used in pacing research. This section will focus on two key issues. First, an evaluation of how adequate pacing measurements are in understanding decision-making processes and second, an introduction to additional decision-making research methods.

Adequacy of pacing measurements for decision-making research in endurance sport

Recording changes in speed or power output throughout an endurance task is relatively simple and is often used in pacing research. However, whereas pacing data is a good measure of the behavioural outcomes of decisions endurance athletes make, it is less useful in revealing anything about antecedent psychological decision-making processes. Segment averaging is by far the most common way by which pacing behaviour has been represented in the literature. This approach first involves defining the epoch of interest, which in previous pacing research has varied between 25 per cent (Micklewright et al., 2015) and 5 per cent (Micklewright et al., 2012), then plotting average speed or power for each segment. This simple method has been helpful in identifying broad patterns of pacing behaviour such as those described by De Koning et al., (2011) and Abbiss and Lauresen (2008), but it cannot adequately capture moment-to-moment decision-making processes. A continuous trace of speed or power changes provide a better indication of momentary outcomes of decisions – however, for several reasons, it is still not perfect. First, change in pace is an outcome of pacing decisions and not a direct measure of underlying psychological processes. A second but related point is that, from the pacing trace, it is impossible to separate deliberate changes in speed or power from intuitive changes that the athlete may not be consciously aware of. Third, as illustrated in Figure 4.1, continuous pacing traces can be complex, making it difficult to differentiate between meaningful changes in speed and drift. Fourth, it is impossible to determine from a pacing trace when a decision to change pace was

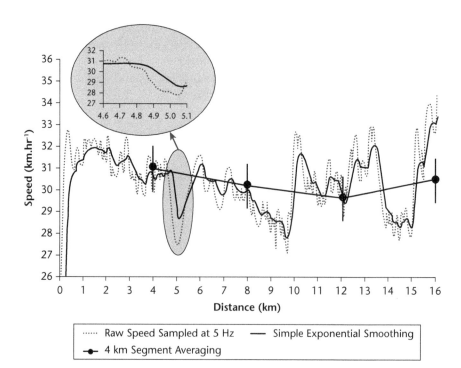

FIGURE 4.1 Example pacing pattern of a 10-mile (16.1 km) cycling time trial with 4 km segment averaging and continuous data with simple exponential smoothing (b)

made since such measures cannot account for the lag between making a decision and implementing it. The final, often overlooked, point, is that a decision not to alter pace, which is still a decision after all, would not be represented on a pacing trace. Figure 4.1 illustrates the difference between segment averaging and continuous pacing measurements and the difficulty of identifying the precise point of a meaningful pacing change, even when methods like moving averages or more sophisticated exponential smoothing are applied owing to the lag between the raw and smoothed data.

Measurements of changing speed or power only tell us about the outcome of a decision but nothing about the psychological processes that led to that decision. Pacing is therefore an outcome not a process indicator and if we are to learn more about how athletes make pacing decisions, we need methods that can capture pre-decisional information processes. This is not easy because information processing and associated thoughts cannot be directly observed and require special process-tracing methods.

Process tracing methods for decision-making in endurance sport

It is useful to distinguish between several information processes relevant to decision-making. The first is information acquisition which refers to how individuals attend to certain cues or information sources. The second process relates to how acquired information or sensory signals are perceived, integrated, and interpreted in ways that lead to a decision. At this point, I am deliberately not differentiating between those information acquisition and integration processes that a participant is consciously controlling, and those that they are not. Both are possible. I will summarise methodological options for investigating information acquisition processes as well as integration and interpretation processes below. A more comprehensive account of these methods is given in the electronic supplement of Micklewright et al. (2017a).

Information acquisition methods

Deception or cue-occlusion methods have typically been used to infer the type of information endurance athletes use in making decisions (Jones et al., 2013; Williams et al., 2014). The rationale is that, if, after altering or removing a source of information pacing or performance changes, it can be inferred that the modified information source has an important contributory role. These experiments have provided a useful way of investigating the influence of certain information on pacing behaviour, but such methods are not without their limitations. One is the necessity to make assumptions about which informational variables to manipulate and direct athletes' attention to compared to simply observing what cues athletes naturally choose to attend to. A further limitation is the assumption of inter-athlete consistency in what they attend to in making decisions rather than adaptive variations in their preference for, uptake and use of certain information sources. These constraints can, in part, be overcome by using process tracing methods that directly measure information uptake. The two I will discuss are active information search (AIS) and eye-tracking.

During the performance of a task, AIS can be used to identify what information participants use, what information they ignore, and the sequence of information they refer to while solving problems (Huber, Huber, & Schulte-Mecklenbeck, 2011). During AIS participants are presented with a scenario incorporating choices about which they are permitted to ask questions before deciding. This method makes it possible to capture deliberative processes regarding what information participants think they need to decide and the sequence in which they refer to, or go back to, information. It reveals nothing about what information was used to decide but does help understand what information was attended to. This method would need adapting for endurance sport research by developing exercise-related AIS scenarios. Although athletes would complete the AIS during non-exercising conditions, the task would still require them to make decisions about whether to increase, decrease, or maintain pace. The ecological validity of AIS could perhaps be improved by asking participants to complete the task in various states of exertion or fatigue.

The most direct way of measuring cue detection and information uptake is to measure eye movements which, with advances in mobile eye-tracking technology, is relatively straight forward (Horsley, Eliot, Knight, & Reilly, 2014). After calibration, eye-trackers simultaneous record from a forward-looking scene camera and a second camera that records corneal reflection (binocular for added precision) enabling eye fixations and saccadic movements to be measured. As such it is possible to ascertain exactly what information athletes look at during an endurance task. Boya et al. (2017) found that, using mobile eye tracking, during a laboratory-based 10-mile time-trial novice cyclists preferred to look at distance feedback whereas experienced cyclists preferred to look at feedback about their speed. This indicates that information acquisition processes may be more adaptive than originally thought. Whereas it is not possible for eye-tracking to reveal how information is used in making decisions, accumulated fixation time and fixation frequency are considered to be measures of object importance (Russo & Leclerc, 1994), whereas average fixation time is considered a measure of processing effort that is sometimes used to discriminate between intuitive and deliberative thinking (Horstmann, Ahlgrimm, & Glöckner, 2009).

Information integration and interpretation methods

Other process tracing methods are needed to understand how athletes use the information they attend to, either in isolation or conjunction with information acquisition methods. Verbal protocols allow participants to speak aloud their thoughts either during a decision-making task, known as a concurrent verbal protocol (Ericsson & Simon, 1980), or soon after the decision-making task has been completed, known as retrospective verbal protocol (Nisbett & Wilson, 1977). Concurrent verbal protocols have become popular because contemporaneous verbalisation of thought processes during a decision-making task is considered a reliable indicator of short-term memory processing and internal deliberation (Bettman, Johnson, & Payne, 1990). However, concurrent verbal protocols are difficult to carry out because, as explained in the gold standard put forward by Ericsson and Simon (1980), the technique requires phasing involving instructing and familiarising participants as well as data recording and data analysis. Perhaps most challenging is the training participants need to carry out to be able to provide continuous verbalisation of a task without gaps of more than 5 seconds. There are different approaches to analysing verbal protocol recordings (Austin & Delaney, 1998) and a framework for identifying decision-making processes from such recording also exists (Harte, Westenberg, & van Someren, 1994).

By comparing solutions an athlete immediately mentions (intuition) with the solution they eventually carry out (deliberation), it may be possible to distinguish intuitive from deliberative processes. There are several threats to the reliability and validity of concurrent verbal protocols in endurance research. First, that a participant's attention to verbalising their thoughts interferes with their decision-making processes, and non-veridicality, where participants either omit some of the decision-making processes or misrepresent such processes. This can be reduced with a sufficiently robust familiarisation phase. Furthermore, while concurrent verbal data during high-intensity exercise can be recorded, researchers should carefully consider the potential effects verbalisation itself has on energetics and performance. An advantage of retrospective verbal protocols is that they do not suffer the same challenges that concurrent verbalisation presents; however, they are more dependent on memory and are therefore prone to recall errors such as distortion, omission, and construction effects (Russo, Johnson, & Stephens, 1989).

One of the known problems of asking participants after an event why they made a decision is the tendency to infer a reason rather than trying to remember their actual thought processes (Nisbett & Wilson, 1977). This is a significant threat to the validity of post-decision surveys and interviews, although this can be minimised by carefully briefing participants beforehand.

There are two main methods for gathering retrospective verbal reports. The first involves a traditional interview which can vary from being unstructured to fully structured during which participants are asked to explain, describe, or rate decision-making processes. The second, known as a cued retrospective verbal reporting, involves simulated recall in which participants are asked to discuss their decision-making processes while watching replayed video footage of themselves performing a problem or task (Omodei, Wearing, & McLennan, 1997). Retrospective verbal reports are advantageous in pacing research because they avoid reactivity, particularly the likelihood that concurrent verbalisation will interfere with the performance of the exercise task and vice-versa. However, unlike concurrent reports, retrospective reporting lacks spontaneity and therefore has a diminished ability to differentiate between intuitive and deliberative pacing decisions. Both concurrent and retrospective verbal protocols are, by their nature, also limited to conscious processes except when pre-conscious, subconscious, or unconscious processes temporarily move into consciousness. Verbal protocol methods represent a powerful way of gathering and analysing subjective decision-making data in dual process pacing research, providing such studies are carefully designed and deployed with rigour. Other process-tracing methods exist that are relevant to decision-making research in endurance sport; however, they are complex and beyond the scope of this chapter. A more detailed discussion of these techniques can be found in the electronic supplement of Micklewright et al. (2017a).

Conclusions

The application of decision-making theory to athletic pacing is a relatively recent phenomenon which has provided a different but complementary perspective on effort regulation during endurance activity which has mostly gravitated around perceived exertion-endpoint interactions. Athletic endurance activity can vary considerably in terms of situational complexity and uncertainty, which may require different approaches to making decisions. Whereas pre-planned pacing strategies executed through intuitive action may work in circumstances of low complexity and low uncertainty, they are unlikely to work in very complex and uncertain endurance task conditions. Heuristics, or cognitive shortcuts, can help endurance athletes making effective pacing decisions in highly complex, uncertain or time-constrained situations. The way in which athletes use heuristics to make decisions varies according to both situational factors and intrinsic factors such as affective state and perception of risk. Whereas pacing measurements have provided good insight about the outcomes of pacing decisions by endurance athletes, we know far less about preceding information processes that result in such decisions. The decision-making approach to endurance sport performance has heuristic potential using process tracing methods such as eye-tracking and think aloud protocols.

References

Abbiss, C. R., & Laursen, P. B. (2008). Describing and understanding pacing strategies during athletic competition. *Sports Medicine, 38*(3), 239–252.

Alhakami, A. S., & Slovic, P. (1994). A psychological study of the inverse relationship between perceived risk and perceived benefit. *Risk Analysis, 14*(6), 1085–1096.

Austin, J., & Delaney, P. F. (1998). Protocol analysis as a tool for behaviour analysis. *The Analysis of Verbal Behavior, 15*(1), 41–56.

Bernoulli, D. (2011). Exposition of a new theory on the measurement of risk. In MacLean, L. C., Thorp, E. O., & Ziemba, W. T (Eds.), *The Kelly capital growth investment criterion: Theory and practice* (pp. 11–24). London: World Scientific Publishing Co., Ltd.

Bettman, J. R., Johnson, E. J., & Payne, J. W. (1990). A componential analysis of cognitive effort in choice. *Organizational Behavior and Human Decision Processes, 45*(1), 111–139.

Bowers, K. S., Regehr, G., Balthazard, C., & Parker, K. (1990). Intuition in the context of discovery. *Cognitive Psychology, 22*(1), 72–110.

Boya, M., Foulsham, T., Hettinga, F., Parry, D., Williams, E., Jones, H., Sparks, A., Marchant, D., Ellison, P., Bridge, C., McNaughton, L. & Micklewright D. (2017). Information acquisition differences between experienced and novice time trial cyclists. *Medicine and Science in Sports and Exercise*, *49*(9), 1884–1898.

Bröder, A. (2003). Decision making with the 'adaptive toolbox': Influence of environmental structure, intelligence, and working memory load. *Journal of Experimental Psychology: Learning, Memory, and Cognition*, *29*(4), 611.

Carrier, D. R., Kapoor, A. K., Kimura, T., Nickels, M. K., Satwanti, Scott, E. C., So, J. K., & Trinkaus, E. (1984). The energetic paradox of human running and hominid evolution [and comments and reply]. *Current Anthropology*, *25*(4), 483–495.

Colom, R., Rebollo, I., Palacios, A., Juan-Espinosa, M., & Kyllonen, P. C. (2004). Working memory is (almost) perfectly predicted by g. *Intelligence*, *32*(3), 277–296.

Coquart, J. B., Eston, R. G., Noakes, T. D., Tourny-Chollet, C., L'hermette, M., Lemaître, F., & Garcin, M. (2012). Estimated Time Limit. *Sports Medicine*, *42*(10), 845–855.

de Koning, J. J., Bobbert, M. F., & Foster, C. (1999). Determination of optimal pacing strategy in track cycling with an energy flow model. *Journal of Science and Medicine in Sport*, *2*(3), 266–277.

de Koning, J. J., Foster, C., Bakkum, A., Kloppenburg, S., Thiel, C., Joseph, T., Cohen, J., & Porcari, J. P. (2011). Regulation of pacing strategy during athletic competition. *PLoS One*, *6*(1), e15863.

de Morree, H. M., & Marcora, S. M. (2010). The face of effort: frowning muscle activity reflects effort during a physical task. *Biological Psychology*, *85*(3), 377–382.

Ericsson, K. A., & Simon, H. (1980). Verbal Reports as Data. *Psychological Review*, *87*: 215–251.

Evans, J. S. B., & Over, D. E. (1996). Rationality in the selection task: Epistemic utility versus uncertainty reduction. *Psychological Review*, *103*(2), 356–363.

Evans, J. S. B. (2003). In two minds: dual-process accounts of reasoning. *Trends in Cognitive Sciences*, *7*(10), 454–459.

Evans, J. S. B. (2010). Intuition and reasoning: A dual-process perspective. *Psychological Inquiry*, *21*(4), 313–326.

Faulkner, J., Parfitt, G., & Eston, R. (2008). The rating of perceived exertion during competitive running scales with time. *Psychophysiology*, *45*(6), 977–985.

Finucane, M. L., Alhakami, A., Slovic, P., & Johnson, S. M. (2000). The affect heuristic in judgments of risks and benefits. *Journal of Behavioral Decision Making*, *13*(1), 1–17.

Foster, C., De Koning, J. J., Hettinga, F., Lampen, J., La Clair, K. L., Dodge, C., Bobbert, M., & Porcari, J. P. (2003). Pattern of energy expenditure during simulated competition. *Medicine and Science in Sports and Exercise*, *35*(5), 826–831.

Garcin, M., Coquart, J., Salleron, J., Voy, N., & Matran, R. (2012). Self-regulation of exercise intensity by estimated time limit scale. *European Journal of Applied Physiology*, *112*(6), 2303–2312.

Gilbert, D. T., & Wilson, T. D. (2007). Prospection: Experiencing the future. *Science*, *317*(5843), 1351–1354.

Gilinsky, A. S., & Judd, B. B. (1994). Working memory and bias in reasoning across the life span. *Psychology and Aging*, *9*(3), 356.

Gigerenzer, G., Todd, P. M., & ABC Research Group. (1999). *Simple heuristics that make us smart*. New York: Oxford University Press.

Gigerenzer, G., & Gaissmaier, W. (2011). Heuristic decision making. *Annual Review of Psychology*, *62*, 451–482.

Haidt, J. (2001). The emotional dog and its rational tail: a social intuitionist approach to moral judgment. *Psychological Review*, *108*(4), 814.

Harte, J. M., Westenberg, M. R., & van Someren, M. (1994). Process models of decision making. *Acta Psychologica*, *87*(2–3), 95–120.

Hey, J. D., & Orme, C. (1994). Investigating generalizations of expected utility theory using experimental data. *Econometrica: Journal of the Econometric Society*, *62*(6), 1291–1326.

Holyoak, K. J., & Simon, D. (1999). Bidirectional reasoning in decision making by constraint satisfaction. *Journal of Experimental Psychology: General*, *128*(1), 3–31.

Horsley, M., Eliot, M., Knight, B. A., & Reilly, R. (2014). *Current trends in eye tracking research*. London: Springer.

Horstmann, N., Ahlgrimm, A., & Glöckner, A. (2009). How distinct are intuition and deliberation? An eye-tracking analysis of instruction-induced decision modes. *Judgement and Decision Making*, *4*(5), 335–354.

Huber, O. S., Huber, O. W., & Schulte-Mecklenbeck, M. I (2011). Determining the information participants need: Methods of Active Information Search. In M. Schulte-Mecklenbeck, A. Kühberger, & R. Ranyard (Eds.), *A handbook of process tracing methods for decision research: A critical review and user's guide* (pp. 65–85). New York & Hove: Psychology Press.

Jones, H. S., Williams, E. L., Bridge, C. A., Marchant, D., Midgley, A. W., Micklewright, D., & Mc Naughton, L. R. (2013). Physiological and psychological effects of deception on pacing strategy and performance: a review. *Sports Medicine*, *43*(12), 1243–1257.

Kahneman, D., & Tversky, A. (1973). On the psychology of prediction. *Psychological Review*, *80*(4), 237.

Kahneman, D., & Tversky, A. (1979). Prospect theory: An analysis of decision under risk. *Econometrics*, *47*, 263–291.

Klaczynski, P. A. (2000). Motivated scientific reasoning biases, epistemological beliefs, and theory polarization: A two-process approach to adolescent cognition. *Child Development*, *71*(5), 1347–1366.

Lerner, J. S., & Keltner, D. (2000). Beyond valence: Toward a model of emotion-specific influences on judgement and choice. *Cognition & Emotion*, *14*(4), 473–493.

Liebenberg, L. (2006). Persistence hunting by modern hunter-gatherers. *Current Anthropology*, *47*(6), 1017–1026.

Lieberman, D. E., Bramble, D. M., Raichlen, D. A., & Shea, J. J. (2007). The evolution of endurance running and the tyranny of ethnography: a reply to Pickering and Bunn. *Journal of Human Evolution*, *53*, 43443–43447.

Loewenstein, G., & Lerner, J. S. (2003). The role of affect in decision making. In R. J. Davidson, K. R. Sherer, & H. H. Goldsmith (Eds.), *Handbook of affective sciences* (pp. 619–642). Oxford: Oxford University Press.

Marcora, S. (2010). Counterpoint: afferent feedback from fatigued locomotor muscles is not an important determinant of endurance exercise performance. *Journal of Applied Physiology*, *108*(2), 454–456.

Mauger, A. R., Jones, A. M., & Williams, C. A. (2010). Influence of exercise variation on the retention of a pacing strategy. *European Journal of Applied Physiology*, *108*(5), 1015–1023.

Micklewright, D., Angus, C., Suddaby, J., St Clair Gibson, A. C. G., Sandercock, G., & Chinnasamy, C. (2012). Pacing strategy in schoolchildren differs with age and cognitive development. *Medicine and Science in Sports and Exercise*, *44*(2), 362–369.

Micklewright, D., Kegerreis, S., Raglin, J., & Hettinga, F. (2017a). Will the conscious–subconscious pacing quagmire help elucidate the mechanisms of self-paced exercise? New opportunities in dual process theory and process tracing methods. *Sports Medicine*, *47*(7), 1231–1239.

Micklewright, D., St Clair Gibson, A., Gladwell, V., & Al Salman, A. (2017b). Development and validity of the rating-of-fatigue scale. *Sports Medicine, 47*(11), 2375–2393.

Micklewright, D., Papadopoulou, E., Swart, J., & Noakes, T. (2010). Previous experience influences pacing during 20 km time trial cycling. *British Journal of Sports Medicine, 44*(13), 952–960.

Micklewright, D., Parry, D., Robinson, T., Deacon, G., Renfree, A., St Clair Gibson, A., & Matthews, W. J. (2015). Risk perception influences athletic pacing strategy. *Medicine and Science in Sports and Exercise, 47*(5), 1026–1037.

Morgan, W. P., & Pollock, M. L. (1977). Psychologic characterization of the elite distance runner. *Annals of the New York Academy of Sciences, 301*(1), 382–403.

Mynatt, C. R., Doherty, M. E., & Dragan, W. (1993). Information relevance, working memory, and the consideration of alternatives. *The Quarterly Journal of Experimental Psychology, 46*(4), 759–778.

Nisbett, R. E., & Wilson, T. D. (1977). Telling more than we can know: Verbal reports on mental processes. *Psychological Review, 84*(3), 231.

Noakes, T. D., St Clair Gibson, A., & Lambert, E. V. (2005). From catastrophe to complexity: a novel model of integrative central neural regulation of effort and fatigue during exercise in humans: summary and conclusions. *British Journal of Sports Medicine, 39*(2), 120–124.

Noorbergen, O. S., Konings, M. J., Micklewright, D., Elferink-Gemser, M. T., & Hettinga, F. J. (2016). Pacing behaviour and tactical positioning in 500-and 1000-m short-track speed skating. *International Journal of Sports Physiology and Performance, 11*(6), 742–748.

Omodei, M., Wearing, A., & McLennan, J. (1997). Head-mounted video recording: A methodology for studying naturalistic decision making. In: R. Flin, E. Salas, & M. Stub (Eds.), *Decision making under stress: Emerging themes and applications* (pp. 137–146). Aldershot, UK: Ashgate Publishing.

Osman, M. (2004). An evaluation of dual-process theories of reasoning. *Psychonomic Bulletin & Review, 11*(6), 988–1010.

Parry, D., Chinnasamy, C., Papadopoulou, E., Noakes, T., & Micklewright, D. (2011). Cognition and performance: anxiety, mood and perceived exertion among Ironman triathletes. *British Journal of Sports Medicine, 45*(14), 1088–1094.

Petty, R. E., & Cacioppo, J. T. (1984). The effects of involvement on responses to argument quantity and quality: Central and peripheral routes to persuasion. *Journal of Personality and Social Psychology, 46*(1), 69.

Renfree, A., Martin, L., Micklewright, D., & Gibson, A. S. C. (2014). Application of decision-making theory to the regulation of muscular work rate during self-paced competitive endurance activity. *Sports Medicine, 44*(2), 147–158.

RunningUSA. (2016) Running USA Annual Marathon Report. Retrieved 20 September 2017 from www.runningusa.org/marathon-report-2017.

Russo, J. E., & Leclerc, F. (1994). An eye-fixation analysis of choice processes for consumer nondurables. *Journal of Consumer Research, 21*(2), 274–290.

Russo, J. E., Johnson, E. J., & Stephens, D. L. (1989). The validity of verbal protocols. *Memory & Cognition, 17*(6), 759–769.

Schoemaker, P. J. H. (2008). Forecasting and scenario planning: The challenges of uncertainty and complexity. In D. J. Koehler, & N. Harvey, (Eds.), *Blackwell handbook of judgment and decision making* (pp. 274–296). Oxford, UK: John Wiley & Sons.

Shiffrin, R. M., & Schneider, W. (1977). Controlled and automatic human information processing: II. Perceptual learning, automatic attending and a general theory. *Psychological Review, 84*(2), 127.

Siegel, D., & Johnson, J. (1992). A preliminary study of pacing in cycling. *Journal of Sport Behavior, 15*(1), 75.

Simon H. A. (1957). *Models of man.* New York: Wiley.

Simon, D., Krawczyk, D. C., & Holyoak, K. J. (2004). Construction of preferences by constraint satisfaction. *Psychological Science, 15*(5), 331–336.

Sloman, S. A. (1996). The empirical case for two systems of reasoning. *Psychological Bulletin, 119*(1), 3.

Slovic, P., Finucane, M. L., Peters, E., & MacGregor, D. G. (2004). Risk as analysis and risk as feelings: Some thoughts about affect, reason, risk, and rationality. *Risk Analysis, 24*(2), 311–322.

Slovic, P., Finucane, M. L., Peters, E., & MacGregor, D. G. (2007). The affect heuristic. *European Journal of Operational Research, 177*(3), 1333–1352.

Smits, B. L., Pepping, G. J., & Hettinga, F. J. (2014). Pacing and decision making in sport and exercise: the roles of perception and action in the regulation of exercise intensity. *Sports Medicine, 44*(6), 763–775.

Stanovich, K. E. (1999). *Who is rational?: Studies of individual differences in reasoning.* NJ: Lawrence Erlbaum Associates.

St Clair Gibson, A. C., Lambert, E. V., Rauch, L. H., Tucker, R., Baden, D. A., Foster, C., & Noakes, T. D. (2006). The role of information processing between the brain and peripheral physiological systems in pacing and perception of effort. *Sports Medicine, 36*(8), 705–722.

St Clair Gibson, A., Swart, J., & Tucker, R. (2018). The interaction of psychological and physiological homeostatic drives and role of general control principles in the regulation of physiological systems, exercise and the fatigue process – The Integrative Governor theory. *European Journal of Sport Science, 18*(1), 25–36.

Swart, J., Lamberts, R. P., Lambert, M. I., Lambert, E. V., Woolrich, R. W., Johnston, S., & Noakes, T. D. (2009). Exercising with reserve: exercise regulation by perceived exertion in relation to duration of exercise and knowledge of endpoint. *British Journal of Sports Medicine, 43*(10), 775–781.

Tucker, R. (2009). The anticipatory regulation of performance: the physiological basis for pacing strategies and the development of a perception-based model for exercise performance. *British Journal of Sports Medicine, 43*(6), 392–400.

Tversky, A., & Kahneman, D. (1973). Availability: A heuristic for judging frequency and probability. *Cognitive Psychology, 5*(2), 207–232.

Tversky, A., & Kahneman, D. (1974). Judgment under uncertainty: Heuristics and biases. *Science, 185*(4157), 1124–1131.

Tversky, A., & Kahneman, D. (1986). Rational choice and the framing of decisions. *Journal of Business*, S251–S278.

Tversky, A., & Kahneman, D. (1991). Loss aversion in riskless choice: A reference-dependent model. *The Quarterly Journal of Economics, 106*(4), 1039–1061.

Tversky, A., & Kahneman, D. (1992). Advances in prospect theory: Cumulative representation of uncertainty. *Journal of Risk and Uncertainty, 5*(4), 297–323.

Ulmer, H. V. (1996). Concept of an extracellular regulation of muscular metabolic rate during heavy exercise in humans by psychophysiological feedback. *Experientia, 52*(5), 416–420.

Venhorst, A., Micklewright, D., & Noakes, T. D. (2018a). Towards a three-dimensional framework of centrally regulated and goal-directed exercise behaviour: a narrative review. *British Journal of Sports Medicine, 52*(15), 957–966.

Venhorst, A., Micklewright, D., & Noakes, T. D. (2018b). Modelling the process of falling behind and its psychophysiological consequences. *British Journal of Sports Medicine*, *52*(23), 1523–1528.

Wang, X. T. (2006). Emotions within reason: Resolving conflicts in risk preference. *Cognition and Emotion*, *20*(8), 1132–1152.

Watson, D. (2000). *Mood and temperament*. New York: Guilford Press.

Williams, E. L., Jones, H. S., Sparks, S., Marchant, D., Micklewright, D., & McNaughton, L. (2014). Deception studies manipulating centrally acting performance modifiers: a review. *Medicine and Science in Sports and Exercise*, *46*(7), 1441–1451.

Wilson, T. D., Lisle, D. J., Schooler, J. W., Hodges, S. D., Klaaren, K. J., & LaFleur, S. J. (1993). Introspecting about reasons can reduce post-choice satisfaction. *Personality and Social Psychology Bulletin*, *19*(3), 331–339.

5

REGULATING EMOTIONS TO GO FASTER!

Andrew M. Lane, Daniel T. Robinson, and Ross Cloak

Introduction

Are there helpful emotions?

People experience a range of emotions but want to feel emotions that they believe will help performance. Sport is an emotion-fuelled environment, whether playing, coaching, or watching. Emotions are subjective feelings experienced in response to events either in the athlete's environment, for example standing on the start line, or in the athlete's mind, such as anticipation of an upcoming event (Lazarus, 2000). Emotions can be pleasant, such as happy and excited, or they can be unpleasant such as sad or angry (Lazarus, 2000). Emotions vary in terms of arousal, for example happiness and sadness associating with low arousal, and excitement and anger associating with high arousal. Emotions usually encompass three types of responses (Baumeister, Vohs, DeWall, & Zhang, 2007; Lane, Beedie, Jones, Uphill, & Devonport, 2012; Lazarus, 2000): physiological, such as changes in respiration and heart rates; cognitive, such as the changes in attention, perception, and information processing priorities; and behavioural, such as staring at an opponent in an attempt to unsettle them, or sprinting at the start of a race due to high anxiety. Athletes experience intense emotions before, during, and after attempts to achieve important goals. Evidence is generally supportive of the predictive effects of pre-competition feelings (Beedie, Lane, & Wilson, 2012; Brick, MacIntyre, & Campbell, 2014, 2015, 2016; Lazarus, 2000).

Emotions can be intense, occupy our minds, change our priorities, alter our physiological states, and guide our learning (Baumeister et al., 2007). Because of these physiological, cognitive, and behavioural processes, emotions can have significant effects on how we perform (Beedie et al., 2012; Wilson, Lane, Beedie, & Farooq, 2012). The link between emotions and performance is most likely influenced through its effect on goals. With goals being a central part of human behaviour (Locke & Latham, 1990; Mansell, 2005), the relationship between the action tendency and the goal the individual pursues is relevant, and this can influence emotions (Lazarus, 2000). People have a hierarchy of goals; for example, being good at sport could be important to one person, but less important to another (Carver & Scheier, 1990; Mansell, 2005). The nature of sport, being time bound where the start and finish are clearly identified, can influence when a person prioritises the results of competition. At the start of competition, where success in competitive sport is the primary goal, emotions increase in intensity in preparation to meet that challenge. With intense emotions come a shift in priorities and feelings of energy because of changes in physiological arousal, the process of mental preparation involves attempts to create a mindset that engenders a belief that goals will be attained (Hanin, 2010; Lane & Terry, 2000).

Emotions intensify during the build-up to competition. We have argued that researchers and practitioners should use discrete emotions such as anger, anxiety, depression, and vigour (Lane & Terry, 2000), rather than combining discrete emotions into broad hierarchical structures of positive and negative affect (Watson & Tellegen, 1985). Lane and Terry (2000) argued that by examining the affective content of discrete emotions, and examining cognitive processes that accompany them, the interaction between emotions becomes important when looking at how they influence action. If the action tendency associated with the emotion is not congruent with the goal, then this prompts emotion regulation strategies to be used (Hanin, 2010; Lane et al., 2012; McCormick, Meijen, Anstiss, & Jones, 2018; Webb, Miles, & Sheeran, 2012). For example, if an athlete feels sad, where the action tendency is to conserve resources, this is not congruent with a goal of marathon running by exercising intensely for several hours. If an athlete feels sad, but wants to run intensely, then the feeling of sadness will need to be regulated. The same athlete might wish to feel energetic and excited, and so would wish to engage in up-regulation strategies. By seeking to intensify a sense of energy, and engendering a belief that the athlete feels able to perform at the desired intensity, this in turn down-regulates feeling of sadness. In this instance, sadness was experienced via anticipating not achieving important goals.

An aspect of the emotion regulation process is that people hold beliefs about whether emotions are helpful or harmful in terms of helping them achieve their goals (Hanin, 2010; Lane et al., 2012). People evaluate how they want to feel and attempt to employ strategies that will change these feelings (Lane, Beedie, Devonport, & Stanley, 2011; Webb et al., 2012). A key question regularly asked about emotion and performance is 'how should I feel if I want to perform better?'

How should I feel if I want to perform better?

Regulation implies there is a standard to reach. For example, a thermostat regulates heat and once room temperature reaches the required temperature, the heating turns off. Monitoring the discrepancy between the current and desired standard drives regulation. With emotion, an example of this could mean that a person identifies that feeling excited associates with good performance and then assesses how excited they feel (Hanin, 2010). If they are less excited than they would like, then it would be desirable for them to engage in strategies to increase excitement. However, the notion that people regulate to a standard is important as it implies there is constant monitoring between the current and desired standard, and that people accurately know how they are feeling and how they would like to feel. With emotions, it is possible that neither is correct. Estimates of current feelings are complicated because people do not have perfect access to inner states; the entire emotional intelligence concept (see Petrides et al., 2016 for a review) is predicated on the basis that some people are better at doing this than others. There appears some credibility in the notion that the ability to identify emotions is an ability that differs between individuals. For example, high scores on an emotional intelligence scale related to experiencing pleasant emotions, low fatigue (Lane & Wilson, 2011), and satisfaction with performance (Lane, Devonport, & Stevens, 2010).

Regulating emotions to help performance is also complicated because the direction, whether to amplify or dampen the emotion, is complex. It is not a case that regulation follows a hedonic model of increasing pleasant emotions and reducing the intensity of unpleasant emotions (Hanin, 2010; Lane & Terry, 2000). Research has highlighted that supposedly unpleasant emotions such as anger, anxiety, and tension are associated with good performance (Beedie, Terry, & Lane, 2000; Cockerill, Nevill, & Lyons, 1991; Hanin, 2010). Research has also found that the same emotion is not always perceived as undesirable, and that people wish to use strategies to increase anger or anxiety based on a belief that this will lead to better performance (Hanin, 2010; Lane, Beedie et al. 2011; Stanley, Lane, Beedie, & Devonport, 2012; Tamir, 2016). Researchers have also sought to identify individual zones of optimal functioning and in this work, it appears both pleasant and unpleasant emotions can be helpful for performance (Hanin, 2000).

In summary, it seems clear that the discrepancy between current and preferred inner states drives regulation. With emotions, it seems there is a mixed currency and that some unpleasant emotions can be functional and help performance even though they feel unpleasant. Evidence suggests people learn to appraise emotions (Baumeister et al., 2007; Hanin, 2010; Lane, Beedie et al., 2011) and so if people wish to regulate emotions to help performance, then they need methods to help identify their current emotions and if these differ from the ideal, then they should consider using strategies to regulate emotions.

If I want to regulate my regulation emotions, what should I do?

What is clear from research and practice is that athletes engage in strategies to regulate emotions. Without providing formal psychological skills training to the participants, research shows that athletes use cognitive strategies that resemble self-talk, imagery, and goal-setting (Stanley, Beedie, Lane, Friesen, & Devonport, 2012; Stevens & Lane, 2001) and use strategies within competition such as listening to music (Lane, Davis, & Devonport, 2011). Research shows that use of psychological skills has positive effects on performance (Thelwell, 2015). Therefore, both emotion and using psychological skills appear to have positive effects on performance. Researchers often assess emotion and psychological skill usage concurrently and then assume the direction of relationship indicates psychological skills usage influences emotion (Gill, Lane, Thelwell, & Devonport, 2011). This is not necessarily the case: experiencing an intense emotion could prompt psychological skill usage. Experiencing an intense unwanted emotion can prompt people to use of regulation strategies (Webb et al., 2012). For practitioners, the commonality and shared variance is less important. Emotions can be regulated via engaging in emotion regulation strategies, and beginning applied work on emotions would seem to be as good a place to start as any. Further, a practically useful way is to investigate the effects of using emotion regulation strategies and psychological skills on emotions to see if there is also an improvement in performance.

In terms of developing experimental strategies to manipulate emotions, our work on the antecedents of emotions in endurance athletes (Lane, Terry, & Karageorghis, 1995a, 1995b; Lane, 2001) and our research into how endurance athletes regulate emotions (Stanley, Beedie et al., 2012) is relevant. Perceived ability, the standard of goal, and course conditions relate to the intensity of emotions, and beliefs that increase the likelihood of goal attainability associate with pleasant emotions. Stanley, Beedie et al. (2012) used an open-ended method to identify what strategies athletes used to regulate pre-competition emotions. They found that cognitive strategies such as self-talk and goals were the most commonly reported. They also found that behavioural strategies such as exercising, talking to others, and distracting yourself, possibly through the use of music, (Karageorghis, Terry, Lane, Bishop, & Priest, 2012) was relevant when regulating emotions. When seen collectively, these results provide a rich evidence base for developing experimental methods to manipulate emotions. They also provide important contextual information on how to manage the environment in which data are collected. As indicated in recent research, the presence of others exercising can influence perceptions of effort (Cohen, Ejsmond-Frey, Knight, & Dunbar, 2010). Our research using a pacemaker as a strategy to help runners achieve their goals and thus manage emotions showed mixed results. Following a pacemaker associated with a reduction in the intensity of unpleasant emotions in some individuals, but an increase in the intensity of the same emotions in others (Fullerton, Lane, & Devonport, 2017). Hence, how you perceive the external environment is important.

Gross and Thompson (2007) proposed a five-category model of antecedent- and response- focused emotion regulation strategies: situation selection, situation modification, attentional deployment, cognitive change, and response modulation (the first four being antecedent-focused; the last, response-focused). Situation selection refers to the process whereby an athlete actively chooses to place him/ herself in one situation rather than another. Situation modification refers to attempts to modify external aspects of the environment. By doing either of these, an athlete may make it more likely that a desirable emotional state is attained or an undesirable one avoided (e.g. walking away from an antagonistic opponent to prevent anger developing, or using humour to diffuse a tense situation). Attention deployment refers to the process whereby an athlete directs his/her attention to influence his/her emotions. That is, when it is difficult to change the situation, the athlete can choose to attend to stimuli that do not negatively impact on emotion (for example, listening to music on headphones to avoid listening to the crowd prior to an event). Cognitive change involves changing the meaning of an event or situation and so it can involve changing an athlete's goals. For instance, an elite runner who has a goal of winning a local race and is expected by others to win and is beaten could re-appraise this as the race being low in importance to them, labelling as a training run, and setting a goal based on self-referenced effort rather than outcome. Response modulation refers to strategies designed to regulate the physiological and cognitive aspects of emotion as directly as possible. Regulating the physiological arousal associated with emotion makes intuitive sense in sport given that optimal arousal levels will vary substantially between endurance events, from the low arousal associated with long endurance events such as a marathon. The process model is appealing for use by practitioners as it provides a theoretical framework to guide work. Anticipating likely emotions and developing a plan to re-appraise the meaning has been found to be effective in running (Lane, Devonport, Stanley, & Beedie, 2016) using an if-then plan (see Wolff, Bieleke, & Schüler, 2019).

What happens to performance when emotions are manipulated or regulated?

More recent work has manipulated environmental cues to manipulate emotions (Beedie et al., 2012) or investigated the effects of interventions to change emotions (Lane, Davis, & Devonport, 2011; Lane et al., 2015; Lane et al., 2016). Beedie et al. (2012) investigated emotion regulation in cycling. This project was developed as an extension of a study which found riders who reported negative emotions when riding at lactic threshold for 2 hours experienced a significant change in physiological responses to that exercise in the form of increased ventilation rate (Lane, Wilson, Whyte, & Shave, 2011). Lane, Wilson et al. assessed emotions using the Brunel Mood Scale (Terry, Lane, & Fogarty, 2003) before and after every 30 minutes during cycling on an ergometer. Lane, Wilson et al. found that riders experiencing unpleasant emotions also experienced greater physiological disturbance, particularly breathing faster and harder. However, from these results, we do not know the direction of changes in respiration and changes in emotion. It is possible that feeling fatigued and increased breathing associated with an increase in unpleasant emotions and, therefore, emotions were responses to the change in physiological states. It was also possible that unpleasant emotions signalled that the participant was struggling to meet the demands of the ride, and emotions were a trigger to breathing harder and thus, increasing respiration would enable riding to feel doable and thus regulate emotion.

Feedback can also influence emotions. Beedie et al. (2012) set out to increase the intensity of emotions during a 10-mile cycle ergometer ride by using false feedback. Beedie et al. gave riders false positive or false negative feedback after each mile. They found false negative feedback associated with intense unpleasant emotions, coupled with significantly higher blood lactic, and greater oxygen usage. Differences in performance were not significant and with a very small overall mean difference. However, how power was produced in the ride was different between conditions. In false negative feedback, riders sought to get back to a pace that would deliver their goals by increasing force on the pedal and this yielded large power spikes in the data, which associated with high lactic acid and oxygen uptake. In contrast, a similar finish time and average wattage use was delivered with a lower oxygen uptake, suggesting that pleasant emotions associated with improved economy, a characteristic that would seem desirable for endurance performance. The response to being behind the performance goals was to produce a surge of effort, but one that was not sustainable and so a dip in watts followed shortly. It is worth noting that differences in performance were driven by the athlete's response to environmental information. Although conducted in a laboratory, there are similar thought patterns in in naturalistic settings, where riders make similar evaluations in conditions far from optimal with the main contenders being the effects of wind, hills, and other riders. The implications from this study suggest that positive perceptions of progress during a race help maintain positive emotions and the behavioural reaction to such as strategy is to ride smoothly, a strategy that delivers an efficient performance.

Our research group followed this study by examining the effects of interventions designed to increase pleasant emotions or increase unpleasant emotions on 1600m running time (Lane et al., 2015). Runners were supported to develop interventions using cognitively based methods including imagery and self-talk. We found that increased anxiety associated with running a fast first lap, slowing and then speeding up for the final lap. In contrast, increasing pleasant emotions associated with three evenly paced laps and speeding up for the final lap. As with Beedie et al. (2012), pleasant emotions associated with faster performance over the final stages. However, as with Beedie et al., there was no difference in overall performance. A consistent feature of the two studies is the notion that unpleasant emotions appear to associate with requiring greater demands in managing effort, results that have implications for performance.

In terms of future research, recent work has found that active training delivered online can help change emotions and improve performance (Lane, Totterdell, et al., 2016). In a study of 44,000 participants, Lane, Totterdell et al. compared and contrasted 12 different interventions including three different techniques (imagery, self-talk, and if-then planning) and four different foci (motivation process, motivation outcome, instruction, and arousal-reduction). They also included a control condition where participants received an informational film in which they were advised to perform the task again, but given no specific guidance on how to improve. All interventions were delivered via watching an instructional film acted and narrated by Olympic Gold Medallist Michael Johnson. Thus, all 13 conditions benefited from the possible positive and motivational effects of receiving encouragement from a potentially inspiring sportsperson. Participants signed up to the project on the basis that they believed they would receive an intervention and were provided with personal feedback from Michael Johnson. The implication from this study is that it is possible to deliver brief active training online, online training leads to changes in emotions in line with theoretical predictions, and such a method offers the potential to overcome challenges of small sample size often seen in other intervention studies (Cugelman, Thelwall, & Dawes, 2011). Few studies, however, compare and contrast the effect of different interventions. Lane, Totterdell et al. (2016) found that self-talk and imagery focused on motivational process associated with an increase in pleasant emotions and improved performance. Such a result is not remarkable, but of greater significance is the fact that active training was delivered online and therefore the reach offered by such an approach is huge. The findings from this study could be used to create interventions for endurance performance; short term outcome focused goals increase emotional arousal and effort, and these associated with faster performance.

In a prequel study to Lane, Totterdell et al. (2016), Lane, Devonport et al. (2016) conducted an online intervention in conjunction with the running magazine, *Runner's World*. Lane, Devonport et al. found performance was significantly better and emotions more positive after the intervention. However, there were two intervention groups and an active-control group, and thus, the intervention training groups were not significantly more advantageous than the control. There were no differences in the effectiveness between an emotion-focused goal intervention, an implementation intention (if-then plan) (Gollwitzer & Sheeran, 2006) and a control condition which encouraged people to do the same emotion regulation strategies they were already doing. Consistent with the approach used by Lane, Totterdell et al. (2016), the control condition involved active training. Consistently, when participants are offered a treatment which they believe will be effective, positive effects are observed. Whereas such a finding might appear unusual or difficult to explain, it is consistent with a wealth of research that has studied placebo effects (Beedie & Foad, 2009). Beedie et al. (2012) have shown that holding a positive belief leads to different outcomes than holding a negative belief even when participants receive the same treatment. And so if all participants receive active training, and 50 per cent of them receive information that endorses the effectiveness of the treatment and 50 per cent are told the treatment is questionable, then these beliefs will play out in the results. Therefore, research that compares interventions that have active training in the control group offer worthwhile findings. Of note, Barwood, Corbett, Wagstaff, McVeigh, and Thelwell (2015) found motivational self-talk associated with improved performance via increased power output. Importantly, Barwood et al. used a 'sham' self-talk intervention, that is, athletes engaged in self-talk that had no theoretical reason to be effective other than participants were aware of an intervention. Online interventions are proposed to be a growing area of applied work and research and facilitated by a number of useful websites such as mood online (http://www.moodprofiling.com/) which allows people to check their mood profile against normative data.

Conclusions

Athletes experience intense emotions before, during, and after competition and emotions provide information on self and the environment. People like to feel emotions that are useful and that will help achieve their goals. Emotional profiles associated with success vary between individuals. In endurance sport, cognitive strategies such as goals, imagery, and self-talk are commonly used by athletes. Intervention work to change emotions has generally supported that teaching usage of these emotions brings about changes in emotions. Whilst emotions have changed, this has not been followed by changes in performance. In terms of how to teach emotion regulation strategies, recent research shows the benefits of online training. Online training has huge potential reach and thus enable wide scale usage and so have potential impact and from this, the capability to test competing interventions.

The support of the Economic and Social Research Council (ESRC) UK is gratefully acknowledged.

(RES-060-25-0044: 'Emotion regulation of others and self [EROS]')

References

Barwood, M. J., Corbett, J., Wagstaff, C. R., McVeigh, D., & Thelwell, R. C. (2015). Improvement of 10-km time-trial cycling with motivational self-talk compared with neutral self-talk. *International journal of sports physiology and performance, 10*(2), 166–171.

Baumeister, R. F., Vohs, K. D., DeWall, C. N., & Zhang, L. (2007). How emotion shapes behavior: Feedback, anticipation, and reflection, rather than direct causation. *Personality and Social Psychology Review, 11*(2), 167–203. doi:10.1177/1088868307301033.

Beedie, C. J., & Foad, A. J. (2009) The placebo effect in sports performance: A brief review. *Sports Medicine, 39*, 313–329.

Beedie, C. J., Lane, A. M., & Wilson, M. (2012). A possible role for emotion and emotion regulation in physiological responses to false performance feedback in 10km laboratory cycling. *Applied Psychophysiology and Biofeedback, 37*, 269–277. doi: 10.1007/s10484-012-9200-7.

Beedie, C. J., Terry, P. C., & Lane, A. M. (2000). The profile of mood states and athletic performance: Two meta-analyses. *Journal of Applied Sport Psychology, 12*, 49–68.

Brick, N., MacIntyre, T., & Campbell, M. (2014). Attentional focus in endurance activity: New paradigms and future directions. *International Review in Sport Exercise Psychology, 7*, 106–134. doi: 10.1080/1750984X.2014.885554.

Brick, N., MacIntyre, T., & Campbell, M. (2015). Metacognitive processes in the self-regulation of performance in elite endurance runners. *Psychology of Sport Exercise, 19*, 1–9. doi: 10.1016/j.psychsport.2015.02.003.

Brick, N. E., MacIntyre, T. E., & Campbell, M. J. (2016). Thinking and action: A cognitive perspective on self-regulation during endurance performance. *Frontiers Physiology, 7,* 159. doi: 10.3389/fphys.2016.00159.

Carver, C. S., & Scheier, M. F. (1990). Origins and functions of positive and negative affect: a control process view. *Psychological Review, 97,* 19–35.

Cockerill, I. M., Nevill, A. M., & Lyons, N. (1991). Modelling mood states in athletic performance. *Journal of Sports Sciences, 9,* 205–212.

Cohen, E., Ejsmond-Frey, R., Knight, N., & Dunbar, R. (2010) Rowers' high: Elevated endorphin release under conditions of active behavioural synchrony. *Biology Letters, 6*(1), 106–108.

Cugelman, B., Thelwall, M., & Dawes, P. (2011). Online interventions for social marketing health behavior change campaigns: A meta-analysis of psychological architectures and adherence factors. *Journal of Medical Internet Research, 13*(1):e17, doi:10.2196/jmir.1367.

Fullerton, C., Lane, A. M., & Devonport, T. J. (2017). How fast can you run a mile? Investigating the role of emotions on self-regulatory behaviour. *Journal of Sports Science and Medicine, 16,* 551–557, http://jssm.org/researchjssm-16-551.xml.xml.

Gill, G., Lane, A. M., Thelwell, R., & Devonport, T. (2011). Relationships between emotional intelligence, psychological skills. *Indian Journal of Fitness, 7,* 9–16.

Gollwitzer, P. M., & Sheeran, P. (2006). Implementation intentions and goal achievement: A meta-analysis of effects and processes. *Advances in Experimental Social Psychology, 38,* 69–119. doi:10.1016/s0065-2601(06)38002-1.

Gross, J. J., & Thompson, R. A. (2007). Emotion regulation conceptual foundations. In J. J. Gross (Ed.), *Handbook of Emotion Regulation* (pp. 3–24). New York: Guilford Press.

Hanin, Y. L. (2000). *Emotions in sport.* Champaign, IL: Human Kinetics.

Hanin, Y. L. (2010). Coping with anxiety in sport. In A. R. Nicholls (Ed.), *Coping in Sport: Theory, methods, and related constructs* (pp. 159–175). Hauppauge, NY: Nova Science Publishers.

Karageorghis, C. I., Terry, P. C., Lane, A. M., Bishop, D. T., & Priest, D. L. (2012). The BASES Expert Statement on the use of music in exercise. *Journal of Sports Sciences, 30,* 953–956. doi:10.1080/02640414.2012.676665.

Lane, A. M. (2001). Relationships between perceptions of performance expectations and mood among distance runners; the moderating effect of depressed mood. *Journal of Science and Medicine in Sport, 4,* 235–249. http://dx.doi.org/10.1016/s1440-2440(01)80013-x.

Lane, A. M., Beedie, C. J., Devonport, T. J., & Stanley, D. M. (2011). Instrumental emotion regulation in sport: relationships between beliefs about emotion and emotion regulation strategies used by athletes. *Scandinavian Journal of Medicine & Science in Sports, 21,* e445–e451. doi: 10.1111/j.1600-0838.2011.01364.x.

Lane, A. M., Beedie, C. J., Jones, M. V., Uphill, M., & Devonport, T. J. (2012). The BASES Expert Statement on emotion regulation in sport. *Journal of Sports Sciences, 30*(11), 1189–1195. doi:10.1080/02640414.2012.693621.

Lane, A. M., Davis, P. A., & Devonport, T. J. (2011). Emotion regulation during running: A test of interventions using music. *Journal of Sports Science and Medicine, 10,* 400–407. www.jssm.org/vol10/n2/22/v10n2-22pdf.pdf.

Lane, A. M., Devonport, T. J., Friesen, A. P., Beedie, C. J., Fullerton, C. L. & Stanley, D. M. (2015). How should I regulate my emotions if I want to run faster? *European Journal of Sports Science.* doi: 10.1080/17461391.2015.1080305.

Lane, A. M., Devonport, T. J., Stanley, D., & Beedie, C. J. (2016). The effects of brief online self-help intervention strategies on emotions and satisfaction with running performance. *Sensoria: A Journal of Mind, Brain & Culture, 12,* 2, doi: http://dx.doi.org/10.7790/sa.v12i2.441.

Lane. A. M., Devonport, T. J., & Stevens, M. (2010). Relationships between emotional intelligence, pre-race and post-race emotions in 10-mile runners. *Athletic Insight*, *2*(3), 205–219. www.athleticinsight.com/Vol12Iss3/Run.htm.

Lane, A. M., & Terry, P. C. (2000). The nature of mood: Development of a conceptual model with a focus on depression. *Journal of Applied Sport Psychology*, *12*, 16–33.

Lane, A. M., Terry, P. C., & Karageorghis, C. I. (1995a). Path analysis examining relationships among antecedents of anxiety, multidimensional state anxiety, and triathlon performance. *Perceptual and Motor Skills*, *81*, 1255–1266.

Lane, A. M., Terry, P. C., & Karageorghis, C. I. (1995b). The antecedents of multidimensional state anxiety and self-confidence in duathletes. *Perceptual and Motor Skills*, *80*, 911–919.

Lane, A. M., Totterdell, P., MacDonald, I., Devonport, T. J., Friesen, A. P., Beedie, C. J., Stanley, D., & Nevill, A. (2016). Brief online training enhances competitive performance: Findings of the BBC Lab UK psychological skills intervention study. *Frontiers in Psychology*, 7:413. doi:10.3389/fpsyg.2016.00413.

Lane, A. M., Whyte, G. P., Shave, R., Barney, S., Stevens, M. J., & Wilson, M. (2005). Mood disturbance during cycling performance at extreme conditions. *Journal of Sports Science and Medicine*, *4*,52–57. http://www.jssm.org/vol4/n1/7/v4n1-7text.php

Lane, A. M., & Wilson. M. (2011). Emotions and emotional intelligence among ultra-endurance runners. *Journal of Science and Medicine in Sport*, *14*, 358–362. http://dx.doi.org/10.1016/j.jsams.2011.03.001

Lane, A. M., Wilson, M., Whyte, G., & Shave, R. (2011). Physiological correlates of emotion-regulation during prolonged cycling performance. *Applied Psychophysiology and Biofeedback*, *36*, 181–184.

Lazarus, R. S. (2000). Cognitive-motivational-relational theory of emotion. In Y. L. Hanin (Ed.), *Emotions in sport* (pp. 39–64). Champaign, IL: Human Kinetics.

Locke, E. A., & Latham, G. P. (1990). *A theory of goal setting and task performance*. Englewood Cliffs, NJ: Prentice-Hall.

Mansell, W. (2005). Control theory and psychopathology: an integrative approach. *Psychology and Psychotherapy: Theory, Research and Practice*, *78*, 141–178.

McCormick, A., Meijen, C., Anstiss, P., & Jones, H. S. (2018). Self-regulation in endurance sports: theory, research, and practice. *International Review of Sport and Exercise Psychology*. doi: 10.1080/1750984X.2018.1469161.

Petrides, K. V., Mikolajczak, M., Mavroveli, S., Sánchez-Ruiz, M-J., Furnham, A., & Pérez-González, J-C. (2016). Recent developments in trait emotional intelligence research. *Emotion Review*, *8*, 335–341.

Stanley, D. M, Lane, A. M., Beedie, C. J., & Devonport, T. J. (2012). "I run to feel better; so why I am thinking so negatively". *International Journal of Psychology and Behavioral Science, 2*(6), 28–213. doi: 10.5923/j.ijpbs.20120206.03

Stanley, D. M., Beedie, C. J., Lane, A. M., Friesen, A. P., & Devonport, T. J. (2012). Emotion regulation strategies used by runners prior to training and competition. *International Journal of Sport and Exercise Psychology*, *10*, 159–171. DOI:10.1080/1612197X.2012.671910

Stevens, M. J., & Lane, A. M. (2001). Mood-regulating strategies used by athletes. *Athletic Insight*, *3*(3), www.athleticinsight.com/Vol3Iss3/MoodRegulation.htm.

Tamir, M. (2016). Why do people regulate their emotions? A taxonomy of motives in emotion regulation. *Personality and Social Psychology Review*, *20*, 199–222.

Terry, P. C., Lane, A. M., & Fogarty, G. J. (2003). Construct validity of the Profile of Mood States—Adolescents for use with adults. *Psychology of Sport and Exercise*, *4*(2), 125–139.

Thelwell, R. (2015). Applied sport psychology. In A. M. Lane (Ed.), *Sport and exercise psychology* (pp. 211–225). London, UK: Taylor & Francis.

Watson, D., & Tellegen, A. (1985). Toward a consensual structure of mood. *Psychological Bulletin, 98*(2), 219–235. http://dx.doi.org/10.1037/0033-2909.98.2.219.

Webb, T. L., Miles, E., & Sheeran, P. (2012). Dealing with feeling: A meta-analysis of the effectiveness of strategies derived from the process model of emotion regulation. *Psychological Bulletin, 138*(4), 77–808. doi:10.1037/a0027600

Wilson, M., Lane, A. M., Beedie, C. J., & Farooq, M. (2012). Accurate 'split-time' feedback does not improve 10-mile time trial cycling performance compared to blind or inaccurate 'split-time' feedback. *Journal of Applied Physiology, 112*, 231–236. doi: 10.1007/s00421-011-1977-1Online First.

Wolff, W., Bieleke, M., & Schüler, J. (2019). Goal striving and endurance performance. In C. Meijen (Ed.), Endurance performance in sport: Psychological theory and interventions (pp. 125–137). Oxon, UK: Routledge.

6

METACOGNITIVE PROCESSES IN THE SELF-REGULATION OF ENDURANCE PERFORMANCE

Noel Brick, Mark Campbell, and Christian Swann

Introduction

What is metacognition?

The Finnish middle- and long-distance runner, and nine-time Olympic gold medallist, Paavo Nurmi, famously pronounced, "[The] mind is everything. Muscle – pieces of rubber. All that I am, I am because of my mind" (cited in Pfitzinger & Douglas, 2001, p. 11). In support of Nurmi's statement, successful endurance athletes often report deliberate engagement of cognitive strategies during critical performance moments. During the final stages of his World Hour record, cyclist Bradley Wiggins employed three attentional strategies to sustain his target pace; (i) relaxation, (ii) focusing on form, and (iii) maintaining a constant pedalling rhythm (Wiggins, 2015). Similarly, successful English Channel swimmers recounted using cognitive strategies such as positive self-talk, relaxation, and strategic distraction to cope with the event's unique challenges (Schumacher, Becker, & Wiersma, 2016). As these examples suggest, endurance athletes often attempt to control their thoughts in a deliberate, goal-driven fashion to regulate performance (i.e., self-regulation). In essence, this requires effective 'thinking' (e.g., engaging cognitive strategies), and a requirement to 'think about thinking' (i.e., meta-cognition; Miller, Kessel, & Flavell, 1970) to plan, monitor, and adapt situationally-appropriate cognitive strategies during endurance performance. Subsequent chapters will provide an overview of cognitive strategies relevant to endurance performance (e.g., Chapter 8 and Chapter 12). The emphasis of this chapter, however, will be to provide an understanding of how endurance athletes might control their thoughts and engage specific attentional strategies to optimise performance.

Metacognition has been defined as an individual's knowledge and cognitions about cognitive phenomena (Flavell, 1979). One approach suggests that metacognition reflects our understanding of what we know and how we use that knowledge to regulate behaviour (e.g., Bransford, Brown, & Cocking, 1999). In this regard, metacognition is considered an important component of effective self-regulation, or the ability to successfully monitor and control one's thoughts and actions in accordance with the demands of a task (e.g., Dinsmore, Alexander, & Loughlin, 2008; Tarricone, 2011). As the earlier examples from cycling and swimming tasks suggest, controlling one's thoughts to optimise performance may include the application of specific cognitive strategies such as motivational self-talk (e.g., Blanchfield, Hardy, de Morree, Staino, & Marcora, 2014) or relaxation (e.g., Caird, McKenzie, & Sleivert, 1999). Later we will examine the importance of metacognition to cognitive strategy selection and implementation. First, however, we will provide an overview of metacognition and each of its constituent parts.

Dimensions of metacognition

Relevant to the present discussion, metacognition can broadly be categorised into two dimensions: knowledge of cognition (or metacognitive knowledge) and regulation of cognition (Baker & Brown, 1984). *Knowledge of cognition* includes declarative knowledge of one's cognitive abilities, knowledge of effective cognitive strategies, and knowledge of task demands or goals (Flavell, 1979). Metacognitive knowledge also concerns interactions amongst these three types of knowledge and, specifically, procedural knowledge of how to use cognitive strategies and conditional knowledge of when and why to use them (e.g., Baker & Brown, 1984; Flavell, 1979; Settanni, Magistro, & Rabaglietti, 2012). As an example of this interaction, to reduce muscular tension during endurance activity, an endurance athlete requires knowledge of effective cognitive strategies (i.e., relaxation techniques), procedural knowledge of how to implement these techniques, and knowledge of when relaxation may, or may not, be effective during task performance (i.e., conditional knowledge).

Regulation of cognition includes *metacognitive skills*, such as planning, monitoring, or reviewing one's cognitions. Metacognitive skills represent the control function of metacognition and the ability to implement cognitive strategies during a task to regulate cognition (e.g., Baker & Brown, 1984; Efklides, 2014). Regulation of cognition also includes *metacognitive experiences* that are based on monitoring processes and facilitate concurrent monitoring during task performance. Metacognitive experiences include any cognitive or affective experiences accompanying cognitive activity (e.g., Flavell, 1979) and comprise metacognitive feelings and metacognitive judgements and estimates. *Metacognitive feelings* inform the individual about task performance in the form of a feeling (e.g., a feeling of task difficulty) and tend to be implicit and nonanalytic in nature (Efklides, 2008, 2014). Alternatively, *metacognitive judgements and estimates* (e.g., judgement about one's performance) are made by the individual and may be the result of both implicit, nonanalytic processes, and explicit, analytic processes (Efklides, 2014). Collectively, awareness of metacognitive experiences, in conjunction with performance, forms a representation of a task (Efklides, 2014). In turn, metacognitive representations provide input to regulate and control cognition (and behaviour) via cognitive or metacognitive skills (Efklides, 2014). To fully explicate these processes, a more practical application of metacognitive skills and metacognitive experiences to cognitive strategy use during endurance performance will be provided later in this chapter (see *Metacognition and endurance activity* section and Figure 6.2).

The relationship between cognition and metacognition can be best understood by applying a framework developed by Nelson and Narens (1990). Within this framework are two related levels; the object-level (i.e., cognition) and the meta-level (i.e., metacognition) (Figure 6.1). In an endurance context, object-level cognitions may include the information athletes attend to and process (e.g., bodily sensations, environmental stimuli). The meta-level, in contrast, consists of metacognitions concerning object-level cognitions. Specifically, the meta-level is responsible for monitoring the object-level and, based on the outcome of monitoring processes, controlling activity of the object-level in a top-down fashion (e.g., Koriat, 2007; Nelson & Narens, 1990). In an endurance context, this may be to alter one's focus of attention, or engage specific cognitive strategies (e.g., motivational self-talk, relaxation). As such, information flowing from the meta-level to the object-level informs the object-level of what to do next (e.g., to maintain ongoing activity, to activate alternative cognitive strategies) (Nelson & Narens, 1990). In line with Flavell's (1979) conceptualisation of metacognition, the meta-level also consists of a model of current goals, and how these goals might be accomplished at the object-level. Ultimately, these goals are accomplished by communication in both directions (i.e., monitoring and control) between the meta-level and the object-level (Nelson & Narens, 1990).

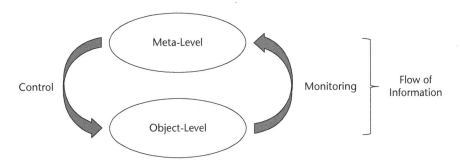

FIGURE 6.1 Illustration of the hierarchical organisation of the meta-level and the object-level (Adapted with permission from Nelson & Narens, 1990)

Metacognition in physical activity and sporting domains

Perhaps unsurprisingly, given its origins in cognitive and developmental psychology, metacognition has received substantial attention in educational and intellectual settings (e.g., Dunlosky & Metcalfe, 2009; Tarricone, 2011). Metacognition may, however, also be important to control action in perceptual-motor (Augustyn & Rosenbaum, 2005), physical activity (Settanni et al., 2012), and endurance activity settings (Brick, MacIntyre, & Campbell, 2015; Nietfeld, 2003). Augustyn and Rosenbaum (2005) noted that intellectual and perceptual-motor tasks rely on similar mechanisms, for example. As such, skilled motor-task performance requires both a knowledge about one's own cognitive functioning and the use of strategies to control cognitive processes (Settanni et al., 2012). In physical activity settings, for example, Settanni et al. (2012) indicated that secondary school pupils who spent more time engaged in physical and sporting activities also scored higher on a *Metacognition Applied to Physical Activities Scale* (MAPAS). This scale measured metacognitive processes such as planning, monitoring, and reflection in a physical activity context. The findings suggested that expertise in physical activities includes proficiency at both motor *and* metacognitive skills (Settanni et al., 2012). Although pupils' stage of cognitive (and metacognitive) development influenced MAPAS outcomes, the authors suggest that domain-specific metacognitions (i.e., in physical activities) are developed with continued experience of physical activity (Settanni et al., 2012).

The role of metacognition in sporting performance has also received some attention. In their review, Martini and Shore (2008) highlighted ability-related differences in the use of metacognition in both academic and psychomotor tasks. Specifically, higher-level sporting performers were inclined to use more planning strategies, to monitor and evaluate their performance more accurately, and have more detailed levels of declarative and procedural knowledge of their activity. These included tasks across a range of sports such as tennis, soccer, and diving. In contrast, lower-level performers tended not to plan, monitor, or evaluate cognitive performance and demonstrated inappropriate or inefficient strategy use (Martini & Shore, 2008). Developing this link between expert performance and metacognitive abilities in the sporting domain, MacIntyre, Igou, Campbell, Moran, and Matthews (2014) proposed that elite athletes are experts not only in movement execution, but also in metacognitive planning, monitoring, and reflection. These authors contended that the breadth and flexibility of expertise in sport, coupled with the breadth and flexibility of processes involved in metacognition and how they are associated with expertise, is a potentially fertile ground to explore human behaviour. Furthermore, MacIntyre et al. (2014) suggest a role for metacognition in both training (e.g., knowledge of when a skill has been acquired) and competitive settings (e.g., self-regulation during competitive scenarios). Collectively, this research provides some support for the importance of metacognition to expert performance across a range of contexts. Despite the emergence of this corpus of literature on metacognition in educational, physical activity, and sporting settings, comparatively little research has investigated metacognition in endurance activities. In the following section, we will provide a brief overview of research addressing the importance of metacognitive processes to endurance performance.

Metacognition and endurance activity

In the first study of metacognitive processes and endurance performance, Nietfeld (2003) examined the relationship between self-reported metacognitive strategy use and the ability of competitive runners to regulate performance during a self-paced running task. Using a *Racing the Mile Questionnaire* (RMQ), Nietfeld (2003) collected data on participants' metacognitive strategy use while racing, or preparing to race (e.g., planning and monitoring of cognitive strategies, cognitive strategy use and adjustment during running, evaluation of cognitive strategy effectiveness). Participants were also asked to describe their thoughts during a typical race. Subsequently, participants completed a one-mile run during which they attempted to run at a pace equivalent to 80 per cent of their personal best time. The findings suggested that participants who reported being more strategic initially tended to be more accurate at monitoring and executing their target pace during the one-mile run (i.e., regulation of cognition during performance). Furthermore, general cognitive ability did not account for the relationship between metacognition and running task performance. Similar to the suggestion of Settanni et al. (2012) for physical activity, Nietfeld (2003) suggested that expert runners operate on intelligent domain-specific strategies (e.g., active self-regulatory strategies; see Chapter 8) that develop as a result of experience.

More recently, Brick et al. (2015) applied a metacognitive approach to understand the influences on, and dynamics of, attentional focus during endurance performance. Interview data from elite runners suggested that metacognitive processes may be fundamental to effective cognitive control during endurance activity. Specifically, the elite runners planned cognitive strategies before running, and evaluated their attentional focus and cognitive strategy use after running. Furthermore, these athletes reported monitoring task performance and sensory stimuli periodically and used this information to apply cognitive strategies in a situationally-appropriate manner during endurance activity (i.e., conditional knowledge of when and why to use attentional strategies; Flavell, 1979). Accordingly, when running felt harder (metacognitive feeling of difficulty), the elite runners reported greater use of active self-regulatory cognitive strategies such as relaxation and motivational self-talk. In contrast, when running tasks were relatively undemanding and felt easier (e.g., long, slow training runs), runners reported greater use of active distraction strategies such as conversing.

Based on these findings, Brick et al. (2015) proposed a metacognitive framework of attentional focus and cognitive control during endurance activity (Figure 6.2). According to this framework endurance athletes may, (i) plan cognitive strategies, or what to monitor, prior to endurance activity. This may be to

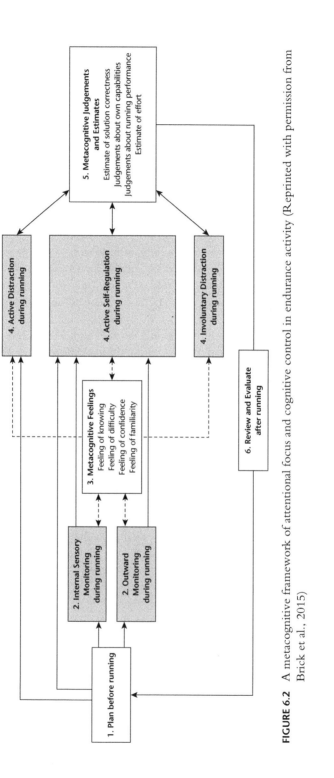

FIGURE 6.2 A metacognitive framework of attentional focus and cognitive control in endurance activity (Reprinted with permission from Brick et al., 2015)

employ a specific pacing strategy, to use motivational self-statements, or to monitor a competitor. Metacognitive planning may be particularly important when an athlete wishes to minimalise interference from environmental (e.g., spectators) or involuntary distractions (e.g., mind wandering) (e.g., Braver, Gray, & Burgess, 2007; Brick, MacIntyre, & Campbell, 2014), for example. During endurance activity, monitoring processes (ii) may directly, or via metacognitive feelings (iii), form a metacognitive representation of the task which, in turn, stimulates cognitive control and the adoption of a cognitive strategy (iv). As an illustrative example, Brick et al. (2015) suggest that internal sensory monitoring (e.g., of effort, breathing), and outward monitoring of task-relevant stimuli (e.g., split-times, distance to go) may generate a metacognitive feeling about that task, such as a feeling of task difficulty (e.g., the task feels harder than expected or desired). Awareness of this feeling, in conjunction with awareness of performance, forms a representation of the task which, in turn, stimulates the initiation of an appropriate cognitive strategy to control cognition. Strategies may include motivational self-talk or relaxing to maintain a goal pace, or movement efficiency, for example. As such, this example supports the notion that efforts to monitor and control thoughts and action link self-regulation and metacognition in an endurance context (e.g., Dinsmore et al., 2008). This interaction between internal sensory monitoring, outward monitoring, and the application of situationally-appropriate cognitive strategies is exemplified by the following account of Eliud Kipchoge's 2017 attempt to break the two-hour marathon barrier (Caesar, 2017):

> But now [4.5 miles to go] his split times began to drift, almost imperceptibly at first, by a second or so a mile. The sub-two was still on, but the prospect was on a knife edge. . . . The turnover of Kipchoge's legs appeared to slow, just a fraction. At times, he appeared to smile broadly – a conscious effort, he later said, to relax and work through the pain.

Subsequent to exerting metacognitive control, an athlete may make metacognitive judgements or estimates (v) regarding the effectiveness of the cognitive strategy employed. Depending on the outcome of this metacognitive judgement, alongside continued monitoring of task performance, the athlete may maintain their attentional focus, or adopt an alternative cognitive strategy. Thus, in an endurance context, this represents the continual flow of information between object-level cognitions (e.g., internal and environmental sensory information) and the meta-level to monitor and control cognitive activity in the pursuit of a goal (Nelson & Narens, 1990). Finally, following performance (Figure 6.2), metacognitive judgements and estimates may further inform review and evaluation processes (vi). At this point, cognitive strategies may be refined, or eliminated, and, as a result, impact on metacognitive planning before subsequent endurance activities (Brick et al., 2015).

Metacognition, and Brick et al.'s (2015) metacognitive framework of attentional focus and cognitive control may also provide some insight to explain why

inexperienced endurance participants may be less proficient at, or may resist implementing, novel self-regulatory strategies (e.g., Okwumabua, Meyers, Schleser,
& Cooke, 1983). Building on the notion that metacognition is a function of
expert performance (e.g., MacIntyre et al., 2014), we (Brick, Campbell, Sheehan,
Fitzpatrick, & MacIntyre, 2018) investigated the metacognitive abilities of novice
recreational endurance runners (i.e., those with approximately 12 months running
experience). In line with findings from other domains (e.g., Martini & Shore,
2008), interview data suggested that novice endurance runners may not possess the
detailed knowledge of task-specific cognitive strategies (i.e., domain-specific metacognitive knowledge), or have as well-developed metacognitive skills as their more
elite counterparts (Brick et al., 2015). Few runners reported planning, reviewing,
or evaluating cognitive strategy use, for example, and many reported difficulties
regulating their cognitions during running. Thus, the findings suggest that an initial challenge for novice participants may be to develop the metacognitive skills,
and knowledge of effective, domain-specific cognitive strategies to occupy and
control attentional resources during endurance activity (e.g., Bigliassi, 2015; Brick
et al., 2014). In support, it has been suggested that learning, adopting, and successfully implementing psychological skills is, in itself, an exercise in metacognition
(Eccles & Feltovich, 2008; MacIntyre et al., 2014). As such, as a novel approach to
psychological skills training, it may be that encouraging the use of metacognitive
skills (e.g., planning, reviewing) and reflection on metacognitive experiences (e.g.,
feelings and judgements), for example, can help to optimise cognitive strategy
acquisition with novice endurance participants. Similar metacognition-augmented
interventions have proven beneficial in other domains (e.g., Moritz et al., 2015)
and may enhance applied practice with endurance participants. It is also likely that
these metacognitive skills may transfer between endurance activities (e.g., running to cycling, etc.). In support, Settanni et al. (2012) reported no difference in
MAPAS score and sport type (individual versus team) in their study. Although further research is needed to support this contention, it suggests that at metacognitive
processes developed through engagement in one activity (e.g., running) may also
transfer to other sporting activities.

Metacognition, flow, and clutch states during endurance activity

There are overlaps between metacognition and self-regulation during endurance
activity, and psychological states underlying excellent performance (cf. Swann
et al., 2017a). Examining these relationships has potential to identify strategies to
induce and prolong such states, as well as providing some context for the study and
application of metacognition and self-regulation (e.g., which strategies are most
useful in specific performance situations?). Building on Csikszentmihalyi's (1975,
2002) classic concept of flow – a highly rewarding state of absorption, enjoyment,
and automaticity – recent evidence suggests that athletes can also experience a
second, distinct psychological state during excellent performance: a more effortful,

intense, demanding "clutch" state (Swann et al., 2017b). Clutch states are highly relevant in an endurance activity context with similarity to the 'end spurt,' and resonate with high profile examples such as the final stages of Bradley Wiggins' World Hour record, and Eliud Kipchoge's sub two-hour marathon attempt described previously. Including participants from endurance activities such as marathon runners and half-ironman triathletes, the occurrence and experience of these states have been outlined in an Integrated Model of Flow and Clutch States (Figure 6.3) (Swann et al., 2017a; see Swann, Crust, & Vella, 2017c for a commentary).

Interestingly, athletes have reported employing different self-regulation strategies during each state (Swann et al., 2017a). In flow, they report using distractive strategies (Brick et al., 2014) such as *positive distractions* to focus attention away from the task at hand and avoid negative or analytical thoughts which may disrupt these states. Conversely, athletes experiencing clutch states report using associative strategies, such as *maintaining perspective, rationalising, setting short-term goals,* and *self-monitoring.* For example, a marathon runner described that during a clutch state she was:

> Thinking positively and thinking, "Yeah, I can do this" . . . but I wasn't so much thinking and telling my legs to do it – I was just telling my head I can do it. I was thinking more "No, I *can* keep this pace," like confident, positive thoughts.
>
> *(Swann et al., 2017a, p. 393)*

Furthermore, the type of goal an athlete pursues is a key factor influencing which state they experience (Schweickle, Groves, Vella, & Swann, 2017). Clutch states involve the commonly-set specific, challenging goals (Locke & Latham, 2013), such as "I need to run the last two kilometres in eight minutes to achieve a personal best." Conversely, flow states involve more exploratory 'open' goals – which have not been articulated in goal-setting theory – such as "see how fast I can run the first five kilometres." Importantly, Schweickle et al. (2017) found that setting open goals in advance of (cognitive) performance led to more flow-like states, whereas setting specific goals in advance led to more clutch-like states. Therefore, the psychological states experienced during endurance performance – and self-regulation strategies employed to manage/prolong them – could potentially be determined *in advance* by setting goals appropriately.

Although relationships between metacognition, self-regulation, and flow/clutch states in sport have been under-studied, there are a number of important implications for future research. It may be the case that flow and clutch states provide a context for understanding which self-regulatory strategies are most appropriate within certain performance situations. Cognitive strategies are also highly promising for the management and maintenance of flow and clutch states, in terms of how athletes should think and regulate their experience to get the most out of these states. Indeed, future work developing flow/clutch interventions should arguably include self-regulation and metacognitive strategies in addition to other

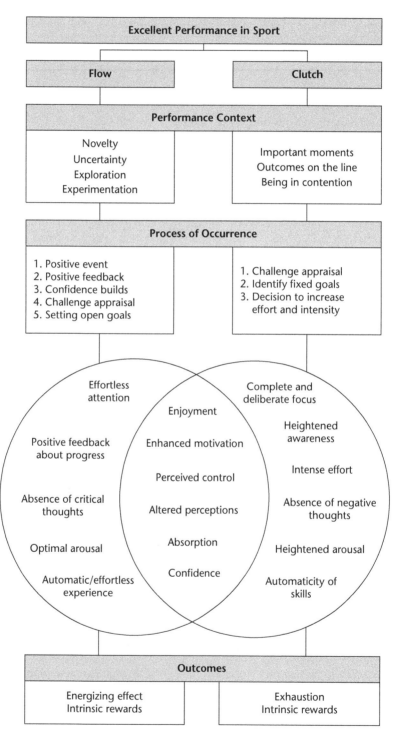

FIGURE 6.3 Integrated model of flow and clutch states in sport (Reprinted from Swann et al., 2017a)

components (e.g., goal-setting), so that athletes are prepared to both induce, and manage, psychological states underlying excellent performance.

Conclusions

A number of research concerns emanate from the present discussion. First is the dominance of research on metacognition during running activities and a comparative lack of investigation into other endurance sports. This may be particularly relevant to the idiosyncratic use of cognitive strategies in other events. With regard to mindfulness, for example, Pineau, Glass, and Kaufman (2014) suggest that immediate judgement of performance may be beneficial to individual sport athletes (e.g., runners, cyclists) to effect performance-related changes (e.g., reacting to competitors). Similar judgements may provoke feelings of frustration and powerlessness in co-active sports such as rowing (i.e., crewed boats), where one individual's ability to impact performance is limited without similar action responses from crew-mates (Pineau et al., 2014). Accordingly, investigation of metacognitive processes to regulate performance in other endurance activities may yield additional insights into cognitive and metacognitive processes unique to each sport.

A second issue pertains to measures of metacognitive processes in endurance participants. Instruments such as the RMQ (Nietfeld, 2003) and the MAPAS (Settanni et al., 2012) were both adapted from scales initially designed for use in educational settings. Accordingly, there is a pressing need to validate measures tailored to the unique demands of endurance activity. Specific to running, these may be developed from existing accounts of the cognitive and metacognitive processes of endurance runners (Brick et al., 2015, 2018). In addition, a further concern relates to data collection methodologies in endurance activity research. Specifically, both questionnaire (Nietfeld, 2003; Settanni et al., 2012) and retrospective, 'career-based' interview methods (Brick et al., 2015) have dominated data acquisition to date. These may be subject to reliability concerns such as memory decay, under-reporting of cognitive processes, and a lack of congruency between reported and actual cognitions (Ericsson & Simon, 1993; Tenenbaum & Elran, 2003). As such, our understanding of the role of metacognition in self-regulation during endurance activity may be enhanced by the adoption of alternative methodologies. These can include analysis of data collected using think aloud protocols, not only to determine the attentional focus of endurance participants (Sampson, Simpson, Kamphoff, & Langlier, 2015; Whitehead et al., 2017), but also to analyse the metacognitive processes underlying cognitive activity. Furthermore, 'event-focused' interviews (e.g., Swann, Keegan, Crust, & Piggott, 2016) may be useful to minimise the delay between endurance performance and recall. This approach samples individuals following a performance of interest, and aims to conduct interviews as soon as possible afterwards (e.g., on average four days later; Swann et al, 2016, 2017a). In doing so, event-focused interviews capture more recent, detailed, and chronological recall than traditional career-based interviews. Although this approach has only been used to study the psychological states underlying excellent performance (i.e., flow and clutch states), it may also be a useful alternative for studying self-regulation and metacognition. Finally, physiological indices such as eye tracking and pupillometry offer precise and non-invasive measures of brain activity during task performance (e.g., Hoeks & Levelt, 1993; Mathôt, Siebold, Donk, & Vitu, 2015). Specifically, pupil size and change in pupil size has been observed to vary systematically in relation to a variety of physiological and psychological factors, including nonvisual stimulation, habituation, fatigue, and level of attentional effort. As such, non-invasive measures of brain activity like pupillometry potentially offer a fruitful avenue for tracking cognitive and metacognitive activity during endurance activity.

This chapter presents a metacognitive perspective to understand self-regulation during endurance activity. Metacognition is considered an important feature of expert performance across many domains. In an endurance context, metacognition may be important for cognitive strategy selection and implementation, for example, a process that may facilitate both optimum endurance performance and endurance exercise adherence. Many issues remain to be addressed, however, to fully develop our understanding of the importance of metacognitive processes during endurance activity.

References

Augustyn, J. S., & Rosenbaum, D. A. (2005). Metacognitive control of action: Preparation for aiming reflects knowledge of Fitts' Law. *Psychonomic Bulletin and Review, 12,* 911–916. http://dx.doi.org/10.3758/BF03196785

Baker, L., & Brown, A. L. (1984). Cognitive monitoring in reading. In J. Flood (Ed.), *Understanding reading comprehension: cognition, language, and the structure of prose* (pp. 21–44). Newark, DE: International Reading Association.

Bigliassi, M. (2015). Corollary discharges and fatigue-related symptoms: The role of attentional focus. *Frontiers in Psychology, 6,*1002. http://dx.doi.org/10.3389/fpsyg.2015.01002

Blanchfield, A. W., Hardy, J., de Morree, H. M., Staino, W., & Marcora, S. M. (2014). Talking yourself out of exhaustion: the effects of self-talk on endurance performance. *Medicine and Science in Sport and Exercise, 46,* 998–1007. http://dx.doi.org/10.1249/MSS.0000000000000184

Bransford, J., Brown, A. L., & Cocking, R. R. (1999). *How people learn: Brain, mind, experience, and school.* Washington, DC: National Academy Press.

Braver, T. S., Gray, J. R., & Burgess, G. C. (2007). Explaining the many varieties of working memory variation: dual mechanisms of cognitive control. In A. R. A. Conway, C. Jarrold, M. J. Kane, A. Miyake, & J. Towse (Eds). *Variation in working memory.* (pp. 76–106). New York, NY: Oxford University Press.

Brick, N. E., Campbell, M. J., Sheehan, R. B., Fitzpatrick, B. L., & MacIntyre, T. E. (2018). Metacognitive processes and attentional focus in recreational endurance runners. *Internal Journal of Sport and Exercise Psychology.* EPub ahead of print.

Brick, N., MacIntyre, T., & Campbell, M. (2014). Attentional focus in endurance activity: New paradigms and future directions. *International Review of Sport and Exercise Psychology, 7,*106–134. http://dx.doi.org/10.1080/1750984X.2014.885554

Brick, N., MacIntyre, T., & Campbell, M. (2015). Metacognitive processes in the self-regulation of performance in elite endurance runners. *Psychology of Sport and Exercise, 19*, 1–9. http://dx.doi.org/10.1016/j.psychsport.2015.02.003.

Caesar, E. (2017, June 29). The epic untold story of Nike's (almost) perfect marathon. Retrieved from https://www.wired.com/story/nike-breaking2-marathon-eliud-kipchoge/ (accessed 23 August 2017).

Caird, S. J., McKenzie, A. D., & Sleivert, G. G. (1999). Biofeedback and relaxation techniques improve running economy in sub-elite long-distance runners. *Medicine and Science in Sports and Exercise, 31*, 717–722. http://dx.doi.org/10.1097/00005768-199905000-00015.

Csikszentmihalyi, M. (1975). *Beyond boredom and anxiety*. San Francisco, CA: Jossey-Bass.

Csikszentmihalyi, M. (2002). *Flow: The psychology of optimal experience* (2nd ed.). New York, NY: Harper & Row.

Dinsmore, D. L., Alexander, P. A., & Loughlin, S. M. (2008). Focusing the conceptual lens on metacognition, self-regulation, and self-regulated learning. *Educational Psychology Review, 20*, 391–409. http://dx.doi.org/10.1007/s10648-008-9083-6.

Dunlosky, J., & Metcalfe, J. (2009). *Metacognition*. London: Sage Publications.

Eccles, D. W., & Feltovich, P. J. (2008). Implications of domain-general "psychological support skills" for transfer of skill and acquisition of expertise. *Performance Improvement Quarterly, 21*, 43–60. http://dx.doi.org/10.1002/piq.20014

Efklides, A. (2008). Metacognition: Defining its facets and levels of functioning in relation to self-regulation and co-regulation. *European Psychologist, 13*, 277–287. http://dx.doi.org/10.1027/1016-9040.13.4.277

Efklides, A. (2014). How does metacognition contribute to the regulation of learning? An integrative approach. *Psychological Topics, 23*, 1–30.

Ericsson, K. A., & Simon, H. A. (1993). *Protocol analysis: Verbal reports as data* (Rev. ed.). Cambridge, MA: MIT Press.

Flavell, J. H. (1979). Metacognition and cognitive monitoring: A new area of cognitive developmental inquiry. *American Psychologist, 34*, 906–911.

Hoeks, B., & Levelt, W. J. (1993). Pupillary dilation as a measure of attention: A quantitative system analysis. *Behavior Research Methods, 25*, 16–26.

Koriat, A. (2007) Metacognition and consciousness. In P. Zelazo, M. Moscovitch & E. Thompson (Eds). *The Cambridge handbook of consciousness* (pp. 289–325). Cambridge University Press

Locke, E., & Latham, G. (2013). *New developments in goal-setting and task performance*. London: Routledge.

MacIntyre, T., Igou, E. R., Moran, A., P., Campbell, M., & Matthews, J. (2014). Metacognition and action: A new pathway to understanding social and cognitive aspects of expertise in sport. *Frontiers in Psychology, 5*, 1155. http://dx.doi.org/10.3389/fpsyg.2014.01155.

Martini, R., & Shore, B. M. (2008). Pointing to emerging parallels in the use of metacognition in cognitive and psychomotor tasks. *Learning and Individual Differences, 18,* 237–247. http://dx.doi.org/10.1016/j.lindif.2007.08.004

Mathôt, S., Siebold, A., Donk, M., & Vitu, F. (2015). Large pupils predict goal-driven eye movements. *Journal of Experimental Psychology: General, 144*, 513–512. http://dx.doi.org/10.1037/a0039168

Miller, P. H., Kessel, F. S., & Flavell, J. H. (1970). Thinking about people thinking about people thinking about. . .: A study of social cognitive development. *Child Development, 41*, 613–623. http://dx.doi.org/10.2307/1127211.

Moritz, S., Thoering, T., Kühn, S., Willenborg, B., Westermann, S., & Nagel, M. (2015). Metacognition-augmented cognitive remediation training reduces jumping to conclusions and overconfidence but not neurocognitive deficits in psychosis. *Frontiers in Psychology, 6,* 1048. http://dx.doi.org/10.3389/fpsyg.2015.01048

Nelson, T. O., & Narens, L. (1990). Metamemory: A theoretical framework and some new findings. In G. H. Bower (Ed.). *The psychology of learning and motivation* (pp. 125–173). New York, NY: Academic Press.

Nietfeld, J. L. (2003). An examination of metacognitive strategy use and monitoring skills by competitive middle distance runners. *Journal of Applied Sport Psychology, 15,* 307–320. http://dx.doi.org/10.1080/10413200390237942.

Okwumabua, T. M., Meyers, A. W., Schleser, R., & Cooke, C. J. (1983). Cognitive strategies and running performance: An exploratory study. *Cognitive Therapy and Research, 7,* 363–370. http://dx.doi.org/10.1007%2FBF01177558.

Pfitzinger, P., & Douglas, S. (2001). *Advanced Marathoning.* Human Kinetics.

Pineau, T. R., Glass, C. R., & Kaufman, K. A. (2014). Mindfulness in sport performance. In A. Le, C. Ngnoumen, & E. Langer (Eds.). *Handbook of mindfulness* (pp. 1004–1033). Oxford, UK: Wiley-Blackwell.

Sampson, A., Simpson, D., Kamphoff, C., & Langlier, A. (2015). Think aloud: An examination of distance runners' thought processes. *International Journal of Sport and Exercise Psychology, 15,* 176–189. http://dx.doi.org/10.1080/1612197X.2015.1069877

Schumacher, J. M., Becker, A. J., & Wiersma, L. D. (2016). Forging ahead: An examination of the experiences and coping mechanisms of channel swimmers. *The Sport Psychologist, 30,* 327–338. http://dx.doi.org/10.1123/tsp.2015-0137.

Schweickle, M., Groves, S., Vella, S., & Swann, C. (2017). The effects of open vs. specific goals on flow and clutch states in a cognitive task. *Psychology of Sport and Exercise, 33,* 45–54.

Settanni, M., Magistro, D., & Rabaglietti, E. (2012). Development and preliminary validation of an instrument to measure metacognition applied to physical activity during early adolescence. *Cognition, Brain, Behaviour. An Interdisciplinary Journal, 16,* 67–87.

Swann, C., Crust, L., Jackman, P., Vella, S., Allen, M., & Keegan, R. (2017a). Psychological states underlying excellent performance in sport: Towards an integrated model of flow and clutch states. *Journal of Applied Sport Psychology, 29,* 375–401. http://dx.doi.org/10.1080/10413200.2016.1272650

Swann, C., Crust, L., Jackman, P., Vella, S., Allen, M., & Keegan, R. (2017b). Performing under pressure: Exploring the psychological state underlying clutch performance in sport. *Journal of Sports Sciences, 23,* 2272–2280. http://dx.doi.org/10.1080/02640414.2016.1265661.

Swann, C., Crust, L., & Vella, S. (2017c). New directions in the psychology of optimal performance in sport: Flow and clutch states. *Current Opinion in Psychology, 16,* 48–53. http://dx.doi.org/10.1016/j.copsyc.2017.03.032.

Swann, C., Keegan, R., Crust, L., & Piggott, D. (2016). Psychological states underlying excellent performance in professional golfers: "Letting it happen" vs "making it happen." *Psychology of Sport and Exercise, 23,* 101–113. http://dx.doi.org/10.1016/j.psychsport.2015.10.008.

Swann, C., Piggott, D., Crust, L., Keegan, R., & Hemmings, B. (2015). Exploring the interactions underlying flow states: A connecting analysis of flow occurrence in European Tour golfers. *Psychology of Sport and Exercise, 16,* 60–69. http://dx.doi.org/10.1016/j.psychsport.2014.09.007.

Tarricone, P. (2011). *The taxonomy of metacognition.* East Sussex: Psychology Press.

Tenenbaum, G., & Elran, E. (2003). Congruence between actual and retrospective reports of emotions for pre- and postcompetition states. *Journal of Sport and Exercise Psychology*, *25*, 323–340.

Whitehead, A. E., Jones, H. S., Williams, E. L., Dowling, C., Morley, D., Taylor, J. A., & Polman, R. C. (2017). Changes in cognition over a 16.1 km cycling time trial using Think Aloud protocol: Preliminary evidence. *International Journal of Sport and Exercise Psychology*, http://dx.doi.org/10.1080/1612197X.2017.1292302.

Wiggins, B. (2015). *Bradley Wiggins: My Hour*. London: Yellow Jersey Press.

7

SELF-EFFICACY AND ENDURANCE PERFORMANCE

Paul Anstiss

Introduction

> *"They are able who think they are able"* – Virgil

Each of us possesses a series of beliefs about ourselves and the world around us. One such belief, which is instrumental in nearly all contexts, is our own perceived capability, which represents what we believe we *can* do. This belief is represented by the psychological construct of 'self-efficacy'. Self-efficacy, importantly, has been consistently associated with improved performance across a wide variety of domains (Bandura, 1997; Feltz, Short, & Sullivan, 2008; Moritz, Feltz, Fahrbach, & Mack, 2000). The purpose of this chapter is to give readers an introduction to self-efficacy, explore its role in endurance performance, and offer direction for future research and applied practice. Before delving any further, it is important to first gain an understanding of the theoretical framework from which self-efficacy first emerged – social cognitive theory.

Social cognitive theory

Social cognitive theory (Bandura, 1997) argues that human functioning occurs through a triadic reciprocal relationship which exists between behaviour (what we do), cognitions (what we think), and the environment (where we are). Importantly, the environment does not just consist of the physical location of where an individual is, but rather it extends to the *social* environment as well (Maddux & Gosselin, 2003). In triadic reciprocal determinism, each component (i.e., the environment, cognitions, behaviour) interacts with each other in a reciprocal manner, and the interaction between these three components helps to explain an individual's behaviour. To demonstrate, consider a runner who performs well in a race (their behaviour). This performance leads them to receiving praise and encouragement from others around them (their environment). This praise and encouragement leads them to have a heightened sense of belief about their own capability (their cognitions). This change in cognition encourages them to seek out a club to train with, in turn further changing their environment and subsequent cognitions and emotions.

Self-efficacy

Self-efficacy refers to the "belief in one's capabilities to organize and execute the courses of action required to produce given attainments" (Bandura, 1997, p.3). It represents a self-appraisal as to what an individual believes they *can* do, not what they *will* do (an intention), or what they *have* done (an experience). How self-efficacy beliefs develop and emerge will be discussed later in the chapter, but it is important to understand that they are dynamic and domain specific beliefs. They are dynamic in that such beliefs can, and do, change based on the information available to an individual. An endurance athlete's self-efficacy will likely change across a season based on their training progression, performance in events, and the feedback they receive from others. Self-efficacy beliefs are also domain specific, meaning they are tied to specific realms of functioning. An individual may have high levels of self-efficacy in their ability as a cyclist, but lower levels of self-efficacy for rugby.

These beliefs help to shape our behaviour and actions in a variety of ways. First, they influence the goals we set ourselves. Research findings have consistently demonstrated that individuals high in self-efficacy set themselves more challenging goals than those with low self-efficacy (Bandura & Locke, 2003; Barz et al., 2016; Locke & Latham, 2002). The setting of goals, however, means very little if individuals are not willing to put in the effort to achieve them. Self-efficacy beliefs have also been linked with effort, with individuals high in self-efficacy being more willing to exert effort into tasks (Feltz et al., 2008). This effort comprises both cognitive effort (e.g., thinking up ways of dealing with problems) as well as physical effort (e.g., pushing ourselves physically) (Feltz et al., 2008). Perhaps most importantly, high levels of self-efficacy have also been positively linked with an individual's perseverance when faced with difficulties or obstacles. For example, individuals high in self-efficacy who failed to reach their target in a treadmill run, put more effort into the next run than those with low self-efficacy (Bueno, Weinberg, Fernández-Castro, & Capdevila, 2008). The setting of goals, the application of effort, and the willingness to persevere are three factors which can help enable success in almost any domain, but these become especially prevalent when we begin to consider the demands of endurance sport.

Individuals do not possess a 'singular' self-efficacy belief; in fact, they possess a variety of different self-efficacy beliefs. Feltz et al. (2008) outlined several different types of self-efficacy which have been measured and examined in the sport psychology literature. Task self-efficacy is the type of self-efficacy most similar to the general definition of self-efficacy, and focuses on the perceived capability for certain performances (e.g., 'How confident are you that you can complete the race in a time of X?'). Self-regulatory efficacy is an individual's belief in their own capability to control their motivations, thoughts, emotions, and behaviours in order to complete a task (e.g., 'How confident are you that you can manage any unwanted emotions during your race?'). Self-regulatory efficacy is also critical when we consider commitment to training programs, especially when there are competing life demands (McCormick, Meijen, & Marcora, 2018). Coping self-efficacy (or ameliorative self-efficacy) refers to an individual's belief in their own capability to cope with threats and difficulties. Coping self-efficacy is also related to how athletes manage unexpected difficulties or changes, such as equipment failure, weather changes, or injury. Being able to manage and deal with such occurrences is critical for helping individuals achieve their potential and reach their goals.

Each of these different self-efficacy beliefs exists across three dimensions: magnitude, strength and generality (Bandura, 1997). The magnitude of self-efficacy beliefs refers to an individual's perception of performance attainments at different levels of difficulty. For example, a runner will report different perceptions of belief in their ability to run a marathon in 4 hours as compared to 3 hours. Strength of self-efficacy beliefs refers to the certainty in that belief, ranging from complete uncertainty to complete certainty. Two athletes might both believe that they are capable of achieving a 3 hour 15 minute marathon, but one may have a greater level of strength in this belief. When discussing self-efficacy beliefs in a sporting context, Bandura often made reference to athletes requiring 'resilient' and 'robust' self-efficacy beliefs (Bandura, 1997). These terms were never truly conceptualised by Bandura, but what they appear to represent is the possession of beliefs which are not easily changed by conflicting information (e.g., a series of poor performances, unexpected weather conditions). Generality focuses on the transferability of efficacy judgements across different tasks. Despite self-efficacy being a domain specific belief, there exists sub-skills which are shared across domains. For instance, although distance running and cycling are two different domains, both require an ability for self-regulation, perseverance, and pacing.

Self-efficacy and related constructs

Research investigating self-efficacy has sometimes mistakenly labelled other psychological constructs as self-efficacy, and failed to differentiate between them. Being able to differentiate between self-efficacy and other related psychological constructs is important, as it helps promote more valid research methodologies. Two constructs which are commonly conflated with self-efficacy are confidence and self-esteem. Both confidence and self-efficacy refer to a judgement on one's own perceived capabilities. The difference lies in their level of specificity and generality. Self-efficacy beliefs are typically focused around specific tasks or domains (e.g., a 10 km runner) whereas confidence tends to be a more general construct (e.g., a confident athlete). Self-efficacy beliefs are better predictors of behaviour and performance than confidence beliefs (Moritz et al., 2000), as they are more specific to individual tasks. The interchangeable use of the terms, whereas problematic in academic research, is unlikely to be a major issue in applied or practical settings. Additionally, the term 'confidence' is more commonly used by both coaches and athletes, and therefore may be more likely to be used in practical and applied settings.

Like self-efficacy, self-esteem represents a judgement by an individual. Whereas the judgement in self-efficacy is in reference to capability, the judgement for self-esteem is one based around worthiness (Schunk & Pajares, 2002). Self-efficacy and self-esteem are likely to be conflated when considering individuals' perceptions on a task that they pride themselves on. An individual, however, can possess low self-efficacy for a particular task without this affecting their self-esteem. A middle distance runner may possess low levels of self-efficacy for marathon running, but as marathon running is not that important to them this low level of self-efficacy will have little impact on their self-esteem. Individuals who possess low levels of global self-esteem, that is they have low levels of self-esteem across a variety of domains, are likely to report lower levels of self-efficacy (Bandura, 1997). This lowering of self-efficacy is hypothesised to occur due to increased attention to the demands and difficulty of the task, and a decreased focus on an individual's abilities.

This first section has provided a brief introduction to the concept of self-efficacy beliefs, the theoretical framework in which they exist, the types of self-efficacy and also their relationship to other similar constructs. The next section of this chapter looks at understanding the development and formation of these self-efficacy beliefs.

Development and formation of self-efficacy beliefs

The development and formation of self-efficacy beliefs occurs through a series of cognitive processes involving the selection, interpretation, and integration of five sources of efficacy information: past experiences, vicarious influences, verbal persuasion, physiological states, and affective states (Bandura, 1997; Feltz et al., 2008). These five sources are involved in three levels of analysis namely; analysis of task requirements, interpretation of causes of previous performance, and assessment of availability of specific resources. This is a constantly occurring process, with changes in self-efficacy occurring as new information about the task and the individual are appraised (Gist & Mitchell, 1992).

As mentioned previously, self-efficacy beliefs are in relation to specific tasks or behaviours. Therefore, the first stage in the formation of a self-efficacy belief is an analysis of the task requirements. An individual will consider what the task requires of them, the difficulties they are likely to encounter, and what will be required of them to achieve different levels of performance. For example, a cyclist will consider the physiological, tactical, and psychological requirements of achieving certain times in an upcoming road race. Perceived task difficulty is likely to be a key factor in this initial stage of formation. To illustrate, a recent study by Sides,

Chow, and Tenenbaum (2017) revealed that changes in perception of task difficulty (e.g., a change in the intensity of a hand-grip exercise) led to lower levels of self-efficacy for that task. In the endurance performance domain these perceptions of task difficulty could relate to a number of factors such as: terrain, other competitors, weather, and familiarity.

As individuals gain more experience with tasks and situations, this assessment of task demands becomes more of an automated process, and individuals are instead likely to rely on their interpretation of the causes of previous performance (Bandura, 1997; Gist & Mitchell, 1992). The attributional analysis of experience, involves individuals seeking to understand why a particular performance level occurred. According to Weiner's attribution theory (1985), individuals attribute their performance across three key dimensions: locus of causality, stability, and controllability. Perceptions of stability and controllability have been demonstrated to be the two most important attributions with regard to self-efficacy (Gernigon & Delloye, 2003).

The last level of analysis requires individual to assess the availability of specific resources or constraints for performing the task. This assessment considers personal factors (e.g., ability level, fitness level, anxiety, available effort, and desire to perform well) as well as situational factors (e.g., competing demands, distractions, difficulties) that would influence performance on the task (Gist & Mitchell, 1992). This assessment of personal and situational factors is also likely to be constantly ongoing during tasks (Gist & Mitchell, 1992). In an endurance performance context, this assessment of personal resources might relate to perceptions of fitness, fatigue, and other various exercise induced sensations (e.g., perception of effort, pain). In order for each of the analyses presented to occur, they need to be based on experiences and perceptions which are identified and internalised from the five proposed sources of self-efficacy.

The sources of self-efficacy

An individual's experiences and success are the most powerful source of self-efficacy information (Bandura, 1997). If these past experiences are perceived to have been successes, this will result in an increase in self-efficacy, whereas if past experiences are perceived to have been failures, this will undermine self-efficacy. Factors such as task difficulty, external support, and occurrences of failure can all contribute to the efficacy value assigned to a past performance (Bandura, 1997). For example, a runner could win an important race, and as such an increase in self-efficacy could be expected. If, however, they feel that this success was only down to other competitors failing to perform, this experience will likely not contribute towards their self-efficacy. Similarly, successes which occur following difficulty or adversity will contribute more to the generation and reinforcement of self-efficacy beliefs rather than more straightforward successes (Bandura, 1997). These past performance experiences, do not only refer to competitive events or races as is often the focus of research and applied work, but also the training process. An athlete who trusts their training program, and the volume of work that they have put into their training will likely have raised self-efficacy for an upcoming event or race.

Vicarious influences are another source of self-efficacy information, and these are based around learning and modelling from others. Although it is hypothesised that vicarious experiences are not as strong a source compared to past performance experiences, such influences are a key contributor to efficacy information, particularly when individuals are novices, and do not have enough of their own experiences to draw on (Bandura, 1997). Watching someone persevere with a difficult task can help develop self-efficacy towards this task, if the observer feels the person they are watching, the modeller, is similar to them (i.e., sex, skill level, age) (Bandura, 1997). This can have implications relating to pacing in endurance events, where individuals may choose to make decisions based on how others around them are performing (Corbett, Barwood, Ouzounoglou, Thelwell, & Dicks, 2012).

Social and verbal persuasions act as a third source of self-efficacy. These can represent feedback and support from coaches and training partners, expectations from others, and self-talk. With regard to the appraisal of verbal persuasion as a source, the expertise and credibility of the provider, the framing of the performance feedback and the degree of disparity between what is said and the individuals own beliefs regarding their capabilities are all influential factors (Bandura, 1997). Support from crowds or members of the public during events can also provide a boost to self-efficacy for those competing (Samson & Solmon, 2011). From an individual perspective, self-talk is a common psychological strategy employed to help regulate thought processes (Van Raalte, Vincent, & Brewer, 2016), and contributes towards enhancing an athlete's self-efficacy.

Physiological states, such as feelings of strength, arousal, pain, fitness, and fatigue, are cognitively appraised by individuals in order to ascertain their ability to successfully meet the task at hand. The sensation itself, such as pain or tiredness, only contributes towards self-efficacy once it has been cognitive appraised. For example, high levels of exertion and exercise induced pain are not likely to cause a decrease in self-efficacy when they are expected, but if they occur when they are not expected (e.g., only a few miles into a marathon), then this will lower self-efficacy as the high level of exertion suggest an individual does not possess the capability to complete the race. The salience of physiological states as a source of efficacy is hypothesised to be dependent on the physical demands of the task (Bandura, 1997), with increased salience for physiological states as physical demands increase. This hypothesis has received some support as Chase, Feltz, and Lirgg (2003) demonstrated that physiological states was the second most cited source of self-efficacy across a basketball season, and Samson (2014) demonstrated that physiological states was the most frequently cited source of self-efficacy for an upcoming marathon. Research, however, has often failed to identify what specific physiological states (e.g., perception of effort, pain, and fatigue) may contribute to or undermine self-efficacy.

The final proposed source of self-efficacy relates to an individual's perceptions of their emotional states. Similarly to physiological states, individuals appraise and interpret their emotional state and consider how this relates to their experiences. Self-efficacy beliefs are often enhanced through positive emotions and decreased through negative emotional states (Bandura, 1997; Martin, 2002). In an endurance context, the experience of positive emotions, such as feelings of happiness, excitement, and calmness have been linked with increased levels of self-efficacy in road wheelchair racing (Martin, 2002). It is difficult, however, to ascertain whether or not these positive emotions were a determinant of the self-efficacy beliefs or an outcome (Martin, 2002).

Overall, when considering the sources of self-efficacy there are two key points to consider. First, information only contributes to self-efficacy once it has been appraised by an individual. Before this appraisal process, information or experiences has no direct influence on self-efficacy (Bandura, 1997). Understanding this appraisal and attributional process, and the tendencies that individuals have, is an important target point for interventions in athletes who possess weak or inaccurate self-efficacy beliefs. Second, although they are presented as distinct entities, the sources of self-efficacy have a significant degree of overlap. Specifically, physiological states and past performance experiences are potentially heavily intertwined in the endurance sport context. Factors such as perception of effort, or exercise-induced pain are likely to influence how an athlete views a prior experience (Samson, 2014). Consider an athlete who finishes in a race in their goal time, but feels like they still have effort and energy in comparison to an athlete who finishes but has feelings of exhaustion and energy depletion. Both athletes will likely be happy with their performance, but the athlete who felt they still had more to give, may have higher self-efficacy in the future.

Self-efficacy and endurance performance

Both narrative (Feltz et al., 2008) and systematic (Moritz et al., 2000) reviews have consistently revealed that self-efficacy is positively associated with sport performance. This relationship between self-efficacy and performance is also apparent across a wide variety of endurance sports. In distance running, Okwumabua (1985) revealed that pre-event self-efficacy strength explained 46 per cent of the variance in marathon performance time. Similar findings for distance running were reported by LaGuardia and Labbé (1993), who found that self-efficacy was negatively correlated with performance time across a range of track running distances (1500 m, 5000 m, 10000 m). Furthermore, self-efficacy has also been demonstrated to be a powerful predictor of performance in Ironman Triathlon. Through regression analysis, Burke and Jin (1996) revealed that self-efficacy was a more powerful predictor of performance for Ironman triathlon than previous performance history, maximal oxygen consumption or measures of sport confidence.

As discussed elsewhere in this book, both perception of effort (Marcora & Bosio, 2007) and perceived exercise-induced pain (Mauger, 2014) are important determinants of endurance performance. Importantly, self-efficacy has been associated with decreased levels of perceived effort (Rudolph & McAuley, 1996) and increased levels of pain tolerance (Baker & Kirsch, 1991; Hutchinson, Sherman, Martinovic, & Tenenbaum, 2008). Additionally, individuals who engage in consistent endurance training have displayed higher pain thresholds and greater levels of self-efficacy in pain management than endurance non-athletes (Johnson, Stewart, Humphries, & Chamove, 2012).

It is important, however, to consider if the possession of a high level of self-efficacy is always beneficial for performance. A growing body of research has begun to argue that given certain situational contexts (e.g., ambiguous performance feedback), self-efficacy can have a null or negative effect on performance (e.g., Halper & Vancouver, 2016). Such null or negative effects of self-efficacy on performance have been demonstrated in muscular endurance tasks (Halper & Vancouver, 2016). Explanations for these negative or null effects are largely grounded in Powers' (1973) perceptual control theory. According to perceptual control theory, when individuals possess high levels of self-efficacy, and performance feedback is ambiguous, they are likely to place less effort into the task, as they believe that performance is easily achievable (Powers, 1973). A key requirement for these negative effects of self-efficacy on performance is a lack of performance feedback. When competing in endurance events or sports, however, athletes often have several sources of feedback information available to them including: comparisons with other athletes, pacers, lap splits, watches, mile markers, and the use of technology (e.g. GPS trackers). The potential for self-efficacy to have a negative effect on endurance performance therefore remains unclear. Despite these potential limitations, the evidence presented throughout this chapter, makes it clear that self-efficacy is an important factor in endurance performance, and that the possession of robust and accurate self-efficacy beliefs is likely to be beneficial for endurance athletes. In order to further our understanding of the role of self-efficacy, three key areas for future research are presented.

Future research

The first area for future research to examine is the measurement of self-efficacy beliefs in endurance performance studies. Self-efficacy measurement in sport psychology typically only focuses on performance, i.e., 'How confident are you that can you complete the race in a time of X?' Although these beliefs are important, Feltz et al. (2008) cautioned against an overreliance on these because performance in sport is multifactorial. Instead, they recommended measuring self-efficacy relating to behaviours that must be carried out to achieve certain performance levels. The development of scales or instruments which look to measure self-efficacy for the wide array of skills and behaviours that must be carried out in endurance performance would be warranted (Anstiss, Meijen, Madigan, & Marcora, 2018). The second direction for future research should be to examine how and why self-efficacy beliefs change during endurance performance. Although measuring self-efficacy during endurance performance poses practical difficulties, recent research suggests that a 'Think Aloud' protocol can be used with runners (Samson, Simpson, Kamphoff, & Langlier, 2017) to gain understanding of their thoughts. Alongside this exploration of cognitions, experimental studies in laboratory settings could look to examine the relationship between self-efficacy and physiological indices such as ventilatory or lactate thresholds. Examining how self-efficacy beliefs may change in relation to physiological feedback would provide further information on the role of physiological states as a source of self-efficacy.

Applied practice

This chapter has predominately discussed the theoretical and research related aspects of self-efficacy. Whereas it is beyond its scope to explore possible interventions to help raise self-efficacy (for reviews see Feltz et al., 2008 and Short & Ross-Stewart, 2008), a key aspect in all applied practice must be a consideration of the experience level of the athlete. Novice, experienced, and athletes returning from injury have different self-efficacy needs that must be considered. For a novice, this is to create an initial sense of self-efficacy and subsequently increasing it gradually. This primarily occurs through gaining experience in the domain, such as through a well-structured training programme, or through providing opportunities for vicarious modelling (Feltz et al., 2008). An intervention for an experienced athlete would instead focus on reinforcing self-efficacy beliefs during difficult periods of an event rather than creating new beliefs. This may involve working out the specific situation or factor which causes a drop in self-efficacy (e.g., a competitor passing them, or unwanted thoughts), and then developing an appropriate strategy for managing this. For an injured athlete, the intervention might sit between the two examples given previously. Reflection and reinforcement of their prior successes and experiences, can help ensure that they remember their perceived capability, whilst incremental training and rehabilitation can help enhance their own capabilities.

Conclusions

This chapter has provided readers with an introduction to self-efficacy. Although there are many 'take-home messages' throughout, one thing that should be remembered is that there are no shortcuts to the development of self-efficacy. High levels of self-efficacy for easy or straightforward tasks are easy to come by. The true challenge is ensuring a robust sense of self-efficacy that remains in the face of obstacles and setbacks. This development of a robust sense of self-efficacy is likely to occur through the accumulation of a variety of experiences, both positive and negative, which the athlete is allowed the opportunity to reflect upon. Future research that looks to gain a better understanding of how these beliefs develop, how they may change during events, and how best to measure them, will be critical in helping the design and delivery of self-efficacy interventions.

References

Anstiss, P. A., Meijen, C., Madigan, D. J., & Marcora, S. M. (2018). Development and initial validation of the Endurance Sport Self-Efficacy Scale (ESSES). *Psychology of Sport and Exercise*, 38, 176–183.

Baker, S. L., & Kirsch, I. (1991). Cognitive mediators of pain perception and tolerance. *Journal of Personality and Social Psychology*, *61*(3), 504–510.

Bandura, A. (1997). *Self-efficacy: The exercise of control*. New York, NY: Freeman.

Bandura, A., & Locke, E. A. (2003). Negative self-efficacy and goal effects revisited. *Journal of Applied Psychology*, *88*(1), 87.

Barz, M., Lange, D., Parschau, L., Lonsdale, C., Knoll, N., & Schwarzer, R. (2016). Self-efficacy, planning, and preparatory behaviours as joint predictors of physical activity: A conditional process analysis. *Psychology & Health*, *31*(1), 65–78.

Bueno, J., Weinberg, R. S., Fernández-Castro, J., & Capdevila, L. (2008). Emotional and motivational mechanisms mediating the influence of goal setting on endurance athletes' performance. *Psychology of Sport and Exercise*, *9*(6), 786–799.

Burke, S. T., & Jin, P. (1996). Predicting performance from a triathlon event. *Journal of Sport Behavior*, *19*(4), 272–287.

Chase, M. A., Feltz, D. L., & Lirgg, C. D. (2003). Sources of collective and individual efficacy of collegiate athletes. *International Journal of Sport and Exercise Psychology*, *1*(2), 180–191.

Corbett, J., Barwood, M. J., Ouzounoglou, A., Thelwell, R., & Dicks, M. (2012). Influence of competition on performance and pacing during cycling exercise. *Medicine & Science in Sports & Exercise*, *44*, 509–515.

Feltz, D. L., Short, S. E., & Sullivan, P. J. (2008). *Self-efficacy in sport*. Champaign, IL: Human Kinetics.

Gernigon, C., & Delloye, J. B. (2003). Self-efficacy, causal attribution, and track athletic performance following unexpected success or failure among elite sprinters. *The Sport Psychologist*, *17*(1), 55–76.

Gist, M. E., & Mitchell, T. B. (1992). Self-efficacy: A theoretical analysis of its determinants and malleability. *Academy of Management Review*, *17*(2), 183–211.

Halper, L. R., & Vancouver, J. B. (2016). Self-efficacy's influence on persistence on a physical task: Moderating effect of performance feedback ambiguity. *Psychology of Sport and Exercise*, *22*, 170–177.

Hutchinson, J. C., Sherman, T., Martinovic, N., & Tenenbaum, G. (2008). The effect of manipulated self-efficacy on perceived and sustained effort. *Journal of Applied Sport Psychology*, *20*, 457–472.

Johnson, M. H., Stewart, J., Humphries, S. A., & Chamove, A. S. (2012). Marathon runners' reaction to potassium iontophoretic experimental pain: Pain tolerance, pain threshold, coping and self-efficacy. *European Journal of Pain*, *16*(5), 767–774.

Laguardia, R., & Labbé, E. E. (1993). Self-efficacy and anxiety and their relationship to training and race performance. *Perceptual and Motor Skills*, 77, 27–34.

Locke, E. A., & Latham, G. P. (2002). Building a practically useful theory of goal setting and task motivation: A 35-year odyssey. *The American Psychologist*, *57*, 705–717.

Maddux, J. E., & Gosselin, J. T. (2003). Self-efficacy. In M. R. Leary & J. P. Tangney (Eds.), *Handbook of self and identity* (pp. 218–238). New York: Springer.

Marcora, S. M., & Bosio, A. (2007). Effect of exercise-induced muscle damage on endurance running performance in humans. *Scandinavian Journal of Medicine & Science in Sports*, *17*, 662–671.

Martin, J. J. (2002). Training and performance self-efficacy, affect, and performance in wheelchair road racers. *The Sport Psychologist*, *16*(4), 384–395.

Mauger, A. R. (2014). Factors affecting the regulation of pacing: current perspectives. *Open Access Journal of Sports Medicine, 5*, 209–214.

McCormick, A., Meijen, C., & Marcora, S. (2018). Psychological demands experienced by recreational endurance athletes. *International Journal of Sport and Exercise Psychology, 16*(4), 415–430.

Moritz, S. E., Feltz, D. L., Fahrbach, K. R., & Mack, D. E. (2000). The relation of self-efficacy measures to sport performance: A meta-analytic review. *Research Quarterly for Exercise and Sport, 71*(3), 280–294.

Okwumabua, T. M. (1985). Psychological and physical contributions to marathon performance: An exploratory investigation. *Journal of Sport Behavior, 8*, 163–171.

Powers, W. T. (1973). *Behaviour: The control of perception*. Chicago, IL: Aldine.

Rudolph, D. L., & McAuley, E. (1996). Self-efficacy and perceptions of effort: A reciprocal relationship. *Journal of Sport and Exercise Psychology, 18*(2), 216–223.

Samson, A. (2014). Sources of self-efficacy during marathon training: A qualitative, longitudinal investigation. *The Sport Psychologist, 28*(2), 164–175.

Samson, A., & Solmon, M. (2011). Examining the sources of self-efficacy for physical activity within the sport and exercise domains. *International Review of Sport and Exercise Psychology, 4*, 70–89.

Samson, A., Simpson, D., Kamphoff, C., & Langlier, A. (2017). Think aloud: An examination of distance runners' thought processes. *International Journal of Sport and Exercise Psychology, 15*, 176–189.

Schunk, D. H., & Pajares, F. (2002). The development of academic self-efficacy. In A. Wigfeild & S. E. Jacquelynne (Eds.), *Development of achievement motivation* (pp. 15–31). San Diego, CA: Academic Press.

Short, S., & Ross-Stewart, L. (2009). *A review of self-efficacy based interventions*. In S. D. Mellalieu & S. Hanton (Eds.), *Advances in applied sport psychology* (pp. 221–280). Abingdon, England: Routledge.

Sides, R., Chow, G., & Tenenbaum, G. (2017). Shifts in adaptation: The effects of self-efficacy and task difficulty perception. *Journal of Clinical Sport Psychology, 11*(1), 34–52.

Van Raalte, J. L., Vincent, A., & Brewer, B. W. (2016). Self-talk: Review and sport-specific model. *Psychology of Sport and Exercise, 22*, 139–148.

Weiner, B. (1985). An attributional theory of achievement motivation and emotion. *Psychological Review, 92*(4), 548–573.

PART II

Psychological interventions in endurance performance

PRELUDE: INTERVENTIONS FOR ENDURANCE PERFORMANCE

Carla Meijen

In the first part of the book, psychological variables that can influence endurance performance, including pain, motivation, perceived effort, pacing, meta-cognition, emotions, and self-efficacy were introduced. The book will now move on to psychological interventions that aim to improve endurance performance. Although there is evidence to suggest that practical psychological interventions, such as goal-setting and imagery, can benefit endurance performance (McCormick, Meijen, & Marcora, 2015), we also need to consider the effect of psychological interventions on other related variables such as coping, emotions, and satisfaction with performance. In this second part of the book, the role of cognitive strategies, goal-striving, imagery, self-talk, and mindfulness will be outlined and evidence for the effectiveness of these interventions will be reviewed.

To put the different interventions of this part in context, I will first provide a background to what psychological interventions are and how these can be used. The word 'intervention' implies that something needs to be fixed, and the use of the concept intervention in such a way often has a negative connotation. I perceive interventions to be broader than this, and in line with Singer and Anshel (2006) I propose that interventions can be used to build on an individual's strengths. Part of this process may be educating endurance performers about a range of psychological techniques that they could benefit from in the future. Psychological interventions are typically described as the use of techniques that can target thoughts, feelings, and behaviours in a certain setting, and these can influence the way a person functions or performs (for example see Brown & Fletcher, 2017; Yeager & Walton, 2011). For example, this can be recalling a successful training session that was particularly challenging, or taking away aspects that prevent goal-achievement, such as using relaxation to reduce pressure (based on Yeager & Walton, 2011). These psychological techniques that can make up an intervention are skills that an individual can learn, and endurance performers can practice psychological techniques to get better at them. Although it is important that the interventions are context specific, psychological interventions can benefit other areas beyond the sporting context (Poczwardowski, Sherman, & Ravizza, 2004).

Who are interventions for?

Psychological interventions can benefit endurance performance, and endurance participants from all age groups and experience levels can use psychological interventions. Those who run a marathon for the first time might find psychological interventions that help to manage nerves useful, whereas an experienced cyclist could benefit from a psychological intervention to manage their race expectations when returning from an injury. The take home message here is that psychological interventions are inclusive, and not just for a certain group.

Traditionally, in a sport psychology context, interventions take the form of an athlete being taught psychological skills over multiple sessions after an accredited sport psychologist has assessed the needs of the athlete (Keegan, 2016). This typically includes a formal intake process and face-to-face interactions between the client and practitioner; one of the strengths of this approach is that there is time for a relationship to develop between the practitioner and athlete which can be an important aspect of initiating change and sport psychology consultancy (Sharp, Hodge, & Danish, 2015). More recently, however, a move towards less traditional intervention approaches is occurring. For example, brief single-session problem solving methods have been introduced at the English Institute of Sport (Pitt, Thomas, Lindsay, Hanton, & Bawden, 2015). In fact, there is some suggestion that 'bigger' interventions are not necessarily better (Yeager & Walton, 2011), although the evidence in sporting contexts for this is limited and of course this also depends on the aim of the intervention. Brief interventions aimed at changing thoughts, feelings, and cognitions can have a long-term effect (Kenthirarajah, Walton, Kenthirarajah, & Walton, 2015), and subsequently this can initiate a change in perception of how a person approaches future situations. Brief contact interventions can occur as interactions between a professional (i.e., sport psychology practitioner) and client (i.e., athlete) that were not specifically planned, but where there are 'teachable' moments helping the client/athlete to have a new or different perspective on the situation, and this can happen in a single interaction (Giges & Petitpas, 2000). A brief intervention may be combined with teaching or incorporating more 'traditional' psychological skills methods.

Brief interventions are also relevant to consider in recreational endurance sport settings, especially where athletes do not have the sources to access professional sport psychology support services but could benefit from sport psychology support. Therefore, it is important to also look at non-traditional intervention approaches such as brief contact interventions. An example of how this can be put into practice will be covered in Chapter 14 where the concept of 'psyching teams' will be explained. This is a concept where mental support is provided to runners before, during, and after long distance running events (Meijen, Day, & Hays, 2017). In addition to brief face-to-face interventions, we may also want to consider the role of alternative means of providing information about psychological skills to a wider audience. For example, through the use of online delivery methods such as video blogs, worksheets, or massive open online courses. Some caution is warranted, however, as there is evidence to suggest that psychosocial interventions, where a coach or practitioner may be involved, are most effective when it comes to benefits on sporting performance (Brown & Fletcher, 2017).

Some points to remember for (brief) interventions.

1. It is important to consider when which type of intervention is appropriate; for example, do not make any major changes close to an event.
2. For brief interventions, focus on one problem, where you build on the athlete's strong points and make small changes that can benefit performance.
3. For longer term interventions, work on the assumption that psychological skills require training, and that there is not necessarily a 'quick' fix (despite the notion of 'brief interventions!). Getting better at a skill requires training, and this is the same for psychological skills. You cannot expect a miracle overnight.
4. It is important to be aware of individual differences. Endurance performers may experience different psychological demands, therefore, what works for one person, does not necessarily work for another endurance performer.

Who should deliver the intervention?

Considering that a significant proportion of recreational endurance performers may not have direct access to professional sport psychology support but could still benefit from training psychological skills, I propose that interventions can also be tailored towards coaches and athletes. Although the content may be provided by a sport psychologist, which is the case for the intervention chapters in this book, it may be the case that the intervention is delivered by a coach, or that an athlete uses online resources or self-help books. We do this, however, with a word of caution. First, it is important to place the interventions that are covered in this book into context, and consider that a certified sport psychologist is trained to work with an athlete on their psychological well-being. There is more to making psychological interventions work than reading about them in a book or journal article. Second, it is is important to use evidence-based practice where it is available. We do acknowledge the challenges that sport psychology, as a field, is facing in establishing this evidence (for example see McCormick et al., 2015), and are encouraging researchers to engage in field research to help strengthen the evidence base. We hope that the following chapters will be useful for giving the reader an overview of the research evidence, as well as some practical applications. The following interventions will be covered: cognitive strategies, goal striving, imagery, self-talk, and mindfulness.

References

Brown, D. J., & Fletcher, D. (2017). Effects of psychological and psychosocial interventions on sport performance: A meta-analysis. *Sports Medicine, 47*(1), 77–99.

Giges, B., & Petitpas, A. (2000). Brief contact interventions in sport psychology. *The Sport Psychologist, 14*(2), 176–187.

Keegan, R. (2016). *Being a sport psychologist.* London: Palgrave.

Kenthirarajah, D. T., Walton, G. M., Kenthirarajah, D., & Walton, G. M. (2015). How brief social-psychological interventions can cause enduring effects. In R. A. Scott & S. Kosslyn (Eds.), *Emerging trends in the social and behavioral sciences* (pp. 1–15). Hoboken, NJ, USA: John Wiley & Sons.

McCormick, A., Meijen, C., & Marcora, S. (2015). Psychological determinants of whole-body endurance performance. *Sports Medicine, 45*(7), 997–1015.

Meijen, C., Day, C., & Hays, K. F. (2017). Running a psyching team: Providing mental support at long-distance running events. *Journal of Sport Psychology in Action, 8*(1), 12–22.

Pitt, T., Thomas, O., Lindsay, P., Hanton, S., & Bawden, M. (2015). Doing sport psychology briefly? A critical review of single session therapeutic approaches and their relevance to sport psychology. *International Review of Sport and Exercise Psychology, 8*(1), 125–155.

Poczwardowski, A., Sherman, C. P., & Ravizza, K. (2004). Professional philosophy in the sport psychology service delivery: building on theory and practice. *The Sport Psychologist, 18*(4), 445–463.

Sharp, L.-A., Hodge, K., & Danish, S. (2015). Ultimately it comes down to the relationship: Experienced consultants' views of effective sport psychology consulting. *The Sport Psychologist, 29*(4), 358–370.

Singer, R. N., & Anshel, M. H. (2006). An overview of interventions in sport. In J. Dosil (Ed.), *The sport psychologist's handbook: A guide for sport-specific performance enhancement* (pp. 63–88). Chichester, UK: John Wiley & Sons.

Yeager, D. S., & Walton, G. M. (2011). Social-psychological interventions in education: They're not magic. *Review of Educational Research, 81*(2), 267–301.

8

ATTENTIONAL FOCUS AND COGNITIVE STRATEGIES DURING ENDURANCE ACTIVITY

Noel Brick, Tadhg MacIntyre, and Linda Schücker

Introduction

Attentional focus and endurance activity

Endurance athletes engage many idiosyncratic attentional strategies to optimise performance. To judge pacing and facilitate concentration, women's marathon world record holder, Paula Radcliffe, revealed how she repeatedly counted to 100 during racing and training events (Radcliffe, 2011). Similarly, successful English Channel swimmers reported using a range of cognitive strategies, such as distraction by mentally planning intricate meals, to cope with fatigue, poor conditions, uncertainty, and associated negative thoughts during the event (Schumacher, Becker, & Wiersma, 2016). The scientific literature on attentional focus and endurance performance originated from a study of the psychological characteristics of endurance runners by Morgan and Pollock (1977). One aspect of this study – the cognitive strategies used by runners – suggested that elite marathoners paid close attention to bodily sensations during running (e.g., muscular sensations, breathing), adjusted pace on the basis of this sensory information, identified other runners to run with or race against, and constantly focused on running in a relaxed manner. These thoughts were categorised as *associative* and contrasted with the *dissociative* strategies of non-elite runners. Morgan and Pollock (1977) suggested non-elites were more likely to engage in dissociative strategies including distractive thoughts such as reconstructing images of past events, or building a house in one's mind, to direct attention away from sensations of exertion.

Although this work provided the foundation for four decades of attentional focus research, the concept of dual categories of association/dissociation has been subject to criticism by some. Specifically, concerns include the use of the term *dissociation*, and its alternative use to describe a clinical pathology involving disturbances in identity, personality, memory, and perception that causes distress and a reduction in daily functioning (American Psychiatric Association, 2013; Masters & Ogles, 1998). Furthermore, it has been suggested that the dichoto- mous conceptualisation may not capture the dynamic intricacies of cognitive activity during endurance performance (Laash, 1994–1995; Salmon, Hanneman, & Harwood, 2010). Consequently, alternative classifications have been proposed to more adequately capture the attentional processes of endurance athletes. An initial attempt was Schomer's (1986) integration of association/dissociation with Nideffer's (1981) theoretical attentional style dimensions (i.e., internal/external and broad/narrow). Consequently, Schomer's (1986) categorisation included, for example, task-related thoughts such as feelings and affects, body monitoring, and pace monitoring, and task-unrelated categories such as reflective thoughts, per- sonal problem solving, and conversational chatter.

The utility of Schomer's (1986) model is demonstrated by the many studies classifying cognitions using this categorisation (e.g., Couture, Jerome, & Tihanyi, 1999; Tenenbaum & Connolly, 2008). Nevertheless, the model has been criticised for overlooking many thoughts endurance athletes might express, such as convers- ing with other runners or setting subgoals during longer-distance events (Stevinson & Biddle, 1998; Summers, Sargent, Levey, & Murray, 1982). Consequently, Stevinson and Biddle (1998) advanced a more comprehensive, two-dimensional categorisation of attentional foci. In this model, associative and dissociative thoughts were recategorised as either *inward* (e.g., breathing, fatigue) or *outward* (e.g., mile-markers, split-times) *monitoring*, and *inward* (e.g., irrelevant daydreams, maths puzzles) or *outward* (e.g., scenery, spectators) *distraction*. This model has also been utilised to categorise endurance participants' attentional focus (e.g., Connolly & Janelle, 2003; Stanley, Pargman, & Tenenbaum, 2007). A number of additional concerns were proposed by Brick, MacIntyre, and Campbell (2014), including a need to reconsider how other associative cognitions are classified (e.g., movement technique). Furthermore, whether inward/outward dimensions most accurately account for the performance outcomes of attentional strategies is debated given the lack of difference between distractive categories, for example, in some stud- ies employing Stevinson and Biddle's framework (e.g., Connolly & Janelle, 2003; Stanley et al., 2007).

Extending Stevinson and Biddle's (1998) categorisation, Brick and colleagues developed a five-category model of attentional focus during endurance activity. Accordingly, associative thoughts were classified into three distinct categories; *active self-regulation* (e.g., pacing strategy, relaxing, optimising technique, cadence/ rhythm) *internal sensory monitoring* (i.e., bodily sensations: breathing, muscle fatigue, etc.), or *outward monitoring* (e.g., task-relevant environmental informa- tion: competitors, split-times, etc.). Brick et al. (2014) also incorporated attention restoration theory (ART; Kaplan, 1995) to recategorise distractive cognitions. Specifically, ART proposes that natural environments may restore cognitive function (e.g., attention) by capturing involuntary attention. This contrasts with the cognitively demanding, directed attention required in settings such as busy urban environments (Berman, Jonides, & Kaplan, 2008). Thus, Brick et al. (2014) proposed *active distraction* (e.g., task-irrelevant, attention-demanding puzzles or environment, conversing, etc.) and *involuntary distraction* (e.g., natural scenery, reflective thoughts, irrelevant daydreams) categories. To summarise the effects of each category, the following sections will provide an overview of the performance (e.g., pacing, movement economy), and perceptual (e.g., affective responses, effort perceptions) outcomes reported in the literature.

Active self-regulatory strategies

Self-regulation represents change to align thinking and behaviour with consciously desired standards or goals (Forgas, Baumeister, & Tice, 2009). As such, *active self-regulation* describes a focus whereby individuals engage cognitive strategies to control thoughts, feelings, and actions during endurance activity. The active self-regulation category also incorporates psychological skills such as goal setting, mental imagery, and self-talk (Brick, MacIntyre, & Campbell, 2015). Given that determinants of pacing strategy (Chapter 4) and psychological interventions focused on goal striving, self-talk, imagery, and mindfulness (Chapters 9, 10, 11, and 12) are discussed elsewhere in this book, this chapter will consider the effects of other active self-regulatory strategies (i.e., cadence/rhythm, optimising movement technique, and relaxing) frequently investigated in attentional focus research.

Focusing on increased cadence (i.e., step frequency) has been shown to improve pace in race walkers compared with a focus on increased stride length or distraction (Clingman & Hilliard, 1990). However, the absence of a control condition in this study limits the applicability of these findings. Similarly, a focus on optimising movement technique using task-relevant statements may improve performance (i.e., pace) beyond baseline or control conditions in swimming (Rushall & Shewchuk, 1989), skiing (Rushall, Hall, Roux, Sasseville, & Rushall, 1988), and running (Donohue, Barnhart, Covassin, Carpin, & Korb, 2001; Miller & Donohue, 2003) tasks, but may also reduce movement economy (Schücker et al., 2016a; see *Internal sensory monitoring* section, this chapter). Interestingly, improved performance whilst engaging active self-regulatory cognitions may not necessarily elevate effort perceptions (e.g., Connolly & Janelle, 2003; Couture et al., 1999; Rushall & Shewchuk, 1989). Given the central role of effort perceptions to regulate performance in models of self-paced endurance activity (e.g., Marcora, 2010; Tucker, 2009), it may be that one mechanism whereby active self-regulatory strategies improve endurance performance is via a reduction in perception of effort. These strategies may do so by competing with effort-related sensory cues (e.g., breathing rate, muscle fatigue), reducing perceptual awareness of these sensations and optimising performance as a result (e.g., Bigliassi, 2015; Brewer & Buman, 2006).

Research investigating the impact of relaxation on endurance performance has also received some attention. Relaxation has been associated with improvements in swimming performance (Spink & Longhurst, 1986), and a reduction in the oxygen cost of running (i.e., improved running economy; e.g., Hatfield et al., 1992).

Furthermore, multimodal psychological skill interventions integrating relaxation, goal setting, imagery, and self-talk have been effective to improve performance during 1600m running (Patrick & Hrycaiko, 1998), and simulated triathlon (Thelwell & Greenlees, 2001, 2003) events. Despite this, many unresolved issues remain regarding the performance effects of relaxation. Most studies have incorporated sophisticated techniques such as progressive muscular relaxation, centring, or biofeedback (e.g., Caird, McKenzie, & Sleivert, 1999; Hatfield et al., 1992). In reality, these techniques may be difficult to learn, and most endurance participants do not have access to the specialist psychological support required to cultivate these skills (e.g., McCormick, Meijen, & Marcora, 2018).

The use of alternative relaxation strategies raises additional concerns. Thelwell and Greenlees (2001, 2003) utilised breathing techniques to induce relaxation in triathletes during simulated competitive events. Despite its intuitive appeal, however, monitoring automated processes such as breathing may, in fact, *reduce* movement economy during endurance activity (Schücker, Knopf, Strauss, & Hagemann, 2014; Schücker, Schmeing, & Hagemann, 2016b; see *Internal sensory monitoring* section). Consequently, alternative strategies requiring minimal training or instruction may be more beneficial to induce a relaxed state and improve movement economy. Recently, Brick, McElhinney, and Metcalfe (2018), reported that smiling improved economy during vigorous intensity running by 2.78 per cent in comparison with frowning and by 2.23 per cent in comparison with a control (normal thoughts) condition. In contrast, conscious relaxation of the upper-body using a common coaching cue to imagine 'holding a crisp [potato chip] between each thumb and forefinger, tight enough to hold it without crushing it', or to hold the fingers in a 'relaxed clench position' (Murphy, 2009, p. 25) did not alter running economy in comparison with frowning and control conditions. Given anecdotal accounts of the use of smiling by elite athletes to relax during competitive performances (Caesar, 2017; Fitzgerald, 2014), the findings of Brick et al. (2018) suggest that periodic smiling may be efficacious to improve movement economy during endurance activity.

Internal sensory monitoring

In contrast to active self-regulatory cognitions, internal sensory monitoring alone may exacerbate effort perceptions and, consequently, decrease pace and performance (e.g., Johnson & Siegel, 1992; Pennebaker & Lightner, 1980; Stanley et al., 2007). Increased effort perceptions may result from an excessive focus on sensory cues and, consequently, increased awareness of effort-related sensations (e.g., Brewer & Buman, 2006; Brick, Campbell, Metcalfe, Mair, & MacIntyre, 2016). This does not imply that internal sensory monitoring is not important to optimise performance, however. Specifically, Brick et al. (2015) suggested that elite endurance runners attend *periodically* to informational aspects of sensory stimuli and use this information to adopt a situationally-appropriate focus of attention. This represents a bottom-up (i.e., stimulus-driven) system of attention allocation (e.g., Buschman & Miller, 2007; Corbetta & Shulman, 2002) whereby an athlete may periodically monitor bodily sensations (e.g., muscular tension) and engage an appropriate cognitive strategy based on the interpretation of this sensory information (e.g., relax to reduce muscular tension). Furthermore, attention may also be redirected in a top-down, goal-driven manner depending on circumstances and need (e.g., Buschman & Miller, 2007; Corbetta & Shulman, 2002). This may be to maintain pace in a competitive situation despite elevated sensations of effort, or to avoid the potentially deleterious effects of distraction on endurance performance (see *Distractive cognitions* section).

A more nuanced understanding of the effects of monitoring bodily sensations was proposed by Schücker and colleagues (Schücker et al., 2014). This approach differentiated between a focus on physical sensations (e.g., effort-related feelings) and on monitoring relatively automated processes (e.g., breathing, running movement). Applying the constrained action hypothesis (Wulf, McNevin, & Shea, 2001), Schücker and colleagues suggested that directing conscious attention to relatively automated processes disturbs automatic control. Consequently, monitoring breathing or running movement may reduce movement economy in comparison with a focus on physical sensations such as effort-related feelings (e.g., Schücker et al., 2014). As indicated previously, this may have implications for attentional strategies commonly used in endurance contexts, such as utilising breathing techniques to promote relaxation.

Conflicting findings regarding a focus on monitoring running movement (i.e., reduced running economy; Schücker et al., 2014, 2016b) and those of a faster pace when optimising running technique (Donohue et al., 2001; Miller & Donohue, 2003) are also noteworthy. The apparent contradictions may reflect differences in the instructions provided in each study, however. Specifically, whereas Schücker and colleagues directed participants' attention to *monitor* "the running movement and . . . to focus on their feet and forward movement of the legs" (Schücker et al., 2016b, p. 208), Donohue and colleagues provided a list of coach-derived *active self-regulatory* instructions to "do actions that would likely result in optimum performance" (Donohue et al., 2001, p. 24). These included cues to keep the hands open and relaxed, focus on technique, and "strike heels against the ground softly" (Miller & Donohue, 2003). The effects of these contrasting instructions on movement economy (i.e., oxygen consumption) and endurance performance (e.g., faster pace) warrants further research attention. More so, whereas some intrinsic biomechanical factors may be important to running economy (e.g., using a preferred, self-optimised, stride length or stride frequency, maintaining arm swing, low thigh antagonist-agonist muscular coactivation), current evidence advises caution when recommending a general economical technique for endurance runners (Moore, 2016).

Outward monitoring

Few studies on the topic of attentional focus have focused on the effects of outward monitoring (e.g., competitors, task-relevant environmental information such as the route, distance) on endurance performance. Those that have, however, have generally indicated positive effects. Williams et al. (2015), for example, noted that cyclists performed faster during a simulated competitive time-trial against a computerised avatar representing cyclists' fastest previous performance than when performing alone. Furthermore, attention was focused more externally when performing the trial, indicating a reduced focus on internal bodily sensations. Similarly, a focus on other task-relevant cues may also be beneficial to endurance performance. Whitehead et al. (2017) reported that attention to distance, speed, and heart rate information (displayed externally) increased over the course of a competitive cycling time-trial amongst club-level cyclists. The authors suggested this may be a deliberate strategy to suppress fatigue-related cognitions (i.e., reduce internal sensory monitoring), or as an input to inform pace-related decision-making (i.e., active self-regulation). Other research supports the informational value of outward monitoring to adopt contextually-appropriate self-regulatory strategies amongst experienced performers. Boya et al. (2017) suggested that expert cyclists focused primarily on speed data (as opposed to distance information by non-experts) to regulate performance during a simulated 16.1 km time-trial. Furthermore, Baker, Côté, and Deakin (2005) reported that under passing conditions (i.e., overtaking, or being overtaken), competitive triathletes reported an increased focus on their own performance (e.g., staying within their limits), or on strategic decisions (e.g., passing decisively). As such, outward monitoring of task-relevant environmental information may influence performance-related decision-making during endurance activities (e.g., Konings, Schoenmakers, Walker, & Hettinga, 2016). Differences between elite and non-elite athletes warrant further attention, however, given that expert endurance athletes may use different information sources (Boya et al., 2017) and cognitive strategies (e.g., active self-regulation versus distraction; Nietfeld, 2003) to regulate performance.

Distractive cognitions

Research on distractive cognitions suggests differential effects for active and involuntary distraction. The majority of studies imposing active distraction strategies such as calculations or word tasks (Fillingim, Roth, & Haley, 1989), conversing (Johnson & Siegel, 1992), or watching videos (Stanley et al., 2007) have typically reported a reduction in effort perception during endurance tasks. This may be at the expense of endurance *performance*, however, and distraction typically results in a reduced intensity when compared with active self-regulatory cognitions (e.g., Clingman & Hilliard, 1990; Connolly & Janelle, 2003).

In contrast, involuntary distraction (e.g., natural scenery) has been shown to increase enjoyment and reduce boredom (Pennebaker & Lightner, 1980), reduce arousal and frustration (Aspinall, Mavros, Coyne, & Roe, 2015), decrease rumination (Bratman, Hamilton, Hahn, Daily, & Gross, 2015), and elevate positive moods (Goode & Roth, 1993; LaCaille, Masters, & Heath, 2004) following endurance activity. Intriguingly, evidence also suggests that distractive cognitions may improve exercise adherence to a greater extent than focusing on bodily sensations alone. Martin et al. (1984), for example, revealed that participants instructed to talk to themselves and "attend to the environment and other pleasant distracting stimuli . . . rather than the ordinary discomforts of exercise" (p. 805) had greater attendance during a 12-week aerobic walking/jogging program (76.6 per cent attendance) than a group instructed to attend to bodily sensations (58.7 per cent attendance). In contrast, Welsh, Labbé, and Delaney (1991) noted no difference in exercise compliance between positive self-statement and distraction groups, and a no-instruction control group during a six-week group-based jogging programme. As such, the findings of Martin et al. (1984) suggest that distractive strategies may be more advantageous than internal sensory monitoring to improve endurance activity adherence. However, Martin and colleagues' (1984) study was limited by the absence of a no-intervention control, and positive self-statements (an active self-regulatory strategy) may be equally effective (Welsh et al., 1991). The paucity of research on the effects of attentional foci on exercise adherence, however, contrasts with the plethora of investigations with performance-related outcomes (e.g., pacing). As such, further exploration of the effects of cognitive strategies on longer-term endurance activity adherence is a worthy avenue for attentional focus researchers. This may be especially relevant given that perceptions of effort are considered an inverse correlate of physical activity (Bauman et al., 2012) and the relatively small positive impact of traditional behaviour change techniques on long-term physical activity behaviour (Samdal, Eide, Barth, Williams, & Meland, 2017).

Conclusions

In their recent review of attentional focus during endurance activity, Brick and colleagues highlighted a number of pressing issues in attentional focus research (Brick et al., 2014). These included a need to study elite endurance athletes, whether control over pacing (i.e., self-controlled versus externally-controlled) influenced performance outcomes, the importance of defining exercise duration by distance or time in experimental settings, and the impact of data collection techniques on attentional focus outcomes. Subsequent research has shed light on some of these concerns. Although the dearth of quantitative studies with elite athletes remains a concern, research on experienced and novice participants highlight the contrasting attentional strategies engaged by expert endurance performers (Boya et al., 2017). The importance of contextual factors was also investigated by Brick et al. (2016) who noted that external control over pacing (e.g., using a pacemaker) may facilitate performance when endurance athletes engage attentional strategies conducive to improved performance and movement economy (e.g., relaxing, optimising running action). Finally, Edwards and McCormick (2017) suggested that exercise intensity distorts time perception and, as such, may impact on pace-regulation during endurance activity. This finding may have additional implications for attentional focus outcomes, particularly considering that studies inconsistently define exercise duration by distance (Miller & Donohue, 2003) or time (Stanley et al., 2007) within the domain.

A multitude of data collection procedures continue to be used by attentional focus researchers. These include concurrent data collection using think aloud (Sampson, Simpson, Kamphoff, & Langlier, 2017; Whitehead et al., 2017), eye-tracking software (Boya et al., 2017), and retrospective interviews conducted immediately post-performance (e.g., Brick et al., 2016). Limitations are inherent in each methodological approach, however, such as possible disruption to natural thought development with some concurrent methodologies, and a tendency to forget with retrospective recall (see Brick et al., 2014). As discussed in Chapter 6, however, data collection may be optimised with greater use and harmonisation of innovative technologies (e.g., eye-tracking) with verbal data-collection methods (e.g., retrospective interviews) to provide additional insights into pace-related decision-making, cognitive strategy use, and cognitive control during endurance activity.

The present chapter also highlights other areas of academic and practical importance requiring attention. These include further exploration of the effectiveness of various relaxation strategies on movement economy and subsequent performance in ecologically valid settings. The apparently contradictory findings regarding a focus on monitoring running movement (Schücker et al., 2014, 2016b) and optimising running technique (e.g., Miller & Donohue, 2003) also demands further attention alongside an explication of mechanisms accounting for the effects of attentional foci on movement economy and other physiological measures (e.g., heart rate) (see Schücker et al., 2016a and Brick et al., 2018 for discussions). In addition, alternative attentional strategies to optimise movement economy should be considered. In this regard, a mindfulness-based approach (see also Chapter 12) might be promising. Mindfulness has been linked to flow experience (e.g., Aherne, Moran, & Lonsdale, 2011) and has been discussed within the framework of attentional focus in endurance activities (Salmon et al., 2010). As a potentially effective attentional strategy, mindfulness might also affect movement economy as a physiological outcome. Finally, investigation of the effects of cognitive strategies on longer-term endurance activity adherence may prove a promising line of enquiry. It may be that strategies typically investigated only in terms of endurance performance outcomes may also have a positive impact on sustained physical activity behaviour.

References

Aherne, C., Moran, A. & Lonsdale, C. (2011). The effect of mindfulness training on athletes´ flow. An initial investigation. *The Sport Psychologist, 25*, 177–189. https://doi.org/10.1123/tsp.25.2.177.

American Psychiatric Association. (2013). *Diagnostic and statistical manual of mental disorders* (5th ed.). Washington, DC: American Psychiatric Publishing.

Aspinall, P., Mavros, P., Coyne, R., & Roe, J. (2015). The urban brain: Analysing outdoor physical activity with mobile EEG. *British Journal of Sports Medicine, 49*, 272–276. http://dx.doi.org/10.1136/bjsports-2012-091877.

Baker, J., Côté, J., & Deakin, J. (2005). Cognitive characteristics of expert, middle of the pack, and back of the pack ultra-endurance triathletes. *Psychology of Sport and Exercise, 6,* 551–558. http://dx.doi.org/10.1016/j.psychsport.2004.04.005.

Bauman, A., Reis, R., Sallis, J., Wells, J., Loos, R., & Martin, B. (2012). Correlates of physical activity: why are some people physically active and others not? *The Lancet, 380,* 258–271. http://dx.doi.org/10.1016/S0140-6736(12)60735-1.

Berman, M. G., Jonides, J., & Kaplan, S. (2008). The cognitive benefits of interacting with nature. *Psychological Science, 19,* 1207–1212. http://dx.doi.org/10.1111/j.1467-9280.2008.02225.x.

Bigliassi, M. (2015). Corollary discharges and fatigue-related symptoms: The role of attentional focus. *Frontiers in Psychology, 6,* 1002. http://dx.doi.org/10.3389/fpsyg.2015.01002.

Boya, M., Foulsham, T., Hettinga, F., Parry, D., Williams, E., Jones, H., . . . Micklewright, D. (2017). Information acquisition differences between experienced and novice time trial cyclists. *Medicine and Science in Sport and Exercise,* http://dx.doi.org/10.1249/MSS.0000000000001304.

Bratman, G. N., Hamilton, J. P., Hahn, K. S., Daily, G. C., & Gross, J. J. (2015). Nature experience reduces rumination and subgenual prefrontal cortex activation. *PNAS, 112,* 8567–8572. http://dx.doi.org/10.1073/pnas.1510459112.

Brewer, B. W., & Buman, M. P. (2006). Attentional focus and endurance performance: Review and theoretical integration. *Kinesiologica Slovenica, 12,* 82–97.

Brick, N. E., Campbell, M. J., Metcalfe, R. S., Mair, J. L., & MacIntyre, T. E. (2016). Altering pace control and pace regulation: Attentional focus effects during running. *Medicine and Science in Sports and Exercise, 48,* 879–886. http://dx.doi.org/10.1249/MSS.0000000000000843.

Brick, N., MacIntyre, T., & Campbell, M. (2014). Attentional focus in endurance activity: New paradigms and future directions. *International Review of Sport and Exercise Psychology, 7,* 106–134. http://dx.doi.org/10.1080/1750984X.2014.885554.

Brick, N., MacIntyre, T., & Campbell, M. (2015). Metacognitive processes in the self-regulation of performance in elite endurance runners. *Psychology of Sport and Exercise, 19,* 1–9. http://dx.doi.org/10.1016/j.psychsport.2015.02.003.

Brick, N. E., McElhinney, M., J., & Metcalfe, R. S. (2018). The effects of facial expression and relaxation cues on movement economy, physiological, and perceptual responses during running. *Psychology of Sport and Exercise, 34,* 20–28. http://dx.doi.org/10.1016/j.psychsport.2017.09.009.

Buschman, T. J., & Miller, E. K. (2007). Top-down versus bottom-up control of attention in the prefrontal and posterior parietal cortices, *Science, 315,* 1860–1862. http://dx.doi.org/10.1126/science.1138071.

Caesar, E. (2017). The epic untold story of Nike's (almost) perfect marathon. www.wired.com/story/nike-breaking2-marathon-eliud-kipchoge/ (accessed: 23 August 2017).

Caird, S. J., McKenzie, A. D., & Sleivert, G. G. (1999). Biofeedback and relaxation techniques improve running economy in sub-elite long-distance runners. *Medicine and Science in Sports and Exercise, 31,* 717–722. http://dx.doi.org/10.1097/00005768-199905000-00015.

Clingman, J. M., & Hilliard, D. V. (1990). Race walkers quicken their pace by tuning in, not stepping out. *The Sport Psychologist, 4,* 23–32.

Connolly, C. T., & Janelle, C. M. (2003). Attentional strategies in rowing: Performance, perceived exertion, and gender considerations. *Journal of Applied Sport Psychology, 15,* 195–212. http://dx.doi.org/10.1080/10413200390213362.

Corbetta, M., & Shulman, G. L. (2002). Control of goal-directed and stimulus-driven attention in the brain. *Nature Reviews Neuroscience, 3(3),* 201–215. http://dx.doi.org/10.1038/nrn755.

Couture, R. T., Jerome, W., & Tihanyi, J. (1999). Can associative and dissociative strategies affect the swimming performance of recreational swimmers? *The Sport Psychologist*, *13*, 334–343.

Donohue, B., Barnhart, R., Covassin, T., Carpin, K., & Korb, E. (2001). The development and initial evaluation of two promising mental preparatory methods in a sample of female cross-country runners. *Journal of Sport Behavior*, *24*, 19–30.

Edwards, A. M., & McCormick, A. (2017). Time perception, pacing and exercise intensity: maximal exercise distorts the perception of time. *Physiology and Behavior*, *180*, 98–102. http://dx.doi.org/10.1016/j.physbeh.2017.08.009.

Fillingim, R. B., Roth, D. L., & Haley, W. E. (1989). The effects of distraction on the perception of exercise-induced symptoms. *Journal of Psychosomatic Research*, *33*, 241–248. http://dx.doi.org/10.1016/0022-3999(89)90052-4.

Fitzgerald, M. (2014). Faces of pain: smile to run better. http://running.competitor.com/2014/04/training/faces-of-pain-smile-to-run-better_14623 (accessed: 19 August 2017).

Forgas, J. P., Baumeister, R. F., & Tice, D. M. (2009). Psychology of self-regulation: an introductory review. In J. P. Forgas, R. F. Baumeister, and D. M. Tice (Eds.), *Psychology of self-regulation: Cognitive, affective, and motivational processes* (pp. 1–17). New York: Psychology Press.

Goode, K. T., & Roth, D. L. (1993). Factor analysis of cognitions during running: Association with mood change. *Journal of Sport and Exercise Psychology*, *15*, 375–389.

Hatfield, B. D., Spalding, T. W., Mahon, A. D., Slater, B. A., Brody, E. B., & Vaccaro, P. (1992). The effect of psychological strategies upon cardiorespiratory and muscular activity during treadmill running. *Medicine and Science in Sports and Exercise*, *24*, 218–225. http://dx.doi.org/10.1249/00005768-199202000-00010.

Johnson, J. H., & Siegel, D. S. (1992). Effects of association and dissociation on effort perception. *Journal of Sport Behavior*, *15*, 119–129.

Kaplan, S. (1995). The restorative benefits of nature: Toward an integrative framework. *Journal of Environmental Psychology*, *15*, 169–182. http://dx.doi.org/10.1016/0272-4944(95)90001-2.

Konings, M. J., Schoenmakers, P. P., Walker, A. J., & Hettinga, F. J. (2016). The behavior of an opponent alters pacing decisions in 4-km cycling time trials. *Physiology and Behavior*, *158*, 1–5. http://dx.doi.org/10.1016/j.physbeh.2016.02.023.

Laash, C. (1994–1995). Cognitive strategies and long-distance running. *Imagination, Cognition and Personality*, *14*, 317–332. http://dx.doi.org/10.2190/UKG1-7W12-66A5-7AQ7.

LaCaille, R. A., Masters, K. S., & Heath, E. M. (2004). Effects of cognitive strategy and exercise setting on running performance, perceived exertion, affect, and satisfaction. *Psychology of Sport and Exercise*, *5*, 461–476. http://dx.doi.org/10.1016/S1469-0292(03)00039-6.

Marcora, S. (2010). Counterpoint: afferent feedback from fatigued locomotor muscles is not an important determinant of endurance exercise performance. *Journal of Applied Physiology*, *108*, 454–456. http://dx.doi.org/10.1152/japplphysiol.00976.2009a108/2/454.

Martin, J. E., Dubbert, P. M., Katell, A. D., Thompson, J. K., Raczynski, J. R., Lake, M., . . . Cohen, R. E. (1984). Behavioral control of exercise in sedentary adults: Studies 1 through 6. *Journal of Consulting and Clinical Psychology*, *52*, 795–811. http://dx.doi.org/10.1037/0022-006X.52.5.795.

Masters, K. S., & Ogles, B. M. (1998). Associative and dissociative cognitive strategies in exercise and running: 20 years later, what do we know? *The Sport Psychologist*, *12*(3), 253–270.

McCormick, A., Meijen, C., & Marcora, S. M. (2018). Psychological demands experienced by recreational endurance athletes. *International Journal of Sport and Exercise Psychology*, *16*(4), 415–430.

Miller, A., & Donohue, B. (2003). The development and controlled evaluation of athletic mental preparation strategies in high school distance runners. *Journal of Applied Sport Psychology, 15*, 321–334. http://dx.doi.org/10.1080/10413200390238004.

Moore, I. S. (2016). Is there an economical running technique? A review of modifiable biomechanical factors affecting running economy. *Sports Medicine, 46*, 793–807. http://dx.doi.org/10.1007/s40279-016-0474-4.

Morgan, W. P., & Pollock, M. L. (1977). Psychologic characterization of the elite distance runner. *Annals of the New York Academy of Sciences, 301*, 382–403. http://dx.doi.org/10.1111/j.1749-6632.1977.tb38215.x.

Murphy, S. (2009). *Marathon and half marathon: from start to finish*. London: A & C Black.

Nideffer, R. M. (1981). *The ethics and practice of applied sport psychology*. New York, NY. Mouvement Publications.

Nietfeld, J. L. (2003). An examination of metacognitive strategy use and monitoring skills by competitive middle distance runners. *Journal of Applied Sport Psychology, 15*, 307–320. http://dx.doi.org/10.1080/10413200390237942.

Patrick, T. D., & Hrycaiko, D. W. (1998). Effects of a mental training package on an endurance performance. *The Sport Psychologist, 12*, 283–299.

Pennebaker, J. A., & Lightner, J. M. (1980). Competition of internal and external information in an exercise setting. *Journal of Personality and Social Psychology, 39*, 165–174. http://dx.doi.org/10.1037/0022-3514.39.1.165.

Radcliffe, P. (2011). *How to run: From fun runs to marathons and everything in between*. London: Simon & Schuster.

Rushall, B. S., & Shewchuk, M. L. (1989). Effects of thought content instructions on swimming performance. *Journal of Sports Medicine and Physical Fitness, 29*, 326–334.

Rushall, B. S., Hall, M., Roux, L., Sasseville, J., & Rushall, A. C. (1988). Effects of three types of thought content instructions on skiing performance. *The Sport Psychologist, 2*, 283–297.

Salmon, P., Hanneman, S., & Harwood, B. (2010). Associative / dissociative cognitive strategies in sustained physical activity: Literature review and proposal for a mindfulness-based conceptual model. *The Sport Psychologist, 24*, 127–156.

Samdal, G. B., Eide, G. E., Barth, T., Williams, G., & Meland, E. (2017). Effective behaviour change techniques for physical activity and healthy eating in overweight and obese adults; systematic review and meta-regression analyses. *International Journal of Behavioural Nutrition and Physical Activity, 14*, 1–14. http://dx.doi.org/10.1186/s12966-017-0494-y.

Sampson, A., Simpson, D., Kamphoff, C., & Langlier, A. (2017). Think aloud: An examination of distance runners' thought processes. *International Journal of Sport and Exercise Psychology, 15*, 176–189. http://dx.doi.org/10.1080/1612197X.2015.1069877.

Schomer, H. H. (1986). Mental strategies and the perception of effort of marathon runners. *International Journal of Sport Psychology, 17*, 41–59.

Schücker, L., Knopf, C., Strauss, B., & Hagemann, N. (2014). An internal focus of attention is not always as bad as its reputation: How specific aspects of internally focused attention do not hinder running efficiency. *Journal of Sport and Exercise Psychology, 36*, 223–243. http://dx.doi.org/10.1123/jsep.2013-0200.

Schücker, L., Fleddermann, M., de Lussanet, M., Elischer, J., Böhmer, C., & Zentgraf, K. (2016a). Focusing attention on circular pedaling reduces movement economy in cycling. *Psychology of Sport and Exercise, 27*, 9–17. http://dx.doi.org/10.1016/j.psychsport.2016.07.002

Schücker, L., Schmeing, L., & Hagemann, N. (2016b). "Look around while running!" Attentional focus effects in inexperienced runners. *Psychology of Sport and Exercise, 27*, 205–212. http://dx.doi.org/10.1016/j.psychsport.2016.08.013.

Schumacher, J. M., Becker, A. J., & Wiersma, L. D. (2016). Forging ahead: An examination of the experiences and coping mechanisms of channel swimmers. *The Sport Psychologist, 30*, 327–338. http://dx.doi.org/10.1123/tsp.2015-0137.

Spink, K. S., & Longhurst, K. (1986). Cognitive strategies and swimming performance: An exploratory study. *Australian Journal of Science and Medicine in Sport, 18*, 9–13.

Stanley, C., Pargman, D., & Tenenbaum, G. (2007). The effect of attentional coping strategies on perceived exertion in a cycling task. *Journal of Applied Sport Psychology, 19*, 352–363. http://dx.doi.org/10.1080/10413200701345403.

Stevinson, C. D., & Biddle, S. J. H. (1998). Cognitive orientations in marathon running and 'hitting the wall'. *British Journal of Sports Medicine, 32*, 229–235. http://dx.doi.org/10.1136/bjsm.32.3.229.

Summers, J. J., Sargent, G. I., Levey, A. J., & Murray, K. D. (1982). Middle-aged, non-elite marathon runners: A profile. *Perceptual and Motor Skills, 54*, 963–969. http://dx.doi.org/10.2466/pms.1982.54.3.963.

Tenenbaum, G., & Connolly, C. T. (2008). Attention allocation under varied workload and effort perception in rowers. *Psychology of Sport and Exercise, 9*, 704–717. http://dx.doi.org/10.1016/j.psychsport.2007.09.002

Thelwell, R. C., & Greenlees, I. A. (2001). The effects of a mental skills training package on gymnasium triathlon performance. *The Sport Psychologist, 5*, 127–141.

Thelwell, R. C., & Greenlees, I. A. (2003). Developing competitive endurance performance using mental skills training. *The Sport Psychologist, 17*, 318–337.

Tucker, R. (2009). The anticipatory regulation of performance: The physiological basis for pacing strategies and the development of a perception-based model for exercise performance. *British Journal of Sports Medicine, 43*, 392–400. http://dx.doi.org/10.1136/bjsm.2008.050799.

Welsh, M. C., Labbé, E., E., Delaney, D. (1991). Cognitive strategies and personality variables in adherence to exercise. *Psychological Reports, 68*, 1327–1335. http://dx.doi.org/10.2466/pr0.1991.68.3c.1327.

Whitehead, A. E., Jones, H. S., Williams, E. L., Dowling, C., Morely, D., Taylor, J. A., & Polman, R. C. (2017). Changes in cognition over a 16.1 km cycling time trial using Think Aloud protocol: Preliminary evidence. *International Journal of Sport and Exercise Psychology*, http://dx.doi.org/10.1080/1612197X.2017.1292302.

Williams, E. L., Jones, H. S., Sparks, A., Marchant, D. C., Midgley, A. W., & McNaughton, L. R. (2015). Competitor presence reduces internal attentional focus and improves 16.1 km cycling time trial performance. *Journal of Science and Medicine in Sport, 18*, 486–491. http://dx.doi.org/10.1016/j.jsams.2014.07.003.

Wulf, G., McNevin, N. H., & Shea, C. H. (2001). The automaticity of complex motor skill learning as a function of attentional focus. *Quarterly Journal of Experimental Psychology, 54*, 1143–1154.

9

GOAL STRIVING AND ENDURANCE PERFORMANCE

Wanja Wolff, Maik Bieleke, and Julia Schüler

Introduction

"I intend to run a sub 2:30 marathon!", "I want to win this competition!", or "I won't let my opponents lure me into an exhausting pace!" These intentions can be considered to reflect goals, and setting goals like these can form the basis for successful endurance performance. This is in line with meta-analytic evidence showing a positive correlation between intentions and subsequent behavior ($r = 0.53$; Sheeran, 2002) and a medium effect of goal setting on endurance performance ($\Delta = 0.34$; McCormick, Meijen, & Marcora, 2015). Yet, these numbers also reflect an experience that every endurance athlete – including the three authors – is probably familiar with: a goal set is not necessarily a goal met.

Gaps between intentions and behaviors are a key research topic in psychology (Sheeran & Webb, 2016). A well-known example is New Year's resolutions: whereas an estimated 40 per cent of Americans make resolutions, less than 10 per cent achieve them (Statistic Brain, 2017). In the domain of physical exercise, only one in two people successfully act upon their intentions (Rhodes & de Bruijn, 2013). To understand this notorious intention-behaviour gap, it is not sufficient to focus on *goal setting* alone, one also has to account for the process of *goal striving* (i.e., translating an intention into goal-directed behaviour; Heckhausen & Gollwitzer, 1987; Kuhl, 1983). People might face a variety of difficulties when pursuing their goals, including failures to initiate goal-directed behaviors, to hedge against internal and external interferences, and to bring goal pursuit to a successful close (Gollwitzer & Oettingen, 2016; Sheeran & Webb, 2016). Overcoming these difficulties requires an effective self-regulation of emotions, thoughts, and actions (Hagger et al., 2016).

Relative to goal setting, the process of goal striving has received little attention from endurance researchers and practitioners alike. This is unfortunate because it creates blind spots in our knowledge about endurance performance. In the present chapter, we discuss the relevance of goal striving for endurance performance, along with common difficulties. Moreover, we introduce the self-regulation strategy of forming implementation intentions (Gollwitzer, 1999, 2014) as a promising tool for dealing effectively with the difficulties of goal striving.

Goal striving and its difficulties

A) Getting started

Failures to initiate goal-directed behaviors are a first obstacle during endurance performance. People struggle with getting started for various reasons: it can be difficult to remember or recognise situations where goal-directed actions can be taken and these actions might be unpleasant or arduous. For example, in road cycling it is important to be well positioned at key moments of a race. Wind, crashes, and features of the course can all split the peloton and many races have been lost because of poor positioning at crucial moments. In 2016, multiple Tour de France champion Chris Froome seemingly lost the Vuelta a España[1] in the 15th stage, to the town of Formigal. Froome's Team Sky did not expect major attacks to happen right at the beginning of the stage. Two favorites in the race, contrary to the expectations of Team Sky, did attack very early and caught Chris Froome and his team by surprise. Here is what Ian Boswell, one of Froome's teammates, had to say about the situation (Hood, 2016):

> We got over that first climb, before you knew it, there was a group with not only just Contador but also with Quintana. When we got over that hill into the flat, we had three riders in the second group, and five riders in the third group. We were chasing full gas in the third group, and the gap just kept going up . . . it just happened so quick. We had just done 14 days of racing, . . . we were toe to toe with Quintana and Froome, and then just 8 km into the race, everything changed. . . . If you let your guard down 10 minutes into the race, there are 15 riders up the road. As teammates, we should have been there. Froome maybe should have followed Quintana. As [a] group, maybe we should have come together. You can't put your finger on it; it is not just one particular incident. It was a perfect storm.

Boswell's account of the event vividly illustrates how missing a single opportunity to act can lead to the loss of a 3-week bike race. Being able to initiate goal-directed behaviours in critical moments during a competition requires that one remembers to act, is ready to seize opportunities as they emerge, and has prepared oneself to act in a goal-directed manner (Sheeran & Webb, 2016). As Team Sky's example illustrates, even these seemingly easy tasks can get overwhelming during an athletic competition, where a host of situational, psychological, and physiological stresses are present simultaneously.

B) Staying on track

Once goal-directed behaviour has been successfully initiated, one has to stay on track. This can be challenging for various reasons. By definition, endurance activities require prolonged effort and athletes can experience various kinds of interferences that might derail successful goal pursuit (McCormick, Meijen, & Marcora, 2018). Some interferences come from a macro level, such as difficulties in investing the time needed for training or struggling to find a training regimen that works. Other interferences act more as micro stressors. For example, before an important event athletes may worry about things going wrong. During competition or training, they may worry about optimising their pacing strategy and staying focused, all while having to deal with the aversive sensations that accompany endurance exercises (McCormick et al., 2018). Sometimes such interferences can be external, as demonstrated by the case of 400-metre Olympic champion Shaunae Miller-Uibo during the 2017 athletic world championships. Miller-Uibo was well on track to win the 400-metre^2 gold medal when she suddenly slowed in the closing meters of the race and eventually even missed out on a medal. After the competition, she reasoned as follows (Kelner, 2017): "I had the race under control and I looked up at the screen and misplaced my foot and completely lost balance". Evidently, even the tiniest interferences from the environment can put an athlete literally off track, and even elite level athletes are not immune to such interferences.

Athletes have to deal with a variety of internal influences as well, such as exercise sensations (e.g., sustaining high levels of pain and exertion), emotions (e.g., not getting frustrated by a head wind in a time trial), intrusive thoughts (e.g., defying worries about the appropriateness of the pacing strategy), or impulses (e.g., keeping the pace despite the urge to slow down). These influences can interfere, for instance, with how effectively athletes monitor their goal progress during the race and adjust to discrepancies. In the 2008 Dubai Marathon, Haile Gebrselassie would have earned one million dollars had he beaten the world record. However, he failed to stick to his pacing strategy and started too fast (first half in 61:27 minutes), and subsequently could not maintain his initial pace (Eder, 2008): "I wanted to do 62 minutes for halfway, and I paid the price in the final stages. You know, everything needs to be perfect, and today, I missed one little thing." As this example suggests, whether or not athletes follow through with a pacing strategy does not only depend on their physiological capacities and the characteristics of the race (Abbiss & Laursen, 2008) but also on subtle psychological and contextual influences.

The regulation of interferences during endurance performance is aggravated by the substantial demands that accompany the activity itself (e.g., Grego et al., 2005; McCormick et al., 2018). These favour automatic over deliberate processes because they require less time, conscious awareness, and cognitive resources (e.g., Brand, Wolff, & Baumgarten, 2015; Evans & Stanovich, 2013). For example, merely thinking about running at high intensity can automatically elicit aversive sensations, although there might be good reasons to evaluate running fast positively (e.g., because one might win a gold medal by doing so). Such automatic processes are generally difficult to control, and this is especially true during an exhausting endurance activity. A similar reasoning pertains to unwanted habits, which can be easily activated by encountering certain situational features (e.g., Snow, 2006) and exert particular influence on behavior under stressful conditions (Schwabe & Wolf, 2009). As an example, consider the 15th stage of the 1998 Tour de France.[3] This stage took place under atrocious conditions and race leader Jan Ullrich lost almost nine minutes on the eventual winner Marco Pantani, reversing what had been a three minutes lead to a six minutes deficit. Crucially, this spectacular loss was not only caused by the rain and the cold; Ullrich simply did not eat in the last part of the stage (Schuele, 2003). Refueling during competition is often a deliberate, preparatory act (i.e., one eats and drinks long before one feels hungry and thirsty). Thus, athletes have to actively decide to refuel even though they might not feel like eating or drinking at the moment (i.e., the automatic habitual response would be not to eat and drink).

C) Bringing goal pursuit to a successful close

Finally, successful endurance performance requires bringing goal pursuit to a successful close. One implication is that athletes should not ease off before having reached their goals. Going back to the case of Miller-Uibo discussed above, one might also argue that the loss of concentration that caused her to lose the 400-metre race reflects a premature easing off before reaching the finish line. This reasoning is supported by research showing that people tend to reduce their efforts when they feel sure about attaining their goal (Louro, Pieters, & Zeelenberg, 2007). Whereas this finding is counter-intuitive, people generally interpret positive feedback on their rate of goal attainment (e.g., feeling good) as a signal that they can attend to something else (Carver, 2003). Recall that in the final moments Miller-Uibo felt that she had the race under control and victory was very likely.

However, successfully closing goal pursuit at times also requires disengaging from futile goal striving (Wrosch, Scheier, Carver, & Schulz, 2003). This can help athletes to save resources (e.g., for the following stages of a competition) and to stay healthy (e.g., avoiding injuries from overextension). The history of endurance sports is full of examples in which athletes failed to disengage, and even died from overextension. Probably the most famous example is the legend of Pheidippides, a messenger who ran about 42 km from the city of Marathon to Athens to deliver news about the victorious battle against the Persians (Pheidippides, n.d.). After delivering the news he collapsed and died.

Thus, to manage the last challenge of goal striving, one has to stay focused until the end while at the same time being able to recognise when further goal striving would be detrimental (Sheeran & Webb, 2016). In addition, one has to make the decision to disengage from a futile goal and then effectively act on this decision (i.e., to stop). The example above underlines that such disengagement is easier said than done when a lot is on the line.

Implementation intentions

So far we have painted a gloomy picture of goal striving in endurance activities. However, our review also shows that athletes can facilitate their goal attainment in various ways: by swiftly attending and responding to emerging opportunities and obstacles, using tailored pacing strategies and shielding them from external and internal interferences, developing favourable automatic evaluations of task demands, monitoring goal progress, and disengaging from futile goals, and so on. In what follows, we introduce research on a simple but highly effective strategy that might help athletes to implement these goal-directed behaviours. It involves mentally linking an opportunity to act or mentally linking an obstacle for goal attainment to a goal-directed behavior in an if-then format: "If I encounter opportunity/obstacle O, then I will perform goal-directed behaviour B!" Making such if-then plans is a self-regulation strategy which is commonly referred to as forming *implementation intentions* (Gollwitzer, 1999) and contrasted from merely setting goals that specify a desired outcome or behavior ("I want to reach outcome O / show behaviour B!"; Triandis, 1977).

Plenty of research has focused on *whether* implementation intentions facilitate goal attainment beyond goal setting and findings of this research generally provide an affirmative answer across several domains (e.g., health, academic, and interpersonal; Gollwitzer, 2014; Gollwitzer & Sheeran, 2006). Other research has focused on *how* implementation intentions achieve these beneficial effects. In a nutshell, implementation intentions automate both the detection of critical situations (opportunities or obstacles) and the initiation of planned behaviors (Webb & Sheeran, 2007), basically putting goal-directed behaviour on autopilot. It is therefore conceivable that athletes using implementation intentions to 'seize the moment' or to overcome obstacles during endurance performance are more likely to attain their goals.

Using implementation intentions to deal with the difficulties of goal striving

When people specify a critical situation (opportunity or obstacle) in the if-part of an implementation intention, this situation becomes mentally activated and receives attentional and perceptual priority (Achtziger, Bayer, & Gollwitzer, 2012; Janczyk, Dambacher, Bieleke, & Gollwitzer, 2015). This makes the situation easy to detect and recognize (Aarts, Dijksterhuis, & Midden, 1999), increasing the probability that planned goal-directed behaviours are initiated in the right place and at the right time. For instance, insufficient rehydration during endurance performance is widespread because many athletes fail to use opportunities to drink, with adverse effects on performance and health (Casa et al., 2000). As we have argued above, the interference of automatic drinking habits might derail goal attainment because it forces people to give up on their goals rather than to stay on track. However, this problem can be tackled with implementation intentions: in one study (Hagger & Montasem, 2009), planning to drink carbohydrate-electrolyte drinks during exercise boosted consumption by more than 50 per cent compared to a control group and significantly improved physiological markers of rehydration. This suggests that athletes could use implementation intentions to replace their drinking habits by recommended rehydration schedules during an endurance performance.

Another feature of implementation intentions is the strong associative link that is forged between the critical situation and the goal-directed behaviour specified in the then-part. This enables behaviour to be initiated immediately, efficiently, and independent of further conscious intent (e.g., Bayer, Achtziger, Gollwitzer, & Moskowitz, 2009; Brandstätter, Lengfelder, & Gollwitzer, 2001; Gollwitzer & Brandstätter, 1997; Wieber & Sassenberg, 2006). These features of automaticity are crucial for successful goal striving. First, implementation intentions are rather independent from resources like time to think or cognitive capacity, which are usually scarce during endurance performance. Second, automating goal directed behaviour puts it on a par with other, potentially unwanted automatic processes such as bad habits.

Successful endurance performance also hinges on warding off both external (e.g., spectators, weather conditions, faulty equipment) and internal (e.g., negative emotions, disruptive thoughts) interferences, which can be accomplished with implementation intentions. First, planning how to ignore involuntarily distractions results in better task performance than merely setting goals to do so (Gollwitzer & Schaal, 1998), which might help athletes to better keep up their concentration (Moran, 1996). Second, implementation intentions can be used to regulate a variety of emotional influences on behaviour (meta-analysis by Webb et al., 2012). For example, professional tennis players who formed implementation intentions to deal with intrusive thoughts, feelings, and physiological states during a critical match enhanced their performance and physical fitness compared to other players (Achtziger, Gollwitzer, & Sheeran, 2008).

Finally, implementation intentions have been shown to facilitate a successful closing of goal pursuit. Behaviours specified in implementation intentions are performed more persistently in the face of difficulties (Freydefont, Gollwitzer, & Oettingen, 2016; Legrand, Bieleke, Gollwitzer, & Mignon, 2017). This effect is commonly associated with the automaticity afforded to behaviors specified in an implementation intention. Yet, implementation intentions are effective only when people are committed to an active superordinate goal (Sheeran, Webb, & Gollwitzer, 2005). For example, when a runner is not committed to the goal of achieving a personal best, implementation intentions tailored to this goal are unlikely to be effective. People also flexibly disengage from implementation intentions when their goals change or when performing the planned behaviour becomes excessively costly (Legrand et al., 2017). This 'flexible tenacity' is important for endurance performance because it might allow athletes to push their limits while avoiding injuries or mistakes resulting from overextension. Implementation intention might also be directly used to avoid overexertion; for instance, by making plans to adapt to changing circumstances or requirements (Doerflinger, Martiny-Huenger, & Gollwitzer, 2017; Wieber, Thürmer, & Gollwitzer, 2015).

Implementation intentions and endurance performance

Taken together, research on implementation intentions suggests they can serve as a highly promising self-regulation tool for dealing with various difficulties with goal striving in endurance performance. They are simple to use (see Figure 9.1) and likely allow athletes to attain their goals even under stressful and demanding circumstances. It therefore comes as no surprise that scientists (e.g., Achtziger et al., 2008; Brick, MacIntyre, & Campbell, 2016; McCormick et al., 2018), athletic institutions (e.g., Calder, 2009), and the popular press (e.g., Gregoire, 2016) alike suggest forming implementation intentions as a strategy for improving endurance performance. However, whereas implementation intentions are known to facilitate engagement in physical activity behaviour (meta-analysis by Bélanger-Gravel, Godin, & Amireault, 2013), surprisingly few studies have tested their effectiveness in the context of a specific endurance activity.

One study (Thürmer, Wieber, & Gollwitzer, 2017) tested whether implementation intentions facilitate performance when groups of three people were required to jointly hold a medicine ball for as long as possible. Groups with the implementation intention "And if our muscles hurt, then we will ignore the pain and tell ourselves: We can do it!" performed longer than groups with a control instruction ("We will ignore our muscle pain and tell ourselves: We can do it!"). Follow-up analyses suggest an increase in communicative interactions among implementation intention group members as a reason underlying this finding. Another study did not find beneficial effects of implementation intentions in an individual static muscular endurance task (Bieleke & Wolff, 2017). Participants who made plans to downregulate their exhaustion during the task ("If the task becomes too strenuous for me, then I ignore the strain and tell myself: Keep going!") failed to outperform participants in a control condition with no such plan. Interestingly, those in the

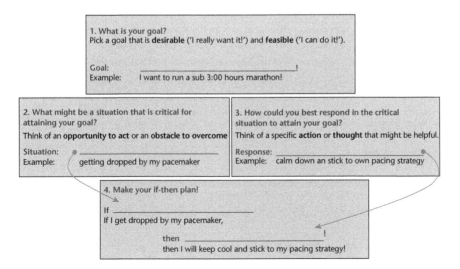

FIGURE 9.1 The steps involved in forming an implementation intention

implementation intention condition became exhausted even more rapidly than those in the control condition but were at the same time willing to reach higher levels of exhaustion. A similar pattern emerged for perceived pain. These results suggest that forming implementation intentions can affect perceived exertion and pain during endurance tasks without necessarily improving performance.

Additional data from our lab complements the findings of Bieleke and Wolff (2017) with data obtained with functional near-infrared spectroscopy (Wolff et al., 2018). Participants this time planned to downregulate perceived pain ("If my arms hurt, then I will ignore the pain and tell myself: Keep going!") before performing the task. Compared to a control condition, this plan did not lead to differences in perceived exhaustion or pain in the implementation intention compared to a control condition; moreover, we again did not observe a difference between conditions regarding endurance performance. Interestingly, the activation of the lateral prefrontal cortex – a brain region associated with effortful control (e.g., Cohen & Lieberman, 2010) – was significantly lower in the implementation intention condition. This is in line with prior neuroimaging research (Gilbert, Gollwitzer, Cohen, Burgess, & Oettingen, 2009) and suggests that implementation intentions might reduce the perceived effort during endurance exercises.

To summarise, to date it is not clear whether implementation intentions can reliably enhance endurance performance during a specific physical activity. Whereas it seems that task relevant processes can indeed be affected (e.g., perceived exertion), additional research has to investigate how implementation intentions must be formed to facilitate performance during a specific endurance activity. This is especially important because the effects of implementation intentions may depend quite strongly on the selected critical situations and behaviours – for instance, when dealing with negative sensations (Schweiger Gallo, McCulloch, & Gollwitzer, 2012). Also, research on implementation intentions has revealed the conditions under which implementations intentions are more, or less, effective. For instance, athletes might find it intuitive to make several plans to attain their goals or to make backup plans in case one plan cannot be acted on – both of which can be detrimental to the effectiveness of implementation intentions (Verhoeven, Adriaanse, de Ridder, de Vet, & Fennis, 2013; Vinkers, Adriaanse, Kroese, & de Ridder, 2015). However, whether such results can be directly transferred to endurance performance is an open question. For instance, we are not aware of any study that tested the effect of implementation intentions on performance in a whole body endurance activity.

Conclusions

Goal setting is an important first step for successful endurance performance, but athletes also have to effectively strive for their goals. During goal striving, athletes are confronted with multiple difficulties: getting started (e.g., recognize and respond to race-defining attacks), staying on track (e.g., not losing concentration during the race), and successfully closing goal pursuit (e.g., pulling out of a race when continuation would be hazardous). Each of these challenges is accompanied by specific psychological demands and successful goal attainment requires that athletes deal effectively with each of them. One promising psychological strategy to facilitate this process of goal striving is to form implementation intentions (i.e., if-then plans).

Implementation intentions facilitate goal striving by allowing people to efficiently attend and respond to critical opportunities and obstacles, thereby enhancing goal attainment across a variety of domains. For instance, they should be helpful for initiating and adhering to a training regimen. Yet, the effects of forming implementation intentions on endurance performance have rarely been investigated. The existing evidence suggests that implementation intentions can indeed affect parameters relevant during endurance activities (e.g., perceived exertion; Marcora, 2008). However, these effects might be unexpected and do not necessarily improve performance. Accordingly, the conditions under which athletes can use implementation intentions to enhance their performance have yet to be explored, especially during whole body endurance activities such as cycling and running. Moreover, research is needed to investigate in which athletic situations implementation intentions are helpful, and the goal-directed behaviours that they can facilitate. Until this research is done, we advise practitioners to test the effects of a specific implementation intention in training settings before using it during a competition.

Notes

1 The Vuelta a España is a three-week stage race and is regarded as one of the most prestigious in road cycling.
2 While 400-metre running does not strictly comply with the operational definition of endurance as adopted in this book, it nevertheless underlines the intricacies of staying on track during an athletic activity.
3 Like the Vuelta a España, the Tour de France is a three-week stage race and is widely regarded as the most prestigious race in road cycling.

References

Aarts, H., Dijksterhuis, A. P., & Midden, C. (1999). To plan or not to plan? Goal achievement or interrupting the performance of mundane behaviors. *European Journal of Social Psychology*, *29*(8), 971–979. doi:10.1002/(SICI)1099-0992(199912)29:8<971::AID-EJSP963>3.0.CO;2-A.
Abbiss, C. R., & Laursen, P. B. (2008). Describing and understanding pacing strategies during athletic competition. *Sports Medicine*, *38*(3), 239–252. doi:10.2165/00007256-200838030-00004.
Achtziger, A., Gollwitzer, P. M., & Sheeran, P. (2008). Implementation intentions and shielding goal striving from unwanted thoughts and feelings. *Personality and Social Psychology Bulletin*, *34*(3), 381–393. doi:10.1177/0146167207311201.
Achtziger, A., Bayer, U. C., & Gollwitzer, P. M. (2012). Committing to implementation intentions: Attention and memory effects for selected situational cues. *Motivation and Emotion*, *36*, 287–300. doi:10.1007/s11031-011-9261-6.
Bayer, U. C., Achtziger, A., Gollwitzer, P. M., & Moskowitz, G. B. (2009). Responding to subliminal cues: Do if-then plans facilitate action preparation and initiation without conscious intent? *Social Cognition*, *27*(2), 183–201. doi:10.1521/soco.2009.27.2.183.

Bélanger-Gravel, A., Godin, G., & Amireault, S. (2013). A meta-analytic review of the effect of implementation intentions on physical activity. *Health Psychology Review*, 7(1), 23–54. doi:10.1080/17437199.2011.560095.

Bieleke, M., & Wolff, W. (2017). That escalated quickly: Planning to ignore RPE can backfire. *Frontiers in Physiology*, 8. doi:10.3389/fphys.2017.00736.

Brand, R., Wolff, W., & Baumgarten, F. (2015). Modeling doping cognition from a dual process perspective. In V. Barkoukis, L. Lazuras, & H. Tsorbatzoudis (Eds.), *The Psychology of Doping in Sport* (pp. 33–43). New York, NY, US: Routledge.

Brandstätter, V., Lengfelder, A., & Gollwitzer, P. M. (2001). Implementation intentions and efficient action initiation. *Journal of Personality and Social Psychology*, 81(5), 946–960. doi:10.1037/0022-3514.81.5.946.

Brick, N. E., MacIntyre, T. E., & Campbell, M. J. (2016). Thinking and action: A cognitive perspective on self-regulation during endurance performance. *Frontiers in Physiology*, 7. doi:10.3389/fphys.2016.00159.

Calder, A. (2009). *Fatigue is no foe with recovery strategies*. Australian Sports Commission. Retrieved from: www.ausport.gov.au/sportsofficialmag/physical_preparation/fatigue_is_no_foe_with_recovery_strategies_in_place.

Carver, C. (2003). Pleasure as a sign you can attend to something else: Placing positive feelings within a general model of affect. *Cognition & Emotion*, 17(2), 241–261. doi:10.1080/02699930302294.

Casa, D. J., Armstrong, L. E., Hillman, S. K., Montain, S. J., Reiff, R. V, Rich, B. S. E., . . . Stone, J. A. (2000). National athletic trainers' association position statement: Fluid replacement for athletes. *Journal of Athletic Training*, 35(2), 212–224.

Cohen, J. R., & Lieberman, M. D. (2010). The common neural basis of exerting self-control in multiple domains. In R. R. Hassin, K. N. Ochsner, & Y. Trope (Eds.), *Self control in society, mind, and brain* (pp. 141–160). New York, NY, US: Oxford University Press.

Doerflinger, J., Martiny-Huenger, T., & Gollwitzer, P. M. (2017). Planning to deliberate thoroughly: If-then planned deliberation increases the adjustment of decisions to available feedback. *Journal of Experimental Social Psychology*, 69, 1–12. doi:10.1016/j.jesp.2016.10.006.

Eder, J. (2008, January 18). *Haile runs 2:04:53 at Standard Chartered Dubai Marathon, by Pat Butcher*. Retrieved from: www.runblogrun.com/2008/01/haile-runs-20453-at-standard-chartered-dubai-marathon-by-pat-butcher.html.

Evans, J. S. B., & Stanovich, K. E. (2013). Dual-process theories of higher cognition: Advancing the debate. *Perspectives on Psychological Science*, 8(3), 223–241. doi:10.1177/1745691612460685.

Freydefont, L., Gollwitzer, P. M., & Oettingen, G. (2016). Goal striving strategies and effort mobilization: When implementation intentions reduce effort-related cardiac activity during task performance. *International Journal of Psychophysiology*, 107, 44–53. doi:10.1016/j.ijpsycho.2016.06.013.

Gilbert, S. J., Gollwitzer, P. M., Cohen, A.-L., Burgess, P. W., & Oettingen, G. (2009). Separable brain systems supporting cued versus self-initiated realization of delayed intentions. *Journal of Experimental Psychology. Learning, Memory, and Cognition*, 35(4), 905–915. doi:10.1037/a0015535.

Gollwitzer, P. M., & Brandstätter, V. (1997). Implementation intentions and effective goal pursuit. *Journal of Personality and Social Psychology*, 73, 186–199. doi:10.1037/0022-3514.73.1.186.

Gollwitzer, P. M. (1999). Implementation intentions: Strong effects of simple plans. *American Psychologist*, 54(7), 493–503. doi:10.1037/0003-066X.54.7.493.

Gollwitzer, P. M. (2014). Weakness of the will: Is a quick fix possible? *Motivation and Emotion, 38*(3), 305–322. doi:10.1007/s11031-014-9416-3.

Gollwitzer, P. M., & Oettingen, G. (2016). Planning promotes goal striving. In K. D. Vohs & R. F. Baumeister (Eds.), *Handbook of self-regulation: Research, theory, and applications* (3rd edn., pp. 223–244). New York: Guilford.

Gollwitzer, P. M., & Schaal, B. (1998). Metacognition in action: The importance of implementation intentions. *Personality and Social Psychology Review, 2*, 124–136. doi:10.1207/s15327957pspr0202_5.

Gollwitzer, P. M., & Sheeran, P. (2006). Implementation intentions and goal achievement: A meta-analysis of effects and processes. *Advances in Experimental Social Psychology, 38*, 69–119. doi:10.1016/S0065-2601(06)38002-1.

Grego, F., Vallier, J. M., Collardeau, M., Rousseu, C., Cremieux, J., & Brisswalter, J. (2005). Influence of exercise duration and hydration status on cognitive function during prolonged cycling exercise. *International Journal of Sports Medicine, 26*(1/02), 27–33. doi:10.1055/s-2004-817915.

Gregoire, C. (2016). Why runners 'hit the wall', and what to do about it. Retrieved from: www.huffingtonpost.com/entry/runners-psychological-mental-obstacles_us_584849 17e4b08c82e8893393.

Hagger, M. S., Chatzisarantis, N. L. D., Alberts, H., Anggono, C. O., Batailler, C., Birt, A. R., . . . Zwienenberg, M. (2016). A multilab preregistered replication of the ego-depletion effect. *Perspectives on Psychological Science, 11*(4), 546–573. doi:10.1177/1745691616652873.

Hagger, M. S., & Montasem, A. (2009). Implementing intentions to drink a carbohydrate-electrolyte solution during exercise. *Journal of Sports Sciences, 27*(9), 963–974. doi:10. 1080/02640410902998262.

Heckhausen, H., & Gollwitzer, P. M. (1987). Thought contents and cognitive functioning in motivational versus volitional states of mind. *Motivation and Emotion, 11*(2), 101–120. doi:10.1007/BF00992338.

Hood, A. (2016, 8 September). *Boswell's first-hand account of how Sky (maybe) lost the Vuelta.* Retrieved from: www.velonews.com/2016/09/news/boswells-first-hand-account-of-how-sky-lost-the-vuelta_420234#oQLRwk0R1tOxvbeA.99.

Janczyk, M., Dambacher, M., Bieleke, M., & Gollwitzer, P. M. (2015). The benefit of no choice: Goal-directed plans enhance perceptual processing. *Psychological Research, 79*(2), 206–220. doi:10.1007/s00426-014-0549-5.

Kelner, M. (2017, 11 August). *Shaunae Miller-Uibo reveals reasons behind her dramatic 400m breakdown.* Retrieved from: www.theguardian.com/sport/2017/aug/10/shaunae-miller-uibo-world-athletics-championships.

Kuhl, J. (1983). *Motivation, Konflikt und Handlungskontrolle.* Heidelberg: Springer.

Legrand, E., Bieleke, M., Gollwitzer, P. M., & Mignon, A. (2017). Nothing will stop me? Flexibly tenacious goal striving with implementation intentions. *Motivation Science, 3*, 101–118. doi:10.1037/mot0000050.

Louro, M. J., Pieters, R., & Zeelenberg, M. (2007). Dynamics of multiple-goal pursuit. *Journal of Personality and Social Psychology, 93*(2), 174–193. doi:10.1037/0022-3514.93.2.174.

Marcora, S. M. (2008). Do we really need a central governor to explain brain regulation of exercise performance? *European Journal of Applied Physiology, 104*(5), 929–931. doi: 10.1007/s00421-008-0818-3.

McCormick, A., Meijen, C., & Marcora, S. (2015). Psychological determinants of whole-body endurance performance. *Sports Medicine, 45*(7), 997–1015. doi:10.1007/s40279-015-0319-6.

McCormick, A., Meijen, C., & Marcora, S. (2018). Psychological demands experienced recreational endurance athletes. *International Journal of Sport and Exercise Psychology. 16*(4), 415–430.

Moran, A. P. (1996). *The psychology of concentration in sport performers: A cognitive analysis.* New York: Routledge.

Pheidippides. (n.d.). In *Wikipedia.* Retrieved from: https://en.wikipedia.org/wiki/Pheidippides.

Rhodes, R. E., & de Bruijn, G. J. (2013). How big is the physical activity intention-behaviour gap? A meta-analysis using the action control framework. *British Journal of Health Psychology, 18*(2), 296–309. doi:10.1111/bjhp.12032.

Schuele, C. (2003, June 5th). *Die Helden-Maschine [The hero machine].* Retrieved from: www.zeit.de/2003/24/Die_Helden-Maschine/komplettansicht.

Schwabe, L., & Wolf, O. T. (2009). Stress prompts habit behavior in humans. *Journal of Neuroscience, 29*(22), 7191–7198. doi:10.1523/JNEUROSCI.0979-09.2009.

Schweiger Gallo, I., McCulloch, K. C., & Gollwitzer, P. M. (2012). Differential effects of various types of implementation intentions on the regulation of disgust. *Social Cognition, 30*, 1–17. doi: 10.1521/soco.2012.30.1.1.

Sheeran, P. (2002). Intention–behaviour relations: A conceptual and empirical review. *European Review of Social Psychology, 12*, 1–36. doi:10.1080/14792772143000003.

Sheeran, P., Webb, T. L., & Gollwitzer, P. M. (2005). The interplay between goal intentions and implementation intentions. *Personality & Social Psychology Bulletin, 31*, 87–98. doi:10.1177/0146167204271308.

Sheeran, P., & Webb, T. L. (2016). The intention–behavior gap. *Social and Personality Psychology Compass, 10*(9), 503–518. doi:10.1111/spc3.12265.

Snow, N. E. (2006). Habitual virtuous actions and automaticity. *Ethical Theory and Moral Practice, 9*(5), 545–561. doi:10.1007/s10677-006-9035-5.

Statistic Brain (2017, 1 January). *New Years Resolution Statistics.* Retrieved from: www.statisticbrain.com/new-years-resolution-statistics/2/.

Thürmer, J. L., Wieber, F., & Gollwitzer, P. M. (2017). Planning and performance in small groups: Collective implementation intentions enhance group goal striving. *Frontiers in Psychology, 8.* doi:10.3389/fpsyg.2017.00603.

Triandis, H. C. (1977). *Interpersonal behavior.* Monterey, CA: Brooks/Cole.

Verhoeven, A. A. C., Adriaanse, M. A., de Ridder, D. T. D., de Vet, E., & Fennis, B. M. (2013). Less is more: The effect of multiple implementation intentions targeting unhealthy snacking habits. *European Journal of Social Psychology, 43*(5), 344–354. doi: 10.1002/ejsp.1963.

Vinkers, C. D. W., Adriaanse, M. A., Kroese, F. M., & de Ridder, D. T. D. (2015). Better sorry than safe: Making a Plan B reduces effectiveness of implementation intentions in healthy eating goals. *Psychology & Health, 30*(7), 821–838. doi: 10.1080/08870446.2014.997730.

Webb, T. L., Schweiger Gallo, I., Miles, E., Gollwitzer, P. M., & Sheeran, P. (2012). Effective regulation of affect: An action control perspective on emotion regulation. *European Review of Social Psychology, 23*, 143–186. doi:10.1080/10463283.2012.718134.

Webb, T. L., & Sheeran, P. (2007). How do implementation intentions promote goal attainment? A test of component processes. *Journal of Experimental Social Psychology, 43*(2), 295–302. doi:10.1016/j.jesp.2006.02.001.

Wieber, F., & Sassenberg, K. (2006). I can't take my eyes off of it – Attention attraction effects of implementation intentions. *Social Cognition, 24*(6), 723–752. doi:10.1521/soco.2006.24.6.723.

Wieber, F., Thürmer, J. L., & Gollwitzer, P. M. (2015). Attenuating the escalation of commitment to a faltering project in decision-making groups: An implementation intention approach. *Social Psychological and Personality Science, 6*(5), 587–595. doi:10.1177/1948550614568158.

Wrosch, C., Scheier, M. F., Carver, C. S., & Schulz, R. (2003). The importance of goal disengagement in adaptive self-regulation: When giving up is beneficial. *Self and Identity, 2*(1), 1–20. doi:10.1080/15298860309021.

Wolff, W., Bieleke, M., Hirsch, A., Wienbruch, C., Gollwitzer, P. M., & Schüler, J. (2018). Increase in prefrontal cortex oxygenation during static muscular endurance performance is modulated by self-regulation strategies. *Scientific Reports, 8*, 15756. doi:10.1038/s41598-018-34009-2.

10

THE THEORETICAL AND APPLIED IMPLICATIONS OF USING IMAGERY TO IMPROVE THE PERFORMANCE AND WELL-BEING OF ENDURANCE PERFORMERS

Sheree McCormick, Francesco di Gruttola, and Maurizio Bertollo

Introduction

Sports performers, sport psychologists, and coaches frequently use mental training techniques to gain the competitive edge in sport. Imagery is one technique that provides athletes with opportunities to improve performance in addition to that achieved through physical practice alone; for example, swimmers may imagine flawlessly performing a tight dolphin kick, triathletes may imagine a smooth and errorless transition, rowers may imagine placing the blade quickly in the water, and marathon runners may imagine finding the depth of physical and mental resources to kick hard in the final stages. The performance increments achieved through imagery may be small, but marginal gains, especially at the elite level, can make the difference between winning or losing, or help secure a personal best. This chapter reviews research related to imagery in sport, in particular self-paced endurance tasks. We provide recommendations on implementing imagery interventions, including guidance on evaluating imagery ability and enhancing the imagery experience.

Defining imagery

Imagery is an experience created in working memory, using information from long-term memory (Decety & Grèzes, 1999; Kosslyn, 2005). In the sports domain, imagery[1] has traditionally been used as a mental training technique in the absence of any movement; however, with respect to endurance sports, evidence suggests that it is often used concurrently with movement (Post, Muncie, & Simpson, 2012; Samson, Simpson, Kamphoff, & Langlier, 2017). Imagery has been defined as a top-down, knowledge driven process that involves the purposeful production of a multi-sensory image, which may include visual, kinesthetic, auditory, tactile, olfactory and/or gustatory details (Bhasavanija & Morris, 2014). Visual details describe what an athlete *sees* in the image, kinaesthetic details relate to what an athlete *feels*, including forces and effort involved in movement, auditory details relate to what an athlete *hears*, and so on. In essence, a middle-distance runner imagining an upcoming race may *feel* her lower limb muscles as being warm and elastic-like, ready to power off with intensity and precision (kinaesthetic), she may *hear* the crack of the starter's gun break the air (auditory), and she may *see* herself take the tangent to curve perfectly and secure her goal position (visual).

Imagery is considered to be most effective when the imagined experience mimics, as closely as possible, the actual performance (Bhasavanija & Morris, 2014). The imagined experience can be generated using two perspectives: in a first person perspective, i.e., individuals imagine the experience as if looking out through their own eyes (also referred to as internal imagery), and in a third person perspective, whereby individuals imagine the experience as if they are observing it from afar i.e., similar to watching the performance of an athlete on a video (also referred to as external imagery; see Callow & Roberts, 2012). When a third person perspective is used, the imagined view can be from any angle e.g., the front, above, behind, or side on. Kinaesthetic sensations can be generated in both perspectives (Callow & Hardy, 2004) and this is recommended to enhance imagery effectiveness. Evidence from the sports literature suggests that a third person perspective may be beneficial for form-based tasks (e.g., gymnastics, dance), whereas a first-person perspective may be more effective for slalom-based tasks (e.g., canoeing, skiing; Callow, Roberts, Hardy, Jiang, & Edwards, 2013). Outside of the sports domain, there is evidence that a third person rather than first person perspective enhances motivation (Vasquez & Buehler, 2007). In applied settings, endurance athletes and coaches are likely to review performances using a third person perspective such as through post-race videos. In these situations, encouraging retrospective inspection of performances through first person perspective imagery could reveal a core component of a skill that is less optimal (Cumming et al., 2016). For example, laboratory-based eye-tracking studies, capturing the gaze of athletes from a first-person perspective, indicate that focus of attention is different between expert and novices in slalom skiing (Decroix et al., 2017) and cycling (Boya et al., 2017). In slalom skiing, experts appear to focus on the timing of actions and novices on the execution of actions, whereas in cycling experts focus on feedback concerning their optimal pacing (i.e., revolutions per minute) and novices on distance. Thus, retrospective inspection of performances using first person perspective imagery and a think-aloud protocol could reveal the core components of the action that the athlete focuses on during performance. In situations where the core components are not optimal for performance, or the athlete reports difficulty in experiencing a 'flow like' state, the Multi-Action Plan (MAP) strategy could be used to identify the optimal attention strategy e.g., focusing their attention on external factors (e.g., metronome) or on the core components of the action (e.g., pacing; Bertollo et al. 2015).

Does imagery work?

Several meta-analyses have reported moderate positive effects of imagery on sport and exercise outcomes (Curran, 2008; Driskell, Copper, & Moran, 1994; Feltz & Landers, 1983). It is generally accepted that imagery practice is not better than physical practice but it can supplement physical practice and is better than no practice at all. Imagery can also be integrated into mental skills training packages and used alongside other psychological techniques such as goal setting, relaxation, and self-talk (Thelwell & Greenlees, 2003).

There is little empirical evidence on the effectiveness of structured imagery training programmes in elite athletes, however, elite athletes are reported to use imagery more and have better imagery ability skills (i.e., the ability to represent sensory information in working memory) than novices (MacInnis, 1987; Weinberg, 2008). In sub-elite and semi-novice athletes, imagery has been shown to improve performance across a wide range of endurance sports including, but not limited to, ultra-distance running (Bull, 1989), triathlon (Thelwell & Greenlees, 2003), swimming (Ferrari, Chirico, & Rasà, 2016; Post et al., 2012), and cycling (Razon, Mandler, Arsal, Tokac, & Tenenbaum, 2014). These studies have traditionally focused on using imagery to enhance performance and modify thought and emotions. More recently, imagery has also been demonstrated to play a role in pain management (Hainline et al., 2017).

How does imagery work?

How can simply imagining an event improve performance outcome? A number of explanations for this phenomenon have been proposed (for a comprehensive summary see Weinberg & Gould, 2014). Here we describe two favoured theories related to sport for which there is a growing evidence base: (i) Lang's Bioinformational theory (Lang, 1979), and (ii) Jeannerod's Functional Equivalence hypothesis (Jeannerod, 1994, 2001).

Bioinformational theory

The Bioinformational theory of emotional imagery (Lang, 1979) proposes that behaviour can be modified by strengthening the sensory details contained in the mental image. Lang refers to the sensory details as 'propositions' of which there are three types: stimulus, response, and meaning. Stimulus propositions describe the situation being imagined (e.g., location, equipment, weather), response propositions describe the athlete's emotional and physiological response to the situation (e.g., heart rate, sweating, muscle tension), and meaning propositions explain how the athlete interprets the response (e.g., challenge vs threat, anxiety vs energy; Cumming et al., 2016). During imagery, the imagined propositions act as a *pseudo-action* causing physiological responses that are similar, but smaller in magnitude, to the real-life action. The physiological responses may include muscle activation, skin responses, and heart rate modulation.

Proposition-based imagery is usually, but not always, generated using written scripts; one or two paragraphs of highly descriptive information that is often co-developed by the athlete and coach/sport psychologist (for an example of proposition-based imagery using stimulus and response propositions see Weinberg & Gould, 2014, p. 306). The athlete is asked to either read the script or listen to an audio recording of it. To guide the development of effective scripts, practitioners can refer to the PETTLEP model (Holmes & Collins, 2001). PETTLEP is an acronym, with each letter relating to an element of the real-life situation that should be reflected in the imagery intervention; Physical, Environmental, Task, Timing, Learning, Emotional, and Perspective. For practical guidance on developing scripts using the PETTLEP model see Wakefield and Smith (2012) and Razon and colleagues (2010). Cooley and colleagues conducted a systematic review of 20 studies that used proposition-based imagery to improve motor performance (Cooley, Williams, Burns, & Cumming, 2013). They reported that researchers tend to use a selection, rather than all, of the seven PETTLEP elements when generating personalised imagery scripts (with Environment and Physical elements most often used) and cautioned that the use of additional propositions could result in a less than optimal imagery experience. Given that the optimum number of propositions to include in an imagery script to enhance endurance is currently unknown, a more conservative approach to imagery script development and training may be prudent. One such approach, explained later in this chapter, is Layered Stimulus Response Training (LSRT; Williams, Cooley, & Cummings, 2013).

Functional Equivalence hypothesis

The Functional Equivalence hypothesis (Jeannerod, 1994, 2001) proposes that some areas of the brain that are activated during physical execution of movement are also activated during imagination of the same movement. The neural equivalence between physical action and imagery is thought to reflect the hidden part of movement such as the goal of the action, the preparation and intention to move, and the effort and force required to complete the action. The idea of functional equivalence is supported by many studies that have repeatedly demonstrated neural, physiological, behavioural, and temporal similarities between physical and imagined actions (for an overview see Lotze & Halsband, 2006) and, more recently, similar attentional strategies (Causer, McCormick, & Holmes, 2013; McCormick, Causer, & Holmes, 2012).

Interestingly, the temporal similarity in the time it takes to physically perform a movement and subsequently imagine the same movement, referred to as mental chronometry, is often used as a marker of imagery ability (for review see Guillot & Collet, 2005). Using mental chronometry, Fusco et al. (2014) reported similar mental and physical execution times when participants imagined light running whilst stepping through the action on the spot (a modified form of imagery referred to as *dynamic imagery*). These findings suggest that endurance athletes could exploit the temporal equivalence phenomenon and use imagery to practice pacing strategy in the absence of physical training. Indeed, Michael Phelps, the most decorated Olympian to date, is said to have been able to imagine executing his 200 m freestyle to within milliseconds of that achieved in competition (Phelps & Abrahamson, 2008).

The function of imagery

Imagery has been conceptualised to serve several motivational and cognitive functions (Paivio, 1985). These include cognitive-specific (CS; imagery of discrete skills), cognitive-general (CG; imagery of tactics, routines, and game plans), motivational-specific (MS; imagery of specific outcome goals, e.g., standing on the podium and receiving a medal), motivational general-mastery (MG-M; imagery relating to an athlete's motivational state), and motivational general-arousal (MG-A; imagery related to arousal control). To date, little fieldwork has examined the effects of specific imagery functions on self-paced endurance tasks, however, Razon et al. (2014) have demonstrated that motivational general imagery decreased ratings of perceived exertion and extended task duration in cycling. Post and colleagues (2012) also reported positive effects using CS imagery to improve performance times in a 1000-yard swim. In their study, one participant reported: "It allowed me to really break down my strokes, so I can focus on them exactly how I wanted to perform them" (Post et al., 2012, p. 332). Paivio's early analytic model (Paivio, 1985) has recently been embedded into a more comprehensive model, the Motor Imagery Integrative Model in Sport (MIIMS; Guillot & Collet, 2008). The MIIMS identifies four distinct outcomes of imagery: (i) motivation, self-confidence, and anxiety; (ii) motor learning and performance; (iii) strategies and problem solving; and, (iv) injury rehabilitation (Figure 10.1). For each desired outcome, the model shows the type of imagery to use (e.g., CS, MG-A) and specific sub-components that influence effectiveness. For example, in Post and colleagues' (2012) study referred to above, an athlete used CS imagery to improve motor performance in the 1000-yard swim. According to the MIIMS, imagery effectiveness could be enhanced by ensuring the imagined stroke rate correlates with its actual time (*temporal equivalence*), the spatial characteristics of the movement are preserved during MI (*spatial and temporal characteristics*), and arousal level is matched to performance conditions (*arousal*).

Imagery and endurance performance

Of the four outcomes listed in the MIIMS model, the outcomes related to *Motivation, Self-confidence, Anxiety*, and *Motor Learning and Performance* appear the most pertinent to this chapter given that one of the key elements in endurance sports is self-regulation: athletes need to balance their pace and perceived effort

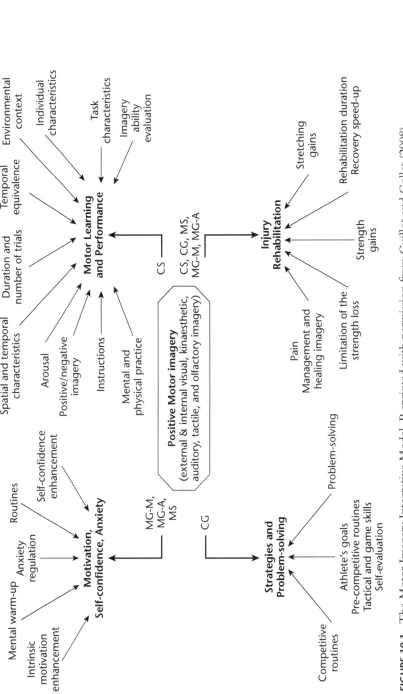

FIGURE 10.1 The Motor Imagery Integrative Model. Reprinted with permission from Guillot and Collet (2008)

appropriately to achieve an optimal level of performance (Brick, MacIntyre, & Campbell, 2016; Schiphof-Godart & Hettinga, 2017). In real-life situations, effort and pace are often regulated through attentional focus (Bertollo et al., 2015). In the following paragraphs, we first highlight the overlap in the literature concerning imagery and attentional focus and then discuss related evidence.

Where to focus one's attention to achieve one's best is a question frequently debated in research. In a classical study, Morgan and Pollock (1977) first introduced the idea of associative and dissociative strategies, associative strategies being those in which one's attention is focused on sensory information (e.g., physical sensations, body temperature, respiration) and dissociative strategies being those in which the sensory cues are ignored in an attempt to block out pain or alleviate boredom (e.g., day dreaming, attending to the scenery). In practice, athletes often employ different attentional strategies depending on task, goal, and level of experience. For an in-depth discussion of attentional strategies, please refer to Chapter 8 in this volume (Brick, MacIntyre, & Schücker).

Since the classical study of Morgan and Pollock (1977), an overlap in the literature concerning imagery and attentional focus has slowly emerged. Bull (1989) noted how an ultra-endurance desert runner attempted to deal with the heat by refocusing his attention and imagining "running through ice and snow (visual imagery) and pretending to feel bitterly cold (kinesthetic imagery)" (p. 258). More recently, Razon and colleagues (Razon et al., 2010, 2014) demonstrated that imagery can exert an ergogenic effect by influencing attention. The authors proposed the terms 'associative' and 'dissociative' imagery to describe the process of using imagery to *prime* an associative or dissociative focus of attention respectively. Razon et al. (2014) and Post et al. (2012) described associative imagery being purposefully used to direct attention away from perceptions of pain to help secure a personal best. For instance, athletes could focus the attention on their own breath (Razon et al., 2014) or the core component of the action/skill (di Fronso, Bortoli, Robazza & Bertollo, 2017; Post et al., 2012). Thus, athletes appear to be able to enhance performance by using imagery to (re)focus their attention on skill execution rather than dwelling on perceptions of pain. Conversely, athletes may also use imagery to (re)focus their attention on positive, but task-irrelevant, thoughts to reduce perceptions of pain. In our applied work, anecdotal evidence provided by one club-level cyclist described how this type of imagery helped him maintain motivation and extend time to exhaustion:

> After over-exerting early during an endurance mountain bike event, and then struggling up a severe climb, I felt an involuntary and overwhelming desire to get off the bike and lie down on the soft grass. It required concerted mental effort to displace this focus of attention onto more positive and distracting thoughts. This worked and the perception of physical pain was much reduced.
>
> *(personal communication, Hulse, S).*

The studies by Post et al. (2012) and Razon et al. (2010; 2014) also demonstrate how imagery can be used in the presence, rather than absence, of movement. This approach could be defined as dynamic concurrent imagery, a form of imagery that has been demonstrated to be effective in sport and clinical settings (Fusco et al., 2014; Guillot, Moschberger, & Collet, 2013). Experimental studies have demonstrated that intense perceptions of pain experienced during exercise can negatively influence the later evaluation of the experience (the so called 'peak-end rule', Hargreaves & Stych, 2013; Redelmeier & Kahneman, 1996). Thus, it is possible that dynamic concurrent imagery, used to refocus attention during peak periods of discomfort, may reduce the moment-to moment perceptions of pain and result in more positive recall (e.g., facilitative imagery) of the event.

Collectively, these findings highlight that in imagery, as in physical performance, focus of attention is idiosyncratic and depends on the characteristics of the athlete, task and environment (Brick, MacIntyre, & Campbell, 2014). Thus, athletes who use dissociative/associative imagery (concurrently or in the absence of movement) should strive for functional equivalence by adopting the attentional style that closely matches that recommended in the real-life situation (Cumming et al., 2016).

Imagery as an effective mental training tool

The extent to which athletes can benefit from imagery depends on their ability to: (i) create vivid images; and, (ii) control them in the desired way (Cumming et al., 2016). Thus, the imagery ability of the athlete should be carefully considered using, for example, objective measures such as mental chronometry, and subjective measures such as the Movement Imagery Questionnaire-3 (Williams et al., 2012), the Vividness of Movement Imagery Questionnaire-2 (Roberts, Callow, Hardy, Markland, & Bringer, 2008), and self-evaluations. Evidence suggests that imagery ability is domain-specific; people imagine actions more clearly and accurately if they are held in their repertoire (Wei & Luo, 2010). For this reason, it might be prudent to assess imagery ability using the same action as that intended to be used in the imagery training programme or intervention (di Gruttola & Sebastiani, 2017). As an example, a cyclist's ability to generate a mental image could be assessed by using a Likert-style self-rating scale of imagery vividness (1 = not very vivid/controlled, 5 = extremely vivid/controlled), and his ability to maintain or manipulate the image could be assessed by comparing the time it takes him to physically cycle and imagine cycling the same distance, for example 1500 m.

For athletes who are less experienced with imagery, less skilled in the physical task, or who have difficulty generating and controlling vivid images, practitioners may wish to use a stepped approach called Layered Stimulus Response Training (LSRT; Williams, Cooley, & Cumming, 2013) to enhance imagery ability. Based on Lang's Bioinformational theory (Lang, 1979), LSRT is a structured exercise programme that involves gradually adding stimulus, response, and meaning propositions to a basic image using a layering approach. As each layer is developed, the athlete is encouraged to reflect on the content and characteristics of the image and to rate its vividness and clarity using a 1–5 rating scale (i.e., 1 = unable to generate any image, 5 = image is perfectly clear and vivid). Reflecting on each layer in this manner can identify core components that are missing from the image, or bring awareness to negative aspects that require reframing.

As an example, a novice triathlete reflecting on the content of her first basic image may reveal: (i) she spontaneously adopts a first person perspective; (ii) her image primarily involves running to a crowded bike rack in a cumbersome wetsuit; and, (iii) she is unable to hold the image in her mind for longer than a few seconds. To help this athlete develop her imagery skills and practice, a stimulus proposition could be added to the next layer e.g., an image of quickly locating the bike and running with it to a clear space. Once the athlete is able to image this scenario clearly and vividly, a third layer could be added such as an image of mounting the bike with ease and passing several other competitors along the way (layer 3). The athlete could also be encouraged to try to generate the image from a third person perspective to see if this improves her ability to control the image (i.e., the length of time she can maintain the image in her mind). Progression could involve reverting back to using a first person perspective and adding in additional response propositions (e.g., the sensation of water on her hands). For practitioners wishing to use LSRT, a detailed case study involving a young female endurance cyclist is provided by Cumming et al. (2016).

Athletes with poorer imagery skills ability may also find it useful to use personal videos highlighting moments of peak or desired performance as an adjunct to imagery practice (Eaves, Riach, Holmes, & Wright, 2016). Alternatively, performing imagery during and/or immediately after performance could *prime* image generation, an approach which may result in more vivid and effective imagery experience. These approaches have been shown to enhance performance and confidence in open skills (i.e., skills used in environments that are constantly changing, for example volleyball) and closed skills (i.e., skills used in predicable environments, for example a free throw in basketball) since the early 1990s (Vealey & Forlenza, 2014) and are fruitful areas to explore with respect to endurance.

Setting up an imagery training programme for endurance athletes

A typical imagery-training programme has four consecutive and interconnected steps (Vealey & Forlenza, 2014) as shown in Figure 10.2:

(1) Introduce imagery to the athlete;
(2) Preliminary assessment of imagery abilities;
(3) Define the objective of the imagery intervention;
(4) Integrate the programme into the athlete's routines.

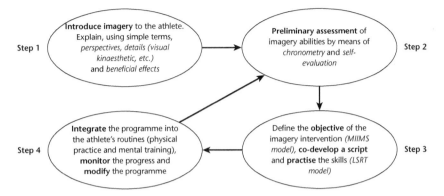

FIGURE 10.2   Tailored imagery programme to meet the needs, abilities and preferences of the athlete

Step 1: Introduce imagery to the athlete

–   Explain the imagery concept to the athlete using simple words and practical examples. An introductory session with, for example, a middle-distance runner, might include the following steps:

   o   Conduct a simple mental chronometry assessment by comparing their physical and mental times of a 200 m and 400 m sprint.
   o   Highlight the similarity in time between the imagined and real-life 200 m, and that both times increase for the 400 m.
   o   Offer an example of how this could be used in training e.g., as part of an interval training set.

–   Convey to the athlete the potential value and benefit of using imagery, provide anecdotal reports or refer to examples provided in this chapter. Razon et al. (2010) provide a description of the important factors to convey to an athlete at the start of an imagery training programme, these include a definition of imagery, how and where it can be used, and critical aspects related to its application (i.e., the vividness and controllability of the image, the external and internal perspectives, the multisensory involvement, and the importance of a frequent practice).

Step 2: Preliminary assessment of imagery abilities

–   Assess imagery ability using a self-report questionnaire e.g., Movement Imagery Questionnaire-3 (MIQ-3; Williams et al., 2012) and mental chronometry (Williams, Guillot, Di Rienzo, & Cumming, 2015).

Step 3: Define the objective of the imagery intervention

- Work with the athlete to agree the imagery outcome. If the outcome is motor learning/performance the **MAP Model** (Bortoli, Bertollo, Hanin, & Robazza, 2012) could be used to identify one or two core components of the skill (di Fronso, Bortoli, Robazza & Bertollo, 2017). Refer to the **MIIMS** (Guillot & Collet, 2008) to determine the most suitable imagery function (CS, CG, MG-A, MG-M, MS) to reach the imagery outcome.
- Begin a structured training programme e.g., LSRT (Williams et al., 2013):

    - Ask the athlete to describe the situation in as much detail as possible (who, what, where, and when). Ask the athlete what they would like to think and feel in this situation and use this information to generate the first basic image (layer one). For self-paced endurance tasks (e.g., swimming or running etc.) imagine the scenario for a limited time (e.g., 30 seconds).
    - Reflect on the image; identify areas for improvement; generate a revised image (layer two).
    - Reflect on the image, identify areas for improvement, generate a revised image (layer three), and so on.

Step 4: Integrate the programme into the athlete's routines

- Establish a regular imagery routine; start with short, high quality imagery sessions that are gradually increased in frequency and duration (Cooley et al., 2013).
- Encourage record keeping in the form of a diary to monitor practice and assess goals.
- Revisit steps 2 and 3 frequently to assess skills and provide feedback on the effectiveness of the imagery programme.

Above all, personalise the imagery training programme so that it meets the needs, abilities, and preferences of the athlete.

Conclusions

Imagery is the process of creating or recreating an image in the mind using all of the senses. It is a mental technique that can improve motor learning and performance directly, and indirectly through enhancing thoughts and emotions. The effectiveness of imagery is determined by the quality of the image generated: images that are vivid and well controlled are the most effective. Imagining situations from different viewing perspectives is recommended and may provide athletes with important information that is not ordinarily available. Structured imagery training programmes can improve imagery ability and enhance motor performance and emotional well-being. LSRT can be embedded into a systematic imagery training programme to support the development and practice of highly personalised imagery. For maximum effect, the athlete's progress and adherence should be monitored and reviewed regularly.

Note

1 Imagery, as referred to in this chapter, encompasses several terms, including: movement imagery; motor imagery; visualisation; mental imagery; kinaesthetic imagery, and exercise imagery. Debate over distinctions between these terms has been a feature of sports psychology for many years (Morris, Spittle, & Watt, 2005). As no generally accepted criterion to distinguish between these terms has been given, the all-encompassing term 'imagery', arguably the most frequent term used by athletes, coaches, sports psychologists, and scholars, has been adopted in this chapter.

References

Bertollo, M., di Fronso, S., Filho, E., Lamberti, V., Ripari, P., Reis, V. M., et al. (2015). To focus or not to focus: Is attention on the core components of action beneficial for cycling performance? *The Sport Psychologist*, *29*(2), 110–119.

Bhasavanija, T., & Morris, T. (2014). Imagery. In A. G. Papaioannou & D. Hackfort (Eds.), *Routledge Companion to Sport and Exercise Psychology: Global Perspectives and Fundamental Concepts* (pp. 356–371). Routledge Handbooks Online.

Bortoli, L., Bertollo, M., Hanin, Y., & Robazza, C. (2012). Striving for excellence: A multi-action plan intervention model for shooters. *Psychology of Sport and Exercise*, *13*(5), 693–701.

Boya, M., Foulsham, T., Hettinge, F., Parry, D., Williams, E., Jones, H., . . . & McNaughton, L. (2017). Information acquisition differences between experienced and novel time trial cyclists. *Medicine and Science in Sports and Exercise*, *49*(9), 1884–1898.

Brick, N., MacIntyre, T., & Schücker, L. (2019). Attentional focus and cognitive strategies during endurance activity. In C. Meijen (Ed.), *Endurance performance in sport: Psychological theory and interventions* (pp. 113–124). Oxon, UK: Routledge.

Brick, N. E., MacIntyre, T. E., & Campbell, M. J. (2014). Attentional focus in endurance activity: new paradigms and future directions. *International Review of Sport & Exercise Psychology*, *7*(1), 106–134.

Brick, N. E., MacIntyre, T. E., & Campbell, M. J. (2016). Thinking and action: A cognitive perspective on self-regulation during endurance performance. *Frontiers in Physiology*, *7*, 159.

Bull, S. J. (1989). The role of the sport psychology consultant: A case study of ultra-distance running. *The Sport Psychologist*, *3*(3), 254–264.

Callow, N., & Hardy, L. (2004). The relationship between the use of kinaesthetic imagery and different visual imagery perspectives. *Journal of Sports Sciences*, *22*(2), 167–177.

Callow, N., & Roberts, R. (2012). Visual imagery perspectives and reference: Conceptualization and measurement. *Journal of Mental Imagery*, *36*(1), 31.

Callow, N., Roberts, R., Hardy, L., Jiang, D., & Edwards, M. G. (2013). Performance improvements from imagery: Evidence that internal visual imagery is superior to external visual imagery for slalom performance. *Frontiers in Human Neuroscience*, *7*, 697.

Causer, J., McCormick, S. A., & Holmes, P. S. (2013). Congruency of gaze metrics in action, imagery and action observation. *Frontiers in Human Neuroscience*, *7*.

Cooley, S. J., Williams, S. E., Burns, V. E., & Cumming, J. (2013). Methodological variations in guided imagery interventions using movement imagery scripts in sport: A systematic review. *Journal of Imagery Research in Sport and Physical Activity*, *8*(1), 13–34.

Cumming, J., Cooley, S. J., Anuar, N., Kosteli, M. C., Quinton, M. L., Weibull, F., & Williams, S. E. (2017). Developing imagery ability effectively: A guide to layered stimulus response training. *Journal of Sport Psychology in Action, 8*(1), 23–33.

Curran, M. (2008). *Imagery – "the icing on the cake". A meta-analytic evaluation of the effect of imagery on sport and exercise.* Toowoomba: University of Southern Queensland.

Decety, J., & Grèzes, J. (1999). Neural mechanisms subserving the perception of human actions. *Trends in Cognitive Sciences, 3*(5), 172–178.

Decroix, M., Wazir, M. R., Zeuwts, L., Deconinck, F. F., Lenoir, M., & Vansteenkiste, P. (2017). Expert – non-expert differences in visual behaviour during alpine slalom skiing. *Human Movement Science, 55*, 229–239.

di Fronso, F., Bortoli, L., Robazza, C., & Bertollo, M. (2017). Performance optimization in sport: A psychophysiological approach. *Motriz: Revista de Educação Física, 23*(4).

di Gruttola, F., & Sebastiani, L. (2017). Questionnaires do not discriminate motor imagery ability of people with different motor expertise. *Revista de Psicología del Deporte, 26*(3), 124–129.

Driskell, J. E., Copper, C., & Moran, A. (1994). Does mental practice enhance performance? *Journal of Applied Psychology, 79*(4), 481–492.

Eaves, D. L., Riach, M., Holmes, P. S., & Wright, D. J. (2016). Motor imagery during action observation: a brief review of evidence, theory and future research opportunities. *Frontiers in Neuroscience, 10.*

Feltz, D. L., & Landers, D. M. (1983). The effects of mental practice on motor skill learning and performance: A meta-analysis. *Journal of Sport Psychology, 5*(1), 25–57.

Ferrari, G., Chirico, F., & Rasà, G. (2016). Examining physical training versus physical and mental training programmes in swimrun semi-professional athletes: A randomised, controlled, trial. *Journal of Health and Social Sciences, 1*(3), 199–210.

Fusco, A., Iosa, M., Gallotta, M. C., Paolucci, S., Baldari, C., & Guidetti, L. (2014). Different performances in static and dynamic imagery and real locomotion. An exploratory trial. *Frontiers in Human Neuroscience, 8*, 760.

Guillot, A., & Collet, C. (2005). Duration of mentally simulated movement: a review. *Journal of Motor Behavior, 37*(1), 10–20.

Guillot, A., & Collet, C. (2008). Construction of the motor imagery integrative model in sport: a review and theoretical investigation of motor imagery use. *International Review of Sport and Exercise Psychology, 1*(1), 31–44.

Guillot, A., Moschberger, K., & Collet, C. (2013). Coupling movement with imagery as a new perspective for motor imagery practice. *Behavioral and Brain Functions, 9*(1), 8.

Hargreaves, E. A., & Stych, K. (2013). Exploring the peak and end rule of past affective episodes within the exercise context. *Psychology of Sport and Exercise, 14*, 169–178.

Hainline, B., Derman, W., Vernec, A., Budgett, A., Deie, M., Dvořák, J., . . . & Moseley, G. L. (2017). International Olympic Committee consensus statement on pain management in elite athletes. *British Journal of Sport Medicine, 51*(17), 1245–1258.

Holmes, P. S., & Collins, D. J. (2001). The PETTLEP approach to motor imagery: A functional equivalence model for sport psychologists. *Journal of Applied Sport Psychology, 13*(1), 60–83.

Jeannerod, M. (1994). The representing brain: Neural correlates of motor intention and imagery. *Behavioral and Brain Sciences, 17*, 187–245.

Jeannerod, M. (2001). Neural simulation of action: a unifying mechanism for motor cognition. *Neuroimage, 14*(1), S103–S109.

Kosslyn, S. M. (2005). Mental images and the brain. *Cognitive Neuropsychology, 22*(3–4), 333–347.

Lang, P. J. (1979). A bio-informational theory of emotional imagery. *Psychophysiology*, *16*(6), 495–512.

Lotze, M., & Halsband, U. (2006). Motor imagery. *Journal of Physiology-Paris*, *99*(4), 386–395.

MacInnis, D. J. (1987). Constructs and measures of individual differences in imagery processing: A review. *Advances in Consumer Research*, *14*, 88–92.

McCormick, S. A., Causer, J., & Holmes, P. S. (2012). Eye gaze metrics reflect a shared motor representation for action observation and movement imagery. *Brain and Cognition*, *80*(1), 83–88.

Morgan, W. P., & Pollock, M. L. (1977). Psychologic characterization of the elite distance runner. *Annals of the New York Academy of Sciences*, *301*(1), 382–403.

Morris, T., Spittle, M., & Watt, A. P. (2005). *Imagery in sport*. Champaign, IL: Human Kinetics.

Paivio, A. (1985). Cognitive and motivational functions of imagery in human performance. *Canadian Journal of Applied Sport Sciences*, *10*(4), 22S–28S.

Phelps, M., & Abrahamson, A. (2008). *No limits: The will to succeed*. London, UK: Simon and Schuster.

Post, P., Muncie, S., & Simpson, D. (2012). The effects of imagery training on swimming performance: An applied investigation. *Journal of Applied Sport Psychology*, *24*(3), 323–337.

Razon, S., Basevitch, I., Land, W., Thompson, B., Biermann, M., & Tenenbaum, G. (2010). Associative and dissociative imagery effects on perceived exertion and task duration. *Journal of Imagery Research in Sport and Physical Activity*, *5*(1).

Razon, S., Mandler, K., Arsal, G., Tokac, U., & Tenenbaum, G. (2014). Effects of imagery on effort perception and cycling endurance. *Journal of Imagery Research in Sport and Physical Activity*, *9*(1), 23–38.

Redelmeier, D. A., & Kahneman, D. (1996). Patients' memories of painful medical procedures: Real-time and retrospective evaluations of two minimally invasive procedures. *Pain*, *66*, 3–8.

Roberts, R., Callow, N., Hardy, L., Markland, D., & Bringer, J. (2008). Movement imagery ability: Development and assessment of a revised version of the vividness of movement imagery questionnaire. *Journal of Sport and Exercise Psychology*, *30*(2), 200–221.

Samson, A., Simpson, D., Kamphoff, C., & Langlier, A. (2017). Think aloud: An examination of distance runners' thought processes. *International Journal of Sport and Exercise Psychology*, *15*(2), 176–189.

Schiphof-Godart, L., & Hettinga, F. J. (2017). Passion and pacing in endurance performance. *Frontiers in Physiology*, *8*, 83.

Thelwell, R. C., & Greenlees, I. A. (2003). Developing competitive endurance performance using mental skills training. *The Sport Psychologist*, *17*(3), 318–337.

Vasquez, N. A., & Buehler, R. (2007). Seeing future success: Does imagery perspective influence achievement motivation? *Personality and Social Psychology Bulletin*, *33*(10), 1392–1405.

Vealey, R. S., & Forlenza, S. T. (2014). Understanding and using imagery in sport. In J. M. Williams & V. Krane (Eds.), *Applied sport psychology: Personal growth to peak performance* (pp. 240–273). New York, NY: McGraw-Hill.

Wakefield, C., & Smith, D. (2012). Perfecting practice: Applying the PETTLEP model of motor imagery. *Journal of Sport Psychology in Action*, *3*(1), 1–11.

Wei, G., & Luo, J. (2010). Sport expert's motor imagery: functional imaging of professional motor skills and simple motor skills. *Brain Research*, *1341*, 52–62.

Weinberg, R. (2008). Does imagery work? Effects on performance and mental skills. *Journal of Imagery Research in Sport and Physical Activity*, *3*(1), 1–21.

Weinberg, R. S., & Gould, D. (2014). *Foundations of sport and exercise psychology, 6E*: Champaign, IL: Human Kinetics.

Williams, S. E., Cooley, S. J., & Cumming, J. (2013). Layered stimulus response training improves motor imagery ability and movement execution. *Journal of Sport and Exercise Psychology*, *35*(1), 60–71.

Williams, S. E., Cumming, J., Ntoumanis, N., Nordin-Bates, S. M., Ramsey, R., & Hall, C. (2012). Further validation and development of the movement imagery questionnaire. *Journal of Sport and Exercise Psychology*, *34*(5), 621–646.

Williams, S. E., Guillot, A., Di Rienzo, F., & Cumming, J. (2015). Comparing self-report and mental chronometry measures of motor imagery ability. *European Journal of Sport Science*, *15*(8), 703–711.

11

SELF-TALK AND ENDURANCE PERFORMANCE

Alister McCormick and Antonis Hatzigeorgiadis

Introduction

'I want to quit' # 'Keep going, you can do this'

'My legs are aching' # 'I'm almost there'

'It's too hot' # 'There's a water station approaching'

'That's it, I'm done' # 'It will get easier soon'

'I can't take it anymore' # 'I will make it'

Endurance events are unique. Athletes are 'alone' fighting against the limits of their body and their mind. The way is long, the time passes slowly, and the mind can't snooze; there is a lot to think about, there is plenty of time to doubt oneself and ruminate but also to reflect upon and praise . . . it's a mind game. The mind is the key and it should be prepared to 'say' all the right things to get you through the event.

> One of my favourites is simple, but effective. It's hard to think too deeply when I'm going to the well, so I just tell myself over and over again: 'You're doing great'. (Ryan Hall, U.S. record holder in the half marathon)
>
> One of my favourite mantras is 'Tough times don't last, but tough people do'. There can be highs and lows in ultras and I like to think of myself as tough, which is why I like this saying. (Ellie Greenwood, two-time IAU 100 km World Champion)
>
> If someone is on my heels or just ahead, then I keep repeating in my head, 'Just keep pushing'. It stops me from easing off even a little bit so that if I slow or if the terrain gets easier, I kick it up a notch. (Ian Sharman, holder of the fastest 100-mile trail time in the U.S.)
>
> *(Havey, n.d.)*

Self-talk refers to what people say to themselves either silently in their head or aloud, automatically or strategically, to stimulate, direct, react to, and evaluate events and actions (Hatzigeorgiadis, Zourbanos, Latinjak, & Theodorakis, 2014). This description first makes a distinction between automatic and strategic self-talk, and then identifies potential functions or purposes of self-talk. Automatic self-talk refers to those things that people say to themselves that are not planned or prepared. Its content can be positive (e.g., 'I can do it'), negative (e.g., 'I'm not in the mood for this'), or neutral in nature (e.g., 'What's my pace?'). Such automatic self-talk can serve to provide direction and stimulate action (e.g., 'Keep the pace') or react (e.g., 'Don't let her go') and evaluate (e.g., 'Screw-up'). In contrast, strategic self-talk refers to use of self-talk that is planned or used in a systematic way to achieve a goal. Strategic self-talk has been categorised depending on its function, mainly as instructional and motivational. Instructional self-talk is used to provide instruction relating to technique or form (e.g., 'Pump your arms'), strategy (e.g., 'Stay with the pack'), movement qualities (e.g., 'Smooth pedalling'), and what to pay attention to (e.g., 'Look out for the trail on the right'). Motivational self-talk is used for motivational purposes such as to psych up (e.g., 'Let's go!'), maximise effort (e.g., 'Give your all!'), build confidence (e.g., 'You can and you will'), and achieve a desired feeling state (e.g., 'Feeling good') (Hatzigeorgiadis, Zourbanos, Galanis, & Theodorakis, 2011).

Recent advances in self-talk theorising have led to new ideas regarding the conceptualisation and origins of self-talk. Latinjak, Zourbanos, Lopez-Ros, and Hatzigeorgiadis (2014) distinguished two broad types of self-talk: goal-directed and spontaneous. Goal-directed self-talk refers to statements that are deliberately used to solve a problem or make progress on a task, and they are used to regulate thoughts, feelings such as emotions, and behaviour. Such self-talk is considered automatic, rather than strategic, because the statements come from the athlete and are not pre-planned. Spontaneous self-talk refers to statements that come to mind unbidden or effortlessly and that are not goal-focused (e.g., 'Silly mistake'). In a somewhat similar fashion, Van Raalte, Vincent, and Brewer (2016) identified (a) an intuitive type of self-talk, that comes to mind spontaneously, focuses awareness on current experiences, and represents the immediate and emotionally-charged reaction to a situation (e.g., 'Damn it, I messed up'), and (b) a rational type of self-talk (e.g., 'Relax your shoulders') based on reason, which is emotionally neutral. Although research is scant on these distinctions between types of self-talk in sport settings, they provide fruitful grounds for enhancing understanding of self-talk in sport and endurance activities.

This chapter gives an overview of the research conducted on self-talk in endurance sports, and identifies priorities for future research. At the end of the chapter, research-informed practical guidance is given on learning to use self-talk to benefit important outcomes such as performance results and satisfaction.

Self-talk research

Providing a framework for the study of self-talk, Hardy, Oliver, and Tod (2009) identified three strands of self-talk research: descriptive research, research on the antecedents of self-talk, and research on the effects of self-talk. Descriptive research describes the qualities of the self-talk, such as its content, frequency, and purpose. Research on the antecedents of self-talk explores personal (e.g., demographic, cultural, or sociopsychological attributes), situational (e.g., importance and difficulty of circumstances, and motivational states), and environmental factors (e.g., coaching behaviour, others' expectancies) that shape and determine people's self-talk. Finally, research on the effects of self-talk examines the effects of using planned self-talk cues or statements on outcomes such as performance, and it examines the psychological mechanisms that explain why self-talk affects performance (Hatzigeorgiadis et al., 2014).

Descriptive research

Research on the content of self-talk used by endurance athletes is useful and warranted, to help identify issues to be dealt with and to further develop effective interventions. Few studies have thoroughly described the self-talk used by people before, during, or after endurance exercise. A notable exception (Van Raalte, Morrey, Cornelius, & Brewer, 2015) explored the self-talk of 483 marathon runners ranging in age, experience, and standard. Most of these runners (88 per cent) reported using self-talk during marathons. They engaged in various types of self-talk that included associative self-talk focusing on their bodies (e.g., 'My breathing is controlled'), positive (e.g., 'You can do it') and negative motivational self-talk (e.g., 'Don't be a wimp, this isn't that hard'), incentive self-talk (e.g., 'I will be able to eat anything I want'), short-term goal-related self-talk (e.g., 'Get to the next mile marker'), dissociative self-talk that served as a distraction (e.g., counting backwards), mantras or repetitive chants (e.g., 'Stride, stride, abide, abide'), and spiritual self-talk (e.g., 'I'm doing this for cancer patients'). Much of the self-talk was motivational in nature, helping the runners to continue despite the exertion and pain encountered when performing over a long distance, therefore identifying an important function of self-talk for endurance performance. Across elite and non-elite competitive standards, the most prevalent types of self-talk were associative, positive-motivational, and incentive self-talk. Nevertheless, differences in self-talk prevalence were evident when comparing elite and non-elite marathon runners, with use of associative self-talk more prevalent in elite runners (43 per cent of runners) than non-elite runners (18 per cent). Associative self-talk was similar to instructional self-talk in other types of sport and reflected runners paying attention to their body and aspects of running such as pace, stride, and form, which are important for performing to their potential (Brick, MacIntyre, & Campbell, 2014). Although it is important that non-elite runners also monitor their pace and form (e.g., so they do not become exhausted before the finish), they may not be motivated by finishing in their fastest time, and focusing on bodily sensations can feel unpleasant and therefore be discouraging.

Other studies have shed light on endurance athletes' use of positive and negative self-talk. Dolan, Houston, and Martin (2011) reported that positive self-talk was the most common mental preparation strategy used during training and in the hour before racing by 401 triathletes. In this study, female triathletes were more likely to use positive self-talk before training (62.4 per cent versus 40.1 per cent) and before racing (56.7 per cent versus 39.6 per cent), compared to males. In addition, in a study with former Olympic cyclists (Kress & Statler, 2007), using positive self-talk was identified as a coping strategy for dealing with exertion pain (e.g., 'Hey, I'm trained for this. I've prepared myself. I can get through this. It will get easier soon. Everybody else is suffering too. If I'm suffering, everyone else must be suffering worse'). Further, ultramarathon runners described using self-talk to cope with the demands of events, and particularly referred to the importance of maintaining positive self-talk throughout events, and specifically during difficult moments (Simpson, Post, Young, & Jensen, 2014). With consideration to negative self-talk, thoughts about quitting (e.g., 'I already did this before... What am I trying to prove by doing this again?') were common for ultramarathon runners and a source of stress (Holt, Lee, Kim, & Klein, 2014). There was a constant battle between positive and negative thoughts throughout the event and especially during the latter stages. In addition, recreational-level runners, cyclists, and triathletes described a desire to stop or slow down and unhelpful self-talk that was persuading them to not continue, when they neared exhaustion during an event. They also described negative self-talk (e.g., 'I'm 30 seconds off what I should be – disaster', 'I've buggered up all that training') when they encountered a range of stressors such as dropping food or a water bottle (McCormick, Meijen, & Marcora, 2018b). In addition, some studies have used a 'think aloud' protocol to examine endurance athletes' thought processes generally (i.e., not limited to their self-talk), which sheds light on what their self-talk would likely relate to. In particular, 10 runners who were running seven or more miles reported thoughts relating to their pace and the distance, relating to pain and discomfort, and relating to environmental factors such as geography and weather, admiration for the environment, wildlife, traffic, and other people (Samson, Simpson, Kamphoff, & Langlier, 2017).

Finally, some studies suggest that many endurance athletes are not fully aware of their self-talk or do not use it deliberately (Buman, Omli, Giacobbi, & Brewer, 2008; McCormick, Meijen, & Marcora, 2018a; Schüler & Langens, 2007; Stanley, Lane, Beedie, Friesen, & Devonport, 2012). For example, few runners identified self-talk as a strategy they use to influence their emotions before they run (Stanley et al., 2012). These studies highlight the potential value of self-talk interventions. Interventions could help athletes to become aware of their self-talk and its consequences, and to intentionally use self-talk statements that match the demands of the endurance event.

Self-talk antecedents

Research on the antecedents of self-talk attempts to identify factors that shape and determine people's self-talk (Hatzigeorgiadis et al., 2014). There is relatively little research on the antecedents of self-talk within endurance sports. One area of relevant research has examined the effects of exercise intensity and duration on a person's thoughts, particularly their focus of attention. In the endurance literature, two broad focuses of attention have been distinguished. Although there are newer classifications (Brick et al., 2014), *association* traditionally refers to when exercisers pay attention to bodily sensations such as their heart rate, breathing, temperature, and muscle fatigue, whereas *dissociation* traditionally refers to when exercisers direct their attention away from these sensations that often feel unpleasant (e.g., Morgan & Pollock, 1977). Research in this area (Aitchison et al., 2013; Hutchinson & Tenenbaum, 2007; Tenenbaum & Connolly, 2008) has required participants to perform at different exercise intensities, and to report or categorise their thoughts. These studies show that people report mostly dissociative thoughts at lower intensities, and thoughts become increasingly associative as the exercise intensity and duration increases, particularly as they near exhaustion. Although research in this area has examined performers' thoughts generally, which includes more than their self-talk such as their focus of attention, the methods used do capture self-talk. The results are also suggestive of what a performer's self-talk is likely to relate to. For example, as a person performs close to their maximum level of effort, their self-talk is likely to relate to whole-body feelings (e.g., pain, fatigue, exertion) and command and instruction to specific body parts or whole-body functioning (Aitchison et al., 2013).

Hatzigeorgiadis and Biddle (2008) reported findings of two studies with middle-distance, cross-country runners that explored anxiety and goal-performance discrepancies as antecedents of negative self-talk. In the first study, they found that cognitive (relating to worry) and somatic anxiety (relating to bodily symptoms) experienced 30 minutes before competing were associated with performance worries during performance (e.g., thoughts that they were not going to achieve their goal). Moreover, they found that runners who perceived their pre-competition anxiety as helpful reported less worries during performance, compared to runners who perceived their anxiety as detrimental. In the second study, goal-performance discrepancy was a stronger predictor of negative self-talk than anxiety. Highlighting the importance of pursuing realistic performance goals, athletes who performed below the standard required to achieve their goal reported more frequent performance worries while performing.

Effects of self-talk

Research examining the effects of self-talk typically uses experimental designs to test whether strategically using instructional or motivational cue words or short phrases improves performance. Laboratory studies provide good evidence that motivational self-talk improves endurance performance. Recreationally-active individuals who received a motivational self-talk intervention showed an 18 per cent increase in their cycling time to exhaustion at 80 per cent of their peak power output (a strenuous workload sustainable for approximately 10 minutes), whereas a control group who did not receive the intervention marginally decreased their time to exhaustion (Blanchfield, Hardy, de Morree, Staiano, & Marcora, 2014).

In other words, people using motivational self-talk persevered with the strenuous cycling for longer before stopping. The strategic self-talk intervention involved using two statements in the early-to-mid stages of the cycling (e.g., 'Feeling good'), and two near exhaustion (e.g., 'Push through this'). In another study (Barwood, Corbett, Wagstaff, McVeigh, & Thelwell, 2015), recreationally-active males who used motivational self-talk increased their power output throughout a 10 km cycling time trial and improved their performance time by 3.75 per cent, whereas a neutral self-talk group maintained similar power outputs and their time increased by 1.30 per cent. The intervention involved identifying negative self-talk they had used (e.g., 'I've worked too hard'), and countering it with positive, motivational statements (e.g., 'I can manage my energy until the end'). In a third study (Wallace et al., 2017), trained cyclists and triathletes who used motivational self-talk performed for 39.4 per cent longer when they were cycling at 80% of their peak power output in an environmental chamber that simulated performing in the heat. A control group marginally decreased their time to exhaustion. Finally, in a similar study in hot conditions (Hatzigeorgiadis et al., 2018), participants cycled at a steady rating of perceived exertion (a 'somewhat hard' to 'hard' intensity) for 30 minutes. Participants using motivational self-talk produced substantially greater power during the final third of the trial compared to control participants.

Complementing laboratory studies that are characterised by experimental control, but that lack ecological validity (i.e., generalisability to real-life settings), two field studies have been conducted at real endurance events. First, Schüler and Langens (2007) examined the effects of using self-talk during a 'psychological crisis' in a marathon. Such a crisis typically occurs after about 30 kilometres (18.6 miles), and is characterised by strong desire to give up, and thoughts about the benefits of stopping (e.g., resting, relaxing) and the costs of continuing (e.g., unbearable exhaustion). For runners experiencing a big psychological crisis, self-talk statements related to self-encouragement (e.g., 'Stay on. Don't give up'), anticipation of positive consequences (e.g., 'I will be proud of myself if I can do it'), and self-calming (e.g., 'Stay calm and you will do it') were effective at buffering against negative effects of a crisis on performance. Second, McCormick, Meijen, and Marcora (2018a) examined the effects of learning to use motivational self-talk in runners completing a 60-mile, overnight ultramarathon. Although there was no performance benefit, which could be explained by the small sample size and variability in performance times, the participants reported finding the intervention helpful and continued to use it six months after their commitment to the research, particularly during endurance events and to a lesser extent in training.

Studies to date have examined the effects of motivational (rather than instructional) self-talk, which is well suited for increasing and maintaining effort during a physically-demanding endurance task. Instructional self-talk could be valuable for managing other demands of endurance events, such as paying attention to other competitors or the environment, or monitoring and controlling pace, stride, form, or technique. Future research could fruitfully examine the effects of instructional self-talk interventions in endurance sports.

Self-talk mechanisms

Various theories discussed in this book explain ways that self-talk could benefit endurance performance. Theories of emotion regulation (Chapter 5) suggest that self-talk can influence how a person evaluates stressful situations they encounter (e.g., adverse weather, injury, mechanical failure), the emotions they experience (e.g., anxiety, frustration, discouragement), and whether these emotions are helpful or harmful (e.g., whether they increase focus or cause distraction). Self-efficacy theory (Chapter 7) suggests that self-talk, as a type of verbal persuasion, can enhance self-efficacy and consequently improve endurance performance. Motivational self-talk could also increase tolerance of exercise-induced pain (Chapter 3). These mechanisms have received some empirical support in sport research on self-talk (for a review, see Galanis, Hatzigeorgiadis, Zourbanos, & Theodorakis, 2016), but have yet to be examined in endurance research on self-talk.

Empirical evidence does exist for mechanisms described by the psychobiological model of endurance performance (Chapter 2), in particular in relation to perception of effort. The psychobiological model suggests that self-talk can improve endurance performance by decreasing perception of effort (how effortful, heavy, or strenuous the exercise feels) or increasing potential motivation (the greatest amount of effort that a person would be willing to offer). Perception of effort plays a role in explaining the effect of motivational self-talk on endurance performance. Blanchfield et al. (2014) found that when participants were using motivational self-talk, their perceived effort was lower than it was at the same time during their baseline performance. In other words, the same workload felt less strenuous. Barwood et al. (2015) and Hatzigeorgiadis et al. (2018) also found support for the role of perceived effort. In both studies, participants who were using motivational self-talk increased their power output (i.e., they were working harder), without perceiving more effort. In contrast, Wallace et al. (2017) did not find that motivational self-talk affected perceived effort. Instead, they found that the eight of nine participants who performed for longer when using motivational self-talk cycled for nearly twice as long (98.6 per cent longer) after reaching a rating of perceived exertion value of 19, which indicates that they are offering their maximal effort or near to it. In other words, using motivational self-talk did not reduce perception of effort, but increased participants' willingness or ability to tolerate near–maximal effort.

Summary

Descriptive research has shed light on the variety of self-talk used by marathon runners and the positive and negative self-talk of other endurance athletes. There is little research specifically on the antecedents of endurance athletes' self-talk, but research has demonstrated that thoughts generally – and seemingly self-talk specifically – become more associative in nature when a person is performing at a higher exercise intensity and as they reach exhaustion. Research on the effects of self-talk demonstrates that strategic use of motivational self-talk improves endurance performance, and perception of effort appears to play an important role.

Directions for future research

Several directions are provided in relation to the three strands of self-talk research. Regarding description and antecedents, we suggest exploring postulations of the new self-talk theoretical models (Latinjak et al., 2014; Van Raalte et al., 2016), particularly how self-talk is conceptualised within these frameworks as spontaneous/ intuitive and goal-directed/rational. Research could explore when, and for what reasons or purposes, endurance athletes experience or use spontaneous or goal-directed self-talk. In addition, they could describe the content of such self-talk in relation to its timing and functions. This research would help identify when and how to intervene to change counterproductive self-talk and promote effective goal-directed self-talk. Preliminary research in non-endurance athletes has provided useful insights (Latinjak et al., 2014).

It is important to theorise and measure potential mechanisms that could explain why self-talk benefits endurance performance (McCormick, Meijen, & Marcora, 2015). Doing so would help us understand how self-talk works, advance our knowledge of the self-talk phenomenon and, importantly, develop additional, effective self-talk interventions. As referred to in the self-talk mechanisms section, above, research could measure the effects of targeted self-talk interventions on emotions, self-efficacy, perceived pain, and perceived effort.

Research has yet to examine the effects of instructional self-talk on endurance performance. Instructional self-talk could help endurance athletes to pay attention to relevant cues (e.g., their breathing, opponent movements), perform technical aspects (e.g., correct running form or bike-handling technique), apply their race strategy, make pacing or tactical decisions, or manage mental and physical fatigue. For example, recent research has shown that instructional self-talk can help counter the effects of ego depletion, which refers to when energy for mental activity is low and self-control is reduced (Gregersen, Hatzigeorgiadis, Galanis, Comoutos, & Papaioannou, 2017).

With regard to long-term interventions, the new line of goal-directed self-talk interventions introduced by Latinjak and colleagues (2016) warrants attention from an applied perspective. Goal-directed self-talk interventions aim to help athletes to come up with alternative goal-directed self-talk in specific, problematic situations that evoke dysfunctional self-talk, such as internally-focused attention when exhausted. Such interventions – for which the purpose and structure are more thoroughly described by Latinjak et al. (2016) – could be accommodated well within the endurance performance setting.

Finally, verbal or written instructions and self-talk workbooks have been used to deliver self-talk interventions. Researchers could examine the effects of self-talk interventions that are delivered in ecologically-valid formats (e.g., websites, online videos, magazine articles) that are preferable for sub-elite endurance athletes, who may not have access to a psychologist (McCormick, Anstiss, & Lavallee, 2018).

Learning to use self-talk

A useful first step is to notice your self-talk and the effects it has on how you feel. Endurance athletes have been encouraged to listen to their self-talk whilst exercising, to notice their self-talk statements, and to notice their effects. A framework like Table 11.1 can be used to record these afterwards (from McCormick, Meijen, & Marcora, 2018a).

For choosing your own strategic self-talk statements, Hatzigeorgiadis et al. (2014) suggested using an IMPACT approach (Table 11.2).

Identify what you want to achieve

Pick self-talk statements based on your needs. Some people may be aiming to enhance their learning by developing new skills, improving their technique, or correcting mistakes. Others may be aiming to enhance their performance by learning how to psych themselves up or cope with exertion and pain. Others may be aiming to have more enjoyable experiences through learning how to cope with stress.

Pick statements based on the demands of the sport too. Although the demands of each sport vary, endurance athletes from a range of sports and events encounter some common demands that self-talk could help them to cope with. They need to persevere despite exertion and pain, make difficult pacing decisions, and cope with a range of stressful situations (McCormick, Meijen, & Marcora, 2018b).

Match self-talk to needs

As a rule, self-talk statements should be brief (a word or a short phrase), memorable, and purposeful for what you want to achieve. It is also important that they

TABLE 11.1 A framework for recording self-talk that you notice you are using

Self-talk statement	Did this statement have a positive, negative, or no effect on how you felt?	Please pick the statements that had the most beneficial effects (✓)
'I've had enough'	Negative	
'Come on, keep going'	Positive	✓

TABLE 11.2 The IMPACT approach to self-talk

I	Identify what you want to achieve
M	Match self-talk to needs
P	Practise different cues with consistency
A	Ascertain which cues work best for you
C	Create specific self-talk plans
T	Train self-talk plans to perfection

TABLE 11.3 Example instructional and motivational self-talk statements

Instructional self-talk	Motivational self-talk
'Pump your arms'	'You're going to dominate today'
'Keep your eyes focused straight ahead'	'This is what you've been training for'
'Run on toes'	'It's time to go to work'
'Drop your shoulders'	'Leave nothing behind'
'High knee lift'	'Come on! Come on! Keep it going!'
'Stick with your plan'	'Smash this!'
'Run through the finish line'	'Keep pushing! You can handle this!'

'feel right' for you personally (Van Raalte, Vincent, & Brewer, 2017). Table 11.3 includes examples of instructional and motivational self-talk statements in running (from McCormick, Meijen, & Marcora, 2018a; Miller & Donohue, 2003). Compare these statements with those that you observed yourself using.

Consider the following when selecting appropriate types of self-talk (Hatzigeorgiadis et al., 2014):

• Instructional self-talk is useful for focusing or directing attention (e.g., 'Watch her going for the overtake') or controlling technical aspects of a movement (e.g., 'Keep your cadence high').
• Motivational self-talk is useful for psyching up (e.g., 'Let's go'), building confidence (e.g., 'Come on, you can do this!'), increasing work rate (e.g., 'Come

TABLE 11.4 An exercise for practising choosing self-talk statements

When would self-talk be helpful?	What do you want to achieve?	What statements could help?
Beginning of performance	Example: Set my own pace despite other competitors.	'Run your own race'
Middle of performance	Example: Maintain good running form.	'Low and loose shoulders'
End of performance	Example: Persevere through high exertion.	'The end's in sight – One last push!'
When having thoughts about withdrawing effort	Example: Continue running, rather than stopping.	'Come on – You can push through this'
After encountering adversity	Example: Cope with getting lost.	'Take your time. There's plenty of time before the cut-off'

on, let's push on'), or maximising effort (e.g., 'Give it all you've got and leave nothing behind').

- Instructional self-talk is useful in the early stages of learning, as verbal cues could help you pay attention to the right things and provide useful technical (e.g., 'Long strides') or tactical instruction (e.g., 'Run your own race'). Motivational self-talk is useful when performing well-learned tasks that you can perform automatically.

How would you complete the exercise in Table 11.4 (p. 162)? What could self-talk help you to achieve, and what statements would you use?

Practise different cues with consistency

The chosen list of self-talk statements should be practised extensively and systematically during training. You can complete something like the below, print it off, and use it to remind yourself of key points before or during training (from McCormick, Meijen, & Marcora, 2018a).

-------------- ✂ --

My self-talk statements are:

Remember:

1. Use these statements often.
2. Use these and similar statements to counter unproductive thoughts.
3. Use these and similar statements during critical moments (e.g., something goes wrong).
4. When might these statements be helpful?

-------------- ✂ --

Ascertain which cues work best for you

Through practice, you can identify statements that work best for achieving your desired goals and gradually refine your self-talk statements. You can complete logs like the below after a training session where self-talk was practised.

List the self-talk statements that you used

Which were particularly helpful?

How did these statements help (e.g., when did they help, what did they help you with)?

List the self-talk statements that were unhelpful

If you found a statement unhelpful, consider replacing it and practising a different statement instead next time.

List the self-talk statements that you intend to use next time

Create specific self-talk plans

Statements can be organised so that a complete self-talk plan is developed for training or an event. This plan could involve using several combinations of self-talk statements to match different situations. It can include statements to use at different distances of a training or competitive performance, and in specific situations. For example, a person taking part non-competitively in a half-marathon may use something like the following:

TABLE 11.5 An example self-talk plan for a half-marathon

When	Self-Talk Statements
First mile	'Enjoy the experience'
Miles 2–3	'Watch your pace'
Middle miles	'How's your running form?'
Towards the end	'Dig deep – You can do it!'
Final mile	'Come on, just one last push!'
Sections with no crowd	'You're doing great. Keep it up!'
If I fall behind my pacer team	'I'm running a good time and may catch them in the last mile'
If the weather is awful	'It's one of those days – Time to adjust my goal'

Train self-talk plans to perfection

You are encouraged to practise your self-talk plan in training and then in endurance events, so that strategic use of appropriate self-talk statements becomes more automatic, and so that strategies are tested and familiar before an important event. For example, a person training for a half-marathon could practise the self-talk that they have prepared for the first mile, miles 2–3, the middle miles, towards the end, and the final mile (as above) during equivalent distances of a preparatory 10 km run. Similarly, a 1,500-metre runner who has planned to use motivational self-talk during the final 200 metres (e.g., 'Keep pushing! Keep pushing!') could practise these statements in repeated, high-intensity intervals during training. Imagery (Chapter 10) could be a valuable psychological skill for practising using self-talk statements to cope with problems that you may encounter during an endurance event (e.g., falling behind a target pace).

References

Aitchison, C., Turner, L. A., Ansley, L., Thompson, K. G., Micklewright, D., & Gibson, A. S. C. (2013). Inner dialogue and its relationship to perceived exertion during different running intensities. *Perceptual and Motor Skills, 117*, 11–30.

Barwood, M. J., Corbett, J., Wagstaff, C. R. D., McVeigh, D., & Thelwell, R. C. (2015). Improvement of 10-km time-trial cycling with motivational self-talk compared with neutral self-talk. *International Journal of Sports Physiology and Performance, 10*, 166–171.

Blanchfield, A. W., Hardy, J., de Morree, H. M., Staiano, W., & Marcora, S. M. (2014). Talking yourself out of exhaustion: The effects of self-talk on endurance performance. *Medicine & Science in Sports & Exercise, 46*, 998–1007.

Brick, N., MacIntyre, T., & Campbell, M. (2014). Attentional focus in endurance activity: New paradigms and future directions. *International Review of Sport and Exercise Psychology, 7*, 106–134.

Buman, M. P., Omli, J. W., Giacobbi, P. R., & Brewer, B. W. (2008). Experiences and coping responses of 'hitting the wall' for recreational marathon runners. *Journal of Applied Sport Psychology, 20*, 282–300.

Dolan, S. H., Houston, M., & Martin, S. B. (2011). Survey results of the training, nutrition, and mental preparation of triathletes: Practical implications of findings. *Journal of Sports Sciences, 29,* 1019–1028.

Galanis, E., Hatzigeorgiadis, A., Zourbanos, N., & Theodorakis, Y. (2016). Why self-talk is effective? Perspectives on self-talk mechanisms in sport. In M. Raab, P. Wylleman, R. Seiler, A.-M. Elbe, & A. Hatzigeorgiadis (Eds.), *Sport and exercise psychology research: From theory to practice* (pp. 181–200). London, England: Academic Press Elsevier.

Gregersen, J., Hatzigeorgiadis, A., Galanis, E., Comoutos, N., & Papaioannou, A. (2017). Countering the consequences of ego depletion: The effects of self-talk on selective attention. *Journal of Sport & Exercise Psychology, 39,* 161–171.

Hardy, J., Oliver, E., & Tod, D. (2009). A framework for the study and application of self-talk within sport. In S. D. Mellalieu & S. Hanton (Eds.), *Advances in applied sport psychology: A review* (pp. 37–74). London, England: Routledge.

Hatzigeorgiadis, A., Bartura, K., Argiropoulos, C., Comoutos, N., Galanis, E., & Flouris, A. D. (2018). Beat the heat: Effects of a motivational self-talk intervention on endurance performance. *Journal of Applied Sport Psychology, 30,* 388–401.

Hatzigeorgiadis, A., & Biddle, S. J. H. (2008). Negative self-talk during sport performance: Relationships with pre-competition anxiety and goal-performance discrepancies. *Journal of Sport Behavior, 31,* 237–253.

Hatzigeorgiadis, A., Zourbanos, N., Galanis, E., & Theodorakis, Y. (2011). Self-talk and sports performance: A meta-analysis. *Perspectives on Psychological Science, 6,* 348–356.

Hatzigeorgiadis, A., Zourbanos, N., Latinjak, A., & Theodorakis, Y. (2014). Self-talk. In A. Papaioannou & D. Hackfort (Eds.), *Routledge companion to sport and exercise psychology: Global perspectives and fundamental concepts* (pp. 370–383). London, England: Taylor & Francis.

Havey, M. L. (n.d.). Positive self talk: Inside the heads of America's top runners. Retrieved 24 August 2017, from www.active.com/running/articles/positive-self-talk-inside-the-heads-of-america-s-top-runners.

Holt, N. L., Lee, H., Kim, Y., & Klein, K. (2014). Exploring experiences of running an ultramarathon. *The Sport Psychologist, 28,* 22–35.

Hutchinson, J. C., & Tenenbaum, G. (2007). Attention focus during physical effort: The mediating role of task intensity. *Psychology of Sport and Exercise, 8,* 233–245.

Kress, J. L., & Statler, T. (2007). A naturalistic investigation of former Olympic cyclists' cognitive strategies for coping with exertion pain during performance. *Journal of Sport Behavior, 30,* 428–452.

Latinjak, A. T., Zourbanos, N., Lopez-Ros, V., & Hatzigeorgiadis, A. (2014). Goal-directed and undirected self-talk: Exploring a new perspective for the study of athletes' self-talk. *Psychology of Sport and Exercise, 15,* 548–558.

Latinjak, A. T., Font-Lladó, R., Zourbanos, N., & Hatzigeorgiadis, A. (2016). Goal-directed self-talk interventions: A single-case study with an elite athlete. *The Sport Psychologist, 30,* 189–194.

McCormick, A., Anstiss, P. A., & Lavallee, D. (2018). Endurance athletes' current and preferred ways of getting psychological guidance. *International Journal of Sport and Exercise Psychology.* DOI: 10.1080/1612197X.2018.1486874.

McCormick, A., Meijen, C., & Marcora, S. (2015). Psychological determinants of whole-body endurance performance. *Sports Medicine, 45,* 997–1015.

McCormick, A., Meijen, C., & Marcora, S. (2018a). Effects of a motivational self-talk intervention for endurance athletes completing an ultramarathon. *The Sport Psychologist, 32,* 42–50.

McCormick, A., Meijen, C., & Marcora, S. (2018b). Psychological demands experienced by recreational endurance athletes. *International Journal of Sport and Exercise Psychology*, *16*, 415–430.

Miller, A., & Donohue, B. (2003). The development and controlled evaluation of athletic mental preparation strategies in high school distance runners. *Journal of Applied Sport Psychology*, *15*, 321–334.

Morgan, W. P., & Pollock, M. L. (1977). Psychologic characterization of the elite distance runner. *Annals of the New York Academy of Sciences*, *301*, 382–403.

Samson, A., Simpson, D., Kamphoff, C., & Langlier, A. (2017). Think aloud: An examination of distance runners' thought processes. *International Journal of Sport and Exercise Psychology*, *15*, 176–189.

Schüler, J., & Langens, T. A. (2007). Psychological crisis in a marathon and the buffering effects of self-verbalizations. *Journal of Applied Social Psychology*, *37*, 2319–2344.

Simpson, D., Post, P. G., Young, G., & Jensen, P. R. (2014). 'It's not about taking the easy road': The experiences of ultramarathon runners. *The Sport Psychologist*, *28*, 176–185.

Stanley, D. M., Lane, A. M., Beedie, C. J., Friesen, A. P., & Devonport, T. J. (2012). Emotion regulation strategies used in the hour before running. *International Journal of Sport and Exercise Psychology*, *10*, 159–171.

Tenenbaum, G., & Connolly, C. T. (2008). Attention allocation under varied workload and effort perception in rowers. *Psychology of Sport and Exercise*, *9*, 704–717.

Van Raalte, J. L., Morrey, R. B., Cornelius, A. E., & Brewer, B. W. (2015). Self-talk of marathon runners. *The Sport Psychologist*, *29*, 258–260.

Van Raalte, J. L., Vincent, A., & Brewer, B. W. (2016). Self-talk: Review and sport-specific model. *Psychology of Sport and Exercise*, *22*, 139–148.

Van Raalte, J. L., Vincent, A., & Brewer, B. W. (2017). Self-talk interventions for athletes: A theoretically grounded approach. *Journal of Sport Psychology in Action*, *8*, 141–151.

Wallace, P. J., McKinlay, B. J., Coletta, N. A., Vlaar, J. I., Taber, M. J., Wilson, P. M., & Cheung, S. S. (2017). Effects of motivational self-talk on endurance and cognitive performance in the heat. *Medicine & Science in Sports & Exercise*, *49*, 191–199.

12

MINDFULNESS IN ENDURANCE PERFORMANCE

Emilie Thienot and Danielle Adams

Introduction

What if we were to state that during your next marathon (or other endurance event), through the development of mindfulness skills, you would be able to: i) notice when you are getting caught up by the pain, fatigue, and other unpleasant sensations (such as thermal discomfort or dyspnoea) you are experiencing; ii) accept the presence of these uncomfortable bodily sensations and iii) redirect your attention to what will help you perform best: breathing, movement form, pacing. This is what mindfulness could help you achieve in your next endurance performance: help you to gain control over your mind, by choosing where you want to focus your attention and reminding yourself why you want to push your limits.

In order to perform at an optimal level, athletes must demonstrate the ability to pay close attention to the present moment and to manage internal and external distractions. In endurance sports, the presence of uncomfortable sensations such as fatigue, exercise-induced muscle pain, joint pain, or cutaneous pain can trigger strong emotional reactions and affect performance by decreasing motivation and effort, altering technique and pacing. External distractions such as other competitors or difficult environmental conditions can also trigger negative emotional reactions and affect the level of effort and engagement in the present moment. Mindfulness techniques can be adopted to assist athletes to become more aware of the internal and external triggers, and manage emotions and attention to alleviate the potential for reactions to interfere with their performance.

This chapter aims to provide a comprehensive understanding of what mindfulness is, and how mindfulness can help endurance performers to optimise their engagement in the present moment. The first part of the chapter will define and explain why mindfulness is relevant for endurance performance. The second part of this chapter will describe how to design a mindfulness intervention to develop mindfulness skills for endurance performers.

Understanding mindfulness

To fully understand the essence of mindfulness, many authors have highlighted the importance of not decontextualising mindfulness from its original Eastern construct (Huxter, 2007). The Buddhist philosophy states that experiencing difficult emotions as well as mental and physical discomfort is part of belonging to the human race. At the core of the Buddhist philosophy is the belief that resisting a full embrace of our human condition can create an addiction to pleasant feelings, and thus suffering. Hence, the pathway to freedom is based on developing more insight and being able to let go of one's automatic reactions (Huxter, 2007). The insight developed through mindfulness meditation was based on the belief that all perceptions should be experienced as impermanent, uncertain, and emptied of assumptions. Following these principles, there should be no need to identify with thoughts, emotions, and bodily sensations: a liberating experience for patients prone to depression (Teasdale et al., 2002). Thus, in Buddhism, mindfulness represents the cultivation of this particular awareness associated with detachment from one's internal experience. The Buddha described three processes involved in mindfulness meditation: i) focusing on the present moment; ii) noticing changes of internal experience and what is triggering these changes; iii) paying a bare attention to the present-experience without clinging to any perceptions (Thanissaro, 1996).

Following Buddhist principles, but without any religious or spiritual connotations, cognitive and behavioural therapies in clinical psychology emphasise the notion that thoughts, emotions, and bodily sensations should be seen as transient events while practicing mindfulness (Teasdale, Segal, & Williams, 2003). Bishop and colleagues (2004) proposed a conceptualisation of mindfulness which characterised it as a metacognitive skill that encompasses two components: attention and acceptance.

Attention

The attention component refers to the ability to intentionally observe one's thoughts, emotions, and bodily sensations as they occur in the present moment, and to regulate one's focus of attention. Bishop and colleagues separated this component into three skills: *sustained attention* (the ability to maintain a state of vigilance over a prolonged period of time), *switching* (the ability to switch the focus from one object to another), and *inhibiting secondary elaborative processing* (the absence of dwelling on the current experience, including rumination and worry). Brown and Ryan (2003), who defined mindfulness as "being attentive to and aware of what is taking place in the present" (p. 822), distinguished the concept of *awareness* from *attention* by defining awareness as an aspect of consciousness that monitors the various internal stimuli (including the five physical senses, the kinaesthetic senses, and the activities of the mind) as well as external stimuli (e.g., environment); whereas attention represents the process of directing the focus of attention on one specific object when the stimulus is sufficiently strong. One may be aware of stimuli without consciously directing the focus of attention toward them (Brown & Ryan, 2003; Brown, Ryan, & Creswell, 2007). For example, a road cyclist in the Tour de France may be aware of the fans standing along the route, but does not focus their attention on them. In their conceptualisation of mindfulness, Brown and colleagues (2007) placed strong emphasis on the self-regulatory characteristic of mindfulness involved in information processing: "the mindful mode of processing involves a voluntary, fluid regulation of states of attention and awareness" (p. 213). In contrast, Brown and Ryan (2003) defined *mindlessness* as a lack of awareness and attention to the present moment characterised by automatic reactions and behavioural responses, and inversely correlated with well-being.

Acceptance

The acceptance component refers to a particular orientation toward one's thoughts, emotions, and sensations by adopting an attitude of openness and receptivity to these experiences (Bishop et al., 2004). This attitude of acceptance is set in opposition to judging, minimising, or attempting to avoid what is experienced in the present moment (Bishop et al., 2004). For example, it can be common in endurance events to start minimising the consequences of not finishing the race via internal self-talk (or decreasing the importance of getting a bad result) when the physical discomfort reaches its peak. Defined as the attempt to minimise, suppress, or replace the thoughts, emotions, and bodily sensations experienced, experiential avoidance has been associated with the development of psychopathology and emotional distress (Hayes & Wilson, 1994). According to the ironic processes theory, rigid and non-flexible attempts to suppress unwanted internal experiences are largely ineffective and can result in increased frequency of unwanted thoughts and emotions (Wegner, Schneider, Carter, & White, 1987). For instance, thinking about not falling on a risky downhill part of a cycle ride may increase the anxiety level and lead to more thoughts in relation to the risk of falling. In contrast, acceptance involves a conscious decision to abandon one's agenda to experience things differently. Ultimately, acceptance can be referred to as an active process of 'allowing' current thoughts, feelings, and sensations in order to be fully experience the present. Bishop and colleagues' conceptualisation appears to be the most complete as it consolidates many of the different mechanisms highlighted in the various models: maintaining awareness in the present moment, regulating the focus of attention, adopting an attitude of acceptance, and disengaging from elaborative thinking processes such as rumination. Drawing from the work of Bishop and colleagues, Shapiro, Carlson, Astin, and Freedman (2006) added a third component to attention and attitude of acceptance, namely *intention*, highlighting the importance of having explicit goals underlining one's mindfulness practice.

The contribution of neuroscience in understanding underlying mechanisms

The last decade has seen that findings from research in cognitive neuroscience helped to provide further clarity and support for the existence of the mechanisms underlying mindfulness (Hölzel et al., 2011). Specifically, brain activity patterns and associated changes in neural structure and function have been observed in association with mindfulness states. The growing body of neuroimaging literature claims that mindfulness practice can enhance cognitive function associated with attention regulation, body awareness, emotion regulation, and detachment of the self (Hölzel et al., 2011). Neuroimaging research using functional magnetic resonance imaging (fMRI) has shown that the anterior cingulate cortex, which enables the detection of distracting stimuli (external or internal) and helps to overcome this distraction, displays increased activation during mindfulness meditation (Hölzel et al., 2007). The implications for endurance performance contexts are potentially significant, considering the importance of detecting internal and external distractions and maintaining focus in the present moment.

The neuroscience of mindfulness and pain

Neuroimaging studies have also demonstrated the impact of mindfulness practice on brain areas involved with body awareness (Haase et al., 2015; Mehling et al., 2009). With regard to physical pain, several studies have shown that mindfulness impacts brain activity in areas involved in pain processing (Grant et al., 2010; Zeidan et al., 2011). By enabling a non-evaluative representation of sensory events, mindfulness is thought to attenuate the subjective experience of pain (Grant, Courtemanche, & Rainville, 2011). Grant and colleagues suggested a functional decoupling of the cognitive-evaluative and sensory-discriminative dimensions of pain associated with practice, possibly allowing meditators to view painful stimuli more neutrally. This suggests a very interesting differentiation for endurance performers: mindful people seem to become more able to notice any sensations that will occur in their body (including pain), but they are able to process these sensations objectively (a non-judgmental reflection of their experience without reacting to it). Other neuroscientific studies have shown that elite athletes become more able to identify, label, and regulate the emotions triggered by unpleasant bodily sensations after attending a 7-week mindfulness intervention (Haase et al, 2015) and mindfulness training facilitates 'emotional recovery' (ability to return to an emotional baseline after an emotion has been triggered) and decreases ruminative processes (Jain et al., 2007).

Mindfulness in endurance performance

Given the prolonged duration of endurance events, arguably the most powerful application of mindfulness to endurance sports is rooted in the Buddhist philosophy that all perceptions should be experienced as impermanent, uncertain, and emptied of assumptions. During an endurance event, an athlete is constantly challenged by various distractions (internal and external) such as fatigue, pain, tough environmental conditions, boredom, performance anxiety, negative thoughts, pacing/perception of effort, and management of technique. Thus, given the prolonged period of time an athlete engages in an endurance sport, the overriding benefit of mindfulness as a meta-cognitive strategy is that the athlete becomes equipped with the ability to notice any sensation that occurs in their body, and thus the capacity to process these sensations objectively in order to appropriately engage in relevant and helpful (internal and external) performance related cues.

Building on the Buddhist philosophy of mindfulness, and in consideration of the requirement to effectively manage the interplay between attention, cognition, and emotion for endurance performance, investigation into the application of shifting attention to useful cues through acceptance, rather than controlling unhelpful emotional states, is worth further attention. Using the Acceptance and Commitment Therapy model (Hayes, Stroshal, & Wilson, 1999), Gardner and Moore (2004, 2017) developed the first mindfulness-based intervention in sport, referred to as Mindfulness-Acceptance-Commitment (MAC). They positioned themselves in opposition to the traditional approaches used in sport psychology interventions by highlighting the importance of modifying one's relationship with the current experience by accepting it rather than aiming to change its content. Gardner and Moore claimed that traditional approaches aimed to negate unwanted objects in consciousness and alter the content of the experience. However, based on Wegner's theory of ironic processes of mental control (in order to negate a certain object, one must evoke it first; Wegner, 1994), they emphasised the paradoxical effect of thought suppression in sport performance. That is, attempts to suppress unwanted thoughts may result in more (rather than less) attentional focus on that specific thought. By simply noticing the cognitive, emotional, and sensory experience without trying to change or avoid its content, one's focus of attention remains on the relevant aspects of the task in order to perform well (Gardner & Moore, 2017). This can have implications for endurance performance, for example in relation to pacing decisions, in line with proposals that mental exertion involving response inhibition can affect the effort-based decision-making process thought to regulate self-paced endurance performance (Marcora, 2010).

Mindfulness and pain/fatigue management

In endurance sport, acceptance of exertion (or exercise-induced) pain seems critical to performance (Fitzgerald, 2015). Recently, researchers have also investigated the relationships between mindfulness, physical effort, and pain perception. Salmon, Hanneman, and Harwood (2010) emphasised the importance of a non-elaborative awareness of sensory cues in sustained physical activity. They hypothesised that mindfulness helps in having a more objective perception of physical sensations and reduces the negative emotional reactions towards the sensations. Salmon and colleagues also highlighted the potential impact of mindfulness processes on de-automating the appraisal process and, therefore, minimising overall stress. A study conducted by Ivanova and colleagues (2014) with a nonathletic female population tested this hypothesis and showed that an acceptance and commitment (ACT) intervention improved exercise tolerance time. More specifically, Ivanova and colleagues showed that the improvements in exercise tolerance induced by a single session ACT intervention (lasting 50 minutes in total) were associated with improvements in perceived effort and ratings of post-exercise enjoyment. Notably, the affect perceived during the task did not vary after the ACT intervention, which may suggest that the acceptance component of the intervention did not alter the negative affect associated with discomfort. In keeping with the psychobiological model of endurance (Marcora, Bosio, & de Morree, 2008), perception of effort is the main limiting factor for endurance performance. According to Ivanova and colleagues, the ACT intervention may have reduced perception of effort indirectly via increasing the perceived ability to perform the high-intensity exercise task, and maybe decreasing the mental effort associated to the need to 'fight against' physical discomfort.

Together, these studies suggest that endurance athletes would benefit by adopting mindfulness techniques in order to be 'equipped' to process discomfort and perceived effort, enhancing their feeling of competency and willingness to face aversive training situations. As a result, developing mindfulness skills may also help to adopt optimal pacing strategy. Pacing requires the continuous selection of the appropriate amount of effort to exert at any given moment (Baron et al., 2009), hence decision-making aspects are crucial (Micklewright, Kegerreis, Raglin, & Hettinga, 2016; Renfree, Martin, Micklewright, & Gibson, 2014; Smits, Pepping, & Hettinga, 2014). The most obvious benefit from an endurance athlete's ability to decrease their mental fatigue through the inhibition of their response to discomfort (thus decreasing their perceived effort), would be that it would allow them to better engage in the planned pacing strategy (Pageaux, Lepers, Dietz, & Marcora, 2014). The relationship between brain neurotransmitters and athletes' pacing behaviours seems to be mediated by the subjective interpretation of their physical state (Marcora & Staiano, 2010), which seems to indicate that an objective perception of pain, as achieved through engagement in mindfulness, would lead an athlete to a more successful adherence to to their pacing strategy.

Mindfulness and flow

Mindfulness has also been associated with the sport-related concept of 'flow' (Moran, 2012). Associated with peak performances (Kimiecik & Stein, 1992), the concept of flow, or optimal experience, has been defined as complete absorption in the current activity (Jackson & Csikszentmihalyi, 1999), and is characterised by nine dimensions: challenge–skill balance, action-awareness merging, clear goals, unambiguous feedback, concentration on task, sense of control, loss of self-consciousness, time transformation, and autotelic experience (Jackson, 1995). According to Jackson (1995), a main facilitator for experiencing the flow state is a present moment and non-self-conscious concentration on the task. It is well-known that present moment strategies in sport help to suspend unnecessary distractions, enhance concentration on the task at hand, and lead to better athletic performances (Orlick, 1990; Ravizza, 2002). In order to demonstrate the link between flow and mindfulness, Kee and Wang (2008), using a cluster analytic approach, showed that a high tendency to be mindful was positively correlated with one's tendency to experience flow. A qualitative study exploring flow experiences in elite swimmers highlighted the presence of an enhanced state of bodily awareness associated to an attitude of acceptance during their race preparation, showing similarities with a mindfulness state (Bernier et al., 2009). Further, Aherne, Moran, and Lonsdale (2011) demonstrated that athletes exposed to a mindfulness-based intervention experienced greater flow. As the flow state can be easily disrupted by environmental stimuli (Jackson, 1995), mindfulness, conceptualised as a meta-cognitive self-regulation process, may be helpful in detecting when the flow state is disrupted and redirecting the focus of attention on optimal goal-relevant cues. After conducting a review of the available research on flow, Landhäußer and Keller (2012) concluded that flow may foster positive affect and even lead to enhanced performance. Interestingly, in their investigation into the relationship between flow and endurance running, Schüler and Brunner (2009) demonstrated that a high flow experience during a marathon race leads to a high motivation to continue running activity in the future, providing further support for the usage of mindfulness to experience flow in training as a means to maintain motivation to train. This notion provides further indication that mindfulness based cognitive strategies adopted during endurance performance lead to reduced mental effort and a subsequent reduction in perceived effort (Ivanova et al., 2014).

Mindfulness and appropriate motor control

Acceptance also reduces the likelihood of the athlete engaging in reinvestment processes (Masters, 1992: see below) which have been shown to result in the breakdown of well-learned motor skills (Jackson & Beilock, 2008); such a breakdown in an experienced endurance runner for example, would result in a less efficient gait. Mindfulness and acceptance approaches are proposed as an antidote to this process by noticing unhelpful shifts in attention to thoughts, feelings, or attentional foci, and instead redirecting attention to more useful, task-relevant cues (Birrer, Röthlin, & Morgan, 2012). Throughout the extended duration of an endurance event, the performer must exercise the most effective control over technique, particularly during times of fatigue. It has been widely proposed that in motor skill execution the need to perform/maintain performance can trigger a 'paralysis by analysis' effect through consciously engaging in the motor control of well-learned skill execution, commonly referred to as reinvestment (Masters, 1992). The tendency to control automatised movements with declarative knowledge is reduced through the ability to accept the current internal state, and athletes could therefore enhance the execution of well-learned technique (motor skill execution) because automatic processes are not interrupted. A further, secondary benefit from the application of mindfulness to endurance sport would be an acceptance that one's happiness does not come as a result of outcomes; such an approach would further alleviate the likelihood of increasing effort.

Enhancing endurance performance through mindfulness intervention

The following 8-week (presented in 4 phases) mindfulness intervention is based on the Mindfulness-Acceptance-Commitment programme developed by Gardner and Moore (2004) combined with the experience and expertise of this chapter's authors. Phase 1 introduces the principles and application of mindfulness to endurance sport, and provides direction to identify performance-relevant attentional cues and commonly experienced distractions. Phase 2 aims to enhance the athletes' understanding of mindfulness through exercises involving self-observation (meta-awareness processes). Phase 3 focuses on developing an understanding and practice of an attitude of acceptance towards the current experience and perceived distractions. Finally, phase 4 is devoted to developing the skill of attention regulation before and during endurance performance, as well as integrating the three mindfulness skills (self-observation, acceptance, and refocusing) into a performance routine (see Appendix 12.1 to read the case study of Elliot, a marathon runner).

Phase 1: Identifying attentional relevant cues and potential distractions

The preliminary step is to clarify what is helpful and what is unhelpful with regard to focus of attention during performance. Part of this process is the clarification of the pacing strategy and what will constitute critical moments relevant to pacing regulation. Self-confrontation and debriefing techniques post-performance facilitate this phase.

Phase 2: Self-observation skills

The second phase aims at developing the ability to efficiently notice when one's focus of attention is not directed at what is relevant in the moment. Two processes are key to enhancing this skill: i) developing an understanding of what self-observation means and feels like; ii) practising the skill of observing oneself in various contexts. Both processes are introduced with practices that are non-sport specific where the intention is to practice generic skills applicable to everyday life for later application to sport/performance (see Figure 12.1 for mindfulness of breathing, teeth brushing exercise, and training application).

What does self-observation mean? 'The sky and the weather' metaphor

The observing self represents the part of your awareness that makes contact with thoughts and feelings yet does not identify with them; the sky and the weather metaphor provides a foundation to explore the observing self.

Your observing self is like the sky; thoughts and feelings are like the weather. The weather changes continually, but no matter how bad it gets, the weather

Mindfulness of the breathing: The aim of this 3-minute exercise is to focus your attention on breathing while noticing your mind wandering. Find yourself a comfortable position, your back straight, gently close your eyes, or keep them open if you prefer. Be focused on your present experience, right here, right now. Bring your attention to your body. Get a sense of the position of your body and the points of contact with the floor, the bed, or the chair.

Then become aware of the fact that you are breathing. Become aware of the movement of the breath as it flows in and out of the body. Notice how it feels. Notice the rise and fall of your rib cage. Notice the air flowing in and out of your nostrils. Notice the rise and fall of your abdomen. Don't try to change or control the rhythm of your breath. Just observe it and allow your breathing to be in its own natural rhythm. When your mind starts to wander, and it will, simply notice it and return to the breath. No commentary, no judgment. Observe the full cycle of each breath. Simply remain present to your breathing. After a short time, you may notice that the mind wanders off to thoughts of the past, or maybe anticipation of the future. As soon as you become aware that the attention has moved off the breath, gently guide it back to the next breath, simply observing your breath in the present moment. Now bring your awareness back to the room, slowly open your eyes, become fully aware of your physical surroundings, and continue your day.

Mindful brushing the teeth exercise: Choose a relatively quiet moment to go in the bathroom and brush your teeth. When you put the toothbrush in your mouth and start to brush your teeth, notice the sensations of the toothpaste on your teeth, the tingling feeling of the menthol, the texture, the smell, the taste, the sensations of brushing ... Be aware of all these sensations as it was the first time that you have ever brushed your teeth, and focus intensively on the task you are doing. You may become aware that other thoughts come into your mind while performing this exercise. That is inevitably going to happen because numerous thoughts come and go in our heads all day, every day. When this happens, please just notice them passing in your mind, without judging them as bad or good, right or wrong. Consider them just simply as an activity in your mind that comes and goes like waves intermittently hitting a shore, or like leaves on a river stream ... And gently bring your attention back to the task of rinsing your mouth.

Mindful training: The goal of this exercise is to expand your mindfulness skills to your training environment, by executing your training session with a mindful attention. Choose 3 training sessions during the week. Before executing the main section of your training session, identify the most relevant cues you want to focus on during the execution to achieve the goal of your session (e.g., breathing; technical cues; specific sensations). The aim is to be very focused on the chosen cues and to notice as quickly as possible when your attention is directed at something else (e.g., fatigue; physical discomfort; boredom; teammates' behaviours). Try to observe what your attention is doing during this exercise. You may become aware that various distractions come into your mind while performing this exercise. That is inevitably going to happen because numerous thoughts, images, feelings come and go in our heads all day, every day. Simply notice them, let them come and go like passing cars, and refocus your attention on your chosen attentional cues as quickly as possible.

FIGURE 12.1 Practice of self-observation

cannot harm the sky in any way. The mightiest thunderstorm, the most turbulent hurricane, the most severe winter blizzard – these things cannot hurt or harm the sky. And no matter how bad the weather, the sky always has room for it. Plus, sooner or later the weather always changes. Sometimes we forget the sky is there, but it is still there. And sometimes we cannot see the sky because is it obscured by clouds. But if we rise high enough above those clouds – even the thickest, darkest thunderclouds – sooner or later we will reach clear sky, stretching in all directions, boundless and pure. More and more, you can learn to access this part of you, a safe space inside from which to observe and make room for difficult thoughts and feelings.

Phase 3: Adopting an attitude of acceptance towards one's current experience

The third phase incorporates the application of a non-judgmental attitude towards disruptive distractions, particularly physical discomfort and negative thoughts. Two processes facilitate an acceptance stance: i) having an understanding of what acceptance means and feels like; ii) practising acceptance in contexts involving physical discomfort and negative thoughts (see Figure 12.2, 'Body scan' and 'Acceptance strategies').

What is acceptance? 'The ball in a pool' metaphor

The ball in a pool metaphor is a description of the counterproductivity of emotional or cognitive avoidance.

Imagine that what you are doing with these thoughts/distressing memories/feelings/physical discomfort is like fighting with a ball in a pool. You don't like them, you don't want them, and you want them out of your life. So, you try to push this ball under water and out of your consciousness. However, the ball keeps floating back to the surface, so you have to keep pushing it down or holding it under the water. This struggling with the ball keeps it close to you and is tiring and futile. If you were to let go of the ball, it would pop up, float on the surface near you and you probably wouldn't like it. But if you let it float there for a while, with your hands off, it would eventually drift away and out of your life. And even if it didn't, at least you'd be better able to enjoy your swim rather than spending your time fighting!

Phase 4: Developing refocusing skills and integrating mindfulness three-step process into competition

The fourth phase aims at enhancing the ability to refocus attention on relevant cues as part of a three-step process: i) self-observation: noticing when the mind is focusing on distractions (i.e., physical discomfort, negative thoughts); ii) acceptance: adopting a non-judgmental and non-reactive attitude towards current distractions;

Body scan: During this 3-minute exercise, you are going to focus on your experience in the present moment. The aim is to quickly scan your body and then focus all your attention on your breathing. Place yourself a comfortable position, your back straight, gently close your eyes, or keep them open if you prefer. Be focused on your present experience, right here, right now. Bring your attention to your body. Get a sense of the position of your body. Scan your whole body, from head to toe ... notice what ever sensations may be in your head; your neck; your spine and back; your arms; your hands; your legs; your feet. Get a sense of the different sensations present in your body. Just observe them, without judging or struggling with them; without trying to control them. Simply allow these sensations to be there. Then bring your awareness to your breathing. For the next few breaths, just notice the rise and fall of your rib cage. Notice the air flowing in and out of your nostrils. Notice the rise and fall of your abdomen. Don't try to change or control the rhythm of your breath. Just observe it and allow your breathing to be in its own natural rhythm. Bring now your awareness back to the room, slowly open your eyes, become fully aware of your physical surroundings, and continue your day.

Acceptance strategies:

❖ **Normalising**
It is okay to feel nervous; it is normal to feel tired or sore; it is okay to feel frustrated. It just tells you that you care about what you are doing.
It is NOT GOOD OR BAD to experience distractions, it is just NORMAL.

❖ **Labelling**
Acknowledge the distraction by labelling it in your mind:
'I am thinking about my opponents '; 'I am feeling frustrated'; 'I am having the thought that I can't make it'; 'I am focusing on how tired I am, instead focusing on my efficient cues'

❖ **Showing self-compassion**
Don't criticise yourself for having certain thoughts or emotions. Don't blame yourself for not being focused on your efficient cues. It happens to everyone. Don't criticise yourself for not being in the perfect state. Be kind to yourself.

❖ **Focusing on the breath :**
As you are observing the feeling, breathe into it and around it. While acknowledging the distraction, focus on your breathing.

❖ **'Letting go' metaphors:**
Thoughts, emotions and sensations are like:
- Passing cars driving past outside your house
- Clouds drifting across the sky / birds flying across the sky
- People walking on the other side of the street
- Suitcases on a conveyor belt
- Waves gently rising onto the beach
- Leaves floating on a stream

You can be aware of the distractions, without focusing on them AND without trying to get rid of them.

FIGURE 12.2 Practice of acceptance

ii) refocusing: quickly regulating the focus of attention on performance relevant-cues in the moment. During this phase, the ability to regulate the attention is strongly underpinned by the level of clarity on what is relevant to perform at their best and what is not.

Assessing the impact of mindfulness interventions in endurance sport

Various tools can be used to assess the impact of mindfulness interventions in endurance sport. Pre- and post-intervention, athletes can complete the 15-item Mindfulness Inventory for Sport (Thienot et al., 2014) which will give an indication of: i) their ability to notice distracting thoughts, emotions, and physical sensations; ii) their ability to adopt a non-judgemental attitude towards their experienced distractions; iii) their ability to refocus quickly on performance-relevant cues. During the intervention, it is recommended to use scales as presented in Appendix 12.2 to regularly assess how much the athletes are able to apply the mindfulness process to a specific task. In combination with self-assessment scales (see Appendix 12.2 for an example), performance indicators can also be used to assess the impact of mindfulness interventions in endurance performance such as pacing consistency through the ability to maintain a certain pace at critical moments of the race and overall time improvement.

Creating sustainable impact through values clarification

A key component of success in sport performance is the meaning that the sport has for the athlete (Fitzgerald, 2015). Clarifying purpose, meaning, and source of motivation is an important ingredient for long-term impact in mindfulness interventions. In order to accept physical discomfort and push through difficult experiences, human beings need to be clear about what their higher purpose is. Endurance athletes need to know what fuels their motivation to train and compete. Being clear about our 'why' and our values enable us to choose what is really important to us over the current discomfort we are experiencing. Elliot (Appendix 12.1) mentions how proud he would feel if he was achieving his target. By exploring this sense of pride further and understanding his sources of motivation, we can unlock his motivation to choose engagement over emotional reaction towards pain. Another element to explore is the importance of his children and how they link with his values and motivation to train and compete. Being more aware of what deeply fuel one's motivation to do something will increase the chance to persevere and find extra resources when the task becomes difficult.

Future research

Whereas the past decade has seen an increase in the knowledge and understanding of the application of mindfulness to sport performance, there still remains uncertainty over the validity of the tool when applied to endurance sports.

This chapter has provided an overview of how the available mindfulness literature can be applied to endurance sport performance. Future research is required to provide clarity on the direct impacts and underlying mechanisms of mindfulness in endurance sport performance. Of particular relevance to endurance sports, a more thorough and conclusive understanding of an athlete's ability to appropriately process pain-related distractions and to explore further the relationship between rate of perceived exertion, mindfulness, motivation, and pacing strategies, during training and competition as a result of mindfulness training is required in order to enhance and refine interventions accordingly.

References

Aherne, C., Moran, A. P., & Lonsdale, C. (2011). The effects of mindfulness training on athletes' flow: an initial investigation. *The Sport Psychologist, 25*, 177–189.

Bernier, M., Thienot, E., Codron, R., & Fournier, J. F. (2009). A multi-study investigation examining the relationship between mindfulness and acceptance approaches and sport performance. *Journal of Clinical Sport Psychology, 3*, 320–333.

Birrer, D., Röthlin, P., & Morgan, G. (2012). Mindfulness to enhance athletic performance: Theoretical considerations and possible impact mechanisms. *Mindfulness, 3*(3), 325–246.

Bishop, S.R., Lau, M., Shapiro, S., Carlson, L., Anderson, N. D., Carmody, J., . . . & Devins, G. (2004). Mindfulness: A proposed operational definition. *Clinical Psychology: Science and Practice, 11*(3), 230–241.

Brown, K. W., & Ryan, R. M. (2003). The benefits of being present: Mindfulness and its role in psychological well-being. *Journal of Personality and Social Psychology, 84*, 822–848.

Brown, K. W., Ryan, R. M., & Creswell, J. D. (2007). Mindfulness: Theoretical foundations and evidence for its salutary effects. *Psychological Inquiry, 18*, 211–237.

Fitzgerald, M. (2015). *How bad do you want it? Mastering the psychology of mind over muscle.* Boulder, Colorado: Velopress.

Gardner, F. L., & Moore, Z. E. (2004). A Mindfulness-Acceptance-Commitment (MAC) based approach to athletic performance enhancement: Theoretical considerations. *Behavior Therapy, 35*, 707–723.

Gardner, F. L., & Moore, Z. E. (2017) Mindfulness and acceptance based interventions in Sport and Performance Contexts. *Current Opinion in Psychology, 16*, 180–184.

Grant, J. A., Courtemanche, J., Duerden, E. G., Duncan, G. H., & Rainville, P. (2010). Cortical thickness and pain sensitivity in Zen meditators. *Emotion, 10*, 43–53.

Grant, J. A., Courtemanche, J., & Rainville, P. (2011). A non-elaborative mental stance and decoupling of executive and pain-related cortices predicts low pain sensitivity in Zen meditators. *Pain, 152*, 150–156.

Haase L., May A. C., Falahpour M., Isakovic S., Simmons A. N., Hickman S. D., . . .& Paulus M. P. (2015) A pilot study investigating changes in neural processing after mindfulness training in elite athletes. *Frontiers in Behavioural Neuroscience, 9*, 229.

Hayes, S. C., Stroshal, K., & Wilson, K. G. (1999). *Acceptance and Commitment Therapy: an experiential approach to behaviour change.* New York: Guilford.

Hayes, S. C., & Wilson, K. G. (1994). Acceptance and commitment therapy: Altering the verbal support for experiential avoidance. *The Behaviour Analyst, 17*, 289–303.

Hölzel, B. K., Lazar, S. W., Gard, T., Schuman-Olivier, Z., Vago, D. R., & Ott, U. (2011). How does mindfulness meditation work? Proposing mechanisms of action from a conceptual and neural perspective. *Perspectives on Psychological Science, 6*, 537–559.

Hölzel, B. K., Ott, U., Hempel, H., Hackl, A., Wolf, K., Stark, R., & Vaitl, D. (2007). Differential engagement of anterior cingulate and adjacent medial frontal cortex in adept meditators and nonmeditators. *Neuroscience Letters*, *421*, 16–21.

Huxter, M. J. (2007). Mindfulness as therapy from a Buddhist perspective, in D. Einstein (Ed.), *Innovations and Advances in Cognitive–Behaviour Therapy* (pp. 43–55). Brisbane: Australian Academic Press.

Ivanova, E., Jensen, D., Cassoff, J., Gu, F., & Knauper, B. (2014) Acceptance and Commitment therapy improves exercise tolerance in sedentary women. *Medicine & Science in Sport & Exercise*, *47*, 1251–1258.

Jackson, S. A. (1995). Factors influencing the occurrence of flow in elite athletes. *Journal of Applied Sport Psychology*, *7*, 135–163.

Jackson, R. C. & Beilock, S. L. (2008). Performance pressure and 'paralysis by analysis': Research and implications. In D. Farrow, J. Baker, & C. MacMahon (Eds.), *Developing elite sports performers: Lessons from theory and practice* (pp. 104–118). London: Routledge.

Jackson, S. A., & Csikszentmihalyi, M. (1999). *Flow in sports: The key to optimal experience and performances*. Champaign, IL: Human Kinetics

Jain, S., Shapiro, S. L., Swanick, S., Roesch, S. C., Mills, P. J., Bell, I., & Schwartz, G. E. (2007). A randomized controlled trial of mindfulness meditation versus relaxation training: Effects on distress, positive states of mind, rumination, and distraction. *Annals of Behavioral Medicine*, *33*, 11–21.

Kee, Y. H., & Wang, C. K. J. (2008). Relationships between mindfulness, flow dispositions, and mental skills adoption: A cluster analytic approach. *Psychology of Sport & Exercise*, *9*, 393–411.

Kimiecik, J. C., & Stein, G. L. (1992). Examining flow experiences in sport contexts: Conceptual issues and methodological concerns. *Journal of Applied Sport Psychology*, *4*, 144–160.

Landhäußer, A., & Keller, J. (2012). Flow and its affective, cognitive, and performance-related consequences. In S. Engeser (Ed.), *Advances in flow research* (pp. 65–85). New York: Springer.

Masters, R. S. W. (1992). Knowledge, knerves and know-how: The role of explicit versus implicit knowledge in the breakdown of a complex motor skill under pressure. *British Journal of Psychology*, *83*, 343–358.

Marcora S. M, Bosio A., & de Morree H. M. (2008). Locomotor muscle fatigue increases cardiorespiratory responses and reduces performance during intense cycling exercise independently from metabolic stress. *American Journal of Physiology-Regulatory, Integrative and Comparative Physiology*, *294*, R874–R883.

Marcora, S. M., & Staiano, W. (2010). The limit to exercise tolerance in humans: mind over muscle? *European Journal of Applied Physiology*, *109*, 763–770.

Mehling, W. E., Gopisetty, V., Daubenmier, J., Price, C. J., Hecht, F. M., & Stewart, A. (2009). Body awareness: Construct and self-report measures. *PLoS ONE*, *4*, e5614.

Micklewright, D., Kegerreis, S., Raglin, J., & Hettinga, F. (2016). Will the conscious subconscious pacing quagmire help elucidate the mechanisms of self-paced exercise? New opportunities in dual process theory and process tracing methods. *Sports Medicine*, *47*, 1231–1239.

Moran, A. P. (2012). Thinking in action: Some insights from cognitive sport psychology. *Thinking skills and creativity*, *7*, 85–92.

Orlick, T. (1990). *In Pursuit of excellence: How to win in sport and life through mental training*. Champaign, IL: Human Kinetics.

Pageaux, B, Lepers, R., Dietz, K. C., & Marcora, S. M. (2014). Response inhibition impairs subsequent self-paced endurance performance. *European Journal of Applied Physiology*, *114*, 1095–1105.

Ravizza, K. (2002). A Philosophical construct: A framework for performance enhancement. *International Journal of Sport Psychology, 33*, 4–18.

Renfree, A., Martin, L., Micklewright, D., & Gibson, A. S. C. (2014). Application of decision-making theory to the regulation of muscular work rate during self-paced competitive endurance activity. *Sports Medicine, 44,* 147–158.

Salmon, P., Hanneman, S., & Harwood, B. (2010). Associative/Dissociative cognitive strategies in sustained physical activity: Literature review and proposal for a mindfulness based conceptual model. *The Sport Psychologist, 24,* 127–156.

Schüler, J., & Brunner, S. (2009). The rewarding effect of flow experience on performance in a marathon race. *Psychology of Sport and Exercise, 10*(1), 168–174.

Shapiro, S. L., Carlson, L. E., Astin, J. A., & Freedman, B. (2006). Mechanisms of mindfulness. *Journal of Clinical Psychology, 62*, 373–386.

Smits, B. L., Pepping, G. J., & Hettinga, F. J. (2014). Pacing and decision making in sport and exercise: the roles of perception and action in the regulation of exercise intensity. *Sports Medicine, 44,* 763–775.

Teasdale, J. D., Moore, R. G., Hayhurst, H., Pope, M., Williams, S., & Segal, Z. V. (2002). Metacognitive awareness and prevention of relapse in depression: Empirical evidence. *Journal of Consulting and Clinical Psychology, 70,* 275–287.

Teasdale, J., Segal, Z. V., & Williams, J. M. G. (2003). Mindfulness and problem formulation. *Clinical Psychology: Science and Practice, 10,* 157–160.

Thanissaro, B. (1996). *The wings of awakening.* Barre, MA: The Dhamma Dana Publication Fund.

Thienot, E., Jackson, B., Dimmock, J., Grove, R., Bernier, M., & Fournier, J. (2014). Development and preliminary validation of the Mindfulness Inventory for Sport. *Psychology of Sport and Exercise, 15,* 72–80.

Wegner, D. M. (1994). Ironic processes of mental control. *Psychological Review, 101*, 34–52.

Wegner, D. M., Schneider, D. J., Carter, S. R., & White, T. L. (1987). Paradoxical effects of thought suppression. *Journal of Personality and Social Psychology, 53,* 5–13.

Zeidan F., Martucci, K. T., Kraft, R. A, Gordon N. S., McHaffie J. G., & Coghill, R. C. (2011). Brain mechanisms supporting the modulation of pain by mindfulness meditation. *The Journal of Neuroscience, 31,* 5540–5548.

APPENDIX 12.1

CASE STUDY OF ELLIOT

An application of mindfulness

Introduction

Elliot is a marathon runner. His performance best is 2 hours and 44 minutes and he has a goal to reduce this to less than 2 hours 40 minutes. During his last marathon, despite appropriate preparation and a physical readiness to achieve his target of 2 hours 39 minutes, Elliot struggled to maintain the required pace from the 30 km point. He started to experience muscular fatigue in his quadriceps and a burning sensation in his lungs; he started to panic and focused on negative thoughts such as "It hurts; I won't be able to finish at this pace; there are still 10 kms to go and I have no more fuel in the tank; maybe I was not as ready as I thought I was; I can't do it". Elliot was focused on the pain experienced and the associated thoughts, which he did not notice for a while; this caused him to decrease his pace significantly and to miss his time-target.

Phase 1 – Identifying attentional relevant cues and potential distractions

Through interview it was identified that Elliot's most relevant cues were: extended hips and contracted core; counting his breathing and feeling the air going in through his nose and out through his mouth; focusing on one km at a time; reminding himself of how proud he will feel to achieve his target; and seeing the look on his children's faces when he passes the finish-line. Elliot's most disruptive distractions were identified as: muscular pain; burning lungs; and lack of self-belief. Elliot was also asked to predict when these potential distractions could most likely occur during his next marathon.

Phase 2 – Practice of self-observation

Over a 2-week period, Elliot practiced mindfulness of breathing four times a week on a recorded audio. He also practiced the teeth brushing exercise at least once a day. In addition, during two training sessions each week Elliot noticed when his focus of attention was not directed at the most relevant cues during his warm-up. Throughout, this phase, Elliot noticed that his mind wandered often during his warm-up. He also became aware during the breathing exercise that his attention was directed to various distractions and he struggled to redirect his attention to breathing. Ultimately, Elliot became aware of what his mind was doing when he was trying to focus on a specific task and he understood that intentionally noticing when the mind is wandering is facilitative to optimal engagement in the task.

Phase 3 – Practice of acceptance

Over a further two weeks, Elliot practised the body scan four times a week. During this period, Elliot realised that he was able to observe uncomfortable physical sensations without engaging. Subsequently, his relationship with physical sensations shifted from evaluative to non-judgmental reflections of current and transitory experience. Every time Elliot trained above threshold, he was able to notice the physical discomfort without judging or reacting emotionally to it, as if he was a curious scientist observing these sensations for the first time. Elliot developed the ability to consciously accept the discomfort as part of his experience and subsequently felt a lot less challenged emotionally. Furthermore, on days when he felt less motivated to train, Elliot started to experience an ability to notice and allow the presence of negative thoughts without engaging or acting up on them.

Phase 4 – Refocusing skills and mindfulness integration

During the following three weeks, Elliot practised a personalised visualisation exercise three times a week which was designed to help him practice the mindfulness three-step process when experiencing physical discomfort and negative thoughts. Elliot also integrated a routine into his performance (in training and competition): A summarised body scan was completed each kilometre, adopting a non-judgmental attitude towards bodily sensations and refocusing by counting his breathing. This routine was also adopted every time he experienced burning lungs and muscular pain in his legs. Elliot also engaged in a mental warm-up before the start of each race which included a reminder of his relevant attentional cues and motivational self-talk relevant to the attitude he wanted to adopt towards physical discomfort (e.g., "the pain will pass, the pride will last").

APPENDIX 12.2

POST-PERFORMANCE (TRAINING OR COMPETITION) SELF-ASSESSMENT

1) To perform this task to the best of your ability, what cues would you have to focus on? (Please list the cues in the boxes below – you don't have to fill up all of them)	2) During the task, were you focusing on these optimal cues? Please circle the appropriate number for each cue on a scale from 1 to 7: 1= Not at all 7= Very much focused on this cue						
	1	2	3	4	5	6	7
	1	2	3	4	5	6	7
	1	2	3	4	5	6	7
	1	2	3	4	5	6	7

3) During the task, were you distracted?

Not at all distracted						Very much distracted
1	2	3	4	5	6	7

4) What were the things that distracted you?

-
-
-

5) During the task, were you AWARE that you were distracted?

Not at all aware						Very much aware
1	2	3	4	5	6	7

6) **During the task, were you judging (e.g., criticising or blaming) yourself and/or what you were experiencing?**

Not at all   Very much

judgmental   judgmental

   1   2   3   4   5   6   7

7) **During the task, were you able to refocus quickly on optimal cues when you were distracted?**

Not at all   Very quickly

   1   2   3   4   5   6   7

PART III

Future directions for research and practice

13

CLINICAL ISSUES IN ENDURANCE PERFORMANCE

Jennifer E. Carter and James Houle

Introduction

A growing body of evidence shows that exercise has positive effects on mental health (Babyak et al., 2000; Kvam, Kleppe, Nordhus, & Hovland, 2016; Wegner et al., 2014). As we often believe in sport, more is better, right? Not so fast. The volume of exercise required for endurance sport may have both positive and negative effects on physical as well as mental health (LeBrun & Collins, 2017; Reardon, 2017; Rice et al., 2016). Despite the decrease in anxiety and depression associated with exercise, the intense pressure to perform as well as reluctance to seek help in endurance athletes can escalate risk for mental health disorders (Roberts, Faull, & Tod, 2016). Endurance athletes may face prevalent mental health disorders such as anxiety and depression. But they also struggle with unique clinical issues such as emotional difficulties as a result of injury. In addition, mental health disorders might look different in endurance athletes. For example, athletes with eating disorders may turn first to compulsive exercise to purge calories because coaches reinforce extra exercise as dedication to the sport. This chapter will explore common and unique mental health disorders in endurance athletes: anxiety, depression, eating disorders, and psychological aspects of injury.

To illustrate how mental health disorders occur uniquely in endurance athletes, here is the story of one university athlete, "Haley" (not a real individual, but a composite of athletes who have presented for counseling):

> I'm Haley and I'm a nineteen-year-old first-year student-athlete at The Ohio State University. I was thirteen when I started distance running. Running is my life. There's nothing like hitting the open road and letting my mind wander, just me and my thoughts. I worry all the time, except when I'm running. Running helps me relax and sleep better. Too bad I've got this

heavy black boot weighing me down after getting another stress fracture. That's why my physical therapist referred me to sport psychology—I've been miserable without running. So you want to know how I got here?

When I was sixteen, I just missed qualifying for the regional meet in the two-mile event. I was really bummed, so I rededicated myself to my training the next summer. And I cut out dessert, since athletes don't need all that sugar. I got super fit and finished fourth in the region when I was seventeen years old. I stopped having my period the summer before my final year in high school, but that's normal for distance runners. For my last high-school cross country season, I won every race until the regional meet, where I finished second! College coaches were calling me all the time and I was thrilled when Ohio State offered me an athletic scholarship. Growing up in a small town in Ohio, I've always dreamed of being a Buckeye. Other parts of my life were going well, too, like school and friends. Well, I stopped hanging out with friends as much because I was so busy, and all they wanted to do was to eat at restaurants. Fattening food like that isn't good for athletes.

Then I got my first stress fracture in my right tibia. It was in March of my last year of high school, right as the track season started. My doctor was skeptical about my return for the season, and unfortunately she was right. Most of my classmates had a blast that spring, but not me. I was so stressed out that I couldn't sleep, and I was so nervous that I started to shake before exams in school. After every argument with my mom, I felt guilty for yelling at her. I tried to run with a weight belt in the freezing water at the local pool, but it was nothing like real running. Weak and unfit, I fell behind my college teammates in training for the fall, but finally my doctor allowed me to run again in late June. I was so happy to put in the miles again and leave for the university in August.

Unfortunately the bottom fell out again my first year at the university. My leg started hurting at the end of cross country season, and the team doctor diagnosed me with my second stress fracture in October. Now it's December and I'm still in this stupid boot. I barely have the energy to drag myself to classes, and I'm really worried about my finals. My coaches ignore me—they probably regret recruiting me. My teammates keep getting faster while I'm stuck doing nothing, and I bet they think I'm faking the injury. The only thing that's going well is sticking to my diet. I try to eat under a thousand calories since I'm not burning anything through exercise. But my physical therapist thinks I'm not eating enough, and I'm hoping you can set him straight.

Anxiety

Haley felt drawn to running because it relaxed her worry and improved her sleep—a good example of how exercise, in particular endurance sport, can decrease anxiety (Boutcher & Landers, 1988; Millet, Groslamber, Barbier, Rouillon, & Candau;

2005; Murphy, Fleck, Dudley, & Callister, 2008; Petruzzello, Landers, Hatfield, Kubitz, & Salazar, 1991). One way that exercise alleviates anxiety is by balancing brain structures (like the anterior cingulate gyrus and basal ganglia) that may be out of balance in anxiety disorders (Wehrenberg & Prinz, 2007). Haley exhibits symptoms of generalized anxiety disorder—chronic worry that interferes with functioning and causes distress (APA, 2013). Haley experiences excessive worry about running, academics, and her teammates' opinions of her. She feels on edge and experiences insomnia. When injury prevents her from running, her worry increases, and she turns to behaviors for temporary anxiety relief (e.g., increased food restriction). Other clinical anxiety disorders that endurance athletes may experience include panic disorder, obsessive-compulsive disorder, and social anxiety disorder.

Athletes may fear the social stigma affiliated with failure, or perceived failure, and feel consumed by a fear of humiliation. Avoiding exercise in order to escape performance scrutiny represents a symptom of social anxiety disorder. Social anxiety disorder can be differentiated from normal sport performance concern by the identification of what the focus of the worry is on (i.e., worry about scrutiny by others versus worry about sport performance; Patel, Omar, & Terry, 2010). In addition to social anxiety (14.7 percent), approximately 7 percent of athletes experience generalized anxiety, and 4.5 percent meet criteria for panic disorder (Gulliver, Griffiths, Mackinnon, Batterham, & Stanimirovic, 2015; Reardon 2017).

To be clear, just because athletes experience stress, nervousness, or worry does not indicate that they have a diagnosable anxiety disorder. A differentiating factor between a disorder and 'nerves' is the impact of anxiety on daily functioning. That is, does the anxiety have a significant impact on social, vocational, and interpersonal effectiveness (APA, 2013)? A certain amount of nervousness is helpful when it comes to performance, especially in elite athletes (Jones, Hanton, & Swain, 1994). For example, when comparing elite and non-elite athletes, Jones and colleagues determined that elite athletes interpreted anxiety as more beneficial than non-elite athletes. Hanin (1980) coined the "zone of optimal functioning" in which a particular level of arousal is necessary to achieve peak performance. One role of a sport psychologist is to assist athletes in finding the right amount of excitement, or nerves, necessary to facilitate their best performance. Findings of research on anxiety in endurance athletes demonstrated that although Ironman triathletes experienced pre-race anxiety, this did not affect their performance. Hammermeister and Burton (1995) did, however, find that triathletes reported more cognitive and somatic anxiety than their single-sport cycling and running counterparts. This seems to indicate that tackling multiple sports can lead to increased anxiety. In addition, pain expectations appear to predict athletes' precompetition anxiety, such that the more athletes believe they will experience pain during exercise (e.g., respiratory distress) the more worry/anxiety they experience prior to competition (Thompson, Eklund, Tenenbaum, & Roehrig, 2009). When comparing short- versus long-term exercise, triathletes experienced decreased anxiety with short-term training (i.e., 23 days) compared to increased anxiety with long-term training (i.e., 59 days; Millet, Groslambert, Barbier, Rouillon, and Candau, 2004). These studies indicate that an athlete's level of pre-competition anxiety is affected by both external factors (e.g., amount of training) and internal factors (e.g., pain expectation).

When Haley starts distance running, she is concerned about doing well but experiences less worry overall (i.e., internal factors). Her injury appears to erase the positive effects of exercise on anxiety. After getting injured, Haley is so "stressed out" that she experiences insomnia and trembling during school exams. As noted earlier, these symptoms do not guarantee a diagnosable anxiety disorder. Sport psychologists need to take into account the context of the anxiety, cultural factors, duration, and extent to which the anxiety affects functioning. These factors assist in making a diagnosis of clinical anxiety. For example, it is understandable that Haley may be nervous when she becomes injured, or that she feels worried that her spot on her team may be affected by her injury. Yet, if individuals around Haley (e.g., coaches, physical therapists, academic counselors) start to see her anxiety leading to difficulties including fatigue, decreased performance (in school, sport or relationships), avoidance of physical therapy, panic attacks, increased irritability, rumination, and/or ritualistic checking behaviors (e.g., washing hands, checking locks), a referral to a mental health provider is warranted. A sport psychologist will assess her history and current functioning to explore an anxiety diagnosis, and refer further to medical providers if needed.

Strong support exists for the beneficial effects of exercise in coping with anxiety. Yet, specific factors associated with endurance sport (e.g., high pressure or pain expectation) may place athletes at risk for heightened anxiety. In the case of Haley, she worried about her running performance, school performance, and others' perceptions. The circumstances that threaten her ability to participate in her endurance sport appear to exacerbate her symptoms of pre-existing anxiety, which in turn relate to her eating behavior and mood.

Depression/mood disorders

Depression is a common mental health disorder affecting over 300 million people of all ages across the globe (World Health Organization, 2017). A key symptom of depression and mood disorders is feeling down and blue, as well as decreased interest in previously desirable activities, worthlessness, apathy, excessive guilt, hopelessness, disturbed sleep and appetite, and suicidal thoughts. Although most athletes will not experience a diagnosable mood disorder, depressed mood can be a response to injury, especially for high performing athletes (Appaneal, 2009). It is evident that injuries have felt devastating for Haley. As with anxiety, exercise is a positive coping mechanism and has an antidepressant effect on mood (Babyak et al., 2000; Kvam et al., 2016). In fact, medical professionals may prescribe exercise before antidepressant medication, given the equal effects of a medication and exercise on mood (Blumenthal et al., 1999; Khazan, 2014). Yet, athletes still experience depression and mood concerns. Although depression may occur in athletes and non-athletes at similar rates, sport-specific risk factors include injury, sport failure, sport retirement, overtraining, and concussion (Reardon, 2017).

Unique factors of endurance sport have been examined in relation to mood disturbance in athletes. For example, endurance athletes may experience over-training syndrome (OTS), a complex group of symptoms including overreaching exercise, decreased sport performance, inflammation in the body, fatigue, and depressed mood (Kreher & Schwartz, 2012). Prescribed rest for athletes can differentiate clinical depression from OTS; rest resolves depression in OTS but not in clinical depression (Reardon, 2017). OTS may lead to overuse injuries that we discuss later in the chapter. Other constructs related to OTS and depression but that are beyond the scope of this chapter include staleness syndrome (Raglin & Kentta, 2005; Weiss, 1995) and fatigued athlete myopathic syndrome (FAMS; Gibson et al., 2000).

In addition to studying the relationship between endurance sport and depression, researchers have examined links between exercise and another mood disorder involving depression: bipolar disorder. Frequent or strenuous exercise may be associated with the onset of manic episodes, which include euphoric, expansive mood, increased energy, decreased need for sleep, and racing thoughts (Sylvia et al., 2013).

Although Haley does not appear to experience a diagnosable mood disorder, injuries have affected her mood. Haley shows signs of her mood declining when she mentions feeling "miserable" without running. Athletes who strongly identify with the athlete role are more at risk for depression after injury (Brewer, 1993), and irritability ("I got into all kinds of arguments, especially with my mom") is often an early sign of depression. She also shows signs of social isolation ("I stopped hanging out with friends"), guilt, hopelessness ("the bottom fell out again"), and fatigue. Fatigue appears to be associated with her decline in mood (i.e., as opposed to potential OTS). An additional factor that may differentiate OTS from a mood concern is that the injury, not excessive training, appears to spark Haley's decline in mood.

The majority of research has supported the benefits of exercise on mood disorders (Kvam et al., 2016; Silveria et al., 2013). Yet, recent research has begun to recognize potential factors associated with endurance sports that are related to depressed and hypomanic/manic mood episodes (Sylvia et al., 2013). In the case of Haley, although it does not appear that she meets criteria for a clinical diagnosis of major depressive disorder (perhaps an adjustment disorder with depressed mood instead), individuals in Haley's network should watch for declining mood or functioning (e.g., hygiene, class attendance, physical therapy compliance, suicidal thoughts).

Eating disorders

Like many athletes, Haley began restricting her food intake with the hope of improving sport performance. Unlike many athletes, Haley's initial dieting developed into an eating disorder (anorexia nervosa). She experiences eating disorder symptoms of food restriction, food preoccupation, depressed mood, distorted body image, social withdrawal, and loss of menses. In addition, she is more irritable (arguing with her mother more), which may result from chronic malnutrition (Keys, Brozek, Henschel, Mickelsen, & Taylor, 1950). These symptoms likely contribute to her athletic injuries.

Unfortunately, Haley's malnutrition increases her risk of injury, particularly stress fractures. Restricting food intake and/or engaging in compulsive exercise can lead to an energy imbalance, which then leads to deleterious health effects. In 2005, the International Olympic Committee issued a consensus statement about the female athlete triad (Drinkwater, Loucks, Sherman, Sundgot-Borgen, & Thompson, 2005). The triad consists of disordered eating, amenorrhea (lack of menstrual cycle for three months or more), and bone density loss/osteoporosis. When there is an energy imbalance, the body enters survival mode and shuts down non-essential operations (Thomas & Heymsfield, 2016). Reproduction is not essential for survival, and women may lose menses. The lower estrogen levels make it difficult for calcium to enter the bones, resulting in brittle bones and an increased risk of stress fractures. The IOC later renamed this syndrome relative energy deficiency in sport (RED-S; Mountjoy et al., 2014), to acknowledge that energy imbalance affects multiple body systems in women *and* men, including metabolic rate, immunity, protein synthesis, and cardiovascular health. For example, lower testosterone levels can lead to decreased bone mass for men. Also, heart rates below 50 beats a minute may indicate a survival emergency, rather than fitness, in athletes who are in a state of energy imbalance (Mountjoy et al., 2014).

How typical is Haley's story—are athletes more at risk for eating disorders than non-athletes? It is true that sport participation can enhance self-esteem and emphasize the body's function instead of form (Wang & Veugelers, 2008), and studies have found decreased prevalence of eating disorders in athletes compared to non-athletes (Carter & Rudd, 2005; Wollenberg, Shriver, & Gates, 2015). However, sport participation involves increased pressures from coaches and teammates (Thompson and Sherman, 2010), revealing uniforms (Greenleaf, Petrie, Carter, & Reel, 2009), voracious appetites (Cooper & Winter, 2017), and the reinforcement of personality factors that coincide with eating disorder risk, such as perfectionism and pain tolerance (Fulkerson, Keel, Leon, & Dorr, 1999). Quite a few studies have indicated increased risk of eating disorders in athletes (Sundgot-Borgen & Torstveit, 2004; Thompson & Sherman, 2014). Level and intensity of sport participation are important in that elite athletes are more at risk for eating disorders than are recreational athletes (Smolak, Murnen, & Ruble, 2000). The severity of symptoms may differ between athletes and non-athletes. For example, Greenleaf et al. (2009) found that female athletes were more likely to exhibit subclinical eating disorder symptoms than meet criteria for clinical eating disorders, but the subclinical symptoms still can lead to substantial health risks.

Anorexia nervosa is the least common eating disorder, but the deadliest. Diagnostic criteria for anorexia nervosa include significantly low body weight, intense fear of weight gain, and body image disturbance. Bulimia nervosa (binge eating and purging) is more common than anorexia nervosa, and binge eating disorder (binge eating without compensatory behaviors) is the most common eating disorder (APA, 2013). About nine out of ten individuals seeking treatment for ano-rexia nervosa and bulimia nervosa are female, whereas about six out of ten seeking treatment for binge eating disorder are female. Female and male athletes may have different risk factors for eating disorders. Perfectionism and appearance orientation appear to be risk factors for female athletes, and drive for muscularity a risk factor for male athletes (Galli, Petrie, Greenleaf, Reel, & Carter, 2014).

Haley's coaches and teammates might be puzzled—if Haley's low weight causes injuries, what stops her from eating more? Neurobiological research shows promise for explaining vexing eating disorder symptoms. Kaye, Fudge, and Paulus (2009) found that individuals with anorexia nervosa have higher levels of serotonin recep-tor activity that cause them to feel agitated. Because the body synthesizes serotonin from food, when individuals with anorexia nervosa restrict their food intake, their brain serotonin activity decreases and they feel a sense of calm. However, their bod-ies obviously do not function well without food. When they try to eat, serotonin receptor activity again skyrockets, leading to distress. Haley feels calm and in control when she restricts her food intake, but her body is not getting what it needs. There are other neurobiological abnormalities in anorexia nervosa such as impaired insula functioning that make it difficult for individuals to know when they are hungry or full (Hill, 2012). The prefrontal cortex, or thinking part of the brain, may over-compensate for the impaired functioning of the insula and other structures in the emotional brain. This overcompensation leads some individuals to maintain excellent cognitive functioning despite the eating disorder (Hill, 2012).

Unbalanced or compulsive exercise is another symptom of eating disorders, which can lead to overuse injuries. One reason endurance athletes like Haley are more at risk for unbalanced exercise is that we applaud athletes who run the extra mile, believing the extra effort is a sign of dedication rather than an eating disorder symptom. If Haley runs through leg pain, fails to take a day off, or secretly pumps out endless push-ups and sit-ups before bed, then she has lost control over her exercise (Stenseng, Haugen, Torstveit, & Høigaard, 2015). Though it is difficult to identify unbalanced exercise in athletes who train hours a day, Powers and Thompson (2008) recommend assessing functional impairment and the quality of exercise. For example, has Haley's exercise interfered with daily activities like school, work, or relationships? As an elite runner, Haley has a strong motivation to exercise for training, but motivations for exercise including punishment, gain-ing permission to eat, and/or burning calories indicate an eating disorder mindset. More balanced motivations include health, training for a sport, stress reduction, fun, and mind–body connection.

Haley's mental health symptoms appear to potentiate each other. Her anxi-ety disorder may have contributed to the development of her eating disorder. Individuals with eating disorders have higher rates of anxiety disorders than the rest of the population (Kaye, Bulik, Thornton, Barbarich, & Masters, 2004). The eat-ing disorder then likely contributed to both depressed mood and athletic overuse injury. Haley's reaction to her injuries is to increase food restriction, which then impairs healing.

Injury

Haley feels distraught at her multiple stress fractures. Psychological reactions to athletic injury often mimic a grief response (Evans & Hardy, 1995), and feelings of denial, sadness/loss, worry, and anger are common. Not only does injury add grief to athletes' lives—it also takes away a primary coping mechanism to handle that grief: exercise. Ask any athlete what it is like to be injured and you will get an earful. Injured athletes experience psychological distress, particularly depression (Brewer, 2007). Depression is a biological illness that is not simply sadness (APA, 2013). Appaneal et al. (2009) found that injured athletes reported more depression symptoms than non-injured individuals, with female athletes reporting more depression symptoms than male athletes across both groups. Specifically, almost ten percent of athletes met criteria for major depressive disorder at one month post-injury, and four percent met criteria at three months post-injury.

Endurance athletes may experience acute injuries, like cycling crashes, heat illness, or weather-related catastrophes. Whereas concussions are more common in contact sports than in endurance sports, sport-related concussions present an increased risk for anxiety and depression (Sandel, Reynolds, Cohen, Gillie & Kontos, 2017). Catastrophic injury can lead to post-traumatic stress disorder (PTSD), which can in turn impair injury rehabilitation (Reardon, 2017). PTSD involves re-experiencing of a traumatic event through flashbacks and nightmares, feeling on edge, and avoidance of trauma stimuli.

Haley's stress fracture is an overuse injury. Overuse injuries occur in low-contact endurance sports like running or swimming, often involve a lack of rest, and are more common in women than in men (Yang et al., 2012). In addition to Haley's malnutrition, her unrelenting worry, driven, Type-A personality (behavior patterns characterized by aspects such as aggressiveness, ambitiousness, restlessness), and unbalanced exercise may have increased risk for her tibia stress fracture (Ekenman, Hassmen, Koivula, Rolf, & Fellander-Tsai, 2001). Athletes like Haley can respond effectively to injury by adhering to injury rehabilitation and setting effective goals (Brewer, 2004), engaging in mental training to improve sport performance (Heil, 1993), and improving their nutrition for healing (Clark, 2014). Haley appears to struggle with nutrition and adherence to rehabilitation. Due to her anxiety and eating disorder, Haley may have rushed her return to running, thus increasing her risk for a further injury. Physical therapists and rehabilitation staff, as well as coaches, benefit from understanding mental health disorders and psychological aspects of injury in order to facilitate return to play.

Conclusions

Although Haley experienced past symptoms of anxiety, depression, eating disorder, and poor recovery from injury, by October of the following year her mental health had improved. The sport psychologist diagnosed Haley with anorexia nervosa and generalized anxiety disorder. At first Haley tried outpatient psychotherapy and nutritional counseling, but she was unable to follow her meal plan and restore a healthy weight. The sport psychologist then referred her for an eight-week intensive outpatient program at a local eating disorder clinic. At the program, Haley had more support to face the fear and agitation of fueling her body. She learned anxiety-management skills, such as mindfulness, cognitive reconstruction, and eliciting social support. She restored weight to a healthy range and resumed her menstrual cycle. Finally, she began a gradual return to running and now competes on her cross-country team as a sophomore.

> I didn't want to do the treatment program and I cried during every group therapy session at first. The meal plan felt like so much food! I struggled to finish my meals and snacks, and some days the eating disorder yelled at me all day long. But I met some cool girls in the program, and I started having more energy to hang out with my friends. I stopped feeling so cold, depressed, and grumpy. The best part was my leg healing! I cherish running and I'm determined not to get another stress fracture. Sometimes I still feel anxious before a test and guilty after I eat, but I use my wise mind or text one of my friends for help. It's been a long road back and nothing will stop me from running down that road to the finish line.

References

American Psychiatric Association (APA). (2013). *Diagnostic and statistical manual of mental disorders* (5th edition). Washington, DC: Author.

Appaneal, R. N., Levine, B. R., Perna, F. M., & Roh, J. L. (2009). Measuring postinjury depression among male and female competitive athletes. *Journal of Sport & Exercise Psychology*, *31*, 60–76.

Babyak, M., Blumenthal, J. A., Herman, S., Khatri, P., Dorainswamy, M., Moore, K., . . . & Krishnan, K. R. (2000). Exercise treatment for major depression: maintenance of therapeutic benefit at 10 months. *Psychosomatic Medicine*, *62*, 633–638.

Boutcher, S., & Landers, D. (1988). The effects of vigorous exercise and anxiety, heart rate, and alpha activity of runners and nonrunners. *Psychophysiology*, *25*(6), 696–702.

Blumenthal, J. A., Babyak, M. A., Moore, K. A., Craighead, W. E., Herman, S., Khatri, P., . . . & Doraiswamy, P. M. (1999). Effects of exercise training on older patients with major depression. *Archives of Internal Medicine*, *159*(19), 2349–2356.

Brewer (1993). Self-identity and specific vulnerability to depressed mood. *Journal of Personality*, *61*(3), 343–364.

Brewer, B. (2004). Psychological aspects of rehabilitation. *Psychology in the Physical and Manual Therapies*, 39–53. doi:10.1016/b978-0-443-07352-6.50009-9.

Brewer, B. W. (2007) Psychology of Sport Injury Rehabilitation, in G. Tenenbaum and R. C. Eklund (Eds.), *Handbook of Sport Psychology*, (3rd edition). Hoboken, NJ: John Wiley & Sons, Inc. doi:10.1002/9781118270011.ch18.

Clark, N. (2014). *Nancy Clarks sports nutrition guidebook*. Champaign, IL: Human Kinetics.

Cooper, H., & Winter, S. (2017). Exploring the conceptualization and persistence of disordered eating in swimmers. *Journal of Clinical Sport Psychology*, *11*, 222–239. https://doi.org/10.1123/jcsp.2016-0038.

Carter, J. E., & Rudd, N. A. (2005). Disordered eating assessment for college student-athletes. *Women in Sport and Physical Activity Journal*, *14*(1), 62–71. doi:10.1123/wspaj.14.1.62.

Drinkwater, B., Loucks, A., Sherman, R., Sundgot-Borgen, J., & Thompson, R. (2005). IOC Consensus Statement on the Female Athlete Triad. www.olympic.org/Documents/Reports/EN/en_report_917.pd.

Ekenman, I., Hassmen, P., Koivula, N., Rolf, C., & Fellander-Tsai, L. (2001). Stress fractures of the tibia: Can personality traits help us detect the injury-prone athlete? *Scandinavian Journal of Medicine and Science in Sports*, *11*(2), 87–95. doi:10.1034/j.1600-0838.2001.011002087.x.

Evans, L., & Hardy, L. (1995). Sport injury and grief responses: A review. *Journal of Sport and Exercise Psychology*, *17*(3), 227–245.

Fulkerson, J. A., Keel, P. K., Leon, G. R., & Dorr, T. (1999). Eating-disordered behaviors and personality characteristics of high school athletes and nonathletes. *International Journal of Eating Disorders*, *26*(1), 73–79. doi:10.1002/(sici)1098-108x(199907)26:1<73::aid-eat9>3.0.co;2-f.

Galli, N., Petrie, T. A., Greenleaf, C., Reel, J. J., & Carter, J. E. (2014). Personality and psychological correlates of eating disorder symptoms among male collegiate athletes. *Eating Behaviors*, *15*(4), 615–618. doi:10.1016/j.eatbeh.2014.08.007.

Gibson, A. S., Lambert, M. I., Collins, M., Grobler, L., Sharwood, K. A., Derman, E. W., & Noakes, T. D. (2000). Chronic exercise activity and the fatigued athlete myopathic syndrome (FAMS). *International SportMed Journal*, *1*(3), 1–8.

Greenleaf, C., Petrie, T. A., Carter, J., & Reel, J. J. (2009). Female collegiate athletes: Prevalence of eating disorders and disordered eating behaviors. *Journal of American College Health*, *57*(5), 489–496.

Gulliver, A., Griffiths, K., Mackinnon, A., Batterham, P. J., & Stanimirovic, R. (2015). The mental health of Australian elite athletes. *Journal of Science and Medicine in Sport*, *18*(3), 255–261.

Hammermeister, J., & Burton, D. (1995). Anxiety and the Ironman: Investigating the antecedents and consequences of endurance athletes' state anxiety. *The Sport Psychologist*, *9*, 29–40.

Hanin, Y. L. (1980). A study of anxiety in sport. In W. F. Straub (Ed.), *Sport psychology: An analysis of athletic behavior* (pp. 236–249). Ithaca, NY: Mouvement.

Heil, J. (1993). *Psychology of sport injury*. Champaign, IL: Human Kinetics.

Hill, L. (2012). ED in the head. *Family eating disorders manual*. Worthington, OH: Published by the author, 47–80.

Jones, G., Hanton, S., & Swain, A. (1994). Intensity and interpretation of anxiety symptoms in elite and non-elite sports performers. *Personality and Individual Differences*, *17*(5), 657–663. doi:10.1016/0191-8869(94)90138-4.

Kaye, W., Bulik, C., Thornton, L., Barbarich, N., & Masters, K. (2004). Comorbidities of anxiety disorders with anorexia nervosa and bulimia nervosa. *American Journal of Psychiatry*, *161*, 2215–2221.

Kaye, W., Fudge, J. L., & Paulus, M. (2009). New insights into symptoms and neurocircuit function of anorexia nervosa. *Nature Reviews Neuroscience*, *10*, 573–584.

Keys, A., Brozek, J., Henschel, A., Mickelsen, O., & Taylor, H. L. (1950). *The biology of human starvation*. Minneapolis, MN: University of Minnesota Press.

Khazan, O. (2014, March 24). For depression, prescribing exercise before medication. *The Atlantic*. Retrieved from www.theatlantic.com/health/archive/2014/03/for-depression-prescribing-exercise-before-medication/284587/.

Kreher, J. B., & Schwartz, J. B. (2012). Overtraining syndrome: A practical guide. *Sports Health, 4*(2), 128–138.

Kvam, S., Kleppe, C. L., Nordhus, I. H., & Hovland, A. (2016). Exercise as a treatment for depression: A meta-analysis. *Journal of Affective Disorders, 202,* 67–86. doi:10.1016/j. jad.2016.03.063.

LeBrun, F., & Collins, D. (2017). Is elite sport (really) bad for you? Can we answer the question? *Frontiers in Psychology, 8,* 324. doi: 10.3389/fpsyg.2017.00324.

Millet, G. P., Groslamber, A., Barbier, B., Rouillon, J. D., & Candau, R. B. (2005). Modelling the relationship between training, anxiety, and fatigue in elite athletes. *International Journal of Sports Medicine, 26,* 492–498.

Mountjoy, M., Sundgot-Borgen, J., Burke, L., Carter, S., Constantini, N., Lebrun, C., . . . Lungqvist, A. (2014). The IOC consensus statement: beyond the Female Athlete Triad—Relative Energy Deficiency in Sport (RED-S). *British Journal of Sports Medicine, 48,* 491–497. doi:10.1136/bjsports-2014-093502.

Murphy, S. M., Fleck, S. J., Dudley, G., & Callister, R. (2008). Psychological and perfor-mance concomitants of increased volume training in elite athletes. *Journal of Applied Sport Psychology, 2,* 34–50.

Patel, D. R., Omar, H., & Terry, M. (2010). Sport-related performance anxiety young female adolescents. *Journal of pediatric Adolescent Gynecology, 23,* 325–335.

Petruzzello, S. J., Landers, D. M., Hatfield, B. D., Kubitz, K. A., & Salazar, W. (1991). A meta-analysis on the anxiety-reducing effects of acute and chronic exercise: Outcomes and mechanisms. *Sports Medicine, 11*(3), 143–182.

Powers, P., & Thompson, R. A. (2008). *The exercise balance.* Carlsbad, CA: Gurze.

Raglin, J., & Kentta, G. (2005). Incidence of the staleness syndrome across a three year period in elite age-group skiers. *Medicine & Science in Sports & Exercise, 37*(5), S48.

Reardon, C. L. (2017). Psychiatric comorbidities in sports. *Neurologic Clinics, 35*(3), 537–548.

Rice, S. M., Purcell, R., De Silva, S., Mawren, D., McGorry, P. D., & Parker, A. G. (2016). The mental health of elite athletes: A narrative systematic review. *Sports Medicine, 46,* 1333–1353. doi: 10.1007/s40279-016-0492-2.

Roberts, C.-M., Faull, A. L., & Tod, D. (2016). Blurred lines: Performance enhance-ment, common mental disorders and referral in the U.K. athletic population. *Frontiers in Psychology, 7,* 1067. doi: 10.3389/fpsyg.2016.01067.

Sandel, N., Reynolds, E., Cohen, P. E., Gillie, B. L., & Kontos, A. P. (2017). Anxiety and mood clinical profile following sport-related concussion: From risk factors to treatment. *Sport, Exercise, and Performance Psychology, 6*(3), 304–323. doi:10.1037/ spy0000098.

Silveria, H., Moraes, H., Oliveira, N., Coutinho, E. S., Laks, J., & Deslandes, A. (2013). Physical exercise and clinically depressed patients: A systematic review and meta-analysis. *Neuropsychobiology, 67*(2), 61–68. doi:10.1159/000345160.

Smolak, L., Murnen, S. K., & Ruble, A. E. (2000). Female athletes and eating problems: A meta-analysis. *International Journal of Eating Disorders, 27,* 371–380.

Stenseng, F., Haugen, T., Torstveit, M. K., & Høigaard, R. (2015). When it's "All about the bike"—Intrapersonal conflict in light of passion for cycling and exercise dependence. *Sport, Exercise, and Performance Psychology, 4(2),* 127–139. doi:10.1037/ spy0000028.

Sundgot-Borgen, J., & Torstveit, M. K. (2004). Prevalence of eating disorders in elite athletes is higher than in the general population. *Clinical Journal of Sports Medicine, 14,* 25–32.

Sylvia, L. G., Friedman, E. S., Kocsis, J. H., Bernstein, E. E., Brody, B. D., Kinrys, G., . . . Nierenberg, A. A. (2013). Association of exercise with quality of life and mood symptoms in a comparative effectiveness study of bipolar disorder. *Journal of Affective Disorders*, *151*(2), 722–727.

Thomas, D. M. & Heymsfield, S. B. (2016). Exercise: Is more always better? *Current Biology*, *26,* R102–R124. doi: http://dx.doi.org/10.1016/j.cub.2015.12.031.

Thompson, B., Eklund, R., Tenenbaum, G., & Roehrig, A. (2009). Expectation of pain as a source of pre-competitive anxiety in athletes. *Journal of Applied Biobehavioral Research*, *13*(4): 181–197.

Thompson, R. A., & Sherman, R. (2010). *Eating disorders in sport*. New York: Routledge.

Thompson, R. A., & Sherman, R. (2014). Reflections on athletes and eating disorders. *Psychology of Sport and Exercise*, *15*, 729–734. doi: 10.1016/j.psychsport.2014.06.005.

Wang, F. & Veugelers, P. J. (2008). Self-esteem and cognitive development in the era of the childhood obesity epidemic. *Obesity Reviews*, *9*, 615–623. doi:10.1111/j.1467-789X.2008.00507.x.

Wegner, M., Helmich, I., Machado, S., Nardi, A. E., Arias-Carrion, O., & Budde, H. (2014). Effects of exercise on anxiety and depression disorders: Review of meta-analyses and neurobiological mechanisms. *CNS & Neurobiological Disorders*, *13*, 1002–1014.

Wehrenberg, M., & Prinz, S.M. (2007). *The anxious brain*. New York: Norton.

Weiss, R. (1995, August 8). Staleness Syndrome. *The Washington Post*. Retrieved from www.washingtonpost.com/archive/lifestyle/wellness/1995/08/08/staleness-syndrome/2dcaf770-0349-4f00-b9ff-46ab1faeb384/?utm_term=.8486c9a3bab8.

Wollenberg, G., Shriver, L. H., & Gates, G. E. (2015). Comparison of disordered eating symptoms and emotion regulation difficulties between female college athletes and non-athletes. *Eating Behaviors*, *18*, 1–6.

World Health Organization (2017, February). *Depression*. Retrieved from www.who.int/mediacentre/factsheets/fs369/en/.

Yang, J., Tibbetts, A. S., Covassin, T., Cheng, G., Nayar, S., & Heiden, E. (2012). Epidemiology of overuse and acute injuries among competitive collegiate athletes. *Journal of Athletic Training*, *47*(2), 198–204. doi:10.4085/1062-6050-47.2.198.

14

APPLICATION TO RECREATIONAL SETTINGS

Working with the public, psyching team activities, and suggestions

Chelsi Day

Introduction

Sport psychology research and practice, as a whole, is largely focused on better understanding and improving the quality of life and performance of high-level performers. This relatively narrow focus misses a key group of individuals participating in sport who devote large amounts of time and energy to training and competing in their free time and who also want to maximize their performance. Since the stakes of their participation and performance are relatively low when compared to their elite counterparts, they are unlikely to have access to sport psychology professionals. When recreational athletes do have access to these services, they may find these to be cost prohibitive. The chapter will discuss the differences between elite and recreational athletes, how recreational endurance athletes can benefit from sport psychology resources, and provide an in depth look at a model of service provision focused on providing such resources called "psyching teams."

Recreational athletes vs. elite athletes

Many coaches, athletes, and professionals identify the mental side of sport as an area deserving of focus and intentional skill building, though this is most often discussed in the context of elite performance. The term "elite athlete" has been used for decades to identify individuals performing at a high level. Despite the wide usage of the term, little consistency is seen in the literature regarding a firm definition (Swann, Moran, & Piggott, 2015). Malcolm Gladwell (2009) popularized years of research by Anders Ericsson suggesting that it takes 10,000 hours to become an expert in any field whereas lay persons often have a more liberal application of the concept, including those who were members of an Olympic team, those who compete at the collegiate level, or anyone who gets paid to perform their sport.

An analysis of available literature suggested that researchers employ a similar breadth of categories to describe what makes an athlete elite (Swann et al., 2015). These included: international/national level participation, significant years of experience, whether participation was defined as professional (i.e., paid for their sport performance), high levels of required training, involvement in talent development programs, participating in regional competition, performance on sport-specific measures including VO_2 peak score, or university level participation.

In contrast, recreation is defined as "an activity that people engage in during their free time, that people enjoy, and that people recognize as having socially redeeming values" (Hurd & Anderson, 2011. p. 9) and this activity is pursued in the "hope that their recreation pursuits can help them to balance their lives and refresh themselves from their work as well as other mandated activities" (p. 10). In short, recreational athletes are engaging in sport for pleasure and are unlikely to be pursuing a path to elite status.

Typically, elite athletes have significantly more financial, corporate, and sometimes personal investment, which may explain why sport psychology services would be more readily utilized to improve performance. For elite athletes, a mental edge may result in greater compensation due to increases in performance and may help explain the research focus on elite athletic performance. Where research is available related to recreational athletes, much of it focuses on differences between elite and recreational athletes in regard to injury, rehabilitation, physiological changes, diet, and supplements. This research is published primarily in journals from allied professions such as sports medicine, nutrition, and strength and conditioning professionals. Despite the lack of much literature on implementation of mental skills training in recreational athletic settings, practitioners are providing these services, notably "psyching teams" which will be explored further in this chapter.

Sport psychology for recreational athletes

One of the largest growing arenas for recreational sport is endurance running events. Over the last 40 years, the growth of participation in marathons and similar events has increased dramatically, as much as 400 percent (Buman, Omli, Giacobbi, & Brewer, 2008; Prins et al., 2016). In 2014, 550,600 runners completed marathons and over 2 million runners completed half marathons in the USA alone (Running USA, 2017), many for the first time (Lemm & Wirtz, 2013) which has led to what some have called the "Second Running Boom" (Murphy, 2013). Reasons cited for the recent increase in participation include, but are not limited to, the increase in number of events available and in easily accessible locations, the desire to compete, an effort to improve and maintain fitness or physical health, an effort to be involved in something bigger than oneself through fundraising, a way to engage in social support experiences (Buman et al., 2008; Jeffery & Butryn, 2012; Havenar & Lockbaum, 2007), and a focus on fun rather than or in addition to performance (Murphy, 2013). Whereas much of the focus of this chapter is on endurance running events, accessibility of and participation in long distance bike races, ultramarathon running, and open water swimming events (sometimes as part of ironman triathlons and sometimes as standalone events) have also grown in popularity and shown increases in participation (Holt, Lee, Kim, & Klein, 2014).

Purpose and justification for service provision

Sport psychology as a field is defined by the American Psychological Association (APA) (n.d.) as "a proficiency that uses psychological knowledge and skills to address optimal performance and well-being of athletes." The broad scope of this definition justifies the provision of these services for recreational endurance athletes, as do the specific benefits and demands of participation at the recreational level.

A common misperception that may be related to the use of the word "recreational" is that recreational endurance athletes are not invested in performance like their elite counterparts but rather that they are focused on enjoyment and completion. However, anecdotal evidence on the number of "tips" lists available on how to run faster or get a personal best time, and the amount of apparel, accessories, and supplements to aid performance, would indicate otherwise (Prins et al., 2016). In addition to tangible items, recreational runners regularly join training groups. As an example, Road Runners Club of America (n.d) alone reports having over 4,000 Certified Coaches and Running in the USA identifies 2,161 different running clubs in the US (n.d.). Given the investment in such resources, it is easy to infer that performance still remains important to recreational runners.

In addition to performance services, the APA identifies addressing the wellbeing of athletes as a relevant component of sport psychology. As noted above, many race participants engage in endurance events as a way to achieve health goals, engage in healthy behaviors, and improve general health and wellbeing. Research indicates that physical activity reduces risks and aids in prevention of many diseases (World Health Organization, 2010) and can reduce depression and anxiety and help with the management of stress (Ridinger, Funk, Jordan, & Kaplanidou, 2012). Additionally, 60 percent of people in the US do not engage in the recommended amount of physical activity, 25 percent engage in no physical activity at all, and 70 percent of marathoners in training drop out prior to the race (Havenar & Lochbaum, 2007). Providing resources to increase enjoyment of and continued engagement in physical activity can help athletes maintain a healthy lifestyle and enhance wellbeing.

Whereas private practitioners may provide services to recreational athletes through fee-for-service or psycho-educational groups, another model currently being utilized around the world provides increased access to sport psychology services to recreational athletes for free. This model, known as "psyching teams," is generally attached to an endurance running event, such as a marathon or half marathon, and provides mental skills interventions to registrants.

Psyching teams as a model to reach recreational endurance athletes

Psyching teams got their start in the mid 80s in New York City when a team of professionals provided mental skills interventions at the start of the New York City Marathon (Meijen, Day, & Hays, 2017) following a charge to find ways to serve the public by "giving psychology away" (Hays & Katchen, 2006; Miller, 1969). With the success in providing these services to marathoners and inspired by the earliest models, students and professionals began developing new and exciting ways to implement psyching teams around the world. The early psyching teams focused on the recruitment of mental health professionals to provide psychological services in parallel ways to medical professionals who had long been providing physical health care services at events. These psyching teams grew and inspired the expansion through North America and beyond.

Despite differences in locations, leadership, organizational models, and strategies for intervention delivery, the general interventions utilized across psyching teams tend to remain the same. Interventions are intended to be brief and solution-focused in nature and align with the idea that an athlete's psychological state can affect their physical state as well as their perception of energy expenditure (Buman et al., 2008). Providing useful interventions requires the ability to build rapport quickly and help the athlete identify areas in which they could benefit from mental skills strategies. The interventions are not typically considered "therapeutic" in nature but rather psychoeducational in a way that allows the athlete to quickly understand and apply the mental strategy to their specific race strategy.

Psyching team interventions

Interventions are provided to race registrants at various points throughout the race weekend and at race-sponsored events in the weeks or months preceding the event. When services occur before race weekend, they are typically in the format of seminars or workshops and offered in person, via social media, or in webinar format (Meijen et al., 2017). Most typically, though, psyching team services occur during the race weekend. For most psyching teams, the race expo is where the greatest number of athletes are reached. A race expo serves as the pre-race registration and/or check in, it is the pre-race event where registrants pick up their race bibs, timing chips, and swag and can walk around the hall where vendors are set up selling or giving away goods and services. During the race expo, psyching team volunteers are either situated at an expo booth where they provide one-on-one or group interventions to those runners who self-select to approach the booth or psyching team members may also walk around the expo speaking to people who are open to efforts to engage. Smaller events may not have an expo, and at those smaller events most of the psyching team services are provided on race day.

The hallmark of psyching team race weekend intervention is the presence of psyching team members along the race course. Volunteers may be present in the corrals and race start talking with athletes and providing in-the-moment strategies. Psyching team members may also stand along the race course to assist with mental skills to overcome challenging moments, and run along with the runners doing this. Finally, there may be volunteers at race finish to assist with medical issues that arise in which psychological intervention is useful or to provide mental support related to outcome (Meijen et al., 2017).

A variety of interventions may be used with a particular athlete in a psyching team setting. The practitioner aims to ask direct questions to identify challenges that the athlete may be experiencing and selects an appropriate intervention based on information gathered. Typically these will also align with the skillset and orientation of the practitioner but ideally these are also grounded in research. McCormick, Meijen, and Marcora (2018) identified seven demand themes that recreational endurance athletes experience. Those that help determine which interventions may be useful are the pre-event stressors, exercise sensations, pacing decisions, and maintaining focus. These themes are expressed to the psyching team in a variety of ways. They are often described as feelings of anxiety or nerves regarding unknowns (pre-event stressors), physiological symptoms (GI distress, fatigue, pain), fears about capability (pacing decisions, first time runners), and the uncontrollable factors of a race (focus despite adversity, weather). Interventions to address these issues should be brief, easy to implement, and informally presented. Print handouts on applicable topics may also be used at expos to help reinforce the intervention, particularly given the brief nature of the contact (Meijen et al., 2017). Whereas a number of different interventions may be useful, Buman et al. (2008) suggest that it may be most useful to identify fewer strategies to minimize the use of resources. Additionally, it is important for the psyching team volunteer to recognize that more anxious athletes may try to use a greater number of coping strategies (Campen & Roberts, 2001) and it may be helpful to encourage them to focus on fewer, more helpful strategies.

Although the interventions below are being presented in isolation, they often integrate with one another to develop a "toolkit" of skills that an athlete can implement during training and competition. Knowing when and how to implement these strategies is equally important to the efficacy as knowing which to select.

Goal setting. Goal setting allows an athlete to maintain focus and direction throughout training and competition and can help an athlete stay motivated (Weinberg, 2010). In most psyching team contexts, the first time the practitioner is meeting with the athlete is within 48 hours of the event. This eliminates the ability to engage in what some might consider traditional strategies for goal setting. One adaptation frequently utilized is asking the athlete to set three concrete goals related to the race outcome. This allows them to consider both the controllable factors and uncontrollable factors without fixating on those things they cannot control. The athlete is encouraged to create one goal that assumes everything goes as planned, a goal that considers uncontrollable factors (weather, physical issues, other runners), and a goal that would be the minimum achievement that would satisfy the athlete (Meijen et al., 2017). This focus helps move an athlete away from high pressure, all-or-none thinking, and allows them to engage in thinking that is both optimistic and realistic. In turn, this can be useful in reducing post-race negative emotional experiences (Holt et al., 2014).

In addition to developing strong outcome goals, it may be useful for a psyching team member to help the athlete develop process goals. Process goals allow an athlete to focus on controllable factors (Weinberg, 2010) that can occur throughout the event. An athlete may be asked to identify goals for various parts of the race that they can focus on through that chunk of time. This "chunking," through process-focused goals, can help athletes avoid mental fatigue and increase their ability to cope, especially in longer races (Holt et al., 2014). It may also help the athlete better anticipate psychological and physiological changes in demands along the course and be able to better adjust. When speaking to runners at a psyching team booth at a marathon, for example, this may be breaking the race down into 3–5 mile pieces.

Self-talk. Understanding how a recreational athlete talks to him or her self can help identify areas of potential intervention and may be a useful area of intervention itself. Whereas the literature can be divisive (Tod, Hardy, & Oliver, 2011), Van Raalte, Morrey, Cornelius, and Brewer (2015) note that utilizing motivational talk can enhance performance. They also suggest that incorporating goals and incentives into the self-talk scripts can motivate and help an athlete persist despite pain and fatigue. They indicate that when self-talk turns to quitting, an athlete is more likely to DNF. When engaging in self-talk as an intervention it is important to expect a battle between positive and negative thinking, especially as the length of the race increases (Holt et al., 2014).

In practice at a psyching team booth, a brief psychoeducational piece often precedes intervention. This allows an athlete to understand the impact of their current self-talk strategies and examine what is useful or not about them. The athlete is then encouraged to think about their training and the race ahead of them to identify the type of self-talk that may be useful for them at different points. This may include goal-focused self-talk in the early miles and mantras and inspirational quotes and ideas in more challenging segments (Meijen et al., 2017). In addition to identifying phrases and strategies, psyching teams often aim to provide visual cues as reminders for the planned self-talk strategies. The goal of the visual cues paired with self-talk can improve the ability to persist in endurance activity longer (Blanchfield, Hardy, & Marcora, 2014). On various psyching teams this may include strategies such as writing words or phrases on a bracelet or athletic tape or by pinning a piece of finish line ribbon to the race bib to serve as the visual cues both passively throughout the race and actively with intentional glancing or touching.

Relaxation. Relaxation as a strategy for arousal control is not a new concept inside or outside of the sport world. When considering pre-event stressors as a relevant area in which to intervene for endurance athletes (McCormick et al., 2015), relaxation is an intervention that can be quickly and broadly applied in a psyching team setting. Specifically, relaxation assists in coping with competitive anxiety and can result in lower levels of general somatic anxiety (Campen & Roberts, 2001;

Kudlackova, Eccles, & Diffenbach, 2013). What relaxes a person can vary between individuals but also within an individual based on circumstances. Breathing exercises and progressive muscle relaxation are two commonly used strategies that are used and relatively easy to explain in psyching team settings (Meijen et al., 2017). Breathing exercises appear to be the most broadly effective with recreational athletes (Kudlackova et al., 2013). In the psyching team setting this typically includes talking the client through a brief breathing exercise, focusing on how to apply it to the specifics of their event. More recently with the advancement of technology, phone apps have also become a useful way to introduce athletes to breathing exercises as well as other relaxation strategies. At the expo, a practitioner can show the athlete the app and assist them in getting it downloaded so that they can walk away with both a handout and an audio/visual guide.

Distraction techniques. As discussed in Chapter 8, distraction techniques may slow a runner's pace but this can reduce perceived effort, thereby allowing the runner to push further. Where elite athletes tend to remain aware of physical factors and experiences, recreational athletes are more oriented toward distraction from physical sensations. Distraction may actually reduce the chance of experiencing "hitting the wall" (Holt et al., 2014). Stevinson and Biddle (1998) found that outward distraction can be key for enjoyment of long distance running, but do recommend engaging in some inward monitoring so as not to be dangerously distracted from the task at hand.

Psyching teams can help athletes identify which physiological components to focus on while developing intentional strategies for outward distraction. These distractions could include, but are certainly not limited to, noticing the signs along the course, looking for familiar faces, taking in the scenery along the course, thinking about plans after the event, and so on.

Mindfulness. Mindfulness has been integrated into sport settings over the last two decades and has been used for both performance enhancement and general wellbeing in athletes (Gardner & Moore, 2017). With the ever-increasing evidence supporting its application, mindfulness interventions can be considered for recreational athletes. Fixation on pain or thoughts of quitting are commonly experienced by distance runners and they report feeling unable to cope with these thoughts (Holt et al., 2014). Not dissimilar from the application of mindfulness in clinical populations such as those with chronic pain, the implementation of mindfulness techniques may allow for acceptance of and effective coping with both pain and fixation on negative experiences during the running event. Implementing mindfulness may also reduce the anxiety reported by recreational athletes as well as pessimism that may come with self-doubting (Scott-Hamilton, Schutte, Moyle, & Brown, 2016).

Within psyching team settings, the contact is brief and the ability to fully educate an athlete on mindfulness is limited. Thus, utilizing print materials and guidance through a basic mindfulness exercise is the most efficient. Particular focus on improving awareness and engaging in non-judgement and self-compassion can aid an athlete in moving through points of particular physical and psychological discomfort during endurance events. The applicability of this intervention beyond race day may allow for increased implementation and adherence.

Imagery. Imagery has long been accepted as a way to both relax the body and mind and to enhance performance. Given that imagery is a skill that often needs to be developed intentionally, engaging in traditional imagery interventions may not be possible when working with recreational endurance athletes during events, depending on when contact is made. In the context of psyching teams, often the practitioner and the athlete are meeting for the first time days or hours before the start of the event. In this case, imagery may look different and focus on small, static images versus more complex mental rehearsal routines (Meijen et al., 2017).

For recreational athletes, particularly first-timers, imagery can increase confidence and can supplement many of the strategies discussed above (Meijen et al., 2017). As high-performing athletes have stated that they find imagery more relevant than recreational athletes (Cumming & Hall, 2002), it is important to utilize imagery for recreational athletes in a way that is clear, approachable, and easily implemented. This may be by imagining a calming, happy place during challenging moments to distance oneself from feelings of worry or may be imagining oneself running strong and calm to pull oneself into a more confident place (Meijen et al., 2017).

Future of psyching teams

According to the psyching teams' website (www.psychingteams.com), recurring psyching teams following the models set out above are only currently implemented at marathons and half marathons and in nine cities worldwide annually. A number of one-time psyching teams have occurred but for a variety of reasons were unsustainable. According to the organizers of the regularly running psyching teams, both volunteers and race directors regularly express interest in expanding the concept of psyching teams. In addition to expansion worldwide, potential for expansion to non-running events exists. With increases in cycling, swimming, triathlon, and adventure racing comes the opportunity to expand psyching teams to these types of events. The potential for growth of these events is endless but relies on providers seeing the value in working with the population and connecting with the idea of giving services away for free as a way to enhance the endurance sport experience.

Case example—Columbus, Ohio, USA

An example of an annual recurring psyching team is the Columbus Marathon psyching team. The Columbus Marathon psyching team was launched in 2013 following the Boston Marathon bombing and a desire to provide support to the running community. In line with the idea of "giving sport psychology away" (Hays & Katchen, 2006), this psyching team was modeled after the Toronto Marathon psyching team in Toronto, Canada, which was the longest consecutive running psyching team in the world. After observing Toronto in action and obtaining the support of the local race director, recruitment of volunteers began.

The model of the Columbus Marathon psyching team was, and remains, one in which sport and clinical psychology professionals, as well as advanced students in these and allied fields, are invited to volunteer. The primary focus is to provide mental skills interventions during the two days of race expo and have a presence at the race start, along the course, and at the finish. Whereas those have remained the core points of contact with race registrants, through the years additional efforts have been made to reach registrants before race weekend. These have included free seminars and workshops in the months leading up to the event, social media videos and memes providing quick tips on mental preparation, guest blog posts on relevant topics on the race blog, and participation in the training kickoff expo event. As the race has utilized innovative ideas, the psyching team has worked to partner with the race in efforts such as recording videos or providing quick tips in writing for the marathon's social media accounts. These creative integrations with the race have led to registrants seeking out the psyching team upon arrival at the expo or at race start and have made the psyching team booth a stable presence. During the expo, the Columbus Marathon psyching team makes contact with over 500 race registrants annually.

The psyching team is identified by a sign at the booth that reads "Let us help you get your head in the race!" The booth table provides various handouts for athletes to review and pieces of ribbon on safety pins. Upon approaching the booth, the athlete is invited over through an opening question such as "Which race are you running?" or "How are you feeling about the race?" This opens the conversation which is then gently turned to identifying areas in which the athlete may benefit from a mental skill intervention. Sometimes these interventions are delivered one-on-one, whereas at other times the psyching team member offers ideas to a small group of runners. The intervention is usually wrapped up with a concrete identification of the skill(s) discussed and the athlete is given a piece of the finish line ribbon. They are instructed to pin this ribbon to their shirt or race bib and use it as a reminder of whatever intervention they engaged in. Each psyching team volunteer may develop their own unique way of moving through this process, but the general structure tends to remain the same.

The expo services are the most consistent and highly utilized aspect of the psyching team at the Columbus Marathon. In addition to these services, some psyching team volunteers are also present on race day. On race morning, volunteers enter the starting corrals and talk with athletes waiting to start, often offering encouragement or in-the-moment relaxation strategies such as breathing exercises or thought reframing to help athletes move into a positive mindset. Other volunteers are arranged along the race course to provide support. At times, they will identify a participant who is struggling and begin running or walking alongside them to provide mental support, in an effort to help them regain their momentum. Finally, volunteers are situated at the race finish area to identify athletes who may need support post-finish. These volunteers may help a disappointed finisher reflect on and reframe the race or process what did not go as planned. Some of the athletes who utilized the psyching team booth will find the volunteers at race finish to recap which strategies they used and share their experience.

Conclusions

The Columbus Marathon psyching team is one model that has developed consistency in presence and services, but is one of many (Day et al., 2014) that have become annual fixtures at endurance running events. As awareness of these opportunities grows, so does opportunity for expansion and evolution of types of events to provides services at and creative ways to reach the recreational endurance athlete population. Recreational endurance athletes can benefit from sport psychology services from both a performance standpoint and a personal standpoint; they are a population that is often overlooked in regard to sport psychology service provision. As the field grows in service providers and visibility, so should the expansion for services for this group. The need is present and the work worthwhile.

References

American Psychological Association. (n.d.). *Sport Psychology*. Retrieved from www.apa.org/ed/graduate/specialize/sports.aspx.

Blanchfield, A., Hardy, J., & Marcora, S. (2014). Non-conscious visual cues related to affect and action alter perception of effort and endurance performance. *Frontiers in Human Neuroscience, (8)*. doi:10.3389/fnhum.2014.00967.

Buman, M. P., Omli, J. W., Giacobbi Jr., P. R., & Brewer, B. W. (2008). Experiences and coping responses of "hitting the wall" for recreational marathon runners. *Journal of Applied Sport Psycholog, 28*, 282–300. doi:10.1080/10413200802078267.

Campen, C., & Roberts, D. C., (2001). Coping strategies of runners: Perceived effectiveness and match to precompetitive anxiety. *Journal of Sport Behaviors, 24*(2), 144–161.

Cumming, J., & Hall, C. (2002). Deliberate imagery practice: The development of imagery skills in competitive athletes. *Journal of Sports Science, 20*(2), 137–145. doi:10.1080/026404102317200846.

Day, C., Hays, K. F., Kamphoff, C., Beachy, E., Christensen, D., & Hutchinson, J. (2014, October). *Giving sport psychology away: Running towards a win-win*. Paper presented at the Annual Conference, Association for Applied Sport Psychology, Las Vegas, NV.

Gardner, F. L., & Moore, Z. E. (2017). Mindfulness-based and acceptance-based interventions in sport and performance contexts. *Current Opinion in Psychology, 16*, 180–184. doi:10.1016/j.copsyc.2017.6.001.

Gladwell, M. (2009). *Outliers: The story of success*. New York: Little, Brown and Co.

Havenar, J., & Lochbaum, M. (2007). Differences in participation motives of first-time marathon finishers and pre-race dropouts. *Journal of Sport Behavior, 30*(3), 270–279.

Hays, K. F., & Katchen, K. (2006). Reaching out, reaching in: Two examples of public education. *Professional Psychology: Research and Practice, 37*(2), 119–124. doi:10.1037/0735-7028.37.2.119.

Holt, N. L, Lee, H., Kim., Y., & Klein, K. (2014). Exploring experiences of running an ultramarathon. *The Sport Psychologist, 28*, 22–35. doi:10.1123/tsp.2013.0008.

Hurd, A. R., & Anderson, D. M. (2011). *The park and recreation professional's handbook*. Champaign, IL: Human Kinetics.

Jeffery, K. A, & Butryn, T.M. (2012). The motivations of runners in a cause-based marathon-training program. *Journal of Sport Behavior, 35*(3), 300–319.

Kudlackova, K., Eccles, D., & Dieffenbach, K. (2013). Use of relaxation skills in differently skilled athletes. *Psychology of Sport and Exercise, 14*(4), 468–475. doi:10.1016/j. psychsport.2013.01.007.

Lemm, K. M., & Wirtz, D. (2013). Exploring "rosy" bias and goal achievement in marathon runners. *Journal of Sport Behavior, 36*(1), 66–81.

McCormick, A., Meijen, C., & Marcora, S. (2015). Psychological determinants of whole-body endurance performance. *Sports Medicine, 45*(7), 997–1015. doi:10.1007/s40279-105-0319-6.

McCormick, A., Meijen, C., & Marcora, S. (2018). Psychological demands experienced by recreational endurance athletes. International Journal of Sport and Exercise Psychology, 16(4), 415–430.

Meijen, C., Day, C., & Hays, K. F. (2017). Running a psyching team: Providing mental support at long-distance running events. *Journal of Sport Psychology in Action, 8*(1), 12–22. doi:10.1080/21520704.2016.1205697.

Miller, G. A., (1969). Psychology as a means of promoting human welfare. *American Psychologist, 24*, 1063. doi:10.1037/h0028988.

Murphy, A. (2013, June 3). Mud, Sweat and Beers. *Sports Illustrated, 218*(23), 54–62.

Prins, P. J., Goss, F. L., Nagle, E. F., Beals, K., Roberston, R. J., Lovalekar, M. T., & Welton, G. L. (2016). Energy drinks improve five-kilometer running performance in recreational endurance runners. *Journal of Strength and Conditioning Research, 30*(11), 2979–2990.

Psyching Teams. (n.d.). Retrieved from www.psychingteams.com/.

Ridinger, L. L., Funk, D. C., Jordan, J. S., & Kaplanidou, K. K. (2012). Marathons for the masses: Exploring the role of negotiation-efficacy and involvement on running commitment. *Journal of Leisure Research, 44*(2), 155–178.

Road Runners Club of America (n.d.). *About RRCA: History*. Retrieved from www.rrca. org/about/history.

Running in The USA (n.d.). *Running club statistics by state*. Retrieved from www. runningintheusa.com/Club/Statistics.aspx.

Running USA (2017). *Running USA half marathon report*. Retrieved from www.runningusa. org/half-marathon-report-2017.

Scott-Hamilton, J., Schutte, N. S., Moyle, G. M., & Brown, R. F. (2016). The relationships between mindfulness, sport anxiety, pessimistic attributions and flow in competitive cyclists. *International Journal of Sport Psychology, 47*, 103–121. doi:10.7352/IJSP.2016.47.103.

Stevinson, C. D., & Biddle, S. J. H. (1998). Cognitive orientations in marathon running and "hitting the wall". *British Journal of Sports Medicine, 32*, 229–235.

Swann, C., Moran, A., & Piggott, D. (2015). Defining elite athletes: Issues in the study of expert performance in sport psychology. *Psychology of Sport and Exercise, 16*(1), 3–14. doi:10.1016/j.psychsport.2014.07.004.

Tod, D., Hardy, J., & Oliver, E. (2011). Effects of self-talk: A systematic review. *Journal of Sport & Exercise Psychology, 33*(5), 666–668.

Van Raalte, J. L., Morrey, R. B., Cornelius, A. E., & Brewer, B. W. (2015). Self-talk of marathon runners. *The Sport Psychologist, 29*(3), 258–260. doi:10.1112/tsp.2014.0159.

Weinberg, R. (2010). Making goals effective: A primer for coaches. *Journal of Sport Psychology in Action, 1*, 57–65. doi:10.1080/21520704.2010.513411

World Health Organization. (2010). *Global recommendations on physical activity for health*. Geneva, Switzerland: WHO Press.

15

PURSUING THE NEXT CHALLENGES

Directions for research on the psychology of endurance performance

Carla Meijen and Alister McCormick

Introduction

In this book we have highlighted the influence of psychological determinants in endurance performance. Psychological determinants of endurance performance that have been covered in this book are mental fatigue and potential motivation, exercise-induced pain, pacing, emotion and mood, self-efficacy, and metacognitive processes. We also covered interventions that can facilitate endurance performance, namely goal-pursuit, self-talk, imagery, metacognitive strategies, and mindfulness. In this chapter we explore some of the recurrent themes in more depth, and make suggestions for where to take the research next. We hope that this will open up new avenues for research, and further spark practitioners' and researchers' interest in the field.

In this book the opportunities for incorporating the psychosocial and psycho-physiological variables of endurance performance, rather than studying these in isolation, is evident. The psychosocial and psychophysiological variables, or determinants when there is a cause-and effect relationship (Bauman, Sallis, Dzewaltowski, & Owen, 2002), help to better understand the *why* of endurance performance, and subsequently inform *how* to implement interventions. For example, if you learn through research that self-efficacy influences how well a person performs, then you could design and test interventions that aim to increase self-efficacy. In general, the research findings in the book highlight that psychological variables play a role in a wide spectrum of endurance activities, and for people taking part in endurance activities at a range of levels, from recreational to elite participants. Furthermore, the use of psychological interventions to enhance endurance performance has been highlighted throughout. Despite these optimistic and exciting findings, we also want to provide a critical view as most of the research designs discussed employed an experimental or observational design.

Researchers are likely to have a preference for particular designs based on their philosophical beliefs; however, overreliance on research designs such as cross-sectional, observational, and 'one-visit experimental study' designs can limit advancing our knowledge (for a discussion on this see McCormick, Meijen, Anstiss, & Jones, 2018). Considering designs such as single-case research designs, narrative enquiries, action research, and randomised controlled trials have the potential to help us to better understand *why* interventions may work. For example, stories of the life of individuals and learning from these stories by better understanding what is going on outside of the 'lab' or 'testing' environment can help to inform interventions. This knowledge can be of benefit for athletes, practitioners, coaches, and researchers alike. Below, we will outline our observations in relation to challenges for research on the determinants of endurance performance and intervention research. When considering the challenges for research on the psychological variables informing endurance performance, these are divided into considerations relating to measurement of endurance performance, the population, mediating and moderating variables, and challenges related to interventions. Finally, suggestions are made for directions the research in the field of endurance performance could take.

Methodological challenges and issues

Measurement considerations

The measure used to examine performance is a key aspect when considering the design of a study. There are various methods of measuring endurance performance in laboratory and field settings. Time-to-exhaustion tests measure the amount of time that a person can perform at a fixed power output or velocity (e.g., 80 per cent of a person's peak power output) before they reach exhaustion. Time trials measure the amount of time that it takes a person to complete a set distance or a fixed amount of work (e.g., time to cycle five kilometres). Constant-duration tests measure the distance or the amount of work that a person can complete in a set duration (e.g., distance run in 30 minutes), and incremental tests measure the highest velocity or power-output increment that a person can reach before exhaustion (Hopkins, Schabort, & Hawley, 2001). The most commonly used protocols in the endurance context are time-to-exhaustion tests and time trials (Currell & Jeukendrup, 2008), with psychology research favouring time trials (McCormick, Meijen, & Marcora, 2015).

When using endurance sport performance measures, researchers should consider the validity, reliability, and sensitivity of the measure (Currell & Jeukendrup, 2008). A valid measure closely resembles the simulated performance, a reliable measure provides a similar day-to-day result when no intervention is introduced, and a sensitive measure can detect small but important changes in performance (Currell & Jeukendrup, 2008). Time trials possess superior reliability compared to time-to-exhaustion tests (Currell & Jeukendrup, 2008), but each is sensitive to the effects of interventions (Amann, Hopkins, & Marcora, 2008). Researchers have debated whether time trials or time-to-exhaustion tests are more valid measures. Performance times in laboratory time trials correlate with performance times in competition time trials (e.g., Russell, Redmann, Ravussin, Hunter, & Larson-Meyer, 2004), and time trials provide a better physiological simulation of real-life performance (Foster, Green, Snyder, & Thompson, 1993; Palmer, Borghouts, Noakes, & Hawley, 1999). These points support time trials over time-to-exhaustion tests. Further, it has been argued that time trials are more valid because, unlike a time-to-exhaustion test, athletes compete in time trials (Currell & Jeukendrup, 2008). Relatively few endurance events, however, are true time trials. During a time trial, athletes perform alone and compete for the fastest time. During most endurance competitions, however, athletes compete head-to-head, and performance outcomes such as qualification or medal winning are determined by an athlete's finishing position relative to others. Although athletes do not perform until exhaustion, they do often maintain the pace of their competitors, such as the eventual winner, until they can no longer do so (de Koning et al., 2011; Hanley, 2014). Competitive endurance events can therefore also resemble a time-to-exhaustion test.

Based on the above, there is a reasonable argument that the aims of the research should therefore determine the choice between a time-to-exhaustion test and a time trial (Amann et al., 2008). A researcher might choose a time trial (or a constant-duration test) when it is desirable for participants to choose their own pacing strategy, such as testing a psychological strategy that could inadvertently distract the performer from their pacing. On the other hand, a researcher may choose a time-to-exhaustion test to determine the mechanisms, such as a change in perceived effort or pain, that cause an intervention to affect endurance performance. Because participants perform these tests at a fixed workload, physiological and psychological responses to the test that could shed light on the mechanisms are not influenced by differences in pacing.

An additional consideration is that few studies have examined the effects of psychological interventions on performance in head-to-head competitive scenarios, in either actual or simulated endurance events (McCormick et al., 2015). When competing against another person, an endurance athlete may be more motivated to offer a maximum effort. They may also respond differently emotionally, because of more being at stake or because of additional sources of stress, which could influence other psychological factors such as their motivation, self-efficacy, what they pay attention to, and how well they concentrate. Whether a time trial, time-to-exhaustion test, or another measure is chosen to measure endurance performance, making the performance situation competitive could support our ability to generalise findings from research to what happens in real-life endurance events (for further discussion, see McCormick, Meijen, Anstiss, et al., 2018).

Mediating and moderating variables

Secondly, a measurement problem that has been previously been highlighted by McCormick et al. (2015) is that researchers often fail to incorporate mediating (helps to explain the relationship, how or why effects have occurred) and moderating (affects the direction or strength of a relationship, for example age or gender) variables in their research design. As a result, the research findings may indicate that a particular intervention is successful in relation to endurance performance, but it is unclear what the psychological underpinning of this is. As an example of measuring mediating variables, perception of effort is typically measured in contemporary research. Motivational self-talk has been shown to reduce perception of effort and improve endurance performance (Blanchfield, Hardy, de Morree, Staiano, & Marcora, 2014), and mental fatigue has been shown to increase perception of effort and undermine endurance performance (Marcora, Staiano, & Manning, 2009). Recently, McCormick, Meijen, Anstiss, et al. (2018) argued that researchers should also measure exercise-induced muscle pain and affective valence (i.e., pleasure versus displeasure), to shed additional light on mediating variables. Relevant psychological theories (overviewed throughout this book) also direct attention towards relevant psychological constructs (e.g., self-efficacy, emotional responses). In relation to moderating variables, experimental research has led to few practical considerations relating to what variables influence whether an intervention has an effect, whether that effect is positive or negative, and how big that effect is. Theoretically informed research is encouraged that aims to shed light on whether variables such as the characteristics of an endurance athlete (e.g., gender, competitive level) or specific situations (e.g., whether the performance is competitive) influence the benefit of an intervention (McCormick et al., 2015).

Recreational populations and elite athletes

The population that has often been used in endurance studies also needs to be considered when interpreting findings of research and translating this to practice. Although some researchers have drawn on experienced endurance athletes, many studies, and lab-studies in particular, have relied on physically active participants who are not regularly taking part in endurance activities (see also McCormick, Meijen, Anstiss, et al., 2018). Although performing the endurance performance task may lead to similar physiological effects (e.g., high heart rate and blood lactate), the psychological investment may be very different when comparing physically active people with endurance athletes (McCormick, Meijen, Anstiss, et al., 2018). Endurance athletes may be more motivated to offer a maximal effort and more familiar with the demands of the task, such as how to pace themselves, meaning that findings could be more likely to generalise to real-life endurance events.

Interventions

When conducting psychological intervention research there are challenges such as how to measure the effectiveness of interventions, as well as deciding which interventions, or psychological techniques, to test. It is evident that these challenges have not escaped the field of endurance performance in sport. Here we discuss some of these challenges.

One issue, both from a methodological and philosophical perspective, is how to define success of interventions and *who* decides what success is – the experimenter, the participant(s), the data? In endurance activities there is typically a measurable time-based performance outcome, and it is no surprise that systematic reviews (for example Brown & Fletcher, 2017; McCormick et al., 2015) have used this to compare interventions and conclude about their effectiveness. We do need to consider, however, whether 'successful' interventions can be defined by a pre-post change in outcome time alone. To explore this further, we will focus on mediating and moderator variables, duration of the intervention/time interval of measuring change, and expectancy effects. Being aware of the difference between efficacy and effectiveness of an intervention (Bishop, 2008; Seligman, 1995) is also needed when evaluating interventions.

First, from systematically reviewing interventions that included a performance measure it was concluded that although there may have been a change in perfor-mance, it was unclear through which psychological mechanisms this change may have occurred (McCormick et al., 2015). This is important, because if a researcher or practitioner sets out to explore if a psychological technique (such as self-talk) used as part of an intervention is intended to target a particular psychological skill (such as self-efficacy) or help change a psychological demand (such as debilitative anxiety), then one will need to measure this change to be able to draw this conclu-sion. Not identifying changes in these psychological factors make the explanations of findings anecdotal and suggestive at best. Measuring psychological factors is needed so that there is theoretical development from a researcher perspective, and accountability from a practitioner perspective.

Furthermore, it is important to have an understanding of who the intervention works for, as well as when the intervention works. This can relate to age groups, levels of participation, gender, as well as cultural background and socio-economic status. For example, the psychological demands experienced by elite level athletes may differ from the recreational athlete (for example see Sanders & Winter, 2016). Brick, MacIntyre, and Schücker (2019) further outline that endurance athletes can use metacognitive strategies at different stages of the event to move towards an appropriate focus of attention. Because of the differences in the experience of novice and expert endurance participants, the application of attentional strategies can be very different. This highlights the notion that there is no 'one-size fits all' strategy. Another, related, issue this raises is how well the findings of endurance performance research that is conducted with physically active, but non-endurance sport, participants translate to the wider endurance sport population. For example, the motivation of 'non-endurance' participants to do well in their endurance activ-ity could be drastically different from those who take part in endurance activities on a regular basis (McCormick, Meijen, Anstiss, et al., 2018).

Third, we need to consider the quality of the intervention, in particular the dura-tion, the multi-modal versus single interventions, and the expectancy (the notion that interventions are supposed to be successful) effect. For example, priming participants about the positive effects of an intervention has the potential to strengthen the psychological effects of an intervention (Szabo & Kocsis, 2017). Although the 'gold standard' in sport psychology delivery is often over a number of sessions with a detailed analysis to understand the psychological needs of the individual (Keegan, 2016), this may not be accessible (or affordable) for non-elite athletes. Alternatively, brief interventions may prove useful for working with populations who do not normally have access to psychological support (see Day, 2019; Meijen, Day, & Hays, 2017), yet challenges remain when systematically examining the effects of brief interventions in this sample because of the anecdotal nature of these activities. Brief interventions are typically built around a strength-based approach, rather than trying to fix something or changing anything dramatically on the day of an event. Making dramatic changes close to an event is not considered good practice when developing psychological skills as it does not give the individual much time to test whether it works for them (Weinberg & Williams, 2010) – compare it to running a marathon wearing brand-new shoes.

In light of these points, we also want to raise awareness of the difference between efficacy and effectiveness of interventions. Efficacy studies focus on comparing some kind of treatment or intervention with a comparison group under controlled conditions, with specific target outcomes and often during a fixed period of time (Seligman, 1995). Although efficacy studies are often considered as a 'gold standard' for measuring the effects of an intervention in a controlled environment, efficacy studies are different from effectiveness studies, where users of an intervention are asked about their experiences and satisfaction with the intervention or treatment (Seligman, 1995) or the interventions are being implemented in a real sporting setting (Bishop, 2008). This difference is important because in intervention studies in endurance sport, conditions outside of the study environment, such as social stressors, motivations of the participants, and preferable ways of providing guidance to endurance athletes, are often not taken into account (McCormick, Anstiss, & Lavallee, 2018; McCormick, Meijen, Anstiss, et al., 2018) and therefore this can influence how success of an efficacy intervention study translates to real life. On a critical note, this is also where they may be a conflict between sport science and (sport) psychology, where the ultimate aim of sport science research is about improving performance in competition, (sport) psychology research is more dispersed and there is an increasing focus on mental health and well-being.

Future directions of research in the field of the psychology of endurance performance

Considering the measurement issues and the challenges inherent in designing intervention research, we propose three areas researchers and practitioners can focus on. Because of the expectancy typically inherent in intervention studies we first provide suggestions on how to account for placebo effects in research designs.

We then discuss alternative research designs less used in endurance performance, such as multiple single case study designs, followed by consideration of qualitative research designs and think-aloud protocols in particular.

Placebo effects and controlled research designs in field settings

Research on the placebo effect demonstrates that a person's belief that they have received a beneficial intervention (even if they have not) is sufficient to improve their performance in an endurance task (Bérdi, Köteles, Szabó, & Bárdos, 2011). It is important for researchers and practitioners to be confident that interventions are effective for reasons beyond a placebo effect. In other areas of sport science, such as nutrition, researchers can demonstrate this by comparing an intervention against a placebo control, which typically appears the same as the intervention but lacks the active ingredients. For example, the intervention and placebo control could both be red pills, or orange-tasting solutions. Finding comparable solutions in sport psychology is challenging, however, and few sport psychology studies have included a placebo control (McCormick et al., 2015). One potential solution would be to have a cover story that the research is comparing different performance-enhancing interventions (perhaps a psychological intervention such as self-talk with a nutrition supplement) in order to compare the mechanisms that they influence (e.g., their effects on exertion, pain, and displeasure). In this example, if the participants are given a placebo instead of a nutritional supplement, then any performance gains through self-talk would need to be greater than the performance gains through the placebo. Comparing a psychological intervention with a traditional placebo still has its challenges, however, as the demands placed on participants are different. For example, a self-talk intervention may involve two weeks of practising a new strategy, whereas the placebo may involve consuming something before performance. The additional demands of practising a strategy could lead to more participants dropping out of the research, compared to the placebo, which introduces bias (Borg, 1984).

An alternative to including a placebo control is including an alternative control treatment. These interventions are similar in duration, perceived value, and procedure to the experimental treatment, but they target completely different outcomes (Borg, 1984). By doing so, they can control for sources of bias relating to differing research drop outs between conditions, as well as occasions where a control group who receive no intervention try to find out (and then use) what the experimental group got (when they are successful, this is called 'contamination'). Although this approach has not been used much in sport psychology research, McCormick, Meijen, and Marcora (2018) compared a motivational self-talk intervention against an alternative control relating to using concentration grids (an exercise where people search for numbers in a grid, to build concentration). The interventions required similar time demands and were delivered using similar workbooks, but the self-talk intervention was intended to benefit performance, and the concentration grid intervention was intended to benefit concentration. The alternative control was judged useful for controlling for bias associated with potential risk of study dropout and for discouraging the control group from asking other participants for the intervention, but notable difficulties were encountered relating to making the concentration grid valuable for participants without it benefiting performance. Additional use of alternative controls is encouraged, although new ideas of how to do it in practice are also encouraged (McCormick, Meijen, & Marcora, 2018).

An additional novelty of the McCormick, Meijen, and Marcora (2018) research was that it measured endurance performance in a real-life endurance event using a randomised, controlled experiment, which no other published studies have done. Much research has shown that psychological interventions can benefit performance in laboratory, non-competitive field settings, and simulated competitions, but there is a lack of high-quality research at real-life endurance events. This type of research is encouraged because, ultimately, we want to know that our interventions are valuable when it really matters. There are notable differences between the typical research conducted to date and real-life events, such as the people being more motivated, encountering additional sources of stress, and experiencing more emotion at real-life events (McCormick, Meijen, Anstiss, et al., 2018), which mean that it is difficult to be confident about how well research findings generalise to real-life events.

Single-case research designs

The use of single-case research methods and designs can be helpful in evaluating interventions and applied practice (Barker, Mellalieu, McCarthy, Jones, & Moran, 2013; Hrycaiko & Martin, 1996), and this can be useful when identifying the effects of brief educational interventions as described in Chapter 14, as well as the interventions outlined in the interventions section. Single-case research designs can enable researchers to study the individual case and conduct experimental investigations with one or multiple athletes and examine the effect on a dependent variable (Barker, McCarthy, Jones, & Moran, 2011). For example, in single-case design (SCD) research, an outcome variable such as performance or a psychological skill such as self-efficacy can be measured on a number of occasions to establish a baseline, and the participant acts as their own control. As such, SCDs can complement controlled group designs, and have the advantage of identifying positive effects for athletes whose effects could be masked in a non-significant group design. This is of particular relevance in real-life sport settings and situations where improvements could be the result of an intervention (Barker et al., 2013).

Single-case research designs also have the advantage of overcoming the issue presented by multimodal interventions (Barker et al., 2013), which is an issue highlighted by other authors in this book, as well as the systematic review (McCormick et al., 2015). SCDs are appropriate in endurance settings, and have been implemented in rowing (Scott, Scott, Bedic, & Dowd, 1999), cycling (Hamilton, Scott, & MacDougall, 2007; Lindsay, Maynard, & Thomas, 2005), running (Patrick & Hrycaiko, 1998), gymnasium triathlon performance (Thelwell & Greenlees, 2001,

2003), and speed-skating (Wanlin, Hrycaiko, Martin, & Mahon, 1997). For a detailed outline on how to conduct single-case design studies we would like to refer the reader to a monograph on the use of SCD research in sport and exercise settings (Barker et al., 2011). Of note, although reversal designs are often considered the 'strongest' design, it can be unethical and challenging to ask an athlete to unlearn a psychological skills intervention (Barker et al., 2013; Hrycaiko & Martin, 1996).

Qualitative research designs and think-aloud protocols

The majority of the research covered in this book has taken a quantitative research design approach, often based on positivist or post-positivist paradigms. This could be because, traditionally, much research in the field of endurance performance has aimed to 'objectify' endurance performance. However helpful this may be for understanding the physiological limits of endurance performance, the context (and relations) as well as a person's actions and emotions play a role in endurance performance, and quantitative research designs may not always be able to capture this fully, although researchers can consider including questionnaires and biomedical markers.

Even within studies that have been labelled as qualitative there has been a 'temptation' to quantify the content. It is of note, however, that some of the methods, such as inter-rater reliability, that were traditionally considered appropriate are now less appropriate and would now not be advocated because of issues that relate to rigour, interpretations of the truth, and emphasis on content over form (for a review see Smith, Caddick, & Williams, 2015; Smith & McGannon, 2018). Notwithstanding these considerations, we also need to acknowledge that some of the early research (such as Morgan & Pollock, 1977) using qualitative methods of collecting data has shaped research in the field of endurance performance. Qualitative research has not typically considered the environment and social-cultural organisational factors – that is, the way endurance athletes 'function' does not happen in isolation, therefore we need to consider the relational aspects and we may want to put more thought into the environment in which an athlete operates, and the sporting culture and sub-culture (Smith et al., 2015).

We would not want to advocate a particular methodological approach. Nevertheless, the majority of endurance-performance studies that have employed a qualitative method to understand more about determinants and psychological skills use in endurance sports utilised interviews, which is representative of the field of sport psychology (Smith et al., 2015). We would therefore suggest that researchers also consider alternative methods that may be more appropriate for their research question and philosophical approach. As an example, researchers can move away from one-off interviews to using multiple interviews, researchers can also consider using observations, surveys, diaries, focus groups, and/or photo-elicitation to name a few (Sparkes & Smith, 2013). Although it is beyond the scope of this chapter to outline each of these methods in detail, we would like to focus on one method, namely think-aloud protocols, which have the potential to measure thought processes in real time.

Think-aloud protocols look to capture 'in-the-moment' data, where individuals verbalise and/or explain their thoughts and actions. Ericsson and Simon (1980) proposed that there are three types of verbalization – levels one and two focus on verbalising thoughts without a direct link made to performance. Level three verbalisation can affect performance because it requires individuals to get involved in (cognitive) processes beyond what they would normally engage in to give the desired type of information asked for by the researcher, and this can influence cognitive processing. As an example, Samson, Simpson, Kamphoff, and Langlier (2017) used a think-aloud protocol to gain an insight into distance runners' thought processes. After a set of three practice tasks, they asked participants familiar with running at least one marathon to run on a treadmill for half an hour while verbalising their thoughts. If participants did not speak out loud for 20 seconds, they were prompted to think aloud. Throughout the task participants were encouraged to verbalise anything that came to mind. After the treadmill trial to test and practice with the think-aloud protocol, participants were asked to record their thoughts during a long run (at least 7 miles) in the subsequent week using a recorder. They identified that thought processes during long runs related to pace and distance, pain and discomfort, and environment. Unfortunately, the authors did not comment on the consistency of the think-aloud recordings during the long run and whether participants recorded their thoughts at least every 20 seconds. Moreover, as they noted that a limitation is that participants may not have shared all their thoughts (such as private thoughts) a follow-up interview with participants about the perceived effectiveness of the protocol may have given the researchers and readers further insight into how to further develop the think-aloud protocol. In one of the few other studies using think-aloud protocols with endurance athletes, Whitehead et al. (2017) reported that cyclists verbalised more thoughts at the initial stages of a 16.1 km time trial compared to the final quarter. As the researchers noted, the study only focused on analysing task relevant thoughts and not all the verbalisations. As a relatively novel method, think-aloud protocols have a place in endurance sports, especially because of the non-contact sport features enabling recording of thoughts to be feasible in a real-life environment, but further refinements in relation to the analysis of verbalised thoughts and protocols are warranted.

Further considerations: The use of online methods

Much of the data collection has been conducted in the lab, or data were collected from questionnaire studies (McCormick, Meijen, Anstiss et al., 2018). The use of online methods such as social media or online interactions (Lane, Devonport, Stanley, & Beedie, 2016) can also be considered when researching and working with endurance athletes. There is some evidence, albeit in its infancy, to suggest that interventions delivered online can be effective (see Webb, Joseph, Yardley, & Michie, 2010). Although delivering interventions in this manner is not that common (yet) in the field of sport psychology, preliminary evidence suggests that endurance athletes are looking for information on the internet (McCormick,

Anstiss, & Lavallee, 2018), and actively seek out sources to aid in their training and competition. Endurance athletes can be part of organised groups, but many train independently from organised settings, and are likely to turn to online sources and social media for advice.

Conclusions

What do the future research directions mean in terms of practical implications for practitioners, coaches, and athletes? We propose three take-home messages. First, there are differences in applying psychological skills when considering the level and intensity of participation and there is no one size fits all. This is not surprising, considering the varying demands and stressors for these groups of athletes/ participants. Building on this, second, understanding and exploring the reasons why people participate in endurance activities is needed when working with endurance athletes, as humans are not machines. This is also important considering that goal pursuit processes are facilitated when individuals are committed to an active and meaningful goal. Third, it is helpful to be aware of the difference between efficacy and effectiveness of interventions when deciding on the success of an intervention. A psychological skills intervention may not show immediate performance effects within a short time frame, but it may be that the athlete is satisfied with the intervention and feels it helped them feel calmer or less nervous: therefore it is helpful to consider whether success of an intervention exceeds beyond performance and could benefit an athletes' mental health for example.

References

Amann, M., Hopkins, W. G., & Marcora, S. M. (2008). Similar sensitivity of time to exhaustion and time-trial time to changes in endurance. *Medicine & Science in Sports & Exercise, 40*, 574–578.

Barker, J. B., Mellalieu, S. D., McCarthy, P. J., Jones, M. V., & Moran, A. (2013). A review of single-case research in sport psychology 1997–2012: Research trends and future directions. *Journal of Applied Sport Psychology, 25*, 4–32.

Barker, J., McCarthy, P., Jones, M., & Moran, A. (2011). *Single case research methods in sport and exercise*. London, UK: Routledge.

Bauman, A. E., Sallis, J. F., Dzewaltowski, D. A., & Owen, N. (2002). Toward a better understanding of the influences on physical activity. *American Journal of Preventive Medicine, 23*(2), 5–14.

Bérdi, M., Köteles, F., Szabó, A., & Bárdos, G. (2011). Placebo effects in sport and exercise: A meta-analysis. *European Journal of Mental Health, 6*, 196–212.

Bishop, D. (2008). An applied research model for the sport sciences. *Sports Medicine, 38*, 253–263.

Blanchfield, A. W., Hardy, J., de Morree, H. M., Staiano, W., & Marcora, S. M. (2014). Talking yourself out of exhaustion: The effects of self-talk on endurance performance. *Medicine & Science in Sports & Exercise, 46*, 998–1007.

Borg, W. (1984). Dealing with threats to internal validity that randomization does not rule out. *Educational Researcher, 13*, 11–14.

Brick, N., MacIntyre, T., & Schücker, L. (2019). Attentional focus and cognitive strategies during endurance activity. In C. Meijen (Ed.), *Endurance performance in sport: Psychological theory and interventions*, pp. 113–124. Oxon, UK: Routledge.

Brown, D. J., & Fletcher, D. (2017). Effects of psychological and psychosocial interventions on sport performance: A meta-analysis. *Sports Medicine, 47*, 77–99.

Currell, K., & Jeukendrup, A. E. (2008). Validity, reliability and sensitivity of measures of sporting performance. *Sports Medicine, 38*, 297–316.

Day, C. (2019). Application to recreational settings: Working with the public, psyching team activities and suggestions. In C. Meijen (Ed.), *Endurance performance in sport: Psychological theory and interventions* (pp. 201–211). Oxon, UK: Routledge.

de Koning, J. J., Foster, C., Bakkum, A., Kloppenburg, S., Thiel, C., Joseph, T., . . . Porcari, J. P. (2011). Regulation of pacing strategy during athletic competition. *PLoS ONE, 6*, e15863.

Ericsson, K. A., & Simon, H. A. (1980). Verbal reports as data. *Psychological Review, 87*, 215–251.

Foster, C., Green, M. A., Snyder, A. C., & Thompson, N. N. (1993). Physiological responses during simulated competition. *Medicine & Science in Sports & Exercise, 25*, 877–882.

Hamilton, R. A., Scott, D., & MacDougall, M. P. (2007). Assessing the effectiveness of self-talk interventions on endurance performance. *Journal of Applied Sport Psychology, 19*, 226–239.

Hanley, B. (2014). Senior men's pacing profiles at the IAAF World Cross Country Championships. *Journal of Sports Sciences, 32*, 1060–1065.

Hopkins, W. G., Schabort, E. J., & Hawley, J. A. (2001). Reliability of power in physical performance tests. *Sports Medicine, 31*, 211–234.

Hrycaiko, D., & Martin, G. L. (1996). Applied research studies with single-subject designs: Why so few? *Journal of Applied Sport Psychology, 8*(2), 183–199.

Keegan, R. (2016). *Being a sport psychologist*. London, UK: Palgrave Macmillan.

Lane, A. M., Devonport, T. J., Stanley, D. M., & Beedie, C. J. (2016). The effects of brief online self–help intervention strategies on emotions and satisfaction with running performance. *Sensoria: A Journal of Mind, Brain & Culture, 12*, 30–39.

Lindsay, P., Maynard, I., & Thomas, O. (2005). Effects of hypnosis on flow states and cycling performance. *The Sport Psychologist, 19*, 164–177.

Marcora, S. M., Staiano, W., & Manning, V. (2009). Mental fatigue impairs physical performance in humans. *Journal of Applied Physiology, 106*, 857–864.

McCormick, A., Anstiss, P. A., & Lavallee, D. (2018). Endurance athletes' current and preferred ways of getting psychological guidance. *International Journal of Sport and Exercise Psychology*. DOI: 10.1080/1612197X.2018.1486874.

McCormick, A., Meijen, C., Anstiss, P. A., & Jones, H. S. (2018). Self-regulation in endurance sports: theory, research, and practice. *International Review of Sport and Exercise Psychology*. DOI: 10.1080/1750984X.2018.1469161.

McCormick, A., Meijen, C., & Marcora, S. (2015). Psychological determinants of whole-body endurance performance. *Sports Medicine, 45*, 997–1015.

McCormick, A., Meijen, C., & Marcora, S. (2018). Effects of a motivational self-talk intervention for endurance athletes completing an ultramarathon. *The Sport Psychologist, 32*, 42–50.

Meijen, C., Day, C., & Hays, K. F. (2017). Running a psyching team: Providing mental support at long-distance running events. *Journal of Sport Psychology in Action, 8*, 12–22.

Morgan, W. P., & Pollock, M. L. (1977). Psychologic characterization of the elite distance runner. *Annals of the New York Academy of Sciences, 301*, 382–403.

Palmer, G. S., Borghouts, L. B., Noakes, T. D., & Hawley, J. A. (1999). Metabolic and performance responses to constant-load vs. variable-intensity exercise in trained cyclists. *Journal of Applied Physiology, 87*, 1186–1196.

Patrick, T. D., & Hrycaiko, D. W. (1998). Effects of a mental training package on an endurance performance. *The Sport Psychologist, 12,* 283–299.

Russell, R. D., Redmann, S. M., Ravussin, E., Hunter, G. R., & Larson-Meyer, D. E. (2004). Reproducibility of endurance performance on a treadmill using a preloaded time trial. *Medicine & Science in Sports & Exercise, 36,* 717–724.

Samson, A., Simpson, D., Kamphoff, C., & Langlier, A. (2017). Think aloud: An examination of distance runners' thought processes. *International Journal of Sport and Exercise Psychology, 15,* 176–189.

Sanders, P., & Winter, S. (2016). Going pro: Exploring adult triathletes' transitions into elite sport. *Sport, Exercise, and Performance Psychology, 5,* 193–205.

Scott, L. M., Scott, D., Bedic, S. P., & Dowd, J. (1999). The effect of associative and dissociative strategies on rowing ergometer performance. *The Sport Psychologist, 13,* 57–68.

Seligman, M. E. P. (1995). The effectiveness of medication: The consumer reports study. *American Psychologist, 50*(12), 965–974.

Smith, B., Caddick, N., & Williams, T. (2015). Qualitative methods and conceptual advances in sport psychology. In S. D. Mellalieu & S. Hanton (Eds.), *Contemporary advances in sport psychology: A review* (pp. 202–225). London: Routledge.

Smith, B., & McGannon, K. R. (2018). Developing rigor in qualitative research: Problems and opportunities within sport and exercise psychology. *International Review of Sport and Exercise Psychology, 11*(1), 101–121.

Sparkes, A., & Smith, B. (2013). *Qualitative research methods in sport, exercise and health: From process to product.* Abingdon, England: Routledge.

Szabo, A., & Kocsis, A. (2017). Psychological effects of deep-breathing: the impact of expectancy-priming. *Psychology, Health & Medicine, 22,* 564–569.

Thelwell, R. C., & Greenlees, I. A. (2003). Developing competitive endurance performance using mental skills training. *The Sport Psychologist, 17,* 318–337.

Thelwell, R. C., & Greenlees, I. A. (2001). The effects of a mental skills training package on gymnasium triathlon performance. *The Sport Psychologist, 15,* 127–141.

Wanlin, C. M., Hrycaiko, D. W., Martin, G. L., & Mahon, M. (1997). The effects of a goal-setting package on the performance of speed skaters. *Journal of Applied Sport Psychology, 9,* 212–228.

Webb, T. L., Joseph, J., Yardley, L., & Michie, S. (2010). Using the internet to promote health behavior change: a systematic review and meta-analysis of the impact of theoretical basis, use of behavior change techniques, and mode of delivery on efficacy. *Journal of Medical Internet Research, 12,* e4.

Weinberg, R. S., & Williams, J. M. (2010). Integrating and implementing a psychological skills training program. In J. M. Williams (Ed.), *Applied sport psychology: Personal growth to peak performance* (pp. 361–391). New York: McGraw-Hill.

Whitehead, A. E., Jones, H. S., Williams, E. L., Dowling, C., Morley, D., Taylor, J. A., & Polman, R. C. (2017). Changes in cognition over a 16.1 km cycling time trial using Think Aloud protocol: Preliminary evidence. *International Journal of Sport and Exercise Psychology.* DOI: 10.1080/1612197X.2017.1292302.

INDEX

Abbiss, C. R. 60
acceptance 170, 172–173, 174, 175, 177–178, 184
Acceptance and Commitment Therapy (ACT) 172–173
active information search (AIS) 62
active self-regulation 85, 86, 114, 115–116, 117
Adams, Danielle 168–182
aerobic exercise 41, 42
affect heuristic 57, 58
afferent feedback 23, 27, 38, 39, 41
Aherne, C. 174
AIS *see* active information search
American Psychological Association (APA) 203
analgesia 42–43
Anderson, D. M. 202
anorexia nervosa 193–195, 196–197
Anshel, M. H. 109
Anstiss, Paul 96–106, 215
anxiety 5, 170, 189, 190–192, 196–197, 203; eating disorders 195; emotion regulation 71, 72, 75; imagery 142, 143; injuries 196; psyching teams 205, 207; relaxation 206; risk perception 56–57; self-efficacy 100; self-talk 157; sensory-discriminative pain 39
APA *see* American Psychological Association
Appaneal, R. N. 196
arousal 70, 74, 76; flow and clutch states 90; imagery 142; involuntary distraction 118; relaxation 206

ART *see* attention restoration theory
associative strategies 5, 113–114, 144, 157
Astin, J. A. 170
Astokorki, A. H. 41–42, 43
attention: attentional deployment 73–74; attentional focus 28, 85–87, 91, 113–120, 144; attentional strategies 4–5, 6, 81, 113–115, 119–120, 139, 144, 216; competition 214; flow and clutch states 90; imagery 144, 145; information acquisition methods 61; internal sensory monitoring 116–117; metacognition 85; mindfulness 168, 169–170, 171–172, 174, 175, 177–179, 183–184; perception of effort 28; pupil size 92; self-talk 157, 162
attention restoration theory (ART) 114
attribution theory 100
Augustyn, J. S. 84
automatic processes 127–128, 129, 130, 174
automatic self-talk 154
availability heuristic 52
awareness 169–170, 171, 184, 207–208

Babel, P. 40
Baker, J. 118
'ball in a pool' metaphor 177
Bandura, A. 97, 98
Barwood, M. J. 76–77, 159
Beedie, C. J. 73, 74, 75
beliefs 71, 76, 96, 97–98, 103, 104
Bertollo, Maurizio 138–152
biases 52

Biddle, S. J. H. 114, 157, 207
Bieleke, Maik 125–137
binge eating disorder 194–195
Bioinformational theory 140–141, 145
biological factors 17, 22–23
bipolar disorder 193
Bishop, S. R. 169, 170
Blanchfield, A. W. 16, 157, 159
body scans 178, 184
Boswell, Ian 126
bounded rationality 50–51
Boya, M. 62, 118
brain 2, 4; anxiety 191; central governor model 3, 22–23; eating disorders 195; implementation intentions 132; mindfulness 170–171; pacing 173; pain perception 38, 43; psychobiological model 17, 23–28; pupillometry 92; stimulation 28
breathing exercises 116, 117, 168, 176, 178, 183–184, 207
Brehm, J. W. 3, 18
Brewer, B. W. 154, 155, 206
Brick, Noel 5, 28, 81–95, 113–124, 144, 145, 155, 157, 216
brief interventions 110–111, 204, 217, 219
Brown, K. W. 169–170
Brunner, S. 174
brushing teeth exercise 176, 184
Buddhism 169, 171, 172
bulimia nervosa 194–195
Bull, S. J. 144
Buman, M. P. 205
Burke, S. T. 102
Burton, D. 191

Cabanac, M. 22
caffeine 21, 26, 29n1
Campbell, Mark 5, 81–95, 114
Carlson, L. E. 170
Carter, Jennifer E. 189–200
central fatigue model 2–3, 16, 21–22
central governor model 3, 16, 22–23, 53
central motor command 24–27
central nervous system (CNS) 2, 29n1
Chase, M. A. 101
Chow, G. 99–100
Chrismas, B. C. 42–43
clinical issues 189–200
Cloak, Ross 70–80
clutch states 88–91, 92
CNS *see* central nervous system
co-active sports 91

cognition: brief interventions 110; metacognition and 82–83; mindfulness 172; social cognitive theory 96–97
cognitive change 73–74
cognitive processes 5, 27, 28; bounded rationality 51; emotional responses 70, 71; uncertainty and complexity 56
cognitive strategies 113–124; emotion regulation 72–73, 77; flow and clutch states 89; metacognition 81, 82–83, 85–88, 91, 92
Collett, J. 42
Columbus Marathon 208–210
competition: decision-making 50; head-to-head 6, 214; pacing decisions 58–59; potential motivation 22; uncertainty and complexity 55
complexity 53–56, 64
compulsive exercise 195
concentration 113, 128, 173, 214, 218–219
concurrent verbal protocols 62–64
confidence: flow and clutch states 90; imagery 142, 143, 208; self-efficacy distinction 98–99; self-talk 154, 162
constant-duration tests 213, 214
constrained action hypothesis 117
controlled research designs 218–219
Cooley, S. J. 141
coping self-efficacy 98
Coquart, J. B. 53
Corbett, J. 76–77
Cornelius, A. E. 155, 206
corollary discharge model 24–25, 27–28
Côté, J. 118
cross-country skiing 1, 15
Csikszentmihalyi, M. 88
cycling 1, 15; attentional focus 81, 139, 169–170; emotion regulation 74–75; eye-tracking 62; goal striving 126; growth in participation 203; high-intensity exercise 20–22; imagery 140, 144, 145; implementation intentions 133; information uptake 58; outward monitoring 118; pacing decisions 57; pain 35, 41–43; psyching teams 208; psychological interventions 6, 110; refueling 128; self-efficacy 98, 99; self-talk 156, 157–158; single-case research designs 219; think-aloud protocols 221

Day, Chelsi 201–211
De Koning, J. J. 53, 60
Deakin, J. 118

decision-making 3, 4, 47–69; intrinsic factors 56–57; methodological considerations 59–64; mindfulness 172; perceived exertion 52–53, 57–59; psychobiological model 18; theoretical developments 49–52; uncertainty and complexity 53–56
Delaney, D. 119
deliberative decision-making 51–52, 63
depression 189, 192–193, 203; eating disorders 195; emotion regulation 71; injuries 196; mindfulness 169
Devonport, T. J. 76
di Gruttola, Francesco 138–152
disengagement 18, 128, 129
dissociative strategies 5, 113–114, 144, 157
distraction 81, 85, 113, 117, 168; active 86, 114, 115, 118; flow 89; involuntary 86, 87, 115, 118–119, 130; mindfulness 171, 176, 178, 179, 183; psyching teams 207; self-assessment 185–186
Dolan, S. H. 155–156
Donohue, B. 117
dopamine 2, 28
dynamic concurrent imagery 145
dyspnea 17, 20–21, 27, 168

eating disorders 189, 193–195, 196–197
ecological rationality 59
Edwards, A. M. 119
Effective Public Health Practice Project Quality Assessment Tool 6
effectiveness/efficacy studies 217
effort: mindfulness 173, 174; regulation of 52; self-efficacy 97; self-talk 162–163; see also perception of effort; work rate
ego depletion 160
EIP see exercise-induced pain
Ekblom, B. 21
elite athletes 201–202, 215, 216; anxiety 191; attentional strategies 5, 113, 119; eating disorders 194; imagery 140; metacognition 84, 85; mindfulness 171; outward monitoring 118; relaxation 116; self-talk 155
emotional intelligence 72
emotions 5, 70–80; decision-making 50, 51, 56–57, 58; emotion regulation strategies 72–74; implementation intentions 130; 'letting go' metaphors 178; mindfulness 168, 169, 170, 171, 172; pain 36, 39–40; real-life events 219; self-efficacy 98, 102; self-regulation 125; self-talk 159, 160; staying on track 127

Enoka, R. M. 25
Ericsson, Anders 201
Ericsson, K. A. 63, 221
evidence-based practice 111
exercise economy 21, 28
exercise-induced pain (EIP) 35–46; see also pain
exercise intensity 157, 159, 165; see also high-intensity exercise
exhaustion 15, 16; central governor model 23; measurement issues 213–214; psychobiological model 18–20, 21, 22, 23; self-talk 157–158; see also fatigue; time-to-exhaustion tests
experiential avoidance 170
expos 204, 207, 209
eye-tracking 58, 62, 64, 92, 120, 139

failure 100, 191, 193
fatigue 4, 171; affect heuristic 58; anxiety 192, 205; brain processes 25–27; central fatigue model 2–3, 16, 21–22; cognitive strategies 113; definition of 15; emotions 72, 74; mental 6, 21–22, 27, 28, 173, 206, 215; mindfulness 168, 172–173, 183; mood disorders 193; overtraining syndrome 193; pain and 36, 37–38, 39; psychobiological model 3, 15–34; pupil size 92; role of the brain 2; self-efficacy 100; see also exhaustion
Faulkner, J. 53
feedback: emotions 75; flow and clutch states 90; self-efficacy 97, 101, 103, 104; unambiguous 173
Feltz, D. L. 97–98, 101, 103
first-person perspective 139, 146
fitness 100
Flavell, J. H. 83
flow 88–91, 92, 120, 139, 173–174
forecasting 54
Foster, J. 42–43
Freedman, B. 170
Froome, Chris 126
Fudge, J. L. 195
Functional Equivalence hypothesis 141–142
Fusco, A. 141–142

Gandevia, S. C. 25–26
Garcin, M. 53
Gardner, F. L. 172, 175
Gebrselassie, Haile 127
generalized anxiety disorder 191, 196–197
Gladwell, Malcolm 201

Glass, C. R. 91
goal setting 6, 125, 132; active self-
    regulation 115, 116; emotion regulation
    72–73; imagery used alongside 140;
    psyching teams 205–206
goals: active and meaningful 222; cognitive
    change 74; emotions 70–71, 77; flow
    and clutch states 89, 90; goal-directed
    self-talk 154, 160; metacognition 83;
    mindfulness 170; psychobiological
    model 16–17; self-efficacy 97; self-
    regulatory processes 8; self-talk 157
goal striving 125–137
Goldbarg, A. N. 21
Gollwitzer, P. M. 131
Grant, J. A. 171
Greenleaf, C. 194
Greenlees, I. A. 116
Greenwood, Ellie 153
Gross, J. J. 73
gross mechanical efficiency 2

Hall, Ryan 153
Hammersmeister, J. 191
Hanin, Y. L. 71–72, 191
Hanneman, S. 172
Hardy, J. 154–155
Harwood, B. 172
Hatzigeorgiadis, Antonis 153–167
Havey, M. L. 153
health benefits of exercise 203
heat 2, 21; *see also* temperature
heuristics 52, 53, 57–59, 64
high-intensity exercise 2; brain processes
    27; mindfulness 173; perception of effort
    20–22; self-talk 157, 159, 165
Hill, A. V. 15
homeostasis 3, 23, 53
Houle, James 189–200
Houston, M. 155–156
Howells, K. 42
Hurd, A. R. 202
hydration 52, 129–130
hyperpnea 27
hypothalamus 2
hypoxia 2, 21

Igou, E. R. 84
Ikai, M. 28
imagery 6, 7, 138–152; active self-
    regulation 115, 116; Bioinformational
    theory 140–141; defining 138–139;
    effectiveness of 140; emotion regulation
    72–73, 75, 76, 77; function of 142;

Functional Equivalence hypothesis
    141–142; as mental training tool
    145–146; psyching teams 208; self-talk
    165; setting up a training programme
    146–148; use of the term 149n1
IMPACT approach 161–165
implementation intentions 126,
    129–132, 133
information acquisition methods 61–62
information integration methods 61, 62–64
inhibition of secondary elaborative
    processing 169
injury 189, 190, 196; decision-making 50;
    depression 192–193; eating disorders
    194, 195; malnutrition 194; pain 36;
    rehabilitation 142, 143; self-efficacy 104
instructional self-talk 154, 155, 157, 158,
    160, 162–163
intentions 125, 126, 129–132, 133, 170
interferences 127, 129, 130
internal sensory monitoring 86, 87, 114,
    116–117, 207
International Olympic Committee
    (IOC) 194
interviews 91–92, 220
intuitive decision-making 51–52, 63
ischaemic exercise 40
Ivanova, E. 172–173

Jackson, S. A. 173
Jin, P. 102
Jones, A. M. 42
Jones, G. 191
judgement and decision-making (JDM) 47,
    48–49

Kahneman, D. 52
Kamphoff, C. 221
Kaufman, K. A. 91
Kaye, W. 195
Kee, Y. H. 173–174
Keller, J. 174
Keltner, D. 56–57
Kipchoge, Eliud 87, 89
knowledge, metacognitive 82
Kress, J. L. 35

Labbé, E. E. 102, 119
labelling 178
lactate 2, 21, 28, 74, 75, 104
LaGuardia, R. 102
Landhäußer, A. 174
Lane, Andrew M. 70–80, 221
Lang, P. J. 140–141, 145

Langens, T. A. 158
Langlier, A. 221
Latinjak, A. T. 154, 160
Laursen, P. B. 60
Layered Stimulus Response Training
    (LSRT) 141, 145–146, 148–149
Lerner, J. S. 56–57
'letting go' metaphors 178
Lirgg, C. D. 101
Lonsdale, C. 174
Lopez-Ros, V. 154
LSRT see Layered Stimulus Response
    Training

MacIntyre, Tadhg 5, 84, 113–124, 216
malnutrition 194, 196
MAP see Multi-Action Plan strategy
MAPAS see Metacognition Applied to Physical
    Activities Scale
marathons 1, 15; attentional strategies 5,
    113; clutch states 89; flow 174; goal
    striving 127; growth in participation
    48, 202–203; imagery 138; mindfulness
    168, 183–184; pain 40; psyching teams
    203–210; psychological interventions
    110; self-efficacy 101; self-talk 8, 155,
    156, 158, 159, 164–165; see also running
Marcora, Samuele 1–11, 15–34, 37, 52,
    102, 115, 133, 172–173, 157, 205
Martin, J. E. 119
Martin, S. B. 155–156
Martini, R. 84
Matran, R. 53
Matthews, J. 84
Mauger, Alexis R. 35–46
maximal oxygen consumption 2, 21, 28,
    37, 202
maximal voluntary contraction (MVC) 15,
    16, 20
McCormick, Alister 1, 6, 8, 15, 116, 119,
    125, 127, 153–167, 205, 212–224
McCormick, Sheree 138–152
McElhinney, M. 116
McVeigh, D. 76–77
measurement 7–8, 213–214; attentional
    focus 120; decision-making 59–64;
    intervention effectiveness 215–217;
    mediating and moderating variables
    214–215; metacognition 91–92;
    mindfulness 179; self-efficacy 103–104
mediators 7, 214–215, 216
meditation 169, 171
Meijen, Carla 1–11, 15, 98, 109–112, 125,
    156, 158, 160, 161, 204, 205, 212–224

memory 51, 52, 56, 138
mental fatigue 6, 21–22, 27, 28, 173,
    206, 215
mental health 189–200, 217, 222;
    see also anxiety; depression
mental skills: imagery 140; psyching teams
    203, 204, 209; recreational athletes 202;
    see also psychological skills
metacognition 5, 8, 81–95, 169, 216
Metacognition Applied to Physical Activities
    Scale (MAPAS) 84, 88, 91
Metcalfe, R. S. 116
methodological issues 59–64, 91–92,
    213–222; see also measurement; research
    designs
Micklewright, Dominic 47–69, 173
MIIMS see Motor Imagery Integrative
    Model in Sport
Miller, A. 117
Miller-Uibo, Shaunae 127, 128
mindfulness 120, 168–182; active self-
    regulation 115; anxiety management
    197; case study 183–184; definitions of
    169, 170; flow 173–174; future research
    179–180; intervention phases 175–179;
    motor control 174; neuroscience
    170–171; pain/fatigue management
    172–173; psyching teams 207–208
Mindfulness-Acceptance-Commitment
    172, 175
moderators 7, 214–215, 216
mood disorders 192–193
Moore, Z. E. 172, 175
Moran, A. P. 84, 174
Morgan, W. P. 5, 28, 113, 144
Morrey, R. B. 155, 206
Morris, M. G. 42
motivation 4, 6–7, 216; competition
    214; to exercise 195; flow and clutch
    states 90; imagery 139, 142, 143,
    144; metacognitive planning 85–87;
    mindfulness 174, 180; pain 39–40;
    potential 3, 17, 18–20, 22, 28, 159;
    real-life events 219; self-talk 154,
    155, 157–158, 159–160, 162–163;
    uncomfortable sensations 168;
    values 179
motivational intensity theory 3, 18,
    20, 22
motivational self-talk see self-talk
motor control 174
Motor Imagery Integrative Model in Sport
    (MIIMS) 142, 148
motor learning 142, 143

motor-related cortical potential (MRCP) 25–26, 29n1
movement economy 115–116, 117, 120
Multi-Action Plan (MAP) strategy 139, 148
multidisciplinary/interdisciplinary approach 1, 3, 43
muscles: central fatigue model 2; central governor model 53; corollary discharge model 24–25; maximal voluntary contraction 15, 16, 20; muscular endurance 1; pain 36–37, 39; psychobiological model 20–21
music 73, 74
MVC *see* maximal voluntary contraction

Narens, L. 83
Nelson, T. O. 83
nerves 110, 191, 205
neurophysiology: implementation intentions 132; pain perception 43; psychobiological model 17, 23–28; *see also* brain
neuroscience 170–171; *see also* brain
Nideffer, R. M. 114
Nietfeld, J. L. 85
Noakes, T. D. 3, 16, 22, 53
nociception 37, 38–39, 41, 43
normalising 178
normoxia 2
Nurmi, Paavo 81
nutrition 21, 28, 196, 197, 218; *see also* malnutrition

obsessive-compulsive disorder 191
Okwumabua, T. M. 102
O'Leary, T. J. 42
Oliver, E. 154–155
online interventions 111, 221–222; emotion regulation 76, 77; psyching teams 204; self-talk 160
OTS *see* overtraining syndrome
outward monitoring 86, 87, 114, 117–118, 207
overextension 130
overtraining syndrome (OTS) 193
overuse injuries 196
oxygen 7, 16, 75; brain processes 23; maximal oxygen consumption 2, 21, 28, 37, 202

pacemakers 73
pacing 3, 5, 98, 171; attentional focus 119, 144; decision-making 47, 49–64; elite athletes 215; goal striving 129; impact of pain on 43; metacognitive planning 85–87; mindfulness 168, 172, 173, 179, 180; muscle cramp 36; research methods 214; self-talk 161; staying on track 127; vicarious experiences 101; worry 127
pain 4, 35–46, 47–48, 171; afferent feedback 39; anxiety about 191–192, 205; brain processes 23, 27, 28; causes of 36–38; definition of 36; imagery 140, 144, 145; impact on pacing and performance 40–43; implementation intentions 132; mediating variables 215; mindfulness 168, 171, 172–173, 180, 183–184, 207; perception of effort 17; perception of pain 38–39, 42, 43; self-efficacy 100, 101, 102–103; self-talk 156, 159, 160, 161; sensory-discriminative and affective-motivational components 39–40; tolerance of 41–42, 103, 194
Paivio, A. 142
panic disorder 191
Pantani, Marco 128
paracetemol 42–43
past performances 100–101, 104
Paulus, M. 195
PBM *see* psychobiological model
peak performance 173
perception of effort 7, 15, 16, 42, 43, 171; active self-regulation 115; brain processes 23–28; central governor model 3, 23; cognitive strategies 119; decision-making 52–53, 57–59; impact of caffeine 29n1; implementation intentions 132; mediating variables 215; psychobiological model 3, 17–22, 23, 28, 159, 173; self-efficacy 100, 102–103; self-talk 159, 160; *see also* effort
perceptual control theory 103
perfectionism 194, 195
peripheral fatigue 16, 21–22
perseverance 97, 98, 101, 179
persuasion 101
PETTLEP model 141
Phelps, Michael 142
Pineau, T. R. 91
placebo effects 3, 16, 42, 218
Pollak, K. A. 37
Pollock, M. L. 5, 28, 113, 144
Post, P. 142, 144–145
post-traumatic stress disorder (PTSD) 196
potential motivation 3, 17, 18–20, 22, 28, 159
power: central governor model 23; decision-making processes 3; feedback

75; inability to produce 15–16; pacing decisions 60–61; pain 42–43; psychobiological model 3, 18; self-talk 76, 158; time-to-exhaustion tests 213
Powers, P. 195
Powers, W. T. 103
practice 4, 201
preparation 5, 71, 155–156
problem-solving 142, 143
process goals 206
propositions 140–141
prospect theory 51–52, 56
prospection 53–54
psyching teams 110–111, 202, 203–210
psychobiological model (PBM) 3, 15–34, 173; biological level of explanation 22–23; brain processes 23–28; manipulations of potential motivation 22; physiological manipulations of perceived effort 20–21; psychological constructs 17–20; psychological manipulations of perceived effort 21–22; self-talk 159
psychoeducational interventions 203, 204, 206
psychological crises 158
psychological interventions 6, 109–112, 212, 214; controlled research designs 218–219; effectiveness and efficacy 215–217, 222; placebo effects 218; single-case research designs 219–220
psychological skills 109–110, 111, 217, 222; emotion regulation 72–73; metacognition 88; qualitative research designs 220; see also mental skills
PTSD see post-traumatic stress disorder
pupillometry 92

qualitative research designs 220

race expos 204, 207, 209
Racing the Mile Questionnaire (RMQ) 85, 91
Radcliffe, Paula 113
rating of perceived exertion (RPE) 17, 21; brain processes 23, 25–27, 29n1; decision-making 52, 53, 56, 57–59; see also perception of effort
Rational Decision-Making Theory (RDM) 49–50
Razon, S. 142, 144–145, 147
recreational (non-elite) athletes 201–211, 215, 216; anxiety 191; attentional strategies 5, 113; eating disorders 194; metacognition 88; outward monitoring 118; self-talk 155, 156, 157–158

RED-S see relative energy deficiency in sport
refocusing 175, 177–179, 184
refueling 128
rehydration 129–130
reinvestment 174
relative energy deficiency in sport (RED-S) 194
relaxation 109, 115–116, 117, 120; imagery used alongside 140; metacognition 81, 82, 83, 85, 87; psyching teams 206–207
reliability 213
representativeness heuristic 52
research designs 8, 212–213; controlled 218–219; qualitative 220; single-case 219–220; see also methodological issues
research quality 6–7
respiration 27, 74–75
response modulation 73–74
rest 193
retrospective verbal protocols 62–64, 120
rewards 6, 18, 22, 90
risk 56–57, 58, 59
RMQ see Racing the Mile Questionnaire
Robinson, Daniel T. 70–80
Rosenbaum, D. A. 84
rowing 1, 15, 91; imagery 138; pain 41; psychological interventions 6; single-case research designs 219
RPE see rating of perceived exertion
running 1, 15; active self-regulation 115; anxiety 5; automatic processes 127–128; clutch states 89; cognitive strategies 113, 120; decision-making 49–51, 57; emotion regulation 75, 76; goal striving 127, 130; growth in participation 202–203; imagery 138, 139, 140, 141–142, 144, 147, 148; implementation intentions 133; internal sensory monitoring 116–117; mental health issues 189–191, 192, 197; metacognition 85, 86, 88, 91; overuse injuries 196; pain 35; psyching teams 110–111, 203–210; psychological interventions 6; relaxation 115–116; self-efficacy 98, 99, 102; self-talk 155, 156, 157, 158, 159, 164–165; single-case research designs 219; think-aloud protocols 221; see also marathons; triathlons
Ryan, R. M. 169–170

Salleron, J. 53
Salmon, P. 172
Samson, A. 101, 221

Schoemaker, P. J. H. 54
Schomer, H. H. 114
Schücker, Linda 113–124, 216
Schüler, Julia 125–137, 158, 174
Schweickle, M. 89
self-assessment 185–186
self-belief 3
self-compassion 178, 207–208
self-control 160
Self, E. A. 3
self-efficacy 6, 96–106, 212; applied
    practice 104; competition 214;
    development and formation of beliefs
    99–100; endurance performance
    102–103; future research 103–104; as
    mediator 7; pain tolerance 41; related
    constructs 98–99; self-talk 159, 160;
    sources of 100–102
self-esteem 98–99, 194
self-observation 175–177, 184
self-regulation 8, 81, 125; active 85, 86,
    114, 115–116, 117; clutch states 89;
    decision-making processes 3; imagery
    142–144; implementation intentions
    131; metacognition 82, 84, 86, 88, 91;
    mindfulness 170; self-efficacy 98
self-talk 6, 8, 16, 153–167, 170, 215; active
    self-regulation 115, 116; antecedents of
    155, 156–157; automatic and strategic
    154; controlled research designs
    218–219; descriptive research 155–156,
    159; effects of 155, 157–158; emotion
    regulation 72–73, 75, 76–77; future
    research 160; imagery used alongside
    140, 165; learning to use 161–165;
    mechanisms 159; metacognition 81, 82,
    83, 85, 87; mindfulness 184; placebo
    effects 218; psyching teams 206;
    psychobiological model 22;
    self-efficacy 101
senses 169
sensory pain 39–40
serotonin 195
Settanni, M. 84, 85, 88
Shapiro, S. L. 170
Sharman, Ian 153
Shore, B. M. 84
Sides, R. 99–100
Simon, H. A. 63, 221
Simpson, D. 221
Singer, R. N. 109
single-case research designs 219–220
situation modification 73–74
situation selection 73

skiing 1, 15, 115, 139
'sky and the weather' metaphor 175–177
social anxiety disorder 191
social cognitive theory 96–97
social media 204, 209, 221–222
speed-skating 219–220
Stanley, D. M. 73
Statler, T. 35
Steinhaus, A. H. 28
Stevinson, C. D. 114, 207
strategic self-talk 154; see also self-talk
strategies 142, 143; see also cognitive
    strategies
strength training 41
stress 126, 191, 203; competition 214;
    implementation intentions 131; micro
    stressors 127; real-life events 219; self-
    talk 156, 159, 161; unwanted habits 128
Stuart, D. G. 25
sustained attention 169
Swann, Christian 81–95
swimming 1, 15; active self-regulation 115;
    cognitive strategies 81, 113; flow 174;
    growth in participation 203; imagery
    138, 140, 142, 148; overuse injuries
    196; pain 35, 41; psyching teams 208;
    psychological interventions 6;
    relaxation 115
switching 169

task difficulty 18, 87, 99–100, 101
task self-efficacy 98
Taylor, J. L. 25–26
Taylor, L. 42–43
teeth brushing exercise 176, 184
teleoanticipation 53
temperature 23, 27, 50; see also heat
Tenenbaum, G. 99–100
Terry, P. C. 71
Thelwell, R. C. 76–77, 116
Thienot, Emilie 168–182
think-aloud protocols 91, 104, 120, 156,
    220–221
third-person perspective 139, 146
Thompson, R. A. 73, 195
thought suppression 172
Thürmer, J. L. 131
time perception 119–120
time-to-exhaustion tests 213–214;
    motivational intensity theory 18; pain
    40–41, 42, 43; psychobiological model
    16, 20, 22
time trials 7, 41–42, 213–214
Tod, D. 154–155

Toronto Marathon 208–209
Totterdell, P. 75–76
triathlons 1, 15; anxiety 191–192; clutch
    states 89; growth in participation 203;
    imagery 138, 140, 146; perceived
    exertion 58; psyching teams 208;
    psychological interventions 6; relaxation
    116; self-efficacy 102; self-talk 155–156;
    single-case research designs 219;
    see also running
Tucker, R. 53
Tversky, A. 52

Ullrich, Jan 128
Ulmer, H. V. 53
ultra-marathons 8, 15, 156, 158, 203
unbalanced exercise 195
uncertainty 53–56, 58, 59, 64, 113

validity of measures 213–214
values clarification 179
Van Raalte, J. L. 154, 155, 206
velocity: central governor model 23;
    decision-making processes 3; inability to
    produce 15–16; psychobiological model
    3, 18; time-to-exhaustion tests 213
verbal encouragement 6
verbal protocols 62–64, 120, 221; *see also*
    think-aloud protocols

vicarious experiences 101, 104
Vincent, A. 154
visual cues 206
visualisation 184
Voy, N. 53

Wagstaff, C. R. 76–77
walking 115
Wallace, P. J. 159
Wang, C. K. J. 173–174
Watkins, S. L. 42–43
Watson, D. 58
Wegner, D. M. 172
Weiner, B. 100
wellbeing 203, 217
Welsh, M. C. 119
wheelchair racing 102
Whitehead, A. E. 118, 221
Wieber, F. 131
Wiggins, Bradley 81, 89
Williams, C. A. 42
Williams, E. L. 118
Wilmore, J. H. 22
Wilson, M. 74
Wolff, Wanja 125–137
work rate 36, 43, 162–163; *see also* effort
worry 5, 127, 157, 191, 208

Zourbanos, N. 154

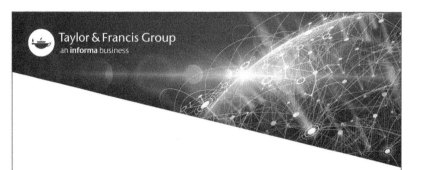